David R. Heise

EDITOR

SOCIOLOGICAL METHODOLOGY

❧1977❧

 Jossey-Bass Publishers
San Francisco · Washington · London · 1977

SOCIOLOGICAL METHODOLOGY 1977
David R. Heise, Editor

Library of Congress Catalogue Card Number LC 76-11879

International Standard Book Number ISBN 0-87589-286-8

Manufactured in the United States of America

JACKET DESIGN BY WILLI BAUM

FIRST EDITION

Code 7619

THE JOSSEY-BASS BEHAVIORAL SCIENCE SERIES

SOCIOLOGICAL METHODOLOGY 1977

EDITOR	David R. Heise
ADVISORY EDITORS	James A. Davis*
	William Mason*
	Patricia Kendall**
	Samuel Leinhardt**
	Elton Jackson***
	Evelyn Kitagawa***

*Term ends with 1977 volume
**Term ends with 1978 volume
***Term ends with 1979 volume

CONSULTANTS

EDITORIAL CONSULTANTS

Michael Allen
Duane Alwin
Ronald Burt
Richard Campbell
Herbert Costner
James Fennessey
Glenn Fuguitt
Arthur Goldberger
Leo Goodman
Roland Hawkes
Thomas Heberlein
Bradley Hertel
Burkart Holzner
Patrick Horan
Stanley Lieberson
Lawrence Mayer

Barry Moriarty
Krishnan Namboodiri
George Rabinowitz
John Robinson
Richard Rockwell
Ronald Schoenberg
Karl Schuessler
John Sharp
Burton Singer
Kent Smith
David Specht
Seymour Spilerman
John Van de Geer
Dennis Willigan
David Wiley

PROLOGUE

Empirical sociology has been grounded largely in cross-sectional surveys of individuals or other social units, in part because cross-sectional studies have several definitive advantages. They tap a broad range of variations so that relationships among variables can be discerned readily; the data gathering operations can be completed efficiently and quickly; properly drawn samples provide information about populations that may be of journalistic or political interest; and over the years a variety of powerful methods have been devised for analyzing cross-sectional data in order to draw out their less obvious theoretical implications. Such advantages adequately rationalize both past and future cross-sectional research projects. Nevertheless, a truncated image of social systems emerges from cross-sectional studies, and sociologists have to turn to other research designs to improve and enrich their theoretical formulations.

Variations over time must be observed in order to develop empirically grounded models of social dynamics, and without such observations, the models that result from data analysis inevitably are static. "Static" is not to be confused with "boring and unimportant" (static principles are, for example, the basis of civil engineering) nor with "recursive" (econometric techniques, for instance, allow us to develop static models of feedback systems). Indeed, static models can even be used to predict how a change in one variable ultimately causes changes in other variables. What a static model does not do, however, is reveal what a system is doing during the period between a change in inputs and the attainment of a new equilibrium. This limitation means that static models do not provide a basis for detailed analyses of developmental processes; static models do not allow us to use a system's structure to predict or explain the over-time configuration of outcomes that occurs in response to continually changing inputs; and from static models alone we cannot say whether changing correlations between time-varying inputs arise from normal system operation or from a change in the system's structure.

The recent surge of interest among sociologists in longitudinal and historical studies hopefully will bring more understanding of social dynamics, but such an accomplishment will not come easily. Longitudinal analysis raises new problems that simply are not relevant in traditional static methodologies—for example, specifying the sources of autocorrelations in the variables and bases of periodic and exponential change over time. Dealing with these problems requires even more careful formulations of research problems than has been the case in cross-sectional research as well as elaborate and sophisticated statistical models for the analysis of data.

This volume provides a heavy concentration of papers dealing with the opportunities and problems that arise in longitudinal and historical research—seven of the nine chapters are related to this theme. Together these works offer a variety of solutions to a variety of problems, and they should be immensely helpful to practicing researchers struggling to comprehend longitudinal data sets. This volume also marks a significant change in the orientation of sociological methodologists toward longitudinal data. In its chapters, longitudinal data are approached predominantly as sources of information about dynamic processes rather than merely as a tack for dealing with problems characteristically arising in cross-sectional research (like defining causal directions). Since some of my own work contributed to the earlier orientation, it is gratifying as an editor to help foster this shift to what promises to be a more productive use of over-time data.

Chapters in this volume also deal with issues other than longitudinal analysis. Chapters one and seven offer important ideas on the use of archives in social research. Chapter six indicates how survey questions about behavior and other personal events should be worded in order to obtain useful information on rates. Chapters seven and eight deal with methodologies involved in network analyses. Chapter nine focuses on the use of statistical tests in least-squares analyses of data. In fact, communicating the full breadth of concerns requires consideration chapter by chapter.

How does one study culture and systems of knowledge that order everyday behavior? Chapter one, "The Epistemological Bases of Social Order: Toward Ethnoparadigm Analysis" by Allen W. Imershein, critically reviews some recent efforts to answer the questions that have been provided in ethnoscience (among anthropologists) and ethnomethodology (among sociologists). Seeking a more powerful framework, Imershein turns to Thomas Kuhn's writings on paradigms to elaborate on how the construct of a paradigm can guide research on the cultural basis of everyday action. Imershein's analysis indicates that an adequate *verstehen* methodology will be historiographic, focusing on crisis points when anomolies arise in an old paradigm, and it will minimize subjectivism by dealing with the actual expressions of persons in the relevant knowledge community (either oral or recorded in documents). Identifying and explicating an emergent paradigm involves searching such historical data for a configuration of new assumptions, exemplars, and rules.

Chapter two, "Estimation in Panel Models: Results on Pooling Cross-Sections and Time Series" by Michael T. Hannan and Alice A. Young, offers a strategy for analyzing multi-wave panel data in the service of parameter estimation. The procedures they propose are addressed specifically to the problem of obtaining meaningful estimates of causal parameters from panel data even in the presence of autocorrelated disturbances and reciprocal causation. Finding analytically that two related methods are equally efficient in large samples, they turn to Monte Carlo analysis to study the small-sample properties of the different estimates. Their analytic results, combined with simulation results, indicate that Ordinary

Least Squares is to be avoided in favor of a modified Generalized Least Squares approach in analyzing panel data.

Simultaneous treatment of causal relations and measurement problems is the central issue treated in Chapter three, "Assessing Reliability and Stability in Panel Models" by Blair Wheaton, Bengt Muthén, Duane F. Alwin, and Gene F. Summers. The authors begin with a review of the early literature on assessing reliability and stability from multi-wave panel studies, turn to an empirical data set that reveals anomolies in the early techniques, and then demonstrate improved procedures for estimating reliabilities and stabilities from panel data by including theoretical specifications of autocorrelations and by using multiple indicators for underlying constructs. The analyses are carried out in the framework of Karl Jöreskog's LISREL model, and one of the auxiliary contributions of the paper is its exemplary work in the analysis of empirical data using LISREL.

Chapter four deals with the problem of analyzing time series data for periods in which interventions or natural events occur that cause new trends or other shifts in variables. In particular, "On Analyzing the Effects of Policy Interventions: Box-Jenkins and Box-Tiao versus Structural Equation Models" has been described by author Douglas A. Hibbs, Jr., as "an expositional piece that outlines Box-Jenkins methods and attempts to show their superiority to econometric methods in certain classes of policy impact problems in sociology and political science." In addition to reviewing the formal features of the methods, Hibbs provides an empirical example estimating the impact of Labour and Conservative governments on unemployment in Great Britain, and he provides copious references to the literature on time series analysis.

"Estimates for Differential Equation Models of Social Phenomena" by Patrick Doreian and Norman P. Hummon (Chapter five) provides three examples illustrating how social process models can be formulated in terms of differential equations, how these can be manipulated mathematically to estimation formats, and how estimations then can be conducted using maximum likelihood procedures applied to over-time data. Distinct technical problems are posed by the examples: one on the relations between a firm's labor turnover and overtime hours, a second dealing with

Peter Blau's theory of formal organizational structure, and a third dealing with sources of public support for Parliamentary parties in Great Britain.

Aage B. Sørensen provides a contribution in the relatively undeveloped area of quasi-longitudinal studies in Chapter six, "Estimating Rates from Retrospective Questions." He demonstrates how the rates of individual events can be estimated from data collected in a single interview in which questions are asked that define durations between occurrences and the time lapsed since the last occurrence. The chapter focuses particularly on an unexpected source of bias in such estimates — interviews tend to intercept longer inter-event durations rather than shorter ones, and Sørensen gives formulas that properly correct for this bias.

"Network Time Series from Archival Records" by Ronald S. Burt and Nan Lin (Chapter seven) points out that evidence of associations can be retrieved from published materials like newspapers, and indeed longitudinal data sets showing patterns and changes in networks can be developed from such sources. Using newspaper reports on actions by government agencies, business corporations, and political parties as an empirical example, the authors discuss specific issues of reliability, including the use of structural equation models to improve estimation of a network time series.

In Chapter eight, Joseph E. Schwartz examines the mathematical basis of clustering methods depending on iterative covariance or correlation analysis. "An Examination of CONCOR and Related Methods for Blocking Sociometric Data" shows that iterative covariance analyses yield no more information than can be extracted from a principal components analysis of the original data matrix — and, in fact, the components analysis provides considerably richer insights into the pattern of clusters. Iterative correlation methods are more complex, but here too he is able to conclude from mathematical and simulation studies that the iteration procedures offer no gains and substantial losses compared to components analysis.

William T. Bielby and James R. Kluegel examine the power of simultaneous statistical tests in Chapter nine, "Statistical Inference and Statistical Power in Applications of the General Linear

Model." When multiple tests are to be performed, the power of the tests depends not only on sample size and the size of the effect to be detected, but also on the covariance structure of the data. The authors point out that while a survey sample of, say, 10,000 may provide more than enough power for many tests, a very much larger sample could be required to deal adequately with some hypotheses.

The 1975, 1976, and 1977 volumes of *Sociological Methodology* constitute my term as editor, and Karl Schuessler now takes over the editorship to guide this periodical into the 1980s. I look forward to his volumes both because I know the care he will give them and because from experience I know what outstanding work he will receive from authors and reviewers.

As a last word, I want to thank my authors, my reviewers, my secretary, Gert Rippy, and my department chairmen, Richard Simpson and Krishnan Namboodiri, for having made my editorship possible.

Chapel Hill, North Carolina   David R. Heise
October 1976

CONTENTS

Editorial Consultants   vi

Prologue
     David R. Heise   vii

1. The Epistemological Bases of Social Order:
Toward Ethnoparadigm Analysis
     Allen W. Imershein   1

2. Estimation in Panel Models: Results on Pooling
Cross-Sections and Time Series
     Michael T. Hannan,
     Alice A. Young   52

3. Assessing Reliability and Stability in
Panel Models
     Blair Wheaton,
     Bengt Muthén,
     Duane F. Alwin,
     Gene F. Summers   84

xiii

4. On Analyzing the Effects of Policy Interventions:
   Box-Jenkins and Box-Tiao versus
   Structural Equation Models
                  Douglas A. Hibbs, Jr.   137

5. Estimates for Differential Equation Models
   of Social Phenomena
                  Patrick Doreian,
                  Norman P. Hummon   180

6. Estimating Rates from Retrospective Questions
                  Aage B. Sørensen   209

7. Network Time Series from Archival Records
                  Ronald S. Burt,
                  Nan Lin   224

8. An Examination of CONCOR and Related
   Methods for Blocking Sociometric Data
                  Joseph E. Schwartz   255

9. Statistical Inference and Statistical Power
   in Applications of the General Linear Model
                  William T. Bielby,
                  James R. Kluegel   283

   Name Index   313

   Subject Index   318

SOCIOLOGICAL
METHODOLOGY
1977

An official publication of

THE AMERICAN SOCIOLOGICAL ASSOCIATION

HANS O. MAUKSCH, *Executive Officer*

❦ 1 ❦

THE EPISTEMOLOGICAL BASES OF SOCIAL ORDER: TOWARD ETHNOPARADIGM ANALYSIS

Allen W. Imershein

FLORIDA STATE UNIVERSITY

The study of the relation between knowledge and behavior has a long standing tradition in both the social sciences and philosophy. The issue took on renewed interest in philosophy with the writings of Wittgenstein (especially 1953, 1958) and the development of ordinary language philosophy (see for example Ryle, 1949; Austin, 1962; Hampshire, 1959; among many) which has only recently begun to have its impact on sociology.[1] The Chomskyan revolution in linguistics has prompted reconsideration of many issues with reverberations well beyond that field. In anthropology the refinements of linguistic anthropology and the development of eth-

---

[1] Several ethnomethodologists, for example, have developed some of their work in direct relation to the writings of Wittgenstein and Austin.

1

noscience, as an offshoot of that area, have provided the context for extensive discussion of issues surrounding how language and behavior are related. Renewed interest and argument has emerged in sociology with the development of ethnomethodology and its critiques of contemporary sociology.

Sociological investigation of knowledge systems and knowledge usage has built only minimally, however, on an extensive discussion which bears direct relation to many of the long standing issues. Kuhn's *Structure of Scientific Revolutions* (1970) has provoked much controversy in philosophical circles (for example, see Lakatos and Musgrave, 1970) and has been used by sociologists to study scientific communities and, more recently, sociology itself (cf. Friedrichs, 1970; Ritzer, 1975). But little attempt has been made to extend some of Kuhn's assumptions and arguments regarding the relation of knowledge and behavior to areas of organized activity beyond the scientific realm (see Warren, 1971; Warren and others, 1974; Imershein, 1974). The aim of this chapter is to lay out the theoretical basis and research methodology for doing just that.[2]

To be sure, there has been much sociological discussion over the relation between at least some aspects of language and behavior, particularly in social psychology. But there has been much less consideration of the relation between behavior as a widely organized (organizational) phenomenon and knowledge as also an ordered phenomenon. Most considerations of this sort are typically cast in a much broader framework: such as Parsons' normative dimension of the cultural system, Weber's Protestant ethic, or Simmel's sociation, to cite some classic examples. But studies cast at a broad cultural level tend to have great difficulty in moving away from vague general statements which may reveal little of the actual ongoing activities of the members of a culture (cf. Anderson and Moore, 1963; Geertz, 1973; Chapter one). The problem of any analytical study of the relation of knowledge and behavior can be characterized as one of having to conduct an investigation which can be conceptualized neither at solely the micro level nor solely at the macro level, but somehow must focus at that in-between level which includes a portion of both. The problem is also one of actually

---

[2]For limited substantive use see, for example, Imershein and Simons, 1976, and Nuehring and Imershein, 1975, for applications to mental health and mental health organizations; Imershein, 1977, for consideration of organizational change; and Imershein, 1976, for an application to the development of medical practice.

carrying out research, of gathering and analyzing data in a systematic manner; for once one moves off the broad cultural plane, one is faced with moving beyond the general theoretical statements to more concrete investigations, a task which seldom has been carried out except at the more narrowly individual micro-analysis level (cf. Nelson, 1972, 1973). Ethnoscience and ethnomethodology are the two primary recent perspectives in the social sciences that have attempted to conduct research at precisely this interstitial level. It is apparent from even a brief consideration of the research carried out in these areas, as is done below, that such investigations almost immediately raise questions not just of the relation between knowledge and behavior, but of how cultural members use their knowledge in relation to the behavior they engage in, a problem which has also been considered variously elsewhere in terms of the use of models (cf. Anderson and Moore, 1960, 1969; Shanin, 1972; for an earlier consideration, see Simmel, 1910). The question, quite properly throughout, is "How?," how is this knowledge used, how are these models employed? And how does one conduct research into these questions? The laying out of a framework to accomplish this task is precisely where Kuhn's considerations become important.

We propose and will argue in the following discussion that many forms of cultural activity and organized change can be considered analogous to the forms of scientific activity and change that Kuhn describes. Elucidation of Kuhn's arguments will therefore form a central part of this chapter. These formulations are of particular interest in relation to those of ethnoscience and ethnomethodology. The research tradition in ethnoscience has focussed upon the knowledge, or more particularly, the language of participants and attempted to relate that to the activities engaged in by them. Ethnomethodological research has tended to focus more on what participants do and relates that to what they know or how they use what they know. We will present a brief explication and critique of these approaches as a useful background for the consideration of Kuhn that follows, and in particular, for how the formulations developed from Kuhn[3] and presented here can resolve some of the issues left unresolved by those research perspectives. Having presented a theoretical and epistemological basis for research, we will

[3]And Wittgenstein.

then consider a methodology which might be developed from this perspective and the ways in which it could be applied. A word of caution: the theoretical and methodological perspective developed here is a formulation that is derived from early stages of ongoing research (primarily in the area of health care and mental health). Given Kuhn's cogent argument that successful research proceeds on the basis of concrete examples rather than formulations of rules, the following discussion must be considered as an attempt to formulate some of what this research perspective might look like, and should in no way be taken as specifically prescriptive for further research. The further development of this perspective and its ultimate success or failure must rest rather with the research use to which it is put and its development on the basis of that concrete usage.

DEVELOPMENT OF THE THEORY
AND TECHNIQUES OF ETHNOSCIENCE

Anthropologists' interest in native language usage and the analysis of the structure of native languages dates back many years, perhaps most notably to Sapir (1921) and to Levi-Strausss' early work (1949). In the course of this development, anthropologists have moved from some sketchy notions of language structures and ethnographic analysis to the specification of fairly sophisticated language models and analytical techniques (see for example, Frake, 1961, 1962, 1964; Goodenough, 1951, 1956, 1965a, 1965b; Lounsbury, 1956, 1964). The merging of linquistic theory with anthropological techniques into an area known as linguistic anthropology has produced a conceptualization of language structures in terms of taxonomies and lexical paradigms (Werner and Fenton, 1970, for an elucidation of these, especially in their more technical aspects; see Sturtevant, 1964, for a less technical discussion). A brief overview of these may be useful.

A lexical paradigm[4] is said to consist of two or more (normally at least three) "segregates," terms which natives use to distinguish similar terms in the same context—to "segregate" items in a given cultural environment. A taxonomy is defined as a more general classificatory system which consists of a set of segregates organized in hierarchical fashion—a given set of related segregates (as in a

---

[4]Not to be confused with scientific paradigm as used below.

lexical paradigm) is classified at a given contrast level by its inclusion under a more general term at the next higher level. The principle analytical technique applied to lexical paradigms has been that of componential analysis, and much attention has been directed at this procedure. Its goal has been to sort out the sets of segregates which form components of a lexical paradigm and to specify the principles which define the dimensions of contrast between these components. In kinship analysis, the most typical example, the anthropologist gathers a set of kinship terms, and then attempts to find how the terms are grouped and what the principles are for grouping them.

A major portion of this research tradition and some of its major outgrowths, characterized by the term *ethnoscience,* is of interest here (Werner and Fenton, 1970; Sturtevant, 1964; Psathas, 1968). Sturtevant has characterized ethnoscience as referring to the "system of knowledge and cognition typical of a given culture" (1964, p. 99). The concern of researchers within this tradition has been with the knowledge of native *speaker-hearers* and with how the natives use this knowledge. Interest has focussed not on what the anthropologist sees and the way he classifies it, but on the language that the native uses to describe and classify his world–on the native's own cognitive categories. While most researchers appear agreed on the use of native informants to elicit proper cultural categories, they disagree over whether the analysis of the principles of classification need be or can be geared to the cognitive world of the native. One position argues that once culturally relevant sets of terms are gathered, the anthropologist should analyze these terms according to their formal linguistic properties to arrive at a "structural reality" or to give a "formal account" (Sturtevant, 1964, p. 109). The other position argues that any analysis must reflect the cognitive world of the native.

CRITIQUE OF COMPONENTIAL ANALYSIS

The cognitive approach to analysis and classification emerged largely from several critiques of componential analysis. Focussing on the application of componential analysis to kinship systems, one criticism pointed out that the analysis typically done of kinship is not one of kinship terms, but of how "kin types are classified by kinship terms" (Schneider, 1965). For example, while uncle and great uncle are equally classified as kin terms, they are not equally relatives; there is a fundamental difference in the character of their being relatives, and the analysis glosses over this fact. Other more general criticisms have questioned whether componential analysis demonstrates anything more than possible relationships; whether some other criteria are needed to decide the relationships upon which natives actually do act, or whether the principles cited in a componential analysis are the same criteria which a native would use in deciding the appropriate term to employ (Wallace, 1965). That is, can the categories or criteria be considered as "cognitively real" (Burling, 1964; Hymes, 1964)? Or, further, are the criteria those that a native does use, given that he could use them (Wallace, 1965)? In sum, critics have argued that a more sophisticated method is required to evaluate what relationships natives do act upon (referred to hereafter as the first critique) and to investigate how natives make decisions regarding the use of terms which organize or classify these relationships (refered to hereafter as the second critique). The overriding issue appears to be how native usage fits into the relation between a *body of knowledge* and a set of observable and orderly native activities.

GOODENOUGH'S RECASTING OF THE PROBLEM

In an attempt to deal with these problems Goodenough (1965b) moves from the analysis of the terms of kinship to a more general consideration of the use of kinship categories as matters of status and role. Considering culture in general and roles in particular as problems of cognitive category usage—as "things that people have in mind" (Goodenough, 1951)—he argues that it is necessary to examine how natives use their own categories to define their own and others' statuses and roles. He thus wishes to move from simple analysis of labels to an analysis of how the labels are used in ongoing activities. He proposes that one must distinguish between the position a person may hold, referred to as a social identity, and the rights and duties which go with that position, referred to as status. The two are practically as well as conceptually distinct, since one may hold a position, as a brother, for example, without honoring the obligations of that position. Furthermore, he argues, the principles which govern the assumption of social identities vary with the persons involved in a situation—one should properly speak of identity relationships and status relationships, the latter being the distribution of rights and duties in an identity relationship. In broadening his analysis Goodenough moved on to investigate the norms which may govern the operation of status relationships in a culture, in particular, the deference patterns in Truk culture. But his use of a scalogram to accomplish a summary analysis and presentation of these deference patterns suffers from the same problems as componential analysis. It is questionable whether Truk natives act in terms of the deference scale he presents. Goodenough offered no justification to support the contention that his description is in fact an accurate representation of their cultural code. Nor can he therefore have offered any solution to the problem of explicating how natives use their own cultural code to engage in this behavior (the second critique of componential analysis cited above).

KEESING'S MODIFICATION: CONSIDERATION OF "OPERATING NORMS"

In an explicit attempt to build upon Goodenough's work, Keesing (1970) approached the problem by considering the "operating norms appropriate to the occupants of paired positions" in addition to examining social identity and status relationships themselves. Seeking the cognitive world of the participants, he argues that in order to collect an accurate categorization of social identities, as well as the rights and duties which go with the positions, one must be able to distinguish between rights and duties which are invariably performed by a participant holding a certain identity position, and those which are only incidental to that performance. One must be able to specify the behavioral entailments, as Keesing puts it, of holding a certain social identity, and only that identity. Without this specification the assignment of rights and duties to a social identity becomes an arbitrary decision made by the observer, and Goodenough's distinction between an identity position and the status of that identity—the rights and duties associated with it—is lost. In addition, if we are to know how native users make decisions regarding what behavior is appropriate to a given social identity—not just what they do but how they go about doing it (second critique above)—we must be able to specify the rules by which native users make these decisions, which Keesing refers to as operating norms. Following this logic, he argues that native actors are continually engaged in the process of constructing composite identities from the lowest level positions that can be said to have invariant behavioral entailments (the participant holding such a lowest level position always performs the same acts). Further, if one assumes that natives build composite identities from these lowest level positions, then one can examine the "operating norms" (rules) which native users follow—both to decide what behavior is appropriate for a given social identity and to combine lower level positions into composite social identities, thus answering the second critique. What then needs to be explicated is a cultural *grammar* for the use of these rules and their application to behavior, and we have a tentative solution to the problem of relating knowledge, behavior, and native usage. At an empirical level, however, this approach is problematic, for native users rarely or only sometimes can specify what rules they are following to engage in their activities. Given this fact and the problems in dealing with it, Keesing concludes that if natives make decisions regarding the use of basic cultural categories, or social identities (kinship terms were the initial examples), investigation into how this is accomplished can be done only indirectly at best, since most of the crucial decisions are unconscious ones (as are the rules). Thus the question of whether the principles cited in a componential analysis are the ones which natives actually use (referred to above as the second critique) is, for the moment, unanswerable. The quest for a way to relate a set of native categories to native behavior in a non-arbitrary way appears stymied.

Not so, at least not entirely. Keesing has moved down a blind alley on the basis of Goodenough's previous mapping, and how that is the case is of particular interest. First, Keesing followed Goodenough's lead in looking for labels for social identities. Indeed, analysis of systems of words (labels) has been the strength of componential analysis. But many native activities may not be specified by social identities, and certainly not necessarily by monolexemically labeled ones. This does not mean that the language describing these activities is not amenable to analysis, although the analysis must differ, at least somewhat, from componential analysis as presently conceived. It cannot be simply an analysis of terms. In fact, at the end of his discussion Keesing suggests that a fruitful alternative might be to examine the staging of "scenes and the sequence of acts that must be performed in staging them, rather than on social identities an actor moves in and out of as he passes through scenes" (1970, p. 450). This is a clear move away from much of the analytical tradition of anthropology and ethnoscience, including Goodenough's arguments. Second, in order to focus on native usage, Keesing followed Goodenough's lead in narrowing analysis to reciprocal identity relationships rather than considering them only as elements in a larger terminological system. But if these elements are taken not just as part of a terminological system but as part of a larger cognitive system which includes descriptions of various activities, and this cognitive system of native usage is subjected as a whole to analysis, then many of the problems encountered by Keesing may be avoided (see below). Insofar as such an approach is necessarily based on native usage, it would satisfy both major critiques of componential analysis. The problem of analysis then would become one of how natives describe their activities and of how they rely on examples, rules, and descriptions to engage in the practices they are observed to engage in. This has been a problem of special concern to ethnomethodologists, and their efforts in this regard will be the focus of the next section.

ETHNOMETHODOLOGY

Ethnomethodologists have argued that the solution to the problem of the social order is to be found in how members go about seeing, describing, and explaining order; accordingly, they set out to investigate how this is done. One of the most important considerations that emerges from an examination of this approach is that the specification of norms, and rules, and the like, can never be sufficient to account for how order is maintained. Thus an examination of the norms, rules, or categories of the actors' usage is in itself insufficient to account for the ordering of their activities. Two alternative formulations have been attempted (for a more extensive discussion of this cf. Imershein, 1974b; also Attewell, 1974): either participants use something in addition to the norms, such as definitions of the situation or interpretive procedures which inform them of how and when the norms should be invoked (McHugh, 1968; Cicourel 1964, 1970a, 1970b); or participants use natural language in everyday descriptions that somehow are seen as orderly (Sacks, 1963; Garfinkel, 1967; Garfinkel and Sacks, 1970), and apparently not themselves subject to analysis beyond that of participants. The first alternative cannot be satisfactory unless one assumes that the individual subject somehow generates his own procedures or meaning or definitions (otherwise these phenomena need to be themselves accounted for). To make this assumption, however, places the explanation into a radical subjectivism, as Mayrl has aptly pointed out (1973), which can ultimately explain very little. One must therefore attempt to account both for these phenomena and for how participants use these phenomena. Interpretive procedures or definitions of the situation cannot be satisfactory solutions however. The invocation of interpretive procedures, insofar as they are like rules, simply places the investigator into a never-ending regressive search for further rules. One needs further rules to know how to follow the initial ones, etc. On the other hand, definitions per se may not be uniformly argeed on nor uniformly applied. If they are uniformly agreed on, how does that make them different from norms as a matter of accounting for differential interpretation of them in different situations—which, after all, was the problem the ethnomethodologists started out with; if they are not uniformly agreed upon then how does one account for the order and regularity that is perceived in their application? At a minimum, a theory of meaning is needed to provide the necessary explanations if this approach is taken.

The alternative approach of focussing on natural language abilities and everyday descriptions may be more fruitful. If these descriptions are a matter of common background knowledge, at least common for all practical purposes, as Garfinkel notes, then the orderliness would emerge somehow out of this commonality. That is, insofar as the descriptions themselves are understood to be ordered—or to be an account of orderly activities—then the use of such descriptions in everyday settings would be seen to be orderly, as long as the activities described were not seen by some participant to be at variance with the description given—that is, when the description, for all practical purposes, is seen by all participants as accurate. If this be the case, then what is needed is an account of the ordered structure of these descriptions, an account of how participants are able to know and use these descriptions, and an account of how or in what way *accuracy* is judged by participants.

This suggests a return to Garfinkel's original research programme in which he critiqued sociology for glossing over many problems with the phrase "common culture" (cf. Garfinkel, 1963). But rather than dispensing with the concept entirely, as Cicourel and McHugh have apparently done, modification to a more concrete and specifiable level appears appropriate. For example, Schutz (1962) noted the commonality of background knowledge relied upon by social actors. The research task would be to examine the structure of this knowledge and the character of its comonality in addition to investigating the subjective usage of this knowledge as Schutz has done.

How this is to be accomplished, however, is still problematic, for analysis of knowledge structures in themselves has not proved especially successful either. The struggles of ethnoscientists with this problem have been noted in the first section of this chapter. Analysis of knowledge structures in terms of systems of words, as in kinship analysis, was deemed inadequate, both because such an approach could not account for how these words might actually be used by natives and because it did not even attempt to account for how natives were *able* to use these words appropriately. Given that proper employment of these terms presumably, but not always, entails enactment of the roles to which the terms refer (again as in kinship analysis), Goodenough argued that one needs to focus upon the dyadic role relationships in addition to the terms which classify these roles. But to account for how these roles are appropriately enacted, Keesing argued that one must find the rules which natives use to make these decisions—and we are back to a parallel of Cicourel's formulation with an ultimately regressive rule search. Note, however, both Goodenough and Keesing have narrowed their analysis in two ways. The analysis has shifted from focussing on a system of terms to focussing on a pair of terms and role relationships, and has consequently narrowed the study of the interrelations within the structures of knowledge; further, it has shifted the analysis from the knowledge structures, *per se,* to an analysis of how they are properly employed by native participants. Thus, an attempt at resolving problems in the study of knowledge structures has resulted in a shift away from studying knowledge structures at all.

We may conclude from this that an analysis of inter-relations in terminology cannot be separated from the meaning of these terms for the native participants who use them. That is, the epistemological question of natives knowing how to use terms properly implies that they know what the terms are and, presumably, what they mean. Further, the problem of meaning cannot be resolved at the level of individual participants, but must somehow be considered in terms of background knowledge of some form that is common to the participants. Any analysis of knowledge structures must presuppose a theory of meaning; one must look at the content as well as the structure of knowledge if one is to account for its proper use. Moreover as was implied above, if one wishes to account for the participants' proper use of terms and related role enactment, insofar as this usage is not radically subjectivist—that is, doesn't rely in some part on common knowledge—then usage is not simply a matter of what participants do, but of what they know—that is, what they know through common background knowledge—how they know, and what they do with what they know. One must focus at an interstitial level between cultural and individual perspectives. If sociology has avoided such epistemological problems, it is not because such epistemological assumptions were unneeded, but because they were assumed from a commonsense world and were neither critically considered nor made explicit. To do the latter is the task of the next sections.

THE PROBLEM OF MEANING IN ETHNOSCIENCE

Already in the background of ethnoscientific research is an implicit theory of meaning. The assumption of lexical constructs such as taxonomies and paradigms has within it a theory of how meaning is assigned or understood. A word in a native culture is understood by classifying it as a segregate in a paradigm or taxonomy. This provides a meaning for the word by showing both what it is and what it is not. First, the procedure shows what the word "is" (what it refers to) by placing it within a set of words which are culturally relevant to a single environmental context. Second, the procedure shows what the word "is not" by distinguishing it from all other relevant words for that context, that is, by contrast.

Componential analysis can be considered an extension of this theory of meaning in that it attempts to discover the rules by which words in a paradigm are contrasted; and thus by contrasting, to give meaning. If this is the case, however, then it is evident that not all anthropologists are agreed on the adequcy of this assumed theory of meaning, and at least some of the critiques of componential analysis (cf. above) may be considered as focussing on the question of meaning. We assume here that the meaning of a word is not primarily a matter of ostensive definition, that is, not a matter of pointing to an object to which the word refers. In the anthropological theory under consideration, meaning is much more a matter of how a word is used in relation to other words. Given this assumption, the question of whether the categories in a componential analysis are "cognitively real" (Burling, 1964) is by implication a question of what the words mean to a native participant. Thus the division of anthropologists over the reality of componential analysis also divides them on a theory of meaning.

FORMAL ACCOUNTS

In a long technical discussion of his approach to ethnoscience, one which may be considered a *formal account,* Werner makes explicit some of the epistemological assumptions ensconced in lexical paradigms and taxonomies (Werner and Fenton, 1970, cf. p. 538 for his statement regarding "formal characterization" as being "central to ethnoscience"). Werner's initial focus is upon culturally appropriate sentences that can be elicited through the use of native informants. To arrive at the cultural knowledge available to a theoretically omniscient native one must consider the set of sentences that is the sum of all sentences (excluding duplication) that might be produced by all natives in that culture. In facing the enormity of that task, Werner shifts his possible research programme from that of analyzing the substance of that knowledge to analyzing the structure of it, and makes a fundamental assumption:

> Since the content of cultural knowledge is largely
> unmanageable the emphasis in this section will be on
> systems for the organization of cultural knowledge. We
> *assume* that knowledge is organized into semantic or
> lexical *fields* (1970, p. 543; *emphasis added*).

Lexical fields have been characterized, thus far, primarily in terms
of lexical paradigms and taxonomies. But the shift in focus from
sentences to terms has strong implications for a theory of meaning
and for an epistemology, as will be noted shortly.

Given the set of culturally appropriate terms that are elicited
from a native informant, Werner also assumes that one should look
for the formal properties inherent in the language rather than
attempt to continue the search for "cognitively real" categories.
Thus, without stating it explicitly, Werner is assuming that
whatever questions arise regarding meaning or epistemology, the
proper place for the investigation of them is in the formal properties
of the language. In this respect he is consistent with Chomsky, to
whom he refers (1965). Both are interested in the theoretical
competence of an ideal omniscient native. In this context he
develops technical statements in set theoretical language of
P-definitions and T-definitions (definitions of terms based on the
lexical paradigm or taxonomy in which they are classified). Having
done this, however, he also notes "the logical primacy of semantic
and lexical fields over definitions" (1970, p. 557). Thus, although a
definition of a word may be technically stated, the meaning of that
word is still logically a matter of its place in the lexical field
(paradigm or taxonomy). The difference between this account and a
"cognitively real" one is that in the latter, meaning is examined
through actual use of the words, or so it is desired; one searches for
how natives actually use their native categories. In the formal
account, however, having elicited the terms, the question of
meaning is entirely a matter of the structure of the language. All
that is important is that one be able to generate culturally
appropriate terms and, ultimately, sentences from one's analysis.
While this cannot yet be accomplished, the possibility is assumed
not to be far off.

CRITIQUE OF THE "FORMAL ACCOUNT" IN ETHNOSCIENCE

It must be apparent to any anthropologist, of whatever persuasion, that native participants do not carry around "in their heads" a table of terms and a set of organizing rules which they consult whenever they need to use one of the terms (an assumption made by componential analysis). The question is one of whether it is useful to conceive of native thought and cognitive process in this fashion. Werner, for example, grants the priority of lexical fields over the definitions of terms in those fields (1970, p. 557), as noted above. But if a native knows the meaning of a term by its place in the field, how analogously does he know the meaning of the rule—how does he know how to follow it? Are there lexical fields for rules as well? And what are the rules for organizing that field, to play out the logic one step further? One might say that one learns the rules so that he need not have to learn each of the words whose use is governed by the rule—that is, using the rules he can "generate" a vocabulary, following Chomsky (1965), and that these rules are somehow prior to and different from the terms whose use they govern. If the question is pressed this far, no one suggests that one is taught these rules explicitly. But if they are not, how are they learned, and how is that different from learning the use of words? It is assumed that they are somehow implicit in learning to use a vocabulary or reside, again as in Chomsky (also Keesing and Cicourel), in the unconscious. But does placing the rules in the unconscious add anything to our explanation besides tying up a theoretical loose end which otherwise would be left lying loose, and embarassingly so? The necessity of rules at this point is highly questionable and, I think, ultimately both untenable and unnecessary. The necessity of rules, at this point at least, apparently results from the classification of knowledge by way of sets of terms. A fundamental assumption of ethnoscience has been that knowledge is organized in terms of lexical fields as in lexical paradigms or taxonomies (Werner, 1970, p. 543; cf. above quote). But is native knowledge learned and organized in that fashion? The discussion to follow will argue that it is not.

A number of assumptions and limitations of the ethnoscientific method suggests that this may be the case. First, the placement of terms in a lexical field depends first upon the specification of a culturally relevant context for a given set of terms. But this is a major assumption which is not accounted for later on in the theory—how does one know what is a culturally relevant context? The anthropologist of course does not, he relies upon the native informant. But how does the native informant know? Now we come again immediately to the question of epistemology. If the native participant's knowledge is organized in a fashion in any way similar to that in lexical paradigms, then he must somehow *already* know the culturally relevant categories to be able to properly use his own knowledge. But if that is the case, then we have a *central* aspect of native knowledge which is *both presupposed and unaccounted for* by the formal account in ethnoscience. Second, Werner notes the "relative inapplicability" of ethnoscientific methods to "verbs and/or abstract concepts" (1970, p. 565). To say the least, such a limitation leaves out major portions of the language of the native user. Does it therefore leave out major parts of his knowledge? Obviously yes, for many things cannot be described without the use of verbs, most activities for example, or without the use of abstract concepts. But also, no, for the set of terms in a lexical paradigm is, I would argue, an abbreviation for the concrete setting in which the term is used. Thus, many activities are assumed in the (largely nominal) categorization of terms. And this fact may be apparent given the necessity of specifying a culturally relevant context (concrete setting) in order to be able to properly categorize or employ the term.

RECAPITULATION

In order to relate knowledge structures to patterned activities it has been argued that one cannot focus solely upon individual activities without falling into a subjectivist account of meaning that is ultimately inadequate. In some sense one must look as well to the background knowledge that individual participants rely upon to accomplish their activities. Moreover, this knowledge, while it may be typically assumed as given by participants, cannot be so assumed by an investigator, but must become a focus for analysis as well. Further, in looking at the background knowledge, it also appears insufficient to look at small portions of this knowledge, such as role sets, as the ethnoscientists have in their search for "cognitive reality." Lastly, it has been argued immediately above that in looking at large portions of knowledge, it will not suffice to examine sets of terms such as lexical paradigms or taxonomies, for this leaves the question of meaning, and ultimately, of use unanswered. Further, it was asserted earlier that one must look at the context as well as the structure of knowledge. It is hopefully apparent from the discussion thus far that one cannot reach many conclusions about how native knowledge is structured without implicitly examining or assuming how it is used. For to understand the knowledge presumably elicited from native informants, one must understand the meaning of at least some of the terms, and assume as well that the native informant knows what they mean; and, in fact, in eliciting the terms one does not ask for the meaning of the terms, but in what context they are used and in what way. Now this is already a matter of looking at the content of native knowledge, and Werner's proposal (for practical reasons) that one can examine only the structure of native language (1970, p. 541) seems undermined at the outset. I believe Werner is correct in stating that lexical paradigms and taxonomies are ways of looking at structure rather than content; but it is not a way of understanding the structure of the *knowledge* under examination, but of understanding the structure of some of the *language,* terminology that is abstracted from that knowledge. That is, the distinction between the content or substance of knowledge and the structure or form of it may itself be a false distinction; at least it has been incorrectly applied. For at no point after the lifting of terms from native sentences has the examination been one of the structure of native knowledge. This is not to say that such abstractions and analyses may not be useful for other purposes (for analyzing some of the characteristics of a language or across languages, for instance). But it does not inform us about native knowledge structures, which is, after all, what we are after here. To acquire an understanding of the structure of native knowledge, we must examine as well the structure of native knowing; an ethnoscience requires an ethnoepistemology.

ON THE CENTRALITY OF MEANING BY EXAMPLE: TOWARD AN ETHNOEPISTEMOLOGY

Wittgenstein (1958) has aptly noted that asking abstract questions about the problem of meaning will often lead us into philosophical puzzles from which there is no escape. More properly, he argues, we must consider such problems in the type of context in which they might likely arise in everyday usage. Thus, to question the meaning of a word is not ordinarily, except for some philosophers, an activity engaged in apárt from some ongoing everyday reading or conversation. Further, it is precisely at this level, everyday ordered usage of the language, that questions of meaning are most important for the present discussion, for an ethnoepistemology. We need to consider what any cultural member might do in considering a problem of word-meaning. That is, we need to be able to cast our discussion at a more specific level than that of general culture and need to be able to deal with particulars; but also we need to consider problems at a more general level than that of specific individuals or groups. We need to focus at an interstitial level concerned with the orderly usage of language, knowledge, and culture.

Attempting to move in such a framework, we can tentatively say that questions of meaning arise among or between cultural members when difficulties in the use of language occur. To take the simplest example, two members carrying on a conversation come to a halt because one does not understand the meaning of what the other has said. How is this resolved? Typically one asks "What do you mean?.," is supplied with an answer, and the conversation continues. Now what is the nature of this answer? Often one may get a definition. But this is helpful only if he understands the meaning of the words in the definition supplied. If he does, then the meaning of one verbal statement which he does understand has clarified the meaning of another one which he did not (cf. Wittgenstein, 1958). It is precisely in this sense that a lexical paradigm may be of use. If one already understands how most of the words in the paradigm are used, then placing another one, whose use was unclear, into that set of words clarifies its use, or at least it may. But suppose the definition is of little help—he still does not understand the word—then what? First, what is being said here? It may be that he understands all the words in the definition, but that still does not help him to understand the word. As Wittgenstein points out, we more accurately could say that he does not understand how the word is used in this context (cf. Wittgenstein, 1958, p. 9f). That is, a word may have different meanings in different contexts, and the definition supplied somehow does not fit in this context, or at least he does not see how it fits. Then what? He may ask for further clarification: "I still don't understand." Note that it would be highly unusual and probably of little help for the person intructing him to say, "Whenever this word is used in this context, here is the rule for how it should be used—or for what it means"—which is approximately what is suggested by the rules searched for in componential analysis. Again, there may be cases where this could be useful, but it is not ordinarily the case.

Then how does he gain clarification in this matter? More than likely, by hearing an example. The person addressing him gives an example of what he means. Why is this helpful, if it is? Because the example provides both a context and the use of the word in that context. If the context is unfamiliar, then the example may be of little help. But if it is familiar, then presumably he knows other words which fit into that context, and can place the word among them. He is at least minimally competent in the culture. For without such competence the question of meaning would be irrelevant from the outset. Questions of meaning presume at least the rudiments of knowledge. Note the similarity here between the placing of a word in an example and in a lexical paradigm; in both cases a culturally relevant context is supplied as are (at least implicitly in the case of the example) other words which might be used in that context. What is different is the abstraction or concreteness, the supplying of the context by rule or by description, and the inter-relation of terms by enumeration or by use in that context, respectively (to name the important distinctions for this argument). What is suggested here is that meaning is supplied by example, that knowing, or the acquisition of knowledge, is accomplished in this manner, and that knowledge is somehow organized in a similar fashion.

In the eliciting of sentences from native informants, does not what is elicited take the form of examples, after all? That is, in order to learn a set of words which might make up a lexical paradigm, the anthropologist will either learn them in the context of concrete situations that are examples of how and where they are used; or the concrete situation will be provided for him in the examples given by the native informant as a description of how the terms are used. The contrast between words within a lexical paradigm may lie in the variations of possible happenings within an example of a given concrete situation, within a culturally relevant context. And these may be characterized more accurately as "scenes" within a given setting, as Keesing at one point has suggested (1970, p. 432; he cites the "scene" of a mortuary feast). Moreover, the problem of handling verbs or abstract concepts (which posed difficulties for analysis in lexical paradigms or taxonomies) may be largely avoided. Certainly the use of verbs is necessary in a description of a set of activities in a scene that is given in an example. Further, the issue is no longer that of individual words per se (nouns or verbs), but rather we are dealing with descriptions of activities and/or concrete situations cast in the form of examples.

A variety of other work stands closely related to the proposal presented here. Sacks' interest in everyday descriptions (1963) is not very far afield. Anderson and Moore's attempt to move from general notions of culture to an analysis of cultural objects (1963) focuses upon learnable and usable elements of a culture which might well be learned and conceived of in terms of cultural examples. Similarly, their concern with folk models (1960) as learning facilitants in interaction may be based on a similar epistemological position and parallels some of the more systematic elements of example usage to be considered below. Clearly Schutz' (1962) cultural typifications fall in line with this scheme. Even Weber's ideal types, if considered at a level of everyday culture rather than as a sociological concept, bears some clear resemblance here. For this discussion of meaning by example is presented not just to elucidate how individual word-meanings are explained, but to point out how concrete examples placed in particular contexts serve as the central elements of any ethnoepistemology, and therefore also as the central elements of our concern with the relation of knowledge, behavior, and native member usage (as will be seen in a more detailed fashion below).

Having argued for the epistemological priority of examples over the terms abstracted from them (perhaps not all that differently from Werner's argument for the priority of lexical fields over definitions drawn from those fields, cf. 1970, p. 557), we must now consider how knowledge codified in and known by means of examples may be organized. Two assumptions will be made here: First, knowledge is organized in a social fashion as well as in a structural fashion. That is to say, a body of cultural knowledge is not universally held, but is socially distributed (cf. Holzner, 1972). Thus to look for over-arching categories or examples which are held by everyone in a culture or which serve as an umbrella for all other knowledge would be misleading and fruitless. Much knowledge, specialized knowledge in particular, may be held only by persons in certain roles. But that the person in this role has this knowledge may be more generally known without knowing the content of the knowledge. Which is to say that if one does not know something in question, one may know who to ask to find out. While this may seem a fairly simple assumption which can be taken for granted, it has important implications for trying to relate knowledge structures that come from different aspects of a culture. It may be the case, for example, that the structural relation between two "bodies" of knowledge can be specified entirely in terms of the occasions when the persons occupying the roles with exclusive access to that knowledge come together in a common activity. Thus, knowledge structures cannot ultimately be separated from activity patterns. A consideration of knowledge structures is necessarily a consideration of knowledge communities (Holzner, 1972, Chapter four). Second, not all examples may be as important as certain ones. That is, for a given set of activities knowledge may be organized around a central concrete example that serves as the basis for similar activities and that covers a wide range of situations, settings, or contexts. And this central example may be commonly relied upon by all participants in that activity. The activity may be a Kwaio mortuary feast; or it may be a piece of current scientific research. The latter case has been discussed at length elsewhere, and will now be considered in some detail as a concrete example of what is to be considered here.

SCIENTIFIC PARADIGMS
AS ETHNOEPISTEMOLOGICAL EXAMPLES

In his much heralded *Structure of Scientific Revolutions*, Kuhn has introduced the concept of scientific paradigm[5] to refer to the

---

[5]Note that this usage is different from that of the anthropologists' reference to lexical paradigms. The identity of terminology is unfortunate (cf. Werner and Fenton, 1970: p. 544).

basis on which scientists commonly engage in research (1970). In *mature* science, or "normal" science as Kuhn refers to it, a paradigm is inculcated into students during their education through their introduction to an accepted way of talking and thinking, common instrumentation, exposure to textbooks demonstrating "the way things are done," etc. That is, a student learns neither a set of rules nor abstract theories which he then applies in research, though he may learn some of these things; rather he is introduced to a common and accepted set of practices, instrumentations, research questions, and the like, all of which are provided by the current reigning paradigm. In Kuhn's words the paradigm

> functions by telling the scientist about the entities that nature does and does not contain and about the ways in which those entities behave. In learning a paradigm the scientist acquires theory, methods, and standards together, usually in an inextricable mixture (1970, p. 109).

Contrary to commonly accepted notions of the more or less unilinear cumulative nature of the growth of science, Kuhn argues that science develops rather by revolutions. A crisis in normal science occurs when an established paradigm encounters puzzles which it is unable to solve ("anomalies," as Kuhn refers to them). Or alternatively, the anomalies are accounted for only by *ad hoc* additions to the existing paradigm. When a new paradigm that can explain these phenomena emerges to challenge the reigning one, scientific research enters a revolutionary stage. The question of which paradigm will win out is not typically solved by a simple empirical test, but by the growth of adherents who find the new paradigm more powerful or useful for doing research. What occurs in the change to a new paradigm is a shift in world view, a gestalt switch, or a conversion experience. To change paradigms is to change a way of thinking, a way of seeing the world (data in particular), and of doing research. Old facts and theories come to be interpreted anew in light of the new paradigm, and the course of science is change in consequence.

After a paradigm shift has occurred, scientific research moves in a new direction. The nature of this new research, how scientific activities will be organized under the new paradigm, is paradigm specific. That is, the questions to be asked, the procedures to be followed, the inter-relation of relevant sectors of the scientific community will all be provided in some form by the new paradigm which now guides research. Thus, we look to the specific content of the new paradigm to account for the re-ordering of scientific activities after a revolution has occurred.

THE STRUCTURE AND USE OF PARADIGMS

Kuhn's original discussion of paradigms (1962, First Edition) was extremely varied, as was aptly pointed out by his may critics (see, for example, Lakatos, 1970; passim); but his later discussion, particularly in the "Postscript" (1970, Second Edition), attempts to clarify and codify this usage primarily in response to his critics, and to one critic in particular who had already codified some of his usage (Masterman, 1970). Despite the similarities, there are some minor but perhaps significant differences between Masterman's and Kuhn's codifications. The latter will be followed here as more consistent with the theoretical discussion given above.[6]

Kuhn recognizes the many ways he has used the term paradigm (22 cited by Masterman) in his initial discussion and, as clarification, finds four components or elements relevant to any usage of the term. First are symbolic generalizations which he characterizes as the formal or formalizable aspects of the paradigm commonly agreed on by members who use the paradigm. They are typically found in symbolic form such as "$f = ma$" or in words such as "elements combine in constant proportion by weight." These are most often considered as laws, but may sometimes be used as definitions as well. Insofar as they are accepted as laws, they tend to define the situation under examination (as falling or not falling under that law, for example; cf. Hanson, 1958, p. 99ff.).

The second component Kuhn refers to is that of "metaphysical paradigms" (presumably following Masterman's terminology at this point). He considers this aspect as shared commitments to certain sets of beliefs about "how the world works," and, more

---

[6]A discussion of the rationale for this choice is important and somewhat relevant to the current discussion, but unfortunately would lead us too far astray at the moment. Suffice it to say that the differences are recognized.

specifically "as beliefs in particular models which among other things supply the group with preferred or permissable analogies or metaphors."

Third, Kuhn refers to shared values of scientific groups. He sees these as more broadly relevant—they are the sorts of values held in common by most scientists, such as those values regarding prediction, the usefulness of quantification, the quest for simplicity and consistency in theories, etc. Values do not necessarily differentiate between holders of different paradigms; scientists adhering to competing paradigms may nevertheless share the same values regarding scientific research (which could not be said regarding the other aspects of paradigms). They may of course apply these values differently, but this might be true within paradigm usage as well. Given that values, *per se,* are not integral to the structure of a paradigm, their relation to patterned activities will be of less concern here.

Last, Kuhn refers to what he still regards as his most important category, exemplars. These are the accepted concrete scientific achievements, the research examples, upon which the everyday practice of science is built. Kuhn places these as the center of a scientific research tradition based upon a paradigm. The symbolic generalizations (for example, the general laws by which science is so often characterized) as well as the theory and procedural rules gain their meaning and are able to be used by scientists by virtue of their employment in the exemplars upon which the scientists rely. This is not to say that the laws do not have use, clearly they do, but they do not have the epistemological status often ascribed to them by analysts of the scientific research process.

In further disagreement with much philosophical and sociological discussion, Kuhn argues that the ordering of research is not primarily, nor need it be, a following of rules; more specifically, one thing a paradigm does not do, or at least not necessarily do, is supply a scientist with a set of rules to carry on research. Kuhn is confusing at this point and, as Masterman notes (1970, pp. 84–85), he is perhaps initially confused. Given this confusion, Kuhn's discussion has sometimes been misread (see Friedrichs, 1970, pp. 4–5, p. 8) and therefore bears close scrutiny. In the course of his discussion he considers whether rules might be found to guide scientific research. But he finally dismisses this possibility:

> Normal science is a highly determined activity,
> but it need not entirely be determined by rules. . . .
> Rules, I suggest, derive from paradigms, but paradigms
> can guide research even in the absence of rules (1970, p.
> 42).

The alternative which Kuhn proposes is that paradigms guide research by direct modeling rather than through the provision of rules. To epistemologically support his contention Kuhn refers here to Wittgenstein's argument regarding family resemblances (Wittgenstein, 1953). The question raised is how it is possible to apply terms like "chair," "leaf" or "game" unequivocally and yet without the apparent use of rules. It is not, Wittgenstein argues, because all three have certain essential elements which we use as criteria to determine whether or not an object is a tree (or a game, or presumably a piece of scientific research). Rather, such things as trees, games, etc. are interrelated in ways similar to how families are interrelated, they share a number of different attributes. Two members at the extremes of a family may have no attributes in common, yet may share attributes with other members at less of an extreme who do have other attributes in common (like two cousins at opposite ends of a family tree). Learning some of the attributes of some of the members of a family usually enables us to recognize other members of the family; just as knowing some games may enable us to immediately recognize others. This does not mean, of course, that we do not make mistakes, but mistakes are possible with any use of knowledge. Kuhn argues that something similar may obtain for scientific research:

> Something of the same sort may very well hold for
> the various research problems and techniques that arise
> within a single normal scientific tradition. What these
> have in common is not that they satisfy some explicit or
> even fully discoverable set of rules and assumptions that
> gives the tradition its character and its hold upon the
> scientific mind. Instead, they may relate by resemblance
> and by modeling to one or another part of the scientific
> corpus which the community in question already recog-
> nizes as among its established achievements (1970, pp.
> 45–46).

It is for precisely this reason that Kuhn places exemplars at the center of the development of scientific research. For modeling becomes possible only with the availability of examples which can be modeled upon. Hence concrete scientific achievements which are (i) "sufficiently unprecedented to attract an enduring group of adherents away from competing modes of scientific activity" and (ii) "sufficiently open-ended to leave all sorts of problems for the redefined group of practitioners to solve" (1970, p.10), provide the basis for an ongoing scientific research tradition. The achievements, in short, provide examples upon which future research is modeled.

But how direct modeling is possible is of crucial importance. For without an explication of this notion Kuhn provides little justification for why modeling, rather than rules, guides scientific research. Again, Kuhn is not that clear on this matter. One of the apparently crucial aspects of a paradigm's utility is the possibility of its being used as a "way of seeing" (1970, p. 117). Examination of this notion may clarify Kuhn's notion of direct modeling based on exemplars. This will be the case especially if we can explain how exemplars, as central to a paradigm, can provide a "way of seeing."

EXEMPLARS AS "A WAY OF SEEING" AND A WAY OF KNOWING

In speaking of using paradigms as a way of seeing Kuhn is trying to say something both about the nature of science and about the nature of perception. Kuhn first wants to reject the view that data remain fixed all the time, and that all that changes with a shift of paradigms is how a scientist interprets data which he views. Rather, he suggests, data are not stable in that way. If there is a difference between what scientists report, it is not because they interpret data differently, but that they see data, literally, in a different way, perhaps even see different data. The shift in perception from one paradigm to another is like a visual gestalt switch. First one sees a duck, then one sees a rabbit. To be sure, for this change to occur other related elements in the 'picture' have changed—the figure is viewed as related to other elements in a way that it was not before, it is seen in a new light. But, data are seen *as data* only by virtue of relying on a paradigm. Furthermore, Kuhn argues, one does not see a figure and then interpret it in the light of a theory to be a rabbit. Rather, one *sees* a rabbit! Kuhn argues that scientists' abilities to recognize certain things as being the same or being like one another is not a matter of rule following, but of perceptual skills which have been acquired by exposure to certain shared examples, they learn to recognize family resemblances rather than engage in a deliberative process of applying rules or criteria. We may conclude that it is through reliance on these perceptual skills that a scientist is able to see a set of data as being like a previously known example, an exemplar (cf. Kuhn, 1974). The use of models is thus part of a process of reasoning analogously *from* a known example *to* a new context in which this research example might be successfully applied (cf. Polanyi, 1966; also cf. Geertz' discussion of "models of" and "models for," 1973, p. 93f.).

ETHNOPARADIGMS

Given scientists' tacit reliance on exemplars and the centrality of exemplars in scientific paradigms, it is possible now to speak of a way that "native" participants engage in patterned activities that is systematically related to the knowledge structures on which they rely. More importantly, we can do so without necessary reference to rules, especially unconscious rules. The question is: to what extent and in what way may this structure of knowledge, knowing, and activity exist beyond the realm of scientific research? That is, does it make sense to speak of and to look for *ethnoparadigms* and/or *ethnoexemplars?* Based on the foregoing arguments, a central assumption of this chapter is, yes it does, and one must look for components of ethnoparadigms in a manner analogous to the components of paradigms cited above.

To consider how these components may be found in ethnoparadigms one is tempted to consider them as elements similar to the principles which are extracted by componential analysis, that is, to see these as formal characteristics of a paradigm to be found consistently across all paradigm usages. In a sense this is correct, for such consistency would seem theoretically appropriate, but in another sense it is not. For the components of a paradigm, and perhaps they are ill-termed as components, *possess* their characteristics as components not by virtue of what they are, but by virtue of how they are used (or how they might be used in the case of a paradigm not yet adopted). Not just any example will do to be an exemplar; it must be a central example, one around which a wide range of activity is or may be organized. Not just any set of laws or symbolic generalizations will do, but they must be able to be used in a certain way; in particular, their meaning is given through their use in examples. Thus, it will not do to substitute ethnoparadigms as the structural units in replacement of the taxonomies and the like of ethnoscience and componential analysis. What this means empirically is that we should not be searching for underlying structures of which participants are unaware, for we are looking for what participants use. To be sure, it may be a tacit usage,[7] but usage nevertheless. The character of this use may be varied; it may be revealed in what participants either say or write. How a sociological observer can make valid imputations or inferences regarding what is or is not an element of usage in a given ethnoparadigm is clearly open to question, and must be considered at greater length shortly. For general purposes, and for simplicity's sake, let us consider basic assumptions, central examples, and specified rules for action as the three primary elements of ethnoparadigm usage following Kuhn's usage of metaphysical aspect, exemplars, and symbolic generalizations (especially as general laws), respectively.

The specification of analytical procedures for ethnoparadigms could lead us in many directions. The rules component of an ethnoparadigm, for example, is that part which is most likely codified into law, if such legal codification has taken place. The basic assumptions, however, probably have the most broad ranging interconnections with other parts of the culture. For such "metaphysical" assumptions are likely to tie in extensively with other cultural aspects. For example, the assumption of professional control in medical practice clearly is linked with a similar assumption in other forms of professional practice and in turn may link with more general cultural conceptual models of the role of the expert. Similarly this expertise may be specified by a set of rules in varying specialized paradigms and in turn codified into law. The whole question of the usage of conceptual models, their relation to cultural values, to conceptions of identity, etc. (cf. Anderson and Moore, 1960; Geertz, 1973; Simmel, 1910), can be brought under analytical scrutiny within this framework, and done so in a systematic manner.

[7]The notion of tacit usage or tacit knowledge is a technical one, taken from Polanyi (1958, 1966), and followed by Kuhn. See Polanyi (especially 1966) or Imershein (1974a, Chapter three) for further explication of this concept.

The problem at this point, at least for this chapter, is one of delimiting the areas of consideration to those for which investigative procedures can be mapped out. The initial focus would appear most appropriately to deal with identification of ethnoparadigms, their use, and the interrelation of the different ethnoparadigmatic components. This analysis in itself, I think, will point us toward further dimensions of this scheme and other possible directions in which it might be powerfully used.

Substantive investigation within this framework, then, will focus initially upon communally held knowledge which provides the structure for a set of organized activities. Kuhn's recent interest in scientific paradigms that characterize professional communities is entirely in line with this focus (Kuhn, 1974). The theoretical discussion presented above and the research procedures derived below were developed as part of a study of proposals for change in the organization of health care delivery (Imershein, 1974a; see also Imershein, 1977). In a similar vein Warren (1971; Warren and others, 1974) has considered competing paradigms for the explanation and resolution of poverty problems. While nowhere relying specifically on Kuhn or the notion of paradigms, Alford's analysis of competing structural interests for health care reform lends itself immediately to this kind of approach (Alford, 1975). In each analysis a set of highly organized and institutionalized activities was challenged and under pressure for change of some sort. All three studies note the differences in language and knowledge used by the competitors in their respective situations, and all three note the difficulties in institutionalizing the proposed changes. Any such investigation will necessarily be considering the "role of knowledge in contributing to social change," as Alford aptly points out (1975, p. 7). The question is: how might one go about doing that in a systematic fashion, given the preceding theoretical discussion? Providing a possible answer to that question is the aim of the discussion to follow (with related examples cited in footnotes).

PROCEDURES FOR RESEARCH

First, how does one find an ethnoparadigm? We can assume that any widely implemented, well-ordered set of activities may be paradigm guided. But the question, "Is there an ethnoparadigm as a whole which guides these activities?,," may be too general to be profitably answered. Discovery procedures should probably focus rather on paradigm elements: assumptions, rules, and exemplars. Clearly, if there is no paradigm, there can be no paradigm change. But when does one have a paradigm, and when does one not have a paradigm? We could answer this arbitrarily; as, for example, when one of the elements is lacking, but answers to more specific questions may be more informative. Consider the following brief overview which will be explicated below.

Paradigms are most easily identified at times of crisis, for, as Kuhn notes, it is at such times that communities tend to focus explicitly on what they have been doing precisely because those activities have become problematic. The problematic character is specified in terms of certain events or aspects of activities which are perceived as improperly occurring; they are anomalous to the situation. Why these events or activities come to be seen as anomalous must relate to the already established paradigm itself, for it is the paradigm which specifies the orderly direction of ongoing activities, and it is this order which has been in some sense disrupted. The anomalous events may also relate to other aspects of the cultural framework in which the activities are enacted. While that possible relation will not be pursued here, it is clearly an area for further consideration. Identification of paradigms, then, can most easily be accomplished in times of change when anomalies come to be apparent. Turning this around into an investigative approach, one could say that if no anomalies can be found, then there is no crisis to be responded to, and no paradigm shift is likely to occur. If the anomalies (in comparison to the rules of the reigning paradigm) can be explained as the result of rule violations under the current paradigm, then no new paradigm is needed. If the assumptions of the new paradigm do not in some sense account for the anomalies, then it is unlikely to differ from the reigning paradigm, and in any case, it will not resolve the crisis. And if the exemplars of the new paradigm do not provide a context for implementation of the proposed rules, then implementation of the paradigm is unlikely to occur. Partial answers to any of the above questions will reveal the weaknesses of the challenging paradigm without necessarily precluding its acceptance and success. What is to be judged as too weak a challenging paradigm is clearly a judgment without any prescribed or prescribable criteria, and can finally be decided only with the ultimate empirical success or failure of the paradigm.

One may begin the search for ethnoparadigms, then, with the appearance of anomalous events in a set of organized activities. They should be apparent by virtue of the participants' proclamations of crisis and their citation of the events which are indicative of that crisis. The anomalies should point first back to the reigning paradigm, for the awareness of crisis is the result of expectations from that paradigm which have been violated; events which should occur, do not; or events which should not occur, do.[8] The anomalies point secondly to the assumptions of the new paradigm, for the discussion which accounts for these anomalies must include a shift of assumptions from the reigning paradigm.[9] Accounting for anomalies is a necessary step, but will not do to resolve the crisis. If such an account is all that is available in the crisis-response under examination, then that response cannot constitute a challenging paradigm, for alternatives to the present anomaly-producing activities are also required. Also necessarily included in that response, and the next ethnoparadigm element to be sought, are examples (or a single example) of the recounting of events in a situation in which the anomalies have been successfully resolved. The presentation of alternative models is absolutely essential. Again, the content of the anomalies will be the cue to find the relevant examples, because it is those anomalous events which led to the alternative examples being presented. These examples serve as the exemplars for the new ethnoparadigm. Either before, after, or scattered throughout the examples may be some of the rules formulated for the new ethnoparadigm. These also will stand in a substantive relation to the anomalies, likely to be either standards to be met or procedures to be followed so as to avoid a situation in which the anomalous events could continue to occur. At a minimum, all of the above elements must be found for a challenging paradigm to exist. More detail on the character of these elements, the context of their use, and the ways they must be inter-related is the focus of the sections to follow.

[8]Extensive evidence has been cited, for example, to argue that health care provided by individually organized professionals is necessarily inadequate (cf. Alford, 1975; Imershein, 1974a).

[9]For example, how an organization of health care that does not assume the dominance and control by individual physicians might resolve the crisis.

SCENES, HISTORY, AND UNITS OF ANALYSIS

We have clearly shifted units of anlysis from the single word units of ethnoscience and componential analysis, but to what? The obvious alternative is to consider sentences, but, again, not just any sentences. They must be sentences that are used in a paradigm either as statements of assumptions, as parts of a description in an example, or as specification of a rule in a set of rules. One must decide, of course, whether a sentence or a set of sentences qualifies as any of these. Clarifying how to make that decision might be accomplished by focussing initially on the most important of these usages— namely, sentences as parts of examples.

It has been argued above that the ordering of what participants are to do in a given setting (the patterning of their concerted activity) is provided by their joint reliance upon common examples of such activity. More specifically, these are examples of scenes of action which provide both roles and the context for those roles. A shift from the words of taxonomies to the scenes of ethnoparadigms may be regarded as a shift from inter-relating words to inter-relating "what happens" in a setting, as that is provided in the scenic example. Note, however, that this is not just any scene, any action, or any description of "what happens," but has the peculiar status of being commonly relied on, for all practical purposes. We are therefore, in a sense, conducting an examination of community structure, a community defined by shared knowledge rather than shared territory. To be commonly relied on implies that participants, while not sharing identical past experiences in the same setting—knowledge on which they now rely—have encountered suficiently similar experiences of the current activity so that they may be considered the same for all practical purposes. To put this differently, while they may not have a common history (though in fact it is possible in some instances that they may), their histories have common characteristics. Further, it is not simply a matter that their pasts or past history are similar, for, if so, they may be totally unaware of that fact. Rather, it is a matter that their "present history" is similar.[10] Participants use elements out of their respective

---

[10]Warren points out that employees of various community service agencies know how to "coordinate" their activities with little explicit agrement needed over specific details. He accounts for this by pointing to their previous exposure to a common set of institutionalized practices (1974, Chapters two and three).

histories in a similar way; they rely on central examples from their past experience to guide their present conduct—they have common ethnoparadigms and exemplars.

Participants' reliance on a shared history suggests that a means of gaining greater knowledge about the organization of their present activities may be through an examination of that common past. This form of historical research into the background of presently organized activities can provide a greater context in which these activities may be seen as organized in a particular fashion. That is, when some organizational aspects of present activities are unclear, an inquiry into the emergence or inception of these activities *as* organized will be useful.[11] Further, as noted above and detailed below, paradigm identification is most directly accomplished through recognition of a situation of anomaly—crisis—response, which is, after all, a historical process. Thus, investigation of a body of knowledge as a possible paradigm is not simply a study of its present structure, but an examination of the history of its use and emergence, at least within the bounds suggested here.

It may be that any ordered body of knowledge has some of the characteristics of a paradigm, however, or could be argued to have some by an enterprising social scientist. The question is, when is the judgment of a body of knowledge as being paradigm-like warranted? As implied above, this is a matter of considering how the body of knowledge is used, or to put it another way, specifying the conditions of its use; further, given the historical dimension just added, it is a matter as well of specifying the conditions for its emergence. The latter consideration may give us the clearest indication of paradigm usage. Emergence is a matter of the beginning of use of a new body of knowledge as a paradigm, or of the replacement of one paradigm by another (a paradigm shift). Such an occurrence may be marked by fairly well-defined events, the emergence of anomalies, that can either be observed or historically reconstructed to provide evidence of paradigm emergence. We may thus cite an initial guideline for discovery procedures in ethnoparadigm research: historically/observationally reconstruct the conditions for and characteristics of paradigm emergence. Probable conditions and characteristics for such an occurrence are as follows.

[11]Cf. Imershein's investigation of the development of the Citizens' Board (1974a, Chapter five); also Alford (1975, Chapter two) and Warren (1974, Chapter seven).

ANOMALIES AND THE HISTORICAL EMERGENCE
OF PARADIGMS

Anomalous events mark the appearance of a crisis in a research tradition and set the conditions for a possible paradigm shift.
The occurrence of these events, unexplained by the reigning paradigm, is both expected and unexpected. It is expected in that
events of a certain sort are not only expected by the paradigm users,
but looked for by them. Many events may be unexpected or unexplained by a paradigm-guided research tradition but are dis-
regarded because they are seen by members of the paradigm community to be irrelevant to the research at hand; in essence such
events are defied by the paradigm as not being data proper for
research. Anomalies appear when data considered proper for research do not appear in the way they are supposed to. In that sense
the events which constitute data are unexpected as well, or as Kuhn
puts it, anomalies are a violation of expectations (1970, Chapter
six). Similarly for ethnoparadigms there is a sense that "given these
conditions, things shouldn't happen this way." Further, the violated
expectations have been generated by the current reigning paradigm,
which is precisely the reason why a crisis occurs.

The occurrence of anomalies does not invariably result in a
shift of paradigms, but it does induce a crisis which in turn may be
resolved in several ways. Events thought to be anomalous turn out
not to be, some fact at first overlooked is discovered to make those
events fall into place, or the reigning paradigm is somehow extended
and modified to include and explain the anomalous events.[12] This
may entail a weakening of the paradigm. For example the expectations it generates may be neither as specific nor as sure as previously;
but if no alternate paradigm appears to explain both the anomalous
events and others already handled by the reigning paradigm, then
at best the old paradigm will be used, and the crisis may continue to
greater or lesser degree. The situation of greatest interest, however,
at least for the purposes at hand, is one in which anomalous events
continue to be recalcitrant, the reigning paradigm is unamenable to
extending over these events, and a new paradigm emerges to challenge the reigning one. Again, whether or not anomalous events are

---

[12]Alford's analysis of the critiques and modifications (or lack of them) of
health care in New York City provides an excellent example of this latter process
(1975).

considered to be recalcitrant and the reigning paradigm not amenable to accounting for them is, at least in part, a decision of some part of the paradigm community. Such decisions are in this sense always "political."

Extending this framework to areas of patterned activities beyond the scientific realm, we may say that the appearance of events, happenings, actions, consequences of patterned action, or the like, which are unexplainable and violate the expectations of participants in a patterned set of everyday activities, may be considered as anomalies indicating a crisis which in turn may precede a paradigm shift.[13] That violated expectations demand a response is nothing new to sociological observation. Sociological commentary on responses to deviant activities has lately been focussed upon the procedures followed by participants to make sense out of these activities (see Scott and Lyman's discussion of accounts, 1968; and McHugh's discussion of explanations of deviance, 1970; both are ethnomethodological investigations into this area). What is of interest here, however, is the importance of the paradigm which provides the necessary background for such expectations of "proper activities" to be held and violated. Note that not all "proclamations of doom" may be considered crises of a paradigm variety. The area must have been previously guided by a paradigm, and, therefore, have been previously well-ordered, for all practical purposes. Further, what is characteristic of a paradigm crisis is that the members of a group who jointly have relied upon a common paradigm are the ones who must recognize the anomalies, for it is they who know how to use the paradigm. Thus, calls for better health care delivery by politicians may indicate little,[14] calls for better health care delivery from physicians (under conditions described earlier in this section) may indicate a paradigm crisis.

How is the sociological observer to decide whether "apparent" or "perceived" anomalies are "actual" anomalies? Further, how is he to validate his decision in reporting it to other scientists? As discussed above, the decision regarding what are and what are not anomalies is not one made by a sociological observer alone, or

---

[13]In the case of health care delivery the availability of medical technology and personnel to provide adequate health care without that result actually occurring may constitute just such violated expectations (cf. Alford, 1975; Imershein, 1974a).

[14]Cf. the problems that Alford cites (1975, Chapter two).

even primarily. The perception of anomalies is a participant's activity, and accurate perception and assessment of *that* activity is the
sociological problem. In one sense this is to say that anything that a
participant decides is an anomaly is, by definition, an anomaly, for
it is a matter of the participant's response to a crisis, not the
sociologist's. It is of course the case that the participant may be
wrong or that he may have contrived the crisis for some other
purpose (perhaps a political purpose). Here is where the obser-
ver/researcher must make his decision: not whether the anomalies
are actual or not, but whether it is reasonable to accept the participants' judgment in that regard. Consider the following two
guidelines for making this research decision and for providing
validation of the decision. First, response to a crisis and the perception of anomalies is not an individualistic affair, but one of a community or group of participants. Observation and/or reconstruction
of the sequence of events/actions which constitutes the perception of
crisis and anomalies may provide evidence of the "actuality" of the
anomalies and the validity of the sociological decision to regard
them as such. This recounting of events would essentially be a
presentation of the common history of the group or characteristics
common to the histories of the participants or groups perceiving the
crisis/anomalies (as discussed above). It is difficult, if not impossible,
to say what would constitute a good "history" of such events, except
that it tells what happened. This is not to say that one cannot say
after the fact whether it is a good recounting of events or not; one in
fact can and must. Other researchers will make similar decisions
based on their own perceptions and abilities to distinguish good
histories (and examples) from not so good ones. One at least wants to
know "what happened." But to provide criteria at this point would
be to invert the relationship between rules and examples presented
in earlier sections. One does not have rules for judging what is a good
example; one makes that judgment by virtue of what the example
(or series of examples put together in a history) reveals about what
happened and what use it can be put to elsewhere. To be sure, we
may have rules of thumb to exclude examples that are not appropriate, and the citation of such a rule may be all that is necessary to
exclude that example. However, the use of those rules rests on the
knowledge of what kinds of examples the rules apply to, and we are
thus back to a consideration of examples and their uses.

As a second guideline we may consider the comparison of the

anomalies perceived by the participants with the reigning paradigm. In a sense, to do this may mean jumping ahead of the paradigm community. That community must make a judgment as to whether the anomalies are resolvable under the reigning paradigm. The point of the comparison suggested here is to make just such a judgement. Kuhn speaks of the incommensurability between competing paradigms—that one sees the world differently through different paradigms, and that to move from one paradigm to another is often a problem of translation. Two participants may view a situation differently; one sees only a minor problem, the other sees an anomaly and a possible crisis.[15] How the latter participant sees this, or these, is obviously relevant to the reigning paradigm, as was stated earlier. Therefore, a second way to evaluate the existence of anomalies is to try to engage in the same sort of comparison as does the active participant. How might this be done?

One way would be to make a *test of consistency* between the anomalies and the symbolic generalizations (rules) of the reigning ethnoparadigm. Further comparisons might be useful, but the central examples or background assumptions of the reigning ethnoparadigm may not be easily discoverable or accessible. Given the extensive elaboration of a reigning paradigm, however, the rules may not only be accessible, but may be the most characteristic part of that body of knowledge, as, for example, in its expression in legal statutes.[16] The question of consistency would be handled as follows. The initial recognition of anomalies may be made on the basis of a variety of largely unspecifiable particulars relied on by participants. But continuation of this judgment would rest as well on an examination of the reigning ethnoparadigm in order to consider whether it may be extended to cover the anomalies, or whether the anomalies may be the result of an inadequate reliance (mistakes, for example) on the paradigm by some of the participants and, therefore, accountable by the paradigm. Thus, if it can be shown by an examination of the rules of the reigning paradigm that the anomalies cannot be explained away as mistakes, then it can be said

[15] For example, two physicians may agree that the country should deliver the best possible health care to its citizens, one sees the medical profession as doing just that, the other does not; and they both mean different things when they say "best possible health care."

[16] For example, state medical practice acts—and the professional code of ethics to which they typically refer.

that there is no necessary inconsistency between the paradigm and the anomalies. Without some inconsistency, the anomalies may not be discounted as being the result of improper use of the paradigm, and the whole paradigm may be brought into question. Recall again that this sociological decision is one analogous to possible community decisions. But it is unlikely that community members might make a detailed pairwise comparison of the cited anomalies and paradigm rules and an examination for rule violation that would be appropriate for sociological investigation. Given this fact, the sociologist's decision may be subject to error in exactly the same sense that community decisions may be subject to debate and disagreement. What constitutes a "correct" decision is finally a matter of community *usage,* not something which is inherent in the language. Again, such community decision-making may relate systematically to other cultural elements used by the community, and would be a fruitful area for investigation beyond the scope of the present discussion.

ANOMALIES, METAPHYSICS, AND BACKGROUND ASSUMPTIONS

The development of a new paradigm in response to the anomalies and crisis can be seen, in part, as the result of a shift in metaphysics or background assumptions, or as a change in the beliefs about "how the world works." It is by virtue of this shift that the anomalies so far unaccounted for may be explained and put into place. That this is the case may only be apparent through the development of concrete examples that serve as exemplars for the new paradigm, a new way of doing things (for example, heath care delivery) that takes into account the anomalies. But a careful examination of the shift in assumptions may reveal the basis on which such changes are made. The question, of course, for the sociological researcher is that of how to ferret out the new assumptions of the challenging paradigm.

The discovery of a change in assumptions may be easier to accomplish if a written document is available, but they can probably be searched out through conversation or interviewing as well.[17]

[17]For examples of the former see Alford's analysis of commission reports (1975, Chapter two), or Imershein's analysis of the Citizens' Board Report (1974a: Chapter five).

The focus again should be on the response to the anomalies. Given that the anomalies have generated a crisis, the first step in the resolution of that crisis is an explanation of why these anomalies occurred. Such an account is necessarily the point of initial arguments in any challenging paradigm, and the assumptions of that argument must form the background assumptions of the remaining portions of that paradigm (for example, exemplars of situated activities in which the anomalous events do not occur).[18] The arguments accounting for the anomalies will, of course, be similar in subject matter to the anomalies. The assumptions must be ferreted out from those arguments. Guidelines for accomplishing that are as follows.

First, one must obviously decide what discussion may be regarded as an argument in response to the anomalies. Again this consists of engaging in a process analogous to that carried out by members of the paradigm community. Second, one must keep in mind the rules of the reigning paradigm. Recall that this is the most obvious part of that paradigm, and some part of those rules will likely be inconsistent with some of the central tenets of the explanatory argument. One could analyze the argument into several component parts or main tenets and then compare these in pairwise fashion with each element in the set of rules for the reigning paradigm, but this might be an unnecessarily long, arduous, and ultimately misleading procedure. It would be long and arduous for obvious reasons, but it would be misleading in that one would likely be already relying on one's knowledge of the rules of the reigning paradigm, and its relation to the arguments in the challenging one, in order to break down those arguments into components. Thus, one would simply be re-analyzing the knowledge one had already "surreptitiously" used to make earlier methodological decisions. Thus, we are necessarily back to a question of careful and reasoned judgment.

Third, one must choose what appear to be the central assumptions of the argument. These are the new assumptions. This choice is again a matter of judgment, this time being at once more

[18]For examples of these with regard to health care cf. explanations of the health care crisis presented by the Citizens' Board and cited by Imershein (1974a, Chapter five); see also the Citizens' Board Report itself (1974, Chapters two and three).

tenuous and less crucial. More tenuous because any number of assumptions may be central to the argument; who is to say which ones are the most central, and on what grounds? Less crucial because most of the assumptions are likely to be inter-related, and, thus, choosing some may imply the others. Again one is working backwards from the anomalies to the statements which account for the anomalies, to the assumptions which underlie these statements. Presumably the anomalies are referenced serially or grouped in sets (categorized), and the statements accounting for them will be similarly grouped. Such ordering of the anomalies is part of the process of placing them in a context in which they are explainable, as a part of these same arguments. The central assumptions should by implicitly or explicitly referenced in each set of statements for each category of anomalies; or if not the exact same assumptions, a set of assumptions which exist in a family relation to each other (see above discussion of family relations). To be sure, the sociologist, like the community member, recognizes an assumption in an argument by virtue of the fact that it cannot be done without and still have the argument intact. This can only be used as a rule of thumb, however, in that another statement of a similar sort might be used as an assumption instead. Given that, one would then have to decide what other statements of a similar nature could still be included if a particular one were done without. One is back, therefore, to a common understanding of the everyday language that is used. The point of the analysis will be to demonstrate that the usage is consistent throughout a set of arguments.[19] If the usage is consistent, however, then the central assumptions are just that, central and used throughout. There is one particular limitation here. The common understanding of everyday language is assumed to be both common and stable; that is a necessary assumption, and one that cannot be avoided. But given the change of activities and the elaboration of a paradigm along with it, say under the new paradigm, the use of the language in that paradigm may also change somewhat. Which is only to say that assumptions not initially regarded as important by either sociologists or participants at the

[19]Alford's analysis is particularly revealing at this point. He cites the contradictions and inconsistencies in the arguments of the commission reports and notes the near impossibility of implementation of the recommendations given this fact.

inception of a paradigm may later be seen to be much more important, given the way in which the activities and the paradigm
develop. In scientific research Kuhn has noted the fact that the full
possibilities for a paradigm's use are rarely seen at its initial inception; such awareness comes only with the growth and extension of
the paradigm. This is not to say that initial decisions are wrong, but
that they are neither ultimately nor totally binding. The paradigm
is subject to development, and so, therefore, is the anlysis of the
paradigm.

RULES AND EXEMPLARS: DISCOVERY AND ANALYSIS

The rules of a paradigm may be the easiest to discover, for
they are the most explicit and probably the most recognized and
stated by the participants. In a written document, they may constitute the recommendations for action, policy guidelines, regulatory
principles, or simply rule-like statements regarding what should be
done (normative directions for action). In well-organized areas of
activity they may take the form of legal statutes or proposals for
same. In that a single rule will rarely do to specify some program of
action, the rules will most likely come in sets and will be recogniza-
ble in this regard. They will also likely be the most clearly and boldly
stated part of the paradigm, for they are the easiest of the three
aspects for participants to codify and communicate. In that there
may be a necessity for legal changes for a structured change in
activity to occur, and given that the rules may be easily translated
into legal statutes, participants using the rules may regard them as
the most important part of the paradigm. If not codified in written
form, the rules can probably be easily elicited by asking for direc-
tives for action in a given setting for which the paradigm is thought
relevant. The problem of collecting a complete set of rules is ob-
viated in the case of a written document, for they are already stated.
In the case of verbal collection, more than one participant may need
to be consulted (as in the case of ethnographic informants), but the
decision regarding completeness is ultimately a participant's decision, not the sociologists'. Again, incompleteness cannot be taken as
a serious problem. First, for a given area of activity, the larger the set
of rules to determine that activity, the greater the likelihood of
overlap and inter-relation between the rules, and the less the need

for additional rules. Second, as argued previously, no area of activity can ever be completely specified by rules, and incompleteness is necessarily the case.

Exemplars may be somewhat more dificult to locate. Often they may be assumed as common knowledge in statements of the rules and not be explicitly stated themselves. In the case of the verbal collection of data the exemplars can most likely be elicited through a simple asking for examples: "In a given situation, what do you do?" If given a rule for what to do, ask for an example of how it might be used. In a written document, examples will most likely be used to illustrate some of the rules being stated.[20] In fact, as indicated in the theoretical discussion above, such illustration is necessary for the rules to be considered meaningful—for participants to know what is meant.[21] The more difficult problem may be in deciding which of the examples are central and most important—which may be peripheral illustrations and which constitute exemplars. If the paradigm is already accepted, the exemplars will likely be those examples which are most often or most consistently cited by participants. At an earlier stage, such decision-making may not be possible, for no exemplar has probably yet emerged to be of central and general usage by participants. Again, this is probably less of a problem than it might seem; for the examples provided are probably all interrelated to one another; they are all similar or may have family resemblences (cf. discussion in earlier section on family resemblences). The more important question is one of what examples are needed to understand the rules of the paradigm in such a way that the rules might be implemented, and that brings us to the question of how these two aspects of a paradigm may be analyzed.

The procedures for analyzing the rules and exemplars of a paradigm have already been implied in the theoretical discussion above. Having already acquired a set of rules and a set of examples, respectively, the main issue is whether the rules are understandable as given. As was argued previously in this chapter, the ultimate way in which a rule may be considered understood is by virtue of a demonstration of how it might be followed, in short, by giving an

[20]See for example the alternatives for health care delivery presented by the Citizens' Board (1973, Chapter four); also see Imershein's analysis of same (1974, Chapter five).

[21]Alford's analysis of commission reports with major undefined terms is a good example of this problem (1975, Chapter two).

example of how the rule is to be followed. Thus the main analytical task is that of finding out whether such provision is made in the examples of the paradigm. Procedurally this may be accomplished by taking each rule from the set of rules and sequentially examining the set of examples to find one which constitutes an example of following the rule. This is a pairwise matching of rules and examples, and may be presented as such for the sake of brevity if nothing else. If there is a problem here, it is probably not one of the rule being not understood, but rather that it may be understood or followed in any number of ways; the example limits this possible usage. Thus understanding the rule may not be a problem for the researcher. Where it is not the case that the rule is unclear, and the context for a single usage is in question, then the researcher's judgment is indeed more dificult. Again, he has no privileged position from which to do this. His position is essentially that of any community member deciding how a rule should be followed and what may constitute an example of its being followed. This is not to say that his decision is arbitrary; it might simply be wrong, or so it could be legitimately argued by other researchers or participants. The best test of the use of the rule could come only with acceptance of the paradigm and implementation or non-implementation of the rule. The best a researcher can probably do at this point is to point out the tenuousness of his decision and to state his reasons for making it the way he did—state how it fits into the rest of the paradigm. The above procedure as a whole must be the crux of the analysis, for no calls for change or programs for action can finally be implemented without concrete examples of how that might be done. As is clearly evident from both Warren's analysis of attempted resoltuions of poverty problems (1974) and Alford's analysis of health care (1975), rules or policy guidelines are simply insufficient for the implementation of new activities.

RECAPITULATION
AND GENERAL CONSIDERATIONS

We have considered at some length the discovery procedures for elements of a paradigm and various kinds of intra- and inter-paradigm analysis:

(1) the examination of the historical context for paradigm usage or paradigm shift;

(2) the discovery of anomalies, reigning paradigm rules, and new paradigm elements;

(3) the relation of anomalies to rules of the reigning paradigm;

(4) the relation of anomalies to assumptions of the new paradigm;

(5) the relation of rules to exemplars of the new paradigm.

It is probable of course that other relations of the paradigm elements can also be analyzed, in particular, the relation of assumptions to rules and exemplars in the new paradigm. Crucial points in the assumptions are likely to be also specified in the rules, and, similarly, these points must be explicated by presentation of examples. Thus we have indirectly analyzed some of the inter-relations (assumptions and exemplars, for example) already, in our analysis of rules and examples. The specification of further research procedures along this line is now in process.

We can make three general assertions about paradigm analysis based on earlier theoretical/methodological discussion. First, it can explain the ordered character of a set of activities that is guided by a given paradigm. Second, it can predict within the limitations discussed above the possibilities for and, to a lesser degree, the likelihood of change (of a paradigm shift). Third, given the possibilities for change, it can predict in detail the character of that change. To be sure, the latter is possible only on the assumption that all other things are equal; that is, if the paradigm is adopted as it stands, then this is what will happen. To specify exactly what that might be one must turn to the substance of the paradigm itself, which would be the point of any given analysis, such as those of Warren (1974), Imershein (1974a), or Alford (1975).

In conclusion, a consideration of the above data selection and data analysis problems highlights the unusual position of any sociologist attempting this type of investigation. The standard canons of reliability, validity, and replicability cannot be applied in any straightforward way. It is not that data gathering or coding in such research lacks reliability; rather, it is a matter of lack of clarity over what exactly constitutes reliability. Presumably the issue is one of reseearchers that are using the same data pool and same procedures being able to make choices which result in the same data being selected and categorized. But what may as well be the issue here is the issue of what constitutes "the same" data or categorization. For example, one researcher may select a slightly different set of statements from one portion of a paradigm (as constituting the assumptions of that paradigm) than does a colleague. In the same research, the problem is one of reliability; in later research, one of replicability. On the one hand it appears that they have chosen different statements. They are not "the same." But on the other hand, if one set of statements taken jointly is *used* in the same way as the assumptions by community members is in the second set of statements (as was suggested in earlier sections), then for all practical purposes it may be possible to consider the two sets of statements as *the same*. The words are not the same, but the usage is. The research problem then is not only one of presenting sets of statements which constitute components of a paradigm, but also one of providing the evidence for how they are used as components in the paradigm. That presentation may be the most crucial aspect for the development of an ordered tradition of research in this area.

Finally, let us briefly consider questions of scope and explanatory power for the perspective presented here. Clearly, only the first and basic elements have been considered, ones which focus on the problem of order from a perspective of change or possible change. Questions of the relation between ethnoparadigm elements in a *stable* setting and, further, their relation to other general elements of a culture or specific elements of a cultural setting remain open as a research challenge. What is hopefully set forth here, and strikingly so, is the primary direction such new efforts should take. An examination of the relation between a body of knowledge and a set of orderly activities can be seen ultimately as one aspect of the classic sociological quest for a solution of the problem of the social order. And what is hopefully made apparent by the discussion in this chapter is that the solution to the problem of the social order cannot be accomplished as Parsons, for example, attempts, by an imposition of sociological categories upon the wide range of levels and activities which Parsons rightly addresses. For any order displayed by that impositon of categories is necessarily one that is *imposed* by the sociologist precisely with and by his categories, and necessarily glosses over the actuality or degree of order that is to be found in the setting, the culture, or the society which is to be studied. The search for universal categories which can be applied to all levels and settings is, in principle, a fruitless search, for it finally cannot provide the explanation that it initially sought. The problem of the social order, as ethnomethodologists have rightly argued, must be seen as solved, if it is at all, only and precisely at the level of everyday activities of the members of the culture under examination. For it is at that level that varying degrees of order obtain or do not obtain, are perceived or not perceived by cultural members, and are observed and commented upon or not observed and commented upon by the sociologist. The interesting question is not simply that there are differences of degrees, for surely that much must be obvious. What is interesting is *how,* in fact, the differences of degree occur. And investigation of that "how" is the point of the research perspective presented in this chapter, albeit only the first few elements of such a perspective. The excitement and challenge lie not so much in the application of the framework as it is already stated herein, but in the exploration of new details and aspects of the approach and in the investigation of where and how it might possibly be extended and applied. It is that possibility, rather than a detailed prescriptions for future research, that the reader should hopefully have left in mind.

REFERENCES

ALFORD, R.

    1975   *Health Care Politics.* Chicago: University of Chicago Press.

ANDERSON, A. R., AND MOORE, O. K.

    1960   "Autotelic Folk-Models." *Sociological Quarterly* 1:203–216.

    1963   "Toward a Formal Analysis of Cultural Objects." In M. W. Wartofsky (Ed.), *Boston Studies in the Philosophy of Science 1961–1962.* Dordrecht-Holland: Reidel.

    1969   "Some Principles for the Design of Clarifying Educational Environments." In David Goslin (Ed.), *Handbook of Socialization Theory and Research.* Chicago: Rand McNally.

ATTEWELL, P.

    1974   "Ethnomethodology Since Garfinkel." *Theory and Society* 1 (Summer):179–210.

AUSTIN, J. L.

    1962   *How to Do Things with Words.* Boston: Harvard University Press.

BALDAMUS, W.

    1972   "The Role of Discoveries in Social Science." In T. Shanin (Ed.), *The Rules of the Game.* London: Tavistock Publications.

BERSHADY, H.
1973   *Ideology and Social Knowledge.* New York: Wiley.

BURLING, R.
1964   "Cognition and Componential Analysis: God's Truth or Hocus-Pocus?" *American Anthropologist* 66:20–28.

CHOMSKY, N.
1957   *Syntactic Structures.* The Hague: Mouton.
1965   *Aspects of the Theory of Syntax.* Cambridge: M.I.T. Press.

CICOUREL, A. V.
1964   *Method and Measurement in Sociology.* New York: Free Press.
1968   *The Social Organization of Juvenile Justice.* New York: Wiley.
1970a "Basic and Normative Rules in the Negotiation of Status and Role." In H. Dreitzel (Ed.), *Recent Sociology No. 2.* New York: Macmillan.
1970b "The Acquisition of Social Structure: Toward a Developmental Sociology of Language and Meaning." In J. Douglas (Ed.), *Understanding Everyday Life.* Chicago: Aldine.

CITIZENS BOARD OF INQUIRY
1971   *Heal Yourself.* Report of the Citizens Board of Inquiry into Health Services for Americans. Published by the Board.
1973   *Heal Yourself.* Second edition. Washington: American Public Health Association.

DOUGLAS, J.
1970   (Ed.), *Understanding Everyday Life.* Chicago: Aldine.

FRAKE, C. O.
1961   "The Diagnosis of Disease among the Subanun of Mindanao." *American Anthropologist* 63:113–132.
1962   "The Ethnographic Study of Cognitive Systems." In S. Tyler (Ed.), *Cognitive Anthropology.* New York: Holt, Rinehart and Winston, 1969.
1964   "Comment on Burling." *American Anthropologist* 66:119.

FREIDSON, E.
1970   *Profession of Medicine.* New York: Dodd, Mead.

FRIEDRICHS, R.
1970   *A Sociology of Sociology.* New York: Free Press.

GARFINKEL, H.
1952   *The Perception of the Other: A Study in Social Order.* Unpublished doctoral dissertation. Department of Sociology, Harvard University.
1963   "A Conception of, and Experiments with, 'Trust' as a Condition of Stable Concerted Actions." In O. J. Harvey (Ed.), *Motivation and Social Interaction.* New York: Ronald Press.

1967   *Studies in Ethnomethodology.* Englewood Cliffs, N.J.: Prentice-Hall.

GARFINKEL, H., AND SACKS, H.,

1970   "On Formal Structures of Practical Actions." In John C. McKinney and Edward Tiryakian (Eds.), *Theoretical Sociology.* New York: Appleton-Century-Crofts.

GEERTZ, C.

1973   *The Interpretation of Cultures.* New York: Basic Books.

GOODENOUGH, W. H.

1951   *Property, Kin, and Community on Truk.* New Haven: Yale University Press.

1956   "Componential Analysis and the Study of Meaning." *Language* 32:195–212.

1965a   "Yankee Kinship Terminology: A Problem in Componential Analysis." *American Anthropologist,* Vol. 67, No. 5, Part 2:259–287.

1965b   "Rethinking Status and Role: Toward a General Model of the Cultural Organization of Social Relationships." In S. Tyler (Ed.), *Cognitive Anthropology.* New York: Holt, Rinehart, and Winston, 1969.

HAMPSHIRE, S.

1959   *Thought and Action.* New York: Viking Press.

HANSON, N. R.

1958   *Patterns of Discovery.* London: Cambridge University Press.

HOLZNER, B.

1972   *Reality Construction in Society.* Cambridge: Schenkman.

HYMES, D. H.

1962   "The Ethnography of Speaking." In T. Gladwin and W. Sturtevant (Eds.), *Anthropology and Human Behavior.* Washington, D.C.: Anthropological Society of Washington.

1964   "Discussion of Burling's Paper." *American Anthropologist* 66:116–119.

IMERSHEIN, A. W.

1974a   *The Social Construction of Medical Practice.* Unpublished doctoral dissertation. Chapel Hill: University of North Carolina.

1974b   "Language, Social Roles, and Social Order: A Review and Critique of Ethnomethodogy." Paper presented at the annual meeting of the Southern Sociological Society.

1976   "The Medicalizing of American Society." *Catalyst,* forthcoming.

1977 "Organizational Change as a Paradigm Shift." *Sociological Quarterly* 18, forthcoming.

IMERSHEIN, A. W., AND SIMONS, R. L.
1976 "Rules and Examples in Lay and Professional Psychiatry: An Ethnomethodological Critique of the Scheff-Gove Controversy." *American Sociological Review* 91:559–563.

KAY, P.
1966 "Comment on Colby." *Current Anthropology* 7:20–23.

KEESING, R. M.
1970 "Toward a Model of Role Analysis." In Raoul Naroll and Ronald Cohen (Eds.), *A Handbook of Method in Cultural Anthropology.* Garden City, N.Y.: The Natural History Press.

KUHN, T. S.
1962 *The Structure of Scientific Revolutions.* Chicago: University of Chicago Press.
1970 *The Structure of Scientific Revolutions.* Second edition. Chicago: University of Chicago Press.
1974 "Second Thoughts on Paradigms." In Frederick Suppe (Ed.), *The Structure of Scientific Theories.* Chicago: University of Chicago Press.

LAKATOS, I., AND MUSGRAVE, A.
1970 (Eds.), *Criticism and the Growth of Knowledge.* Cambridge: Cambridge University Press.

LEVI-STRAUSS, C.
1949 *The Elementary Structures of Kinship.* New York: Beacon Press. English edition published in 1969.
1963 *Structural Anthropology.* New York: Basic Books.
1966 *The Savage Mind.* Chicago: University of Chicago Press.

LOUNSBURY, F. G.
1956 "A Semantic Analysis of the Pawnee Kinship Usage." *Language* 32:158–194.
1964 "The Structural Analysis of Kinship Semantics." *Proceedings of the Ninth International Congress of Linguists.* The Hague: Mouton. Also in S. Tyler (Ed.), *Cognitive Anthropology.* New York: Holt, Rinehart, and Winston.

MASTERMAN, M.
1970 "The Nature of a Paradigm." In Imre Lakatos and Lakatos and Alan Musgrave (Eds.), *Criticism and the Growth of Knowledge.* Cambridge: Cambridge University Press.

MAYRL, W. W.

1971   *Subjectivism and Social Analysis: An Inquiry into the Methodological Foundations of Ethnomethodology.* Unpublished doctoral dissertation. Department of Sociology, State University of New York at Buffalo.

1973   "Ethnomethodology: Sociology Without Society." *Catalyst* 7 (Winter): 15–28.

MC HUGH, P.

1968   *Defining the Situation.* New York: Bobbs-Merrill.

1970   "A Common Sense Conception of Deviance." In J. Douglas (Ed.), *Deviance and Respectability.* New York: Basic Books.

NELSON, B.

1972   "Communities, Societies, Civilizations: Postmillenial Views on the Masks and Faces of Change." In M. Stanley (Ed.), *Social Development.* New York: Basic Books.

1973   "Civilization Complexes and Intercivilizational Encounters." *Sociological Analysis* 34 (Summer):79–105.

NUCHRING, E., AND IMERSHEIN, A. W.

1975   "Open Systems, Organizational Research, and the Sociology of Knowledge." Paper presented at the annual meeting of the Southern Sociological Society.

PSATHAS, G.

1968   "Ethnomethods and Phenomenology." *Social Research* 35 (September): 550–520.

POLANYI, M.

1958   *Personal Knowledge.* Chicago: University of Chicago Press.

1959   *The Study of Man.* Chicago: University of Chicago Press.

1966   *The Tacit Dimension.* New York: Doubleday.

1969   *Knowing and Being.* Marjorie Greene (Ed.). Chicago: University of Chicago Press.

RITZER, G.

1975   *Sociology: A Multiple Paradigm Science.* Boston: Allyn and Bacon.

RYLE, G.

1949   *The Concept of Mind.* New York: Barnes and Noble.

SACKS, H.

1963   "Sociological Description." *Berkeley Journal of Sociology* 8:1–16.

SAPIR, E.

1921   *Language: An Introduction to the Study of Speech.* New York: Harcourt Brace Jovanovich.

SCHNEIDER, D. M.

1965   "American Kin Terms and Terms for Kinsmen: A Critique of Goodenough's Componential Analysis of Yankee Kinship

Terminology." *American Anthropologist.* Vol. 67, No. 5, Part 2:288–308.

SCHUTZ, A.
1962 *Collected Papers I: The Problems of Social Reality.* The Hague: Martinus Nijhoff.

SCOTT, M., AND LYMAN, S.
1968 "Accounts." *American Sociological Review* 33 (February):46–62.

SHANIN, T.
1972 (Ed.) *The Rules of the Game: Cross-disciplinary Essays on Models in Scholarly Thought.* London: Tavistock.

SIMMEL, G.
1910 "How Is Society Possible?" *American Journal of Sociology* 16:372–391.

STURTEVANT, W. C.
1964 "Studies in Ethnoscience." *American Anthropologist* 66 (June): 99–131.

TYLER, S. A.
1969 (Ed.), *Cognitive Anthropology.* New York: Holt, Rinehart and Winston.

WALLACE, A. F. C.
1965 "The Problem of the Psychological Validity of Componential Analyses." *American Anthropologist.* Vol. 67, No. 5, Part 2:229–248.

WALLACE, A. F. C., AND ATKINS, J.
1960 "The Meaning of Kinship Terms." *American Anthropologist* 62:58–80.

WARREN, R. L.
1971 "The Sociology of Knowledge and the Problems of the Inner Cities." *Social Science Quarterly* 52 (December): 469–491.

WARREN, R. L., ROSE, S. M., AND BERGUNDER, A. F.
1974 *The Structure of Urban Reform.* Lexington: D. C. Heath.

WERNER, O., AND FENTON, J.
1970 "Method and Theory in Ethnoscience or Ethnoepistemology." In Raoul Naroll and Ronald Cohen (Eds.), *A Handbook of Method in Cultural Anthropology.* Garden City, N.Y.: The Natural History Press.

WITTGENSTEIN, L.
1953 *Philosophical Investigation.* New York: Macmillan.
1958 *The Blue and Brown Books.* New York: Harper and Row.

Received July 29, 1975.

ESTIMATION IN PANEL MODELS: RESULTS ON POOLING CROSS-SECTIONS AND TIME SERIES

Michael T. Hannan

STANFORD UNIVERSITY

Alice A. Young

CARNEGIE-MELLON UNIVERSITY

INTRODUCTION

Panel designs, in which the same sample of units is observed at more than one point in time, are becoming increasingly common in sociological research. Yet, many of the central meth-

*This research was supported by NSF Grant-32065. Aage Sørensen, Neil Henry, and Arthur Goldberger made helpful comments on an earlier version.

odological issues that arise in such designs are not yet well understood. We address ourselves to three related issues: (1) alternatives in the formulation of panel designs, (2) estimation problems in conventional panel designs, and (3) estimation in "pooled" panels. The key design issue concerns the treatment of panels with multiple "waves" of observations. The estimation problems arise due to the likelihood that errors in a panel design will be autocorrelated. A *pooled* model in which all waves are analyzed in a single model is advocated as a possible solution to both design and estimation problems for multi-wave panels. Since there is no treatment of pooled models in the sociological literature, we discuss the estimation issues in some detail. Finally, we present results of a Monte Carlo simulation of the behavior of alternative estimators for pooled models.

PANEL MODELS IN SOCIAL RESEARCH

The increased popularity of panel analysis reflects both the wider availability of comparable data over time and intellectual concerns in social science. We briefly consider two quite different motivations for adopting panel designs.

The first, and perhaps most pervasive, attraction of panel designs is their use as a methodological strategy for unraveling reciprocal causation. It is widely known that the presence of "causal loops" greatly complicates cross sectional analysis. In particular, ordinary least squares regression is inappropriate for such cases. Researchers faced with suspected reciprocal causal structures are usually advised to use simultaneous equations estimators (two-stage least squares). These procedures resolve the problem by using *instruments* — that is, variables that are not involved in the feedback cycle but have causal effects on some but not all of the variables in the cycle.[1] If a set of instruments can be found that exhibit the proper pattern of relationships with variables in the model, simultaneous equations procedures will resolve the analytic difficulty caused by feedback. But, the value of the instrumental variables strategy depends heavily on the researcher's knowledge of the rela-

---

[1] A good nontechnical discussion of the identification problem in both static and dynamic models is presented by Blalock (1969, Chapters four and five).

tionships of instruments to variables in the model.[2] If one does not have such detailed knowledge of the behavior of the system, it is tempting to look for alternative solutions.

It has apparently occured to many social researchers to use longitudinal (or intertemporal) variation to disentangle reciprocal causal effects. More precisely, it is suggested that lagged values of variables involved in feedback loops be treated as instruments. This is the logic underlying Lazarsfeld's famous sixteen-fold table for panel analysis (Lazarsfeld, 1972; Boudon, 1968) and the "cross-lag correlation" design proposed by Pelz and Andrews (1964), and Campbell and Stanley (1963). In both cases one begins with a pair of variables X and Y, assumed to causally affect each other. To evaluate the effect of X on Y one regresses Y on lagged X and lagged Y, and to evaluate the effect of Y on X one regresses X on lagged Y and lagged X. In each case, the lagged dependent variable is treated as an instrument.[3]

Duncan (1969, 1972) has correctly deflated the more over-blown claims for the power of this method. He showed, for example, that in the presence of both lagged and instantaneous causal effects, the use of only lagged dependent variables as instruments will not suffice to identify the structure—that is, yield a unique solution in terms of causal or structural parameters. Further, introducing lagged dependent variables gives rise to a number of estimation difficulties. As we will see below, lagged dependent variables are not proper instruments when the disturbances are autocorrelated. Yet, one should not overlook the possible advantages of the strategy of using lagged variables as regressors. The addition of inter-temporal variation cannot decrease one's knowledge of the causal structure. The central methodological problem of panel analysis is to expolit inter-temporal variation in such a way as to simplify causal inference.

    [2]It appears that one pays a very heavy price for using "improper" instruments. More precisely, instrumental variables methods seem to suffer more seriously from specification error than do the more straightforward ordinary least squares procedures. See, for example, the simulations reported by Blalock, Wells and Carter (1970) and Hurd (1972).

    [3]Whether or not a lagged dependent variable will serve as a useful instrument for unraveling patterns of reciprocal causation depends entirely on the autocorrelation of disturbances. When the disturbances are uncorrelated the lagged values are perfectly appropriate instruments.

A closely related motivation for panel analysis arises from work with models containing unobservable variables. Such models confront measurement and other analytic difficulties by inserting both measured and unmeasured variables into structural equations models. The use of unobservables will ordinarily lead to problems of identification unless strong restrictions are placed on the model. One possibility that occurred to a number of sociologists (Heise, 1969; Blalock, 1970; Duncan, 1972; Hannan and others, 1974) was to measure the same variables at multiple points in time and presume that the causal relations under study are time-invariant. Under a limited number of conditions this strategy leads to identification of multi-variable multiwave panel models containing unobservables. The main point for present purposes is that this use of the panel design has essentially the same motivation as Lazarsfeld's: use temporal variation to eliminate identification problems.

A second, perhaps deeper, motivation for panel analysis is an interest in dynamics. Sociology has been overwhelmingly preoccupied with static models of social organization and social behavior. In recent years, however, the limitations of a completely static approach have begun to make an impression, and a number of sociologists are experimenting with dynamic formulations. Dynamic models are typically analyzed in other sciences by the study of a single unit over many time periods. Unfortunately, many research areas in social science do not contain observational series that are sufficiently rich for time series analysis.[4]

Under at least some conditions one can study dynamics with short time series by analyzing panel observations. Coleman (1968) has made this clear in the following way. Consider the following differential equation:

$$\frac{dY}{dt} = a + bY + cX \qquad (1)$$

This equation relates the rate of change in some variable Y to its own level and to some casual variable X, and is explicitly dynamic. To estimate (1) it is necessary to relate it to observations made at

[4]The usual assertion is that at least thirty time periods must be observed for meaningful time series analysis.

discrete time intervals. The usual procedure is to integrate (1) to yield the expression:[5]

$$y_t = (a/b)(e^{b\Delta t} - 1) + e^{b\Delta t}y_{t-k} + (c/b)(e^{b\Delta t} - 1)x_{t-k} \qquad (2)$$

This may be rewritten as

$$y_t = a^* + b^* y_{t-k} + c^* x_{t-k} \qquad (3)$$

Coleman suggests collecting panel observations for at least two periods, say t and $t-k$, and estimating (3) by ordinary least squares. Then one can use (2) to transform estimates of (3) into estimates of the parameters of the differential equations.[6]

The estimation form of Coleman's model is identical to that most frequently used in estimating cross-lag correlations. The points of similarity are the inclusion of lagged values of the dependent variables and the dependence on panel observations. Given these similarities, the dominant concerns of both strategies can be reasonably well represented by the following two equation models (for N individuals at T periods):

$$y_{it} = \beta_0 + \beta_1 y_{i,t-1} + \beta_2 x_{i,t-1} + u_{it}$$

$$(i = 1, ..., N; \ t = 1, ..., T) \qquad (4)$$

$$x_{it} = \gamma_0 + \gamma_1 x_{i,t-1} + \gamma_2 y_{i,t-1} + w_{it}$$

Here the introduction of lagged dependent variables in both equations gives rise to the dynamic character of the model. Further, they serve as instruments (or perhaps only pseudo-instruments) for estimating and testing. We take the model in (4) as the methodological point of reference. All that follows is addressed to researchers who, for one reason or another, are interested in estimating models similar to (4).

CONSTRUCTION OF MULTI-WAVE PANEL MODELS

The sociological literature offers little in the way of didactic

[5]We are assuming here that X is fixed over time. For other cases see Coleman (1968).

[6]Coleman's method involves substituting ordinary least squares estimates of (3) into (2). This procedure involves non-linear operations on the estimators. Unfortunately, least squares estimators do not retain optimal statistical properties under such transformations. Maximum likelihood estimation is clearly preferable.

treatments of the handling of multi-wave panels.[7] Let.us consider the major alternatives in the context of a substantive example. Suppose a researcher, interested in the effects of ethnic heterogeneity on levels of political violence, collects observations for a sample of N nations for the years 1950, 1955, 1960, 1965, and 1970. If the appropriate causal lag is five years, the data yield four usable lag periods: 1950–55, 1955–60, 1960–65, end 1965–70. The question is how to utilize all four waves.

This situation seems to admit of three main alternatives (other than ignoring some of the data completely):

A. *Average observations over time and analyze the averages.* For example, in the regression of levels of violence on ethnic diversity, the dependent variable for each nation would be the average level of violence for five different periods, etc. Thus the $5N$ observations are compressed into N observations. Procedures like this always result in a loss of statistical efficiency (an increase in the standard error of estimators). Further, grouping over time or over units gives rise in many cases to complicated aggregation problems (cf. Theil, 1954; Hannan, 1971).

B. *Conduct separate analyses for each lag period.* For example, estimate the model for 1950–55 (with N observations), then again for 1955–60, and so forth. As in the previous case, this procedure sacrifices statistical efficiency. It does, however, avoid aggregation problems. An advantage of this procedure is that it may uncover changes in the causal structure over time. If the nature of the relationship among variables is changing over time, estimated causal effects will differ from period to period. Any such time non-stationarity can be very damaging to inference. To check for such problems, one should conduct analysis in this form before moving to the alternative discuesed below. If the causal structure does not appear to be constant over the entire period, there is no point in pooling observations. In such cases, the analyst must first attempt to identify the source of the change in causal structure and, if possible, modify the model to take its effects into account.

---

[7] Recently, a number of researchers (Duncan, 1972; Kenny, 1973; Hannan, Rubinson, and Warren, 1974) have applied path analysis to the estimation of multi-wave panels containing unobservable variables. But even three-wave panels produce unwieldy algebraic structures. We fear that this work has done nothing to encourage researchers to employ multiple waves.

There is a major difficulty that cannot be addressed within this and the previous strategy. The source of the difficulty is autocorrelation of disturbances. Disturbances will tend to be autocorrelated if the variables omitted from the model are stable over time (cf. Heise, 1970). For example, we might expect the repressive power of the state to be relatively stable over the period of observation. If this variable were not included in the model, its presence in the disturbance would tend to make the errors autocorrelated.

Whenever a lagged dependent variable is included in the model, the errors will be correlated with at least one of the regressors, and ordinary least squares regression will be biased and inconsistent. The problem with the two approaches just discussed is that, although the analyst may acknowledge the existence of autocorrelation in the disturbances, he does not have enough information to test for such effects or to modify the analysis to take the problem into account. This limitation, together with the possibility of gains in efficiency when all the observations are used in a single model, is the main motivation for considering the next alternative.

C. *Pool the lag structures into a single model (more generally pooling the time series of cross-sections)*[8] For example, conduct a least squares analysis on all $5N$ observations simultaneously. The data may be arranged such that the pooled dependent variable consists of the political violence scores for the first nation in 1955, 1960, 1965, and 1970; then the four scores for the second nation at those same times; and so on for all N nations. Observations for each independent variable are arranged analogously. More generally, there are NT observations for each regressor (N individuals, or other elementary units, each measured at T points in time).

Unlike the previous case, only a single set of structural or causal parameters is estimated. The single set of parameters are substantively meaningful only if the analyst has reason to believe that the causal structure does not undergo change during the observation period. Whether or not it is desirable to employ such a strong hypothesis depends on the purposes of the analysis. However,

[8]The pooling of cross-sections and time series has been discussed for some time in the econometrics literature. See, for example, Kuh (1959), Balestra and Nerlove (1966), Wallace and Hussain (1969), Maddala (1971) and Nerlove (1971). We rely heavily on this literature in the analytic discussion that follows.

deductively oriented sociologists with abstract theoretical concerns ought to welcome the opportunity to formulate and test such "ahistoric" hypotheses.

If restriction to a single set of causal parameters is appropriate, the pooling method yields a considerable gain in efficiency. It is immediately obvious, however, that one does not have $4N$ independent outcomes. Rather, the amount of independent variation lies somewhere between that contained in N and $4N$ independent observations. We shall see below that the magnitude of autocorrelation of disturbances determines whether it is closer to N or $4N$. When the autocorrelation of disturbances approaches unity, one gains very little new information from each additional wave. When the autocorrelation approaches zero, each new wave contains essentially as much new information about the causal structure as the previous wave.

Pooled models allow explicit consideration of autocorrelation problems. This is its main advantage over the other alternatives mentioned. To evaluate the potential contribution of pooled models we must proceed more formally. In the next section we state the conditions under which pooling is a useful procedure and collect analytic results on estimation in pooled models. In so doing, we will continue to contrast pooled models with the other two alternatives considered here.

ANALYTIC RESULTS ON NERLOVE-TYPE POOLED MODELS

In this section we collect available analytic results on pooled models. The simplest models are considered first. The complications are introduced, first singly and then jointly. The models considered are those that arise in the cross-lag correlation and Coleman approaches. We begin with the following one-equation model:

$$y_{it} = \beta_0 + \beta_1 y_{i,t-1} + \beta_2 x_{i,t-1} + u_{it}$$

$$(i = 1, \ldots, N; \ t = 1, \ldots, T) \qquad (5)$$

where the $x_{i,t-1}$'s are stochastic,[9] and the u_{it}'s are unobservable disturbances with

$$u_{it} = \mu_i + v_{it}, \text{all } i, t$$

$$E\mu_i = Ev_{it} = 0, \text{all } i, t$$

$$E\mu_i v_{i't} = 0, \text{all } i, i', \text{and } t$$

$$E\mu_i \mu_{i'} = \begin{cases} \sigma_\mu^2, i = i' \\ 0, \text{otherwise} \end{cases}$$

$$Ev_{it} v_{i't'} = \begin{cases} \sigma_v^2, i = i', t = t' \\ 0, \text{otherwise} \end{cases}$$

$$E\mu_i x_{i't} = 0, \text{all } i, i', \text{and } t$$

$$Ev_{it} x_{i't'} = 0, \text{all } i, i', t, \text{and } t'$$

$$Ev_{it} y_{i',t-1} = 0, \text{all } i, i', \text{and } t$$

With one exception, these are the usual least squares assumptions. The peculiar feature of this model is the specification of the disturbance. It contains a unit-specific component μ_i and the usual random component v_{it}. In other words, the model contains an unobserved variable μ_i which is constant for each individual but varies across individuals. This term summarizes all of the unobserved causes of Y which are relatively constant over time. In our substantive example, the factors summarized in μ_i might include specific historical experiences such as the nature of the elite at the time of state formation, or perhaps features of the legal system. Whatever the substantive context it is quite likely that some such unobserved variables will be operating. To the extent that they remain constant over time, they will conform to the model outlined above.

It is quite natural to extend the model to incorporate time-specific effects. These are effects that vary from period to period but are constant across units within any period. For example, the level of

---

[9]It is more usual to begin with a framework in which the x_{it-1} are fixed. But, our point of reference is with the cross-lag model in which x_{it-i} is necessarily a stochastic variable. All of the same results hold at least for special cases when we allow the x_{it-1} to be stochastic, but we must evaluate not expectations but the limits of probability distributions (denoted *plim*).

political violence in every polity might be affected in the same way by widespread economic booms or busts. More generally, the introduction of time-specific error components is likely to be useful when ever all (or most) units a affected by environmental variations in the same sorts of ways.

As long as the time-specific effects behave similarly to the μ_i defined above, no additional analytic issues arise when both types of effects are included. Consequently, there is no need to complicate the algebra in the discussion which follows by including time-specific terms.

The model stated in (5) and (6) contains what amounts to a factor-analytic structure for the disturbances (Goldberger, 1973a, p. 17). In particular, disturbances for the same unit are correlated at the same magnitude no matter how distant they are in time. Unfortunately, we do not yet have sufficient experience with panel analysis utilizing varieties of estimation techniques over a wide enough class of substantive situations to know how appropriate this error specification will be to researchers. This assumption may be unrealistic in long time series (where the more usual autoregressive scheme will probably be more appropriate). In relatively short series, as commonly found in panel analysis, the assumption may be a good approximation. One aim of this paper is to stimulate interest in the examination of such problems.

It will be convenient to employ matrix expressions for (5–6):

$$\mathbf{y}_t = \mathbf{Q}_t \boldsymbol{\beta} + \mathbf{u}_t \tag{8}$$

where

$$\mathbf{y}_t = (y_{11}, y_{12}, ..., y_{1T}, y_{21}, ..., y_{2T}, ..., y_{N1}, ..., y_{NT})'$$

$$\mathbf{y}_{t-1} = (y_{10}, y_{11}, ..., y_{1,T-1}, y_{20}, ..., y_{2,T-1}, ..., y_{N0}, ..., y_{N,T-1})'$$

$$\mathbf{x}_{t-1} = (x_{10}, x_{11}, ..., x_{1,T-1}, x_{20}, ..., x_{2,T-1}, ..., x_{N0}, ..., x_{N,T-1})'$$

$$\mathbf{u}_t = (u_{11}, u_{12}, ..., u_{1T}, u_{21}, ..., u_{2T}, ..., u_{N1}, ..., u_{NT})'$$

$$\mathbf{Q}_t = (\iota, y_{t-1}, x_{t-1}) \quad \{\text{where } \iota \text{ is an } NT \times 1 \text{ vector of ones}\},$$

and

$$\boldsymbol{\beta} = (\beta_0, \beta_1, \beta_2)'$$

Further,

$$
E\mathbf{uu}' = \sigma^2
\begin{bmatrix}
\mathbf{A} & \mathbf{0} & . & . & . & \mathbf{0} \\
\mathbf{0} & \mathbf{A} & & & & \mathbf{0} \\
. & & . & & & . \\
. & & & . & & . \\
. & & & & . & . \\
\mathbf{0} & \mathbf{0} & . & . & . & \mathbf{A}
\end{bmatrix}
\tag{8}
$$

an $(NT \times NT)$ martix, where

$$
\sigma^2 = \sigma_\mu^2 + \sigma_v^2, \quad \rho = \sigma_\mu^2/(\sigma_\mu^2 + \sigma_v^2)
$$

and

$$
\mathbf{A} =
\begin{bmatrix}
1 & \rho & . & . & . & \rho \\
\rho & 1 & & & & \rho \\
. & & . & & & . \\
. & & & . & & . \\
. & & & & . & . \\
\rho & \rho & . & . & . & 1
\end{bmatrix}
\tag{9}
$$

a $(T \times T)$ matrix.

It is helpful in presenting available analytic results to begin with special cases of (7) before considering the model in its entirety. We begin with the case in which the lagged dependent variable does not appear in the model $\beta_1 = 0$.

Case 1: $\beta_1 = 0$

When the lagged dependent variable does not appear in the model, it is reasonable to expect that the disturbances will be uncorrelated with regressors. As we have formulated the model in (6) this will be the case. Consequently, the *ordinary least squares estimator* (*OLS*), $\beta_{OLS} = (\mathbf{Q}_t'\mathbf{Q}_t)^{-1}\mathbf{Q}_t'\,y_t$, is consistent.

To consider the efficiency of *OLS* we must refer to the variance-covariance matrix of the disturbances, $E\mathbf{u}_t\mathbf{u}_t'$. *OLS* is efficient if and only if $E\mathbf{u}_t\mathbf{u}_t' = \sigma^2\mathbf{I}$, that is, if the variance-covariance matrix of disturbances has constant variance and all zero covariances. Clearly, by (8) and (9), *OLS* is efficient if and only if $\rho = 0$.

At this point it is natural to search for a consistent estimator which avoids the problem in the disturbances. The existence of such an estimator is suggested by the fact that we can transform (8) in such a way as to produce "well-behaved" disturbances. What we need is to find a matrix Ω which when applied to (7) yields

$$\Omega^{-1/2}\mathbf{y}_t = \Omega^{-1/2}\mathbf{Q}'_t\boldsymbol{\beta} + \Omega^{-1/2}\mathbf{u}_t \tag{10}$$

$$E[\Omega^{-1/2}\mathbf{u}_t\,\mathbf{u}'_t\,\Omega^{-1/2}] = \sigma^2\mathbf{I} \tag{11}$$

Nothing in the causal structure has been changed and we can apply ordinary least squares to (10). Because of (11) *OLS* applied to the transformed model is now an efficient estimator. The gain in efficiency relative to *OLS* applied to (7) arises from the explicit consideration of correlated error.

The procedure suggested in (10) is an application of the widely useful *generalized least squares (GLS)* approach to estimation. The application of *GLS* to pooled models is commonly advocated in the econometric and biometric literatures (Nerlove, 1971; Searle, 1971).

Since we will make continued reference to the *GLS* estimator we need a somewhat more formal representation. The *GLS* estimators is defined as

$$\boldsymbol{\beta}_{GLS} = (\mathbf{Q}'_t\,\Omega^{-1}\mathbf{Q}_t)^{-1}\mathbf{Q}'_t\,\Omega^{-1}\mathbf{y}_t \tag{12}$$

where

$$\Omega^{-1} = \begin{bmatrix} \mathbf{A}^{-1} & 0 & . & . & . & 0 \\ 0 & \mathbf{A}^{-1} & . & . & . & 0 \\ . & & . & & & \\ . & & & . & & \\ . & & & & . & \\ 0 & 0 & . & . & . & \mathbf{A}^{-1} \end{bmatrix}$$

and (cf. Hannan and Young, 1974)

$$\mathbf{A}^{-1} = (1/\eta)(\mathbf{I}_T - \mathbf{ll}'/T) + (1/\xi)(\mathbf{ll}'/T) \qquad (13)$$

where $\eta = (1 - \rho), \xi = (1 - \rho) + T\rho$, and $\mathbf{l}$ is a $(T \times 1)$ vector of ones.

The form of the *GLS* transformation (13) can be intuitively motivated as follows. The peculiar feature of pooled models is the use of both cross-sectional (between-unit) and longitudinal (within unit) variation to estimate causal parameters. The richness of the data presents an implicit choice, how to weight one type of variation relative to another. Generalized least squares uses ρ to weight the two types of information. To see this, consider the case where $\rho = 0$. Then $\mathbf{A}^{-1/2} = \mathbf{I}_T$ and observations are transformed in (10) by an identity transformation. *GLS* reduces to *OLS* where cross-sectional and time series variation are weighted proportionately to N and T (see Maddala, 1971). At the other extreme, when $\rho = 1$, $\mathbf{A}^{-1} = \mathbf{II}'/t^2$. It is easy to show that this transformation averages observations over time for each unit (as in the first of the broad approaches discussed in Section III). The result is a regression on grouped observations where all of the weight is placed on cross-sectional variation. In cases where ρ takes on a value $0 \leq \rho \leq 1$, *GLS* weights time series variation inversely to ρ. Such a weighting seems appropriate since ρ measures *redundancy* in the time series. The more redundancy, the lower the weight attached to longitudinal variation.

The gain in efficiency of *GLS* relative to *OLS* arises because *GLS* uses a weighting based on population or sample information, rather than an arbitrary weighting (cf. Goldberger, 1973b). Such a gain can be realized only if ρ is known *a priori* or can be estimated from sample data in a consistent (or unbiased) manner. There are no realistic cases where sociological researchers will have prior knowledge of ρ. So we turn to a discussion of procedures for estimating ρ.

The most widely used procedures for estimating ρ involve introducing dummy variables for each unit into (7):

$$\mathbf{y}_t = \mathbf{Q}_t\boldsymbol{\beta} + \boldsymbol{\Delta\mu} + \mathbf{v}_t \qquad (14)$$

where $\boldsymbol{\mu}$ is an $((N - 1) \times 1)$ vector containing the μ_i, and $\boldsymbol{\Delta} = (\boldsymbol{\delta}_1, \boldsymbol{\delta}_2, \ldots, \boldsymbol{\delta}_{N-1})$ and $\boldsymbol{\delta}_i$ is an $(NT \times 1)$ vector with ones corresponding to observations on unit i and zeroes elsewhere. We point out below that estimates of $\boldsymbol{\mu}$ can be used to construct a useful estimator of ρ.

But before moving to that discussion, we consider (14) more closely. Notice that the μ_i's that give rise to the correlation of disturbances have been shifted out of the disturbance. The remaining portion of the disturbance, $\mathbf{v}_t$, is well-behaved. In particular, $E\mathbf{v}_t\mathbf{v}_t' = \sigma_v^2\mathbf{I}$. So *OLS* applied to (14) is an asymptotically efficient estimator (cf. Amemiya, 1967). We refer to this estimator as least squares with dummy variables (*LSDV*).

In cases where N is moderately large, calculation of *LSDV* by direct methods will be either costly or impossible within conventional regression programs. An alternative approach is more generally useful. Express all observations as deviations from each unit's mean and apply *OLS*. The estimates of $\boldsymbol{\beta}$ are identical to those obtained using (14) directly and $\hat{\boldsymbol{\mu}}$ can be recovered by operations analogous to those used in recovering the constant in regressions with deviation scores (see Hannan and Young, 1974).

The results of *LSDV* can be used to calculate $\hat{\rho}$ as follows. To estimate $\hat{\rho}$ we need an estimate of σ_v^2. Nerlove (1971) suggests

$$\hat{\sigma}_\mu^2 = \sum_{i=1}^{N} (\hat{\mu}_i + \sum_{i=1}^{N} \hat{\mu}_i /N)^2/N$$

An obvious estimator of σ_v^2 is the sum of squared residuals from the *LSDV* regression divided by NT. Then

$$\hat{\rho} = \hat{\sigma}_\mu^2/(\hat{\sigma}_\mu^2 + \hat{\sigma}_v^2). \tag{15}$$

Nerlove chose ρ in (15) over a maximum likelihood estimate to avoid negative values of ρ (which are implausible in most applications). Unfortunately the estimator in (15) is upwardly biased (at least in small samples) with the magnitude of the bias inversely related to ρ.

Recall that *GLS* requires consistent estimates of ρ. The bias in $\hat{\rho}$ does not, however, appear to unduly damage the resulting *GLS* estimators (Amemiya, 1967). We study this issue further below. To acknowledge the fact that we are using estimates of ρ rather than the true values, it is more precise to refer to this estimator

$$\hat{\boldsymbol{\beta}}_{MGLS} = (\mathbf{Q}_t' \, \hat{\boldsymbol{\Omega}}^{-1} \mathbf{Q}_t')^{-1}\mathbf{Q}_t' \, \hat{\boldsymbol{\Omega}}^{-1}\mathbf{y}_t$$

as *modified* generalized least squares (*MGLS*).

We are interested in comparisons between *MGLS* and *LSDV*. Amemiya (1967) has proven for the limiting case of $N = 1$ that *GLS* and *LSDV* are both asymptotically efficient. But, the weighting of cross-sectional and time series variation seems more arbitrary than in *MGLS* (Maddala, 1971; Nerlove, 1971). Further, since one loses a degree of freedom in the estimation of each μ_i in *LSDV, LSDV* appears to "waste" degrees of freedom relative to *GLS*. Nerlove's (1961) simulation also suggests that *GLS* is more efficient than *LSDV* in small samples. We investigate the small sample behavior of the two estimators below.

Only one further issue remains to be discussed for the case $\beta_1 = 0$. We have assumed throughout that disturbances are uncorrelated with lagged *X*. In many substantive cases this will not be true. When lagged *X* is correlated with μ, *OLS* is inconsistent but both *MGLS* and *LSDV* are consistent. Since the correction for ρ cleans the equation of this specification bias, the choice among estimators involves not only effiniency but also consistency considerations when the factor denoted μ_1 may be correlated with the regressor.

Case 2: $\beta_2 = 0$

Since the μ_i's affect y_{it} at every period, it is clear that the lagged dependent variable is correlated with the disturbance. *OLS* applied to this model is inconsistent and (for $\rho > 0$), $\hat{\beta}_1$ is biased upwards. *OLS* gives "credit" to lagged **y** for the causal effects of μ_i. The stronger the effects of μ_i relative to lagged **y**, the greater the upward bias. In most realistic cases the upward bias is quite high.

Since both *MGLS* and *LSDV* take μ_i into account (*LSDV* directly and *MGLS* via $\hat{\rho}$), they are both consistent estimators of β. Again, both estimators are asymptotically efficient and choice between the two depends on knowledge of finite sample properties.

Case 3: $\beta_1 \neq 0, \beta_2 \neq 0$

The "full" model does not introduce new complications. It is worth pointing out that the presence of $\mathbf{x}_{t-1}$ tends to lessen upward bias in β_1 estimated by *OLS* (Malinvaud, 1971, p. 558). And, if β_1, β_2 and ρ are all positive, $\hat{\beta}_1$ and $\hat{\beta}_2$ will be negatively correlated (Johnston, 1971, p. 161). So upward bias in *OLS* estimates of β_1 will tend to bias $\hat{\beta}_2$ downward. This means the *OLS* applied to (7) will ordinarily lead one to overstate the lagged effects of the dependent variable and understate the effects of other (positively correlated) independent variables. As in Case 2, both *MGLS* and *LSDV* are consistent and asymptotically efficient estimators for this case.

The full model admits another approach to estimation. Inconsistency in *OLS* estimates arises only from the correlation of μ and $\mathbf{y}_{t-1}$. Since we have assumed $\mathbf{x}_{t-1}$ to be uncorrelated with μ, $\mathbf{x}_{t-2}$ is a proper "instrument" for $\mathbf{y}_{t-1}$. *Instrumental variables (IV)*, estimators for β_1 and β_2, are calculated by first regressing $\mathbf{y}_{t-1}$ on $\mathbf{x}_{t-2}$ and then substituting $\hat{\mathbf{y}}_{t-1}$, the predicated or "fitted" values from the first stage, into (7). Then *OLS* applied to this revised model is *IV* and gives consistent estimators. Since the *IV* estimator does not correct for the correlated errors, *IV* is less efficient than either *MGLS* or *LSDV*.[10] For these reasons, *IV* has little to recommend for the model defined here.

In all three cases analytic considerations lead to a clear-cut choice of *MGLS* or *LSDV* over *OLS* (or *IV*). But analytic results may not be directly useful for social researchers working with small samples. Both *MGLS* and *LSDV* are *asymptotically* efficient (meaning that they attain the minimum possible variability in an infinite sample). But it is important to know how the two compare in moderate and small samples. Further, the consistency results are also large-sample results. It is conceivable that *OLS* may out-perform *MGLS* and *LSDV* in terms of bias and mean squared error in small or moderate samples.

Nerlove (1971) applied a maximum likelihood procedure to a model similar to (8) with very disappointing results. While there is no reason to expect the method of maximum likelihood to be useful in small samples, Nerlove's method may not have been optimal. We are conducting further work in this area, but for the moment we omit any treatment of maximum likelihood.

Case 4: Continue to focus on (7) but assume that (7) is one equation in a two-equation system composed of (7) and $\mathbf{x}_t = \gamma_0 + \mathbf{y}_{t-1}\gamma_1 + \mathbf{x}_{t-1}\gamma_2 + \mathbf{w}_t$

The addition of this second equation to (7) completes the "cross-lag" structure so widely used in social research. Our concern is with properties of estimators of β_1 and β_2 when (7) does not stand alone but is embedded in the full causal structure The main consequence is to complicate the role of $\mathbf{x}_{t-1}$. Because of the causal feedback, $\mathbf{x}_{t-1}$ will no longer be uncorrelated with $\mathbf{u}_t$ (in fact $\mathbf{x}_t$

---

[10] Note that, also, *IV* wastes a whole wave of observations in the first stage. This exacerbates the inefficiency of *IV*.

can be written as an explicit function of $\mathbf{u}_t$). OLS will no longer necessarily understate the causal importance of $\mathbf{x}_{t-1}$, as in Case 3. Rather, it becomes much more difficult to evaluate complications arising in OLS. Since neither GLS nor $LSDV$ applied to (7) correct for the correlation of $\mathbf{x}_{t-1}$ with $\mathbf{u}_t$, neither are consistent estimators.

This latest complication is an instance of the familiar simultaneous equations bias (see Goldberger, 1973a, p. 4). No single-equation method (such as OLS, $MGLS$, $LSDV$, or even "true" GLS) copes with the problem. As mentioned earlier, a number of simultaneous equation estimation procedures are available for such situations.

In the case at hand, however, no statistical procedure will resolve the difficulty as the model stands. All of the causal variables are involved in the feedback and, thus, every regressor is correlated with the two disturbances. No instruments exist for consistent "first-stage" estimation as was described for Case 3.

Suppose that a proper instrument for $\mathbf{x}_{t-1}$ does exist; that is, suppose that the analyst can find a variable $\mathbf{z}$ that is correlated with $\mathbf{x}_{t-1}$ but is uncorrelated with the disturbance $\mathbf{u}_t$. We make reference again to the instrumental variables method. In the first stage, regress $\mathbf{x}_{t-1}$ on $\mathbf{z}$ to produce $\hat{\mathbf{x}}_{t-1}$. Then replace $\mathbf{x}_{t-1}$ in (7) with $\hat{\mathbf{x}}_{t-1}$ and use OLS.

If there were no correlated errors in (7), use of IV would eliminate all inconsistency. But the errors in (7) are correlated, and the lagged dependent variable will continue to be correlated with the disturbance. Only if $\mu = 0$ will IV give consistent estimates.

It is, however, true that IV corrects for the feedback or simultaneity aspect of the estimation problem. It seems natural, then, to combine IV with one of the methods which corrects for the pooled disturbance correlations $MGLS$ or $LSDV$. In fact, both composite estimators, IV-$MGLS$ and IV-$LSDV$, are consistent. Neither IV-$MGLS$ nor IV-$LSDV$ are maximally efficient. In general, estimators that make use of restrictions sequentially are less efficient than those that use them simultaneously.[11] It will be important to develop applications of more efficient estimators for this case. In

---

[11] Estimators that use constraints sequentially are termed "limited-information" estimators, while those that use them jointly are called "full-information methods." The latter are always more efficient than the former when the constraints hold in the population.

what follows, we restrict our attention to the two synthetic estimators *IV-GLS* and *IV-LSDV*.

To summarize this section, we note first that pooling cross-sections in the "full" cross-lag model involves both the time series bias discussed earlier and simultaneous equations bias. The combination of the two types of bias has not (as far as we know) been discussed in the literature. None of the widely used estimators (*OLS, LSDV, MGLS*, or *IV*) are consistent in this case. We find that a combination of *IV* and *LSDV* or *IV* and *MGLS* leads to consistent estimation. Neither synthetic estimator is asymptotically efficient.

Throughout the discussion of the four cases we have relied on large-sample theory. As we mentioned earlier, it is important for empirical researchers to obtain some information about the behavior of such estimators in small and moderate sized samples. Two issues are important here: we want to compare the efficiency of the various consistent estimators in finite samples, and we also want to compare the performance of the consistent estimators with those of inconsistent estimators (*OLS* for example) which may have smaller mean squared error in small samples (cf. Hurd, 1972). Since these issues have not yet been dealt with analytically, we turn next to a Monte Carlo simulation.

STRUCTURE OF THE SIMULATION

A. The Model. The following model allows us to study both types of bias discussed above:

$$\mathbf{y}_t = \mathbf{y}_{t-1}\beta_1 + \mathbf{x}_{t-1}\beta_2 + \mathbf{u}_t \tag{16}$$
$$\mathbf{x}_{t-1} = \mathbf{z}_{t-1}\gamma + \mathbf{w}_{t-1}$$

where the $\mathbf{u}_t$ behave as specified in (3), and

$$\rho = \sigma_\mu^2/(\sigma_\mu^2 + \sigma_v^2)$$
$$\mathrm{Cov}(u_{it}w_{i,t-1}) = \psi, \qquad E\mathbf{w}_t\,\mathbf{w}_t' = \sigma_w^2\,\mathbf{I}$$

Although we have not simulated the full cross-lag model, allowing the disturbances from the two equations to be correlated ($\psi \neq 0$) introduces exactly the same type of simultaneous equations bias we identified in the discussion of Case 4.

We chose to restrict our attention to panels with five waves and fifty observations per wave ($T = 5$ and $N = 50$, for example). Two of the parameters of the model, β_2 and γ, are fixed (at unity) and the remaining parameters were varied as follows:

$$\rho = 0, .25, .5, .75, .9, .95$$

$$\gamma = 0, .5, .9$$

$$\beta_1 = .3, .8$$

For each of the thirty-six combinations of values of ρ, ψ, and β_1, we generated one hundred samples with $N = 50$, $T = 5$. The properties of the samples is the focus of our investigation. Further details of the simulation and the routines used for calculating estimators are presented in Hannan and Young (1974).

   B. The Estimators. The estimators studied are those described above. Here we restate the main asymptotic results (and note methods of calculation where they are not obvious).

   (1) *Ordinary least squares (OLS)* applied to (8). Consistent and efficient when $\rho = 0$ and $\psi = 0$; inconsistent otherwise.

   (2) *Least squares with individual constants (LSDV)* applied to (18) by introducing dummy variables for each unit. Consistent and asymptotically efficient when $\psi = 0$, inconsistent otherwise.

   (3) *Modified generalized least squares (MGLS)* applied to (18) with $\hat{\rho}$ calculated as in (15) from an *LSDV* first stage. Consistent and asymptotically efficient when $\psi = 0$; inconsistent otherwise.

   (4) *"True generalized least squares (GLS)* applied to (18) using known values of ρ. Minimum variance consistent estimator.

   (5) *Instrumental variables (IV)* applied to (18) with x_{t-1} replaced by "fitted values" from a regression of x_{t-1} on z_{t-1}. Consistent when $\rho = 0$; inconsistent otherwise.

   (6) *IV-LSDV* by applying *LSDV* to (18) in which x_{t-1} has been replaced by fitted values. Consistent but not asymptotically efficient regardless of values of ρ and ψ.

   (7) *IV-MGLS* by applying *GLS* to (18) with x_{t-1} replaced by fitted values and using $\hat{\rho}$ calculated from *IV-LSDV* estimates of u_t. Consistent but not asymptotically efficient.

FINDINGS

We report our findings in three forms. First, for each combination of ρ and ψ we calculate *mean errors* (*ME*) for each estimator. For example, the mean error of $\hat{\beta}_1$ is

$$\frac{1}{100} \sum_{i=1}^{100} (\hat{\beta}_1 - \beta_1)$$

The *ME* is a summary of tendency toward directional error. Second, we likewise compute *mean squared errors* (*MSE*): the *MSE* of $\hat{\beta}_1$ is

$$\frac{1}{100} \sum_{i=1}^{100} (\hat{\beta}_1 - \beta_1)^2$$

The *MSE* summarizes both absolute amount of error and the variability of the estimator.

Third, to simplify the reporting of tendencies in the behavior of the estimators we present results of regressions of mean squared errors on the parameter values. The regressions take the following form:

$$MSE = \pi_0 + \pi_1 \rho + \pi_2 \psi + \pi_3 (\rho * \psi)$$

The multiplicative term $(\rho * \psi)$ is introduced as a simple device for locating interaction effects.[12]

1. $\psi = 0$. First we consider the "pure" pooling problem. That is, we examine those conditions in which there is no simultaneous equations bias. Our simulation at this point corresponds closely with Nerlove's (1971). However, he set $N = 25$ and $T = 10$, while we have $N = 50$ and $T = 5$. Few social science panel investigations yield even five waves of observations.

Attention should be focused on the single-equation methods (*OLS, LSDV,* and *MGLS*). First, notice the very poor performance of *OLS* estimates of both β_1 and β_2. Tables 1 and 2 make clear the very strong effect of ρ on the behavior of *OLS*.[13] But the tendency is more marked for estimates of β_1 than for β_2 as expected. *OLS* estimates of β_1 are biased upwards and estimates of β_2 respond with a smaller downward movement. As we noted above, the positive correlation of

[12] Other regression equations containing terms in ρ^2, ψ^2 and $(\rho * \psi)^2$ were also examined. These equations did not change the analysis below and are therefore, not reported here.

[13] Results for $\rho = 0.95$ were so similar to those for $\rho_1 = 0.9$ that they are not shown in Tables 1, 2, 3, 6, or 7.

y_{t-1} and x_{t-1} yields a negative correlation between $\hat{\beta}_1$ and $\hat{\beta}_2$. Thus any factor which biases $\hat{\beta}_1$ upwards will bias $\hat{\beta}_2$ downward and the reverse. While results for parameter values $\beta_1 = 0.8$ and $\beta_1 = 0.3$ are qualitatively the same, the latter case produced much greater upward bias in estimates of β_1. These results are consistent with those reported by Malinvaud (1970).

TABLE 1.
Mean Error of Estimate for $\hat{\beta}_1$ ($\psi = 0$)

$\beta_1 = 0.80$

$\rho =$	0.00	0.25	0.50	0.75	0.90
OLS	0.00*	0.09	0.13	0.16	0.17
LSDV	−0.13	−0.10	−0.07	−0.04	−0.02
MGLS	−0.06	−0.02	0.00	0.01	0.01

$\beta_1 = 0.30$

$\rho =$	0.00	0.25	0.50	0.75	0.90
OLS	0.00	0.12	0.23	0.33	0.38
LSDV	−0.12	−0.10	−0.08	−0.05	−0.02
MGLS	−0.07	−0.04	−0.02	−0.01	0.00

* Figures have been rounded; values listed as .00 actually range between .0003 and .0049.

TABLE 2
Mean Error of Estimate for $\hat{\beta}_2$ ($\psi = 0$)

$\beta_1 = 0.80$

$\rho =$	0.00	0.25	0.50	0.75	0.90
OLS	0.01	−0.03	−0.04	−0.05	−0.06
LSDV	0.00*	0.00	0.00	0.00	0.00
MGLS	0.01	0.00	0.00	0.00	0.00

$\beta_1 = 0.30$

$\rho =$	0.00	0.25	0.50	0.75	0.90
OLS	0.01	−0.02	−0.04	−0.05	−0.06
LSDV	−0.01	−0.01	0.00	0.00	0.00
MGLS	0.01	0.00	0.00	0.00	0.00

*Figures have been rounded; values listed as 0.00 actually range between 0.0003 and 0.0049.

Turn next to a consideration of the estimators designed to deal with the pooled model. MGLS always has smaller mean error than *LSDV*. The difference between the two estimators is small for $\hat{\beta}_2$ but quite large in estimating $\hat{\beta}_1$.

Examination of mean errors in Table 1 shows that *LSDV* appears to *overcorrect* for the presence of autocorrelated error in the sense that estimates of $\hat{\beta}_1$ undershoot the mark. The likely explanation is that LSDV attributes to the individual dummy variables μ part of the causal effect of the lagged y.

There is a slight tendency for *MGLS* as well to underestimate β_1. The explanation certainly differs from that which applies to *LSDV*: attention should be focused on the role of $\hat{\rho}$ from (15) in *MGLS*. As may be seen in Table 3, $\hat{\rho}$ is biased upwards. The upward bias in $\hat{\rho}$ decreases with increases in ρ, and the downward bias in the *MGLS* estimates of β_1 decreases with increasing ρ. This latter observation is consistent with the explanation that upwardly biased $\hat{\rho}$ values produce an overcorrection which will lead to underestimates of β_1.

TABLE 3
Mean Error of Estimate of $\hat{\rho}$ ($\psi = 0$)

$\beta_1 = 0.80$					
$\rho =$	0.00	0.25	0.50	0.75	0.90
MGLS	0.32	0.32	0.22	0.20	0.03
$\beta_1 = 0.30$					
$\rho =$	0.00	0.25	0.50	0.75	0.90
MGLS	0.23	0.22	0.15	0.07	0.02

Table 4 summarizes the quality of the one-equation estimators for the pure pooling problem. The *OLS*, *LSDV* and *MGLS* estimators have the same rank-order of quality as found in Table 1 and 2. The true *GLS* estimator is shown as a benchmark, since it is asymptotically efficient and consistent and employs the true value of ρ. Two items of interest may be found in estimates from the *GLS* estimation. First, the low values of the mean squared error indicate low amounts of sampling error in the simulation. Second, bias in the estimation of $\hat{\rho}$ appears to have little effect upon the quality of the *MGLS* estimator, since the differences between *GLS* and *MGLS* are small.

It is simple to summarize our findings for the pure pooling case. Modified generalized least squares consistently outperforms *LSDV*. Both *MGLS* and *LSDV* are far superior to *OLS*. The use of the convenient $\hat{\rho}$ from (15) does not appear to incur great costs, particularly with high values of ρ. Presumably most sociological investigators do face high ρ values.

2. $\psi \neq 0$. We next introduce simultaneous equations bias into the structure just examined. Since our attention is focused on the estimation of panel models we do not investigate "pure" simultaneous equations bias but only the combination of the two sources of error.

TABLE 4

Mean Squared Error Averaged over All Conditions
(where $\rho \neq 0, \psi = 0$, and the number of cases $= 1000$)

	$\hat{\beta}_1$	$\hat{\beta}_2$
OLS	0.059	0.005
LSDV	0.005	0.001
MGLS	0.003	0.001
GLS	0.002	0.001

TABLE 5

Mean Squared Error Averaged over All Conditions
(where $\rho \neq 0, \psi \neq 0$, and the number of cases $= 2000$)

	$\hat{\beta}_1$	$\hat{\beta}_2$
OLS	0.038	0.144
LSDV	0.003	0.124
MGLS	0.001	0.131
IV	0.065	0.156
IV-LSDV	0.074	0.266
IV-MGLS	0.019	0.089

In broad terms we find that allowing $\psi \neq 0$, that is, introducing simultaneous equations bias involving x_{t-1}, produces very large magnitudes of error, particularly in estimates of $\hat{\beta}_2$. A comparison of the single-equation estimators in Tables 4 and 5 shows that the presence of the simultaneity problem produces relatively small changes in the average mean square error of $\hat{\beta}_1$, but quite large increases in the *MSE* of $\hat{\beta}_2$. There exists no benchmark estimator comparable to the *GLS* in Table 4 with which to compare the results of this part of the simulation. Here *GLS* is no longer consistent, as already noted. One could construct an IV-GLS estimator using fitted values of $\mathbf{X}_{t-1}$ and the known "true" values of ρ, but this estimator is not asymptotically efficient. This latter estimator would thus not allow one to distinguish between the potential inefficiency of an IV estimator and sampling error within the simulation.

We begin with another contrast of the single-equation methods. First, OLS is inferior over the range of parameter values to $MGLS$ and to $LSDV$ (in Table 5). Thus, the choice among single-equation methods is between $MGLS$ and $LSDV$. Both estimators, in these cases, tend to underestimate β_1 and overestimate β_2, as may be seen in Tables 6 and 7. But, $LSDV$ underestimates β_1 more than does $MGLS$ while $MGLS$ overestimates β_2 more than does $LSDV$.

TABLE 6
Mean Error of Estimate for $\hat{\beta}_1$ ($\beta_1 = .8$)

$\psi =$	0.00	0.00	0.00	0.00	0.00
$\rho =$	0.00	0.25	0.50	0.75	0.90
OLS	0.00	0.09	0.13	0.16	0.17
$LSDV$	-0.13	-0.10	-0.07	-0.04	-0.02
$MGLS$	-0.06	-0.02	0.00	0.01	0.01
IV	0.00	0.10	0.14	0.17	0.18
IV-$LSDV$	-0.30	-0.28	-0.27	-0.25	-0.24
IV-$MGLS$	-0.17	-0.14	-0.12	-0.10	-0.09
$\psi =$	0.50	0.50	0.50	0.50	0.50
$\rho =$	0.00	0.25	0.50	0.75	0.90
OLS	-0.02	0.07	0.11	0.14	0.15
$LSDV$	-0.12	-0.10	-0.08	-0.05	-0.03
$MGLS$	-0.07	-0.04	-0.02	-0.01	-0.01
IV	0.00	0.10	0.14	0.17	0.18
IV-$LSDV$	-0.33	-0.32	-0.31	-0.28	-0.26
IV-$MGLS$	-0.20	-0.17	-0.15	-0.13	-0.11
$\psi =$	0.90	0.90	0.90	0.90	0.90
$\rho =$	0.00	0.25	0.50	0.75	0.90
OLS	-0.03	0.05	0.09	0.12	0.14
$LSDV$	-0.09	-0.08	-0.07	-0.05	-0.03
$MGLS$	-0.06	-0.04	-0.04	-0.03	-0.03
IV	0.00	0.10	0.14	0.16	0.18
IV-$LSDV$	-0.36	-0.34	-0.33	-0.31	-0.28
IV-$MGLS$	-0.22	-0.19	-0.17	-0.15	-0.12

TABLE 7
Mean Error of Estimate for $\hat{\beta}_2$ ($\beta_1 = .8$)

$\psi =$	0.00	0.00	0.00	0.00	0.00
$\rho =$	0.00	0.25	0.50	0.75	0.90
OLS	0.01	−0.03	−0.04	−0.05	−0.06
LSDV	0.00	0.00	0.00	0.00	0.00
MGLS	0.01	0.00	0.00	0.00	0.00
IV	−0.02	−0.24	−0.32	−0.37	−0.38
IV-LSDV	0.62	0.59	0.56	0.52	0.50
IV-MGLS	0.37	0.31	0.27	0.23	0.21
$\psi =$	0.50	0.50	0.50	0.50	0.50
$\rho =$	0.00	0.25	0.50	0.75	0.90
OLS	0.43	0.37	0.29	0.19	0.11
LSDV	0.41	0.35	0.29	0.21	0.13
MGLS	0.43	0.38	0.31	0.22	0.14
IV	−0.03	−0.24	−0.33	−0.38	−0.40
IV-LSDV	0.69	0.67	0.64	0.59	0.55
IV-MGLS	0.42	0.36	0.32	0.28	0.24
$\psi =$	0.90	0.90	0.90	0.90	0.90
$\rho =$	0.00	0.25	0.50	0.75	0.90
OLS	0.77	0.69	0.57	0.41	0.25
LSDV	0.74	0.65	0.53	0.38	0.24
MGLS	0.77	0.67	0.54	0.38	0.24
IV	−0.04	−0.25	−0.33	−0.38	−0.41
IV-LSDV	0.71	0.69	0.66	0.62	0.57
IV-MGLS	0.43	0.38	0.34	0.30	0.26

The behavior of the estimators over combinations of ρ and ψ is at least as interesting as the gross comparisons between estimators. It is most convenient to focus on the regression results presented in Tables 8 and 9. Since results of regressions for the case $\beta_1 = 0.3$ were similar to those for $\beta_1 = 0.8$, only the latter are presented here.

Consider first MSE in estimates of $\hat{\beta}_1$. As in the case $\psi = 0$, OLS reacts differently to increases in ρ than does LSDV and MGLS. As ρ increase MSE (in $\hat{\beta}_1$) for OLS increases but the corresponding MSE for LSDV and MGLS decreases. One would expect that an estimator such as OLS which does not correct for an analytical difficulty such as ρ would do increasingly worse in the face of greater values of ρ. Further, increases in ψ do not have a particularly strong direct effect on any of the three single-equation estimators. But, the

TABLE 8

Regression of Mean Squared Error in $\hat{\beta}_1$ on the Parameters

(The number of cases $= 1800, \beta_1 = 0.8$)

Mean Squared Error in:	R^2
$OLS = 0.0002 + 0.0309\rho + 0.0027\psi - 0.0181(\rho^*\psi)$ $\quad\quad\quad (0.0003) \quad (0.0004) \quad (0.0005)$	0.92
$LSDV = 0.0171 - 0.0189\rho - 0.0088\psi + 0.0114(\rho^*\psi)$ $\quad\quad\quad (0.0004) \quad (0.0004) \quad (0.0006)$	0.68
$MGLS = 0.0032 - 0.0038\rho + 0.0003\psi\dagger + 0.0005(\rho^*\psi)\dagger$ $\quad\quad\quad (0.0002) \quad (0.0002) \quad (0.0003)$	0.45
$IV = 0.0024 + 0.0325\rho - 0.0008\psi\dagger + 0.0013(\rho^*\psi)\dagger$ $\quad\quad\quad (0.0005) \quad (0.0005) \quad (0.0008)$	0.88
$IV\text{-}LSDV = 0.0919 - 0.0383\rho + 0.0481\psi = 0.0235(\rho^*\psi)$ $\quad\quad\quad (0.0033) \quad (0.0038) \quad (0.0057)$	0.33
$IV\text{-}MGLS = 0.0293 - 0.0211\rho + 0.0213\psi - 0.0156(\rho^*\psi)$ $\quad\quad\quad (0.0016) \quad (0.0018) \quad (0.0028)$	0.36

†Null hypothesis $\pi = 0$ not rejected at 0.001 level.

TABLE 9

Regression of Mean Squared Error in $\hat{\beta}_2$ on the Parameters

(The number of cases $= 1800, \beta_1 = 0.8$)

Mean Squared Error in:	R^2
$OLS = -0.0419 + 0.0414\rho + 0.6612\psi - 0.6529(\rho^*\psi)$ $\quad\quad\quad (0.0055) \quad (0.0060) \quad (0.0092)$	0.92
$LSDV = -0.0377 - 0.0388\rho + 0.6043\psi - 0.6013(\rho^*\psi)$ $\quad\quad\quad (0.0048) \quad (0.0052) \quad (0.0080)$	0.92
$MGLS = -0.0381 + 0.0383\rho + 0.6380\psi - 0.6539(\rho^*\psi)$ $\quad\quad\quad (0.0047) \quad (0.0052) \quad (0.0079)$	0.93
$IV = 0.0378 + 0.1408\rho + 0.0202\psi\dagger + 0.0142(\rho^*\psi)\dagger$ $\quad\quad\quad (0.0120) \quad (0.0132) \quad (0.0202)$	0.19
$IV\text{-}LSDV = 0.4471 - 0.1866\rho + 0.1910\psi - 0.0997(\rho^*\psi)\dagger$ $\quad\quad\quad (0.0311) \quad (0.0343) \quad (0.0523)$	0.10
$IV\text{-}MGLS = 0.1667 - 0.1124\rho + 0.0898\psi - 0.0586(\rho^*\psi)\dagger$ $\quad\quad\quad (0.0139) \quad (0.0154) \quad (0.0234)$	0.15

†Null hypothesis $\pi = 0$ not rejected at 0.001 level.

combined effects of ρ and ψ cannot be completely accounted for by the two additive effects. That is ρ and ψ "interact" to produce consequences which cannot be anticipated from consideration of the distinct effects of each. And these interaction effects are opposite in sign for *OLS* as opposed to *LSDV* and *MGLS*. Combinations of high ρ and ψ values decrease *MSE* (of $\hat{\beta}_1$) for *OLS* but increase *MSE* for the other two estimators. This means that the quality of the *LSDV* and *GLS* estimators are damaged by the joint presence of the two analytic difficulties (autocorrelation and simultaneity) while that of *OLS* is actually improved. But, recall that *LSDV* and *MGLS* are still superior to *OLS* even at high levels of ρ and ψ. In other words, while the differences between *OLS* and either *MGLS* or *LSDV* decreases as ρ and ψ increase, the ranking of the estimators does not change.

Estimation of β_2 involves a very different pattern. Increases in both ρ and ψ increase mean squared error for all three estimators. But the ψ effects are many magnitudes greater. Surprisingly, we find strong negative interaction effects for all three estimators. In fact, the slopes of the interaction effects are in each case similar in magnitude to those of ψ. This is quite interesting because it suggests that the biasing effects of simultaneity can be considerably offset by the presence of autocorrelation. In other words, although each problem is damaging in isolation from the other, the combination of the two tends to be less damaging to inference than at least the pure simultaneity. Examination of Table 7 makes this plain.

Next, consider the instrumental variables (*IV*) estimator. It is consistent only when $\rho = 0$. Tables 8 and 9 show that increases in ρ increase the *MSE* for both $\hat{\beta}_1$ and $\hat{\beta}_2$ for the *IV* estimator. It seems reasonable that *IV* is sensitive to increases in the problem that it does not correct (that is, increases in ρ). Conversely, *IV* is designed to deal with nonzero values of ψ, and the *MSE* of the *IV* estimator does not appear to depend systematically on either ψ or ($\rho * \psi$).

The overall performance of the *IV* estimator is in sharp contrast with the single-equation methods, as may be seen by a return to Table 5. Although *OLS, LSDV, MGLS,* and *IV* are all inconsistent when $\rho \neq 0$ and $\psi \neq 0$, they differ considerably in quality. The *IV* estimator is the least efficient of the four methods.

Finally, we turn to the estimators which are consistent when both $\rho \neq 0$ and $\psi \neq 0$, *IV-LSDV* and *IV-MGLS*. The most important result is the astounding contrast between *IV-LSDV* and *IV-MGLS*. While *IV-MGLS* has by far the *lowest* average *MSE* for $\hat{\beta}_1$ and $\hat{\beta}_2$ across conditions *IV-LSDV* has the *highest MSE* averages for both $\hat{\beta}_2$ and $\hat{\beta}_2$. Thus, over the combinations of parameter values studied,

IV-LSDV has nothing to recommend it. At the same time IV-MGLS is clearly superior to all other methods studied in the condition $\rho \neq 0, \psi \neq 0$.

Despite the radical differences in quality, IV-LSDV and IV-MGLS appear to have qualitatively similar performances in the face of changes in parameter values. Both IV-LSDV and IV-MGLS systematically underestimate β_1 and overestimate β_2, as may be seen in Tables 6 and 7. In each case, according to Tables 8 and 9, ρ has a negative effect, ψ a positive effect, and $(\rho * \psi)$ an insignificant effect.

CONCLUSIONS

The cross-lag panel model is of central importance to research which focuses upon dynamic causal processes. This model involves lagged X, reciprocal causation, and lagged dependent variables. Most often the estimation of panel models involves both time series and simultaneous equations problems. Social researchers attracted to the cross-lag model must learn to deal with the combination of the two problems.

We began with the premise that multi-wave data such as that used in the cross-lag panel model can often be best exploited when pooled into a single estimation. We limited our attention to pooling of cross-sections where there are individual-specific but not time period-specific components to error. This model of error components deals with stability in disturbances due only to time-invariant properties of sample units. It is likely to be a good approximation when the omitted unit-specific causes of Y change considerably more slowly than X and Y.

Whether pooling results in improved inference depends on at least three things. It depends on the stability of the causal processes over all waves of observations. It depends on one's ability to model the peculiar error characteristics of pooled data. And, finally, it depends on one's ability to design and modify statistical models to cope with the complicated error structures. Our research focused on the third issue.

The disturbance structure of a pooled model makes OLS inappropriate even when there is no reciprocal causation (that is, no possibility of simultaneous equations bias). In this restricted case, both LSDV and MGLS are consistent and asymptotically efficient estimators. Choice between the two (and between either and the inconsistent *OLS*) depends on their small-sample properties. Our simulation yields results which agree with Nerlove's (1971) simulation even though here $N = 50$ and $T = 5$, while he used $N = 25$ and $T = 10$. We find, in particular, that the performance of *OLS* is poor enough to cast doubt on the many published panel studies which do not correct for autocorrelation. Further, while both *LSDV* and *MGLS* surpass *OLS,* the modified generalized least squares procedure is superior. In fact *MGLS* estimates, using biased estimates of ρ, are quite close to those of "true" *GLS.*

We also analyzed the intersection of the autocorrelation problem with simultaneity. Both *IV-LSDV* and *IV-MGLS* procedures are consistent but not asymptotically efficient estimators for the "full" cross-lag model. Since the behavior of the two "synthetic" estimators has apparently not been previously studied, we have no a priori information concerning their small sample behavior. We find the *IV-MGLS* procedure vastly superior to *IV-LSDV* over the whole range of parameter combinations. Further, the *IV-MGLS* procedure very plainly outperforms the inconsistent estimators studied.

Our results offer strong support for the view that application of the modified generalized least squares approach to panel estimation is preferable to the available alternatives. This appears to be true both when *MGLS* is used to correct for the "pure" pooling problems and when *MGLS* is used in combination with an instrumental variables estimator to deal with the combination of time series and simultaneous equations complications.

REFERENCES

AMEMIYA, T.

    1967 "A Note on the Estimation of Balestra-Nerlove Models." Technical Report No. 4. Stanford University, Institute for Mathematical Studies in the Social Sciences.

BALESTRA, P., AND NERLOVE, M.

    1966 "Pooling Cross-Section and Time Series Data in the Estimation of a Dynamic Model: The Demand for Natural Gas." *Econometrica* 34 (July): 585–612.

BLALOCK, H. M., JR.

1969   *Theory Construction: From Verbal to Mathematical Formulations.* Englewood Cliffs, N.J.: Prentice-Hall.

BLALOCK, H. M., JR., WELLS., C. S., AND CARTER, L. F.

1970   "Statistical Estimation with Random Measurement Error." In E. F. Borgatta and G. W. Bohrenstedt (Eds.), *Sociological Methodology 1970.* San Francisco: Jossey-Bass.

BOUDON, R.

1968   "A New Look at Correlation Analysis." In H. M. Blalock, Jr. and A. Blalock (Eds.), *Methodology in Social Research.* New York: McGraw-Hill, pp. 199–235.

CAMPBELL, D. T., AND STANLEY, J. S.

1963   *Experimental and Quasi-Experimental Design for Research.* Chicago: Rand McNally.

COLEMAN, J. S.

1968   "The Mathematical Study of Change." In H. M. Blalock, Jr. (Ed.), *Methodology in Social Research.* New York: McGraw-Hill, pp. 428–478.

DUNCAN, O. D.

1969   "Some Linear Models for Two-Variable Panel Analysis." *Psychological Bulletin* 72 (September): 177–182.

1972   "Unmeasured Variables in Linear Models for Panel Analysis." In H. Costner (Ed.), *Sociological Methodology 1972.* San Francisco: Jossey-Bass, pp. 36–82.

GOLDBERGER, A. S.

1973a   "Structural Equation Models: An Overview." In A. S. Goldberger and O. D. Duncan (Eds.), *Structural Equation Models in the Social Sciences.* New York: Seminar Press.

1973b   "Efficient Estimation in Overidentified Models: An Interpretive Analysis." In A. S. Goldberger and O. D. Duncan (Eds.), *Structural Equation Models in the Social Sciences.* New York: Seminar Press.

HANNAN, M. T.

1971   *Aggregation and Disaggregation in Sociology.* Lexington, Mass.: Heath Lexington.

HANNAN, M. T., RUBINSON, R., AND WARREN, J. T.

1974   "The Causal Approach to Measurement Error in Panel Analysis: Some Further Contingencies." In H. M. Blalock (Ed.), *Measurement in the Social Sciences.* Chicago: Aldine.

HANNAN, M. T., AND YOUNG, A. A.

1974   "Estimation of Pooled Cross-Section and Time Series Models: Preliminary Monte Carlo Results." Paper presented at Conference on Policy Research: Methods and Implications, University of Wisconsin, Madison.

HEISE, D. R.

1969   "Separating Reliability and Stability in Test-Retest Correlations." *American Sociological Review* 34 (February): 93–101.

1970   "Causal Inference from Panel Data." In E. Borgatta and G. Bohrnstedt (Eds.), *Sociological Methodology 1970.* San Francisco: Jossey-Bass, pp. 3–27.

HENDERSON, C. R.

1971   "Comment on 'The Use of Error Components Models in Combining Cross-Section with Time Series Data.'" *Econometrica* 39 (March): 397–401.

HURD, M. D.

1972   "Small-Sample Estimation of a Structural Equation with Autocorrelated Errors." *Journal of the American Statistical Association* 67 (September): 567–573.

JOHNSTON, J.

1972   *Econometric Methods.* New York: McGraw-Hill.

KENNY, D. A.

1973   "Cross-Lagged and Synchronous Common Factors in Panel Data." In A. S. Goldberger and O. D. Duncan (Eds.), *Structural Equation Models in the Social Sciences.* New York: Seminar Press.

KNUTH, D. E.

1969   *The Art of Computer Programming.* Vol. 2. Reading, Mass.: Addison-Wesley.

KUH, E.

1959   "The Validity of Cross-Sectionally Estimated Behavior Equations in Time Series Application." *Econometrica* 27 (April): 197–214.

LAZARSFELD, P. F., PASANELLA, A. K., AND ROSENBERG, M.

1972   *Continuities in the Language of Social Research,* Section IV. New York: The Free Press.

MADDALA, G. S.

1971   "The Use of Variance Components Models in Pooling Cross-Section and Time Series Data." *Econometrica* 39 (March): 341–358.

MALINVAUD, E.

1970   *Statistical Methods of Econometrics.* New York: American Elsevier.

NERLOVE, M.

1971   "Further Evidence on the Estimation of Dynamic Economic Relations from a Time Series of Cross-Sections." *Econometrica* 39 (March):359–382.

PELZ, D. C., AND ANDREWS, F. M.

1964 "Causal Priorities in Panel Study Data." *American Sociological Review* 29 (December): 836–848.

SEARLE, S. R.

1968 "Another Look at Henderson's Methods of Estimating Variance Components." *Biometrics* 24 (December):749–778.

1971 "Topics in Variance Component Estimation." *Biometrics* 27 (March):1–76.

THEIL, H.

1954 *Linear Aggregation of Economic Relations.* Amsterdam: North-Holland.

WALLACE, T. D., AND HUSSAIN, A.

1969 "The Use of Error Components Models in Combining Cross Section with Time Series Data." *Econometrica* 37 (January): 55–72.

WILEY, D. E., AND WILEY, J. A.

1970 "The Estimation of Measurement Error in Panel Data." *American Sociological Review* 35 (February): 112–117.

Received February 19, 1975.

$\approx 3 \approx$

ASSESSING RELIABILITY
AND STABILITY
IN PANEL MODELS

Blair Wheaton

YALE UNIVERSITY

Bengt Muthén

UNIVERSITY OF UPPSALA

Duane F. Alwin

INDIANA UNIVERSITY

Gene F. Summers

UNIVERSITY OF WISCONSIN-MADISON

*This research was supported in part by the College of Agricultural and Life Sciences, University of Wisconsin-Madison, and the National Institute of Mental Health, PHS Research Grant MI-19689. We wish to acknowledge the helpful comments of George Bohrnstedt and David Heise on an earlier draft of this paper. We, of course, assume responsibility for any errors that remain.

84

INTRODUCTION

The proper interpretation of multiple time-point data has become a subject of increasing interest among sociologists. One concern has been with models that incorporate a single variable measured at two or more points in time. For example, Heise (1969; see also Wiley and Wiley, 1970) has dealt with a model that includes unreliability (random measurement error) in the observed variables and instability over time in the underlying "true score" variable for variables with single indicators. Heise's purpose in setting forth this type of model is to caution researchers to avoid misleading interpretations of simple test-retest correlations, and towards this purpose he provides an operational distinction between the reliability and stability of variables measured over time. Wiley and Wiley (1970) and Werts, Jöreskog, and Linn (1971) discuss the identification and estimation of reliability and stability parameters in these models under less restrictive sets of assumptions. Others (Costner, 1969; Blalock, 1970; Hauser and Goldberger, 1971) have discussed single variable multi-wave models where the variable has multiple indicators at each time point. In this case more information is available for estimating reliability and stability. Included in the treatment of both types of single variable panel models is a concern with *measurement specification*; that is, a measurement model is explicitly represented for the relationship between observed measures and their underlying constructs and for the relationships among observed measures.

A second concern with the interpretation of panel data has been in the context of the multi-wave multi-variable case (Bohrnstedt, 1969; Duncan, 1969; Heise, 1970). This second focus is important because it takes more seriously the issue of theoretical specification. By *theoretical specification* we mean the specification of the pattern of relationships among the underlying constructs. Inasmuch as this second concern is not explicitly the issue of measurement error, it lacks the special virtues of the literature cited above. Both concerns are essential in any proper interpretation of panel data, especially when observed variables are fallible. Discussions by Heise (1970), and Duncan (1972, 1975) have dealt with the issues of measurement specification and theoretical specification, but their primary concern is not with estimation issues.[1] Hannan, Rubinson, and Warren (1974) have also discussed panel models with both theoretical and measurement specifications made explicit, but their treatment of identification and estimation issues does not emphasize that given an efficient estimation procedure there are clear advantages to overidentification. A recent paper by Jöreskog and Sörbom (1976a) provides a useful and comprehensive statistical treatment of a number of types of panel models with illustrative examples. This chapter shares the orientation of Jöreskog and Sörbom to the analysis of panel data and follows the approach to estimation introduced by Jöreskog (1973; see also Jöreskog, 1976).

The purpose of the present chapter is to suggest some strategies that will improve both the measurement and the theoretical specification of models using panel data and incorporating the estimation of reliability and stability parameters. It is especially important to point out that the resulting flexibility in the specification procedure greatly increases the usefulness of panel data while providing a potential solution to some of the common problems with their use. Following the lead of Heise (1969) and the Wileys (1970), our discussion emphasizes the necessity of incorporating the issue of unreliability of measurement in any general model for the analysis of panel data. Also, following Duncan (1969) and others, we encourage the thorough specification of causal relationships among the theoretical variables included in multiple-wave data.

We begin our discussion by reconsidering the original single-variable three-wave model proposed by Heise (1969). It has become clear that for many purposes such single-variable models are inadequate at the level of theoretical specification, resulting in biased estimates of reliability and stability parameters in such models. Also involved in the issue of the theoretical specification of relationships among unobserved constructs is the reconceptualization of stability, since in the multivariate case the stability parameter is a partial regression coefficient rather than a correlation.

---

[1] A third literature dealing with panel analysis has addressed the issue of assessing causal priority of variables in multi-wave data using "cross-lagged" correlations (Pelz and Andrews, 1964; Rozelle and Campbell, 1969; Kenny, 1973). Others (Bohrnstedt, 1969; Duncan, 1969; Heise, 1970) have shown that this issue can be addressed in a more conventional regression framework.

We then go on to examine a set of models that are more completely specified, estimating the parameters of these models via a technique that allows us to estimate causal (structural) relations among unobserved constructs with multiple indicators (Jöreskog, 1976; Jöreskog and Sörbom, 1976b). Of special interest here is the fact that issues of specification at each level must be considered in the development of properly specified panel models.

THE SINGLE-VARIABLE THREE-WAVE MODEL

The original single-variable three-wave model set forth by Heise (1969) is presented in Figure 1. First, the model states that at each point in time ($t = 1, 2, 3$) the observed variable x_t, is a perfect linear, additive function of two uncorrelated components: a true (reliable) component X_t, and a random error component e_t, assumed to be measurement error. Second, the model states that at

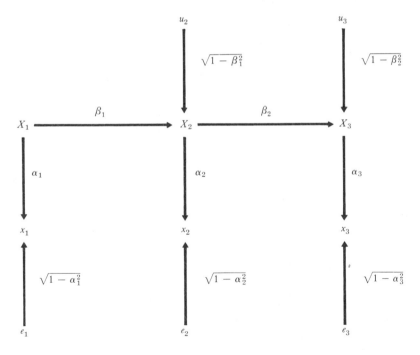

Figure 1. A Representation of the Single-Variable Three-Wave Panel Model.

each point in time the true underlying variable X_t is a perfect linear additive function of two uncorrelated components: the true variable at the previous point in time, and a random disturbance representing sources of change or instability in the true variable over time. We have represented the effects of a true score on the observed score at a particular point in time as α_t, and the effects of a true score at a particular point in time on the true score at a subsequent point in time as $\beta_j (j = 1, 2)$. In order to identify the reliability and stability parameters Heise (1969) assumes $\alpha_1 = \alpha_2 = \alpha_3$, which provides for a straightforward algebraic solution for α_t and the stability parameters β_1 and β_2. Wiley and Wiley (1970) point out that this solution does not make use of all the available information in the data, since it analyzes the correlation matrix instead of the variance-covariance matrix. The Wileys note that it is sufficient to assume that $\text{Var}(e_1) = \text{Var}(e_2) = \text{Var}(e_3)$, then the variance of the unobserved true variable need not be equal across time. In this case we need not assume $\alpha_1 = \alpha_2 = \alpha_3$ in order to identify these parameters. Werts, Jöreskog, and Linn (1971) have pointed out that if the single-variable model is extended to four (or more) time points, unequal reliabilities and the stabilities for the internal measures (excluding the first and the last) can be identified without having to assume equality in the error variances.

Note that the reliability of a particular observed score at a given point in time is defined as α_t^2 (see Lord and Novick, 1968), where for any t:

$$\alpha^2 = p_{xX}^2 = \frac{\text{Var}(X)}{\text{Var}(x)} = \frac{\sigma_X^2}{\sigma_X^2 + \sigma_E^2} \tag{1}$$

where σ_X^2 = true score variance, and σ_E^2 = measurement error variance. There is a more general definition of reliability, which we will introduce later, of which this definition is a special case.

These single-variable models do have a number of assumptions in common:

(1) The true and error components of the observed score are uncorrelated, and error components of any observed score are uncorrelated with all other true variables.

(2) Measurement errors at different points in time are uncorrelated.

(3) Disturbance terms are uncorrelated with the true variables at prior points in time.

(4) The system is assumed to be lag-1; that is, there is no direct linear effect of the true variable at time 1 on the true variable at time 3.

Problems with assumptions (1) and (2) have been discussed in a number of other papers (Blalock, 1970; Althauser and Heberlein, 1970; Costner and Schoenberg, 1973; Alwin, 1974). For our present purposes, assumption (1) expresses the measurement model used in this paper, and we will address problems resulting when the other assumptions do not hold.

An important potential problem with the single-variable model described above is one of bias in the estimates of the stability parameters. We mean by this that some external variable, say Y, is a determinant of the underlying true variable at two or more points in time; and, as a result, we may spuriously attribute stability to the underlying true variable. This possibility (assuming Y is perfectly measured) is represented in the diagram in Figure 2.

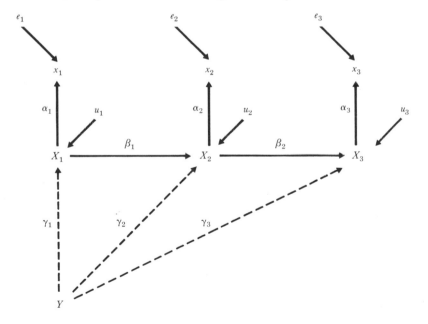

Figure 2. The Operation of an Excluded Variable in the Single-Variable Model.

Using the conventional algorithms of path analysis and assuming standardized data, we can solve for Heise's stability parameters in this model as follows (using the notation β'_1 and β'_2 for Heise's parameters):

$$\beta'_1 = \frac{\rho_{13}}{\rho_{23}} = \frac{\alpha_1 \alpha_3 (\beta_1 \beta_2 + \gamma_1 \gamma_3 + \gamma_1 \gamma_2 \beta_2)}{\alpha_2 \alpha_3 (\beta_2 + \gamma_3 \gamma_2 + \gamma_3 \gamma_1 \beta_1)}$$

$$= \frac{\alpha_1 (\beta_1 \beta_2 + \gamma_1 \gamma_3 + \gamma_1 \gamma_2 \beta_2)}{\alpha_2 (\beta_2 + \gamma_3 \gamma_2 + \gamma_3 \gamma_1 \beta_1)}$$

$$\beta'_2 = \frac{\rho_{13}}{\rho_{12}} = \frac{\alpha_1 \alpha_3 (\beta_1 \beta_2 + \gamma_1 \gamma_3 + \gamma_1 \gamma_2 \beta_2)}{\alpha_1 \alpha_2 (\beta_1 + \gamma_1 \gamma_2)}$$

$$= \frac{\alpha_3 (\beta_1 \beta_2 + \gamma_1 \gamma_3 + \gamma_1 \gamma_2 \beta_2)}{\alpha_2 (\beta_1 + \gamma_1 \gamma_2)}$$

Note from the above equations that β'_1 will equal β_1 when $\gamma_1 \gamma_3 = \gamma_1 \gamma_2 = \gamma_2 \gamma_3 = 0$ and $\alpha_1 = \alpha_2$. Also note that β'_2 will equal β_2 when $\gamma_1 \gamma_2 = \gamma_1 \gamma_3 = 0$ and $\alpha_2 = \alpha_3$, suggesting the possibility of bias when Y is related to X. Heise (1969) discusses the possibility, but does not present data bearing on the issue. Likewise, reliability estimates in such a model may be affected. Using Heise's assumptions ($\alpha_1 = \alpha_2 = \alpha_3 = \alpha$) for simplicity, it is clear that under most conditions

$$\alpha' = \frac{\rho_{12} \rho_{23}}{\rho_{13}} \neq \sqrt{\frac{\alpha^2 (\beta_1 + \gamma_1 \gamma_2)(\beta_2 + \gamma_2 \gamma_3 + \beta_1 \gamma_1 \gamma_3)}{(\beta_1 \beta_2 + \gamma_1 \gamma_3 + \gamma_1 \gamma_2 \beta_2)}}$$

where α' is the estimate resulting from the Heise model. Therefore, in cases where other variables cause X, the Heise estimates of reliability and stability may be biased.[2]

Figure 2 introduces a new complexity in the definition and interpretation of stability. In single-variable models, the stability (standardized to a path coefficient) is automatically the total correlation between successive true variables. In the multivariate case,

[2] These principles can also be illustrated with the Wiley and Wiley (1970) model, since it is very similar to that proposed by Heise. The proofs in this case are much more cumbersome, and we will not deal with them here.

the stability parameters we will use are partial regression coefficients. This is not only a shift in operational definition, it also points to the need for a clarification of the concept of stability. Care must be taken first to specify the unit of analysis under discussion. The stability parameter is intended to represent the amount of true change in a variable across time, and in this chapter what we mean by "true change" is change of individuals' positions in the distribution relative to one another. This means that we do not address the issue of constant change over time, as reflected by changes in the intercept. Constant change of the group as a whole is another issue, which can be addressed in the context of "system" differences but is not central to the question of the relative change between individuals—which is implicit in our application of the stability concept.

We contend that the simple change definition (operationalized as a correlation) can lead to misleading interpretations of stability. It is obvious from Figure 2 that part of this inter-temporal true score correlation is not due to the effect of the variable at t on the same variable at $t + 1$. Stability, as we define it, is concerned with the amount of change or lack of change in X_{t-1} and due to X_t alone; that is, the degree to which one's score on X_t is, in fact, the source of one's score on X_{t+1}. The change in X_2 and X_3 in Figure 2 caused by other agents should be interpreted separately from the stability of that variable. Such a notion of stability is implicitly recognized by Heise when discussing potential sources of distortion to stability estimates (1969, pp. 99–101).

We conclude, from the preceding discussion, that it is essential that causal models representing processes measured in panel data be correctly specified at the theoretical level—as well as the measurement level—if one is to place any confidence in estimates of the "true" stability of variables. Our orientation leads us to explore first the possibility that certain concomitant variables may be causally related to the single variable measured at three points in time in single indicator models. Also, however, by using multiple indicators for each construct we introduce the possibility of estimating correlations between error terms for the observed measures, and we create more information for the estimation of the stability parameters (Costner, 1969; Blalock, 1970). This "over-identification" in multiple indicator models is useful precisely because it results in more than one estimate of the stability parameter. Given a procedure for combining these separate estimates, the estimation of such models is enhanced. A general procedure for obtaining efficient estimation in overidentified models of the type considered here is available using a maximum-likelihood solution (Jöreskog, 1973, 1976; Jöreskog and Sörbom, 1976b), and we will make use of this method below.

THE SPECIFICATION AND ESTIMATION OF RECURSIVE MODELS IN PANEL DATA

Discussions of the analysis of panel data by Duncan (1969) and Heise (1970) consider the problems inherent in making inferences from sample data in panel situations where the variables contain measurement error. Neither treatment incorporates specification of the measurement error in the variables as a part of the model to be estimated. More recent papers by Duncan (1972, 1975) develop several models for the two-wave two-variable situation that incorporate unobserved constructs and, thereby, implicitly deal with the issue of random measurement error. Also, Hannan *et al.* (1974) specify both random and nonrandom measurement errors in a series of three-wave models. We can extend these discussions using different estimation assumptions and placing them in the context of the reliability-stability issue.

We will discuss first an "unexplicated" confirmatory factor analytic model (hereafter referred to as a *CFA* model). By "unexplicated" we mean simply that we do not specify a causal system for the covariances among unobserved constructs. Later, we will distinguish this form of *CFA* from the "explicated" *CFA* model in which we postulate a causal structure among unobserved constructs, which is intended to account for the covariances and variances among these constructs. The unexplicated *CFA* model deals only with the issue of measurement specification, whereas the explicated model deals with both measurement and theoretical specification. From an econometric perspective, the explicated model could be regarded as a structural equation model extended to include multiple indicators.

Explicated confirmatory factor analytic models provide a number of advantages in estimating reliability-and-stability models with panel data. First, these methods take into account random measurement error in that the amount of this type of error is estimated directly in the model. Second, in the case of multiple indicators, certain measurement error correlations can also be estimated. Third, causal relationships between abstract constructs can be interpreted directly rather than through inference from measured variable relationships. Fourth, the postulated structure relating observed measures to unobserved constructs and unobserved constructs to each other can be tested for fit to the observed variance-covariance matrix. Fifth, the model is thus very amenable to use as a theory construction tool (see the discussion by Burt, 1973). And, sixth, the issue of reliability and stability can be addressed within the context of a general model that has increased specification flexibility and, thus, increases our chances of accurately estimating these parameters. Specifically, the models we will suggest can be used to incorporate and estimate the effects of three possible sources of distortion to reliability and stability estimates; including the effects of excluded causal variables in the Heise and Wileys' models, the effects of correlations between exogenous constructs in the model and endogenous disturbance terms (or, alternatively, violation of the lag-1 assumption), and the effects of correlated measurement error.

An example of an unexplicated *CFA* model appears in Figure 3. The well-known covariance structure implied by this model (Jöreskog, 1969) can be expressed as:

$$\Sigma = \Lambda \Phi \Lambda' + \Theta^2 \qquad (2)$$

where Σ is a $p \times p$ population variance-covariance matrix for $p = 7$ variables, composed of three types of matrices: matrix Λ is a $p \times m$ factor pattern matrix expressing the p observed variables as a linear function of m unobserved constructs; matrix Φ is an $m \times m$ matrix of unobserved construct covariances and variances; and matrix Θ^2 is a $p \times p$ diagonal matrix of residual error variances for the observed variables.[3] Each of these parameter matrices may contain *fixed* parameters that are assumed known *a priori*, and the other parameters in

[3] In this case, the paths for the error terms are assumed to be 1 (as in the factor analytic model), and we can then identify the variance of the error term. This is equivalent to representing the Θ_i as the path coefficients for the measurement terms with the variance of the e_i equal to 1.

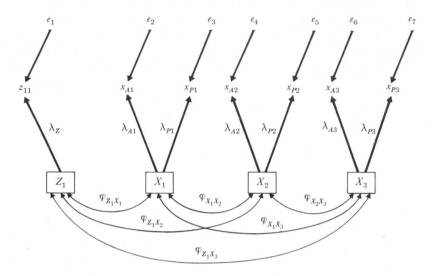

Figure 3. A Two-Variable Three-Wave *CFA* Measurement Model.

the model are then estimated. Estimated parameters can be of two types: *free* parameters that are unknown and not assumed equal to any other unknown parameters in the model, and *constrained* parameters that are set equal to other unknown parameters. The consequences of restricting certain parameters can be tested for efficacy by a χ^2 goodness of fit test in the case where we restrict more parameters than are needed for identification.

In the model presented in Figure 3, there are several zero entries in matrix Λ, indicated by the absence of direct effects from certain unobserved constructs to certain observed variables (for example, X_3 to x_{P2}). The prespecification of certain zero entries in the Λ matrix allows a covariance between factors (or "constructs," in our terminology) to be identified and to be estimated. Thus a zero effect of X_3 on x_{P2}, for instance, is not evidence of a lack of covariance; rather, there is an association between x_{P2} and X_3 due to the fact that x_{P2} is a measure of another construct, which itself *is* directly related to X_3.

If we feel that a particular causal structure underlies the unobserved variances and covariances in Figure 3, and we have a time-ordering established for our variables, we can postulate an

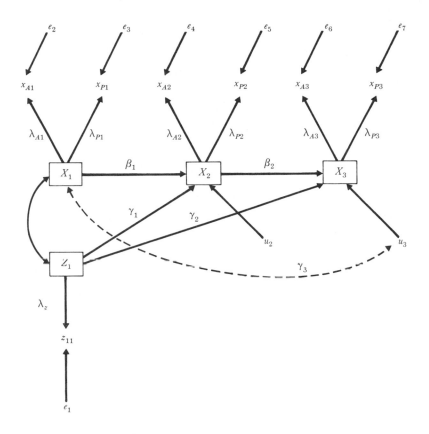

Figure 4. Explicated Causal Model for the CFA Model in Figure 3.

explicated *CFA* model as in Figure 4. This model will be important in our subsequent analysis. We will consider first the version of Figure 4 in which $\gamma_3 = 0$.[4] This is an explicated model containing an overidentifying restriction on the variance-covariance matrix for the constructs in addition to the restrictions on the Λ matrix.

Following Jöreskog (1976), we can express the relationships in Figure 4 as follows, first for the relations between constructs and their measures:

[4] We specify γ_3 as the correlation between X_1 and u_3 and not the direct effect of X_1 on X_3 for reasons to be stated later.

$$
\begin{bmatrix} x_{A2} \\ x_{P2} \\ x_{A3} \\ x_{P3} \end{bmatrix} = \mu + \Lambda_y \begin{bmatrix} X_2 \\ X_3 \end{bmatrix} + \begin{bmatrix} e_4 \\ e_5 \\ e_6 \\ e_7 \end{bmatrix} \tag{3}
$$

$$
\begin{bmatrix} z_{11} \\ x_{A1} \\ x_{P1} \end{bmatrix} = \nu + \Lambda_x \begin{bmatrix} Z_1 \\ X_1 \end{bmatrix} + \begin{bmatrix} e_1 \\ e_2 \\ e_3 \end{bmatrix} \tag{4}
$$

where μ and ν are the respective mean vectors for the measures $\Lambda_{y(p \times m)}$ = the factor loading matrix for all observed measures of endogenous unobserved constructs, p = the number of observed measures and m = the number of endogenous constructs, and $\Lambda_{x(q \times n)}$ = the factor loading matrix for all observed measures of exogenous unobserved constructs, q = the number of observed measures, and n = the number of exogenous constructs; and second, for the relations between constructs,

$$
B \cdot \begin{bmatrix} X_2 \\ X_3 \end{bmatrix} = \Gamma \begin{bmatrix} Z_1 \\ X_1 \end{bmatrix} + \begin{bmatrix} u_2 \\ u_3 \end{bmatrix} \tag{5}
$$

where $B_{(m \times m)}$ is a coefficient matrix for the relationships among endogenous constructs, and $\Gamma_{(m \times n)}$ is a coefficient matrix for relationships between exogenous and endogenous constructs.

In applying this model, we begin with the following assumptions: the expectation for all unobserved constructs is defined to be zero, that is, $E(Z_1) = E(X_1) = E(X_2) = E(X_3) = 0$; the expectation of the disturbances is also zero, that is, $E(u_2) = E(u_3) = 0$; the expectation of the observed variable vector is μ, ν; measurement errors are uncorrelated with each other and with all constructs in the model; exogenous constructs and disturbance terms for endogenous constructs are uncorrelated; and B is nonsingular. We designate $\Phi_{(n \times n)}$ as the variance-covariance matrix of exogenous constructs, $\psi_{(m \times m)}$ as the variance-covariance matrix for disturbance terms, Θ_ε as a diagonal matrix of error standard deviations for the p observed measures of endogenous constructs, and Θ_δ as a diagonal matrix of error standard deviations for q observed measures of exogenous constructs. We will then obtain the population variance-covariance matrix for the observed measures $(x_{A2}, x_{P2}, x_{A3}, x_{P3}, z_{11}, x_{A1}, x_{P1})'$ as (Jöreskog, 1976):

$$\Sigma = \tag{6}$$

$$\begin{bmatrix} \Lambda_y(B^{-1}\Gamma\Phi\Gamma'B'^{-1} + B^{-1}\Psi B'^{-1})\Lambda_y' + \Theta_\varepsilon^2 & \text{symmetric} \\ \hline \Lambda_x\Phi\Gamma'B'^{-1}\Lambda_y' & \Lambda_x\Phi\Lambda_x' + \Theta_\delta^2 \end{bmatrix}$$

We should make it explicit that the variance-covariance matrix of exogenous constructs is

$$T_1 = \text{Var}\begin{pmatrix} Z_1 \\ X_1 \end{pmatrix} = \Phi$$

that the variance-covariance matrix of endogenous constructs is

$$T_2 = \text{Var}\begin{pmatrix} X_2 \\ X_3 \end{pmatrix} = B^{-1}\Gamma\Phi\Gamma'B'^{-1} + B^{-1}\Psi B'^{-1}$$

and that the covariance matrix between exogenous and endogenous constructs is

$$T_3 = \text{Cov}\left[\begin{pmatrix} Z_1 \\ X_1 \end{pmatrix}, \begin{pmatrix} X_2 \\ X_3 \end{pmatrix}\right] = E\left[\begin{pmatrix} Z_1 \\ X_1 \end{pmatrix} (X_2 X_3)\right] = \Phi\Gamma'B'^{-1}$$

Then we write Σ in simplified form:

$$\Sigma = \begin{bmatrix} \Lambda_y(T_2)\Lambda_y' + \Theta_\varepsilon^2 & \text{symmetric} \\ \hline \Lambda_x(T_3)\Lambda_y' & \Lambda_x(T_1)\Lambda_x' + \Theta_\delta^2 \end{bmatrix}$$

$$= \begin{bmatrix} \Lambda_y & 0 \\ 0 & \Lambda_x \end{bmatrix} \cdot \begin{bmatrix} T_2 & \text{sym} \\ T_3 & T_1 \end{bmatrix} \tag{7}$$

$$\cdot \begin{bmatrix} \Lambda_y & 0 \\ 0 & \Lambda_x \end{bmatrix}' + \begin{bmatrix} \Theta_\varepsilon^2 & 0 \\ 0 & \Theta_\delta^2 \end{bmatrix}$$

which is in a form analogous to our expression for Σ (equation (2)) for the unexplicated *CFA* model.

Our object is to fit this matrix to the corresponding sample variance-covariance matrix S by an appropriate choice of parameter estimates. We use the following fitting function (Jöreskog, 1976):

$$F = \tfrac{1}{2}[\log|\Sigma| - \log|S| + \text{tr.}\,(S\Sigma^{-1}) - (p + q)] \tag{8}$$

which will be minimized with respect to the elements in

$$\Lambda_y, \Lambda_x, B, \Gamma, \Phi, \Psi, \Theta_\varepsilon, \Theta_\delta$$

With the additional assumption of a multivariate normal distribution for the observed variable vector, the assumptions stated earlier ensure that minimizing F is equivalent to maximizing the likelihood of the sample values; that is, our parameter estimates will be *ML*-estimates with optimal large-sample properties. This additional assumption is not an unreasonable approximation for the data we will use, and our sample size seems large enough ($N = 932$) for large-sample properties to be relevant. The model as represented in Figure 4 may be conveniently estimated using the fitting function above via the Jöreskog and Sörbom computer program LISREL (1976b). For the case in which we impose restrictions on the relationships among constructs, the *ML*-estimates have the property of optimal efficiency compared to the ordinary least squares estimates. In some cases in which this part of the model is just-identified, the estimates are in fact the same. LISREL can be applied as easily in both situations. However, the method of analysis used by LISREL is especially advantageous in the case that the researcher has theoretical reasons for imposing restrictions *a priori* on relationships among constructs.

Using LISREL, we can also obtain a χ^2 goodness of fit test (see Jöreskog, 1973, p. 90) for any overidentified model, with degrees of freedom equal to the number of distinct elements in $S[(p + q) \cdot (p + q + 1)/2]$ minus the number of different parameters to be estimated. The χ^2 value for a model is determined by both the sample size and the minimum value of our fitting function F_0 as follows:

$$\chi^2_{df} = 2(N - 1) \cdot F_0 \tag{9}$$

This means that we are testing the null hypothesis (H_0) that the Σ matrix for a particular constrained model is correct as specified against the alternative (H_1) that an unconstrained Σ matrix (which is, of course, still positive definite and symmetric) is the correct model. Obviously, the Σ matrix under H_1 will reproduce the S matrix perfectly, and $F_1 = 0$. In practice, this hypothesis testing procedure implies that larger values of χ^2 reflect poorer fit for the model under H_0.

The χ^2 test statistic is very often significant in samples of large size, suggesting rejection of the proposed model. Thus, it is used frequently in a descriptive fashion to decide between models on the basis of *relative* fit to the data. In applying this χ^2, we will want to assess varying χ^2/d.f. ratios across models in order to get a rough indication of fit per degree of freedom. For our sample size, we judge a ratio of around 5 or less as beginning to be reasonable, based on our experience in inspecting the sizes of residuals which accompany varying χ^2 values. The residuals matrix is the difference between the Σ matrix of the estimated variances and covariances implied by the model and the observed variance-covariance matrix (S). In order to give an indication of the kinds of residuals that accompany different χ^2/d.f. ratios we will present such information at various points in the discussion.

EMPIRICAL ESTIMATION OF RECURSIVE MODELS FOR PANEL DATA

The Data

The empirical examples that we present to illustrate the estimation techniques suggested in the foregoing section make use of data from a longitudinal study of the effects of industrial development in a rural region in Illinois. The study was designed such that the data were collected on the same variables at three points in time (1966, 1967, and 1971) in each of two regions — an experimental region where a Jones & Laughlin Steel Corporation cold rolling mill was being constructed, and a control region where there was no such development taking place. For purposes of the present analyses the two samples are combined, producing a total of 932 cases.[5]

[5] See Summers *et al.* (1969) for a further description of the research setting and O'Meara (1966) for a detailed description of the sampling design.

Beginning with a traditional "social structure and personality" perspective, our original interest was in the reliability and stability of measured attitudes and the possible effects of'selected social status factors on these attitudes over time. The initial interest in the stability of attitudes stemmed from a concern with whether social psychological variables (such as alienation and expressed social distance toward minority groups) are either highly volatile and, therefore, amenable to change, or are relatively stable over time. The following attitude scales were administered at all three points in time: an *alienation scale,* composed of items from Srole (1956) and items developed for this study by Summers; an *anomia subscale* of the above scale, from Srole (1956); a *powerlessness subscale* from the alienation scale, comprised of the items developed by Summers; a *religious importance scale,* measuring the degree to which the individual attaches importance to religion in his own life and composed of items from the scale developed by Snell and Middleton (1961); a *Latin American social distance scale* from Bogardus (1925), composed of a summated 6-item scale, each item was coded with a dichotomous acceptance-rejection designation; and a *Negro social distance scale,* a modification of items in Bogardus (1925), also a summed 6-item scale wherein each item was coded with a dichotomous acceptance-rejection designation.

In addition, two measures of the respondent's current socioeconomic position are also included in the present analysis: the respondent's educational attainment is expressed as years of schooling completed, and the status of the respondent's occupation is expressed in terms of the Duncan Socioeconomic Index *(SEI),* using the average *SEI* of the major census occupational grouping in which his occupation falls. For those not currently in the labor force, the *SEI* score for their last full-time job was used.

Single-Indicator Models

In Table 1 we present the estimates of reliability and stability of each of the six attitude measures in a single-variable model using the computational formulae of both Heise (1969) and Wiley and Wiley (1970). It is remarkable that, given the time period involved (from one to four years), the stability of these social psychological variables appears to be rather high. It appears also that three different reliability coefficients estimated from the Wileys' model are

TABLE 1
Reliabilities and Stabilities Estimated from Both Single-Indicator Models for Six Selected Attitudes.

| | Heise Model | | | | Wiley and Wiley Model | | | | | |
| | Reliabilities | Stabilities | | | Reliabilities | | | Stabilities | | |
	$\alpha^{2}*$	β_1	β_2	$\beta_1 \cdot \beta_2$	α_1^2	α_2^2	α_3^2	β_1	β_2	$\beta_1 \cdot \beta_2$
Alienation	0.75	0.97	0.81	0.79	0.78	0.75	0.76	0.95	0.80	0.76
Anomia	0.71	0.94	0.79	0.74	0.74	0.71	0.73	0.92	0.78	0.72
Powerlessness	0.64	0.98	0.81	0.79	0.69	0.64	0.67	0.94	0.80	0.75
Religious importance	0.68	0.82	0.77	0.63	0.63	0.68	0.50	0.85	0.91	0.77
Latin American social distance	0.43	1.15	0.96	1.11						
Negro social distance	0.52	1.08	0.96	1.03						

*In this table, estimated parameters will not include "^" notation, although it is to be understood that they are sample estimates.

usually similar over time points. Heise's assumption of constant reliability may indeed be reasonable for these variables. As Wiley and Wiley (1970) note, their time 2 reliability coefficient is equal to Heise's overall reliability—an assertion which is empirically demonstrated by the estimates presented in Table 1.

However, there are some problems with these results. In computing the parameter estimates in the two versions of the single-variable panel model for "Latin American social distance" and "Negro social distance" some unexpected results were obtained. For these variables some of Heise's stabilities exceed unity, and for corresponding coefficients in the Wiley models negative variances were obtained in the disturbances for the true score variables at times 2 and 3. This makes the application of the Wiley formulas problematic. Of course, given some sampling error, these results are possible and would then lead to the interpretation that the variable in question is, in fact, perfectly stable. However, such an interpretation is not convincing without first testing alternative explanations.

The above discussion suggests the possibility that, at least for certain variables, single-variable models may be inappropriate in the sense that some of the assumptions are not met and that they are, therefore, misspecified in important ways. In particular, we are concerned first with the possibility that important causal variables are excluded from these single-variable models (that is, assumption (3), noted earlier, is violated).[6] This circumstance is not, however, limited to the cases in which the stability estimates exceed unity in Heise's model. Even those stability estimates that are within reasonable limits may be biased upward, and this is a possibility we wish to explore. For instance, the estimated stabilities for alienation in Table 1 are 0.95 to 0.97 for β_1 and 0.80 to 0.81 for β_2 in the two models, respectively, and we feel these results demand closer inspection as well.

Before we proceed, however, it is important to illustrate the limitations imposed on alternative specifications by three-wave single-indicator models. Using LISREL, rather than the computational formulae, we can find reliability and stability estimates for the just-identified Wileys' model. In the case of the "Latin American

[6] We shall retain the lag-1 assumption in its original form, and choose to relax assumption (3) instead, where it is possible.

social distance" variable, for instance, we estimate the following parameters: $\alpha_1^2 = (0.654)^2$, $\alpha_2^2 = (0.639)^2$, $\alpha_3^2 = (0.727)^2$, $\beta_1 = 1.031$, and $\beta_2 = 0.981$. Both of the stability paths are close to one. The question is whether we can assess with other models the plausibility of these estimates. The first step might be to estimate a model as in Figure 2, adding a variable with proven theoretical and empirical relevance to the phenomenon of expressed social distance. Our inclination, then, is to assess the effects of "years of education" in this model, assuming that social distance towards minority groups (or "out groups") is itself a proxy for generalized prejudice. The correlations underlying this model are contained in Table 2. Without presenting the results of the whole model, we need only mention that effects of education as measured in 1966 on later states of social distance are essentially zero (where we apply the criterion for statistical significance that a coefficient should exceed twice its standard error).[7] Thus, changes in estimates of stability are minor.

In cases where the added variable's effects are unsuccessful, or only partially successful—and if we want to asses the potential influence of other causal variables which could distort the stability estimates via indirect paths between X_1 and X_3—we can specify the model so that $p_{X_1 u_3} \neq 0$.[8] However, without imposing further restrictions, the model is under-identified in the single indicator case. It should be pointed out that there is more than one way to render the model just-identified, and we have no statistical criteria for deciding between these models. The resulting estimates are affected by the particular restrictions we choose, and the fit to the observed data is perfect for each model. It may be useful to impose some contrasting over-identifying restrictions on the model in order to test their efficacy with the χ^2 test.

If we want to estimate $p_{X_1 u_3}$ (a path which stands for other possible sources of further distortion to the stability estimates), we

[7] The LISREL program produces estimates of the asymptotic standard errors, and in a large sample such as ours the above ratio has an approximate normal distribution.

[8] This relaxes the third assumption we began with in applying LISREL. This can be done by specifying u_3 as an extra exogenous construct correlated with X_1 and causing X_3 with the unstandardized path fixed to one. It should be noted that this parameter does not constitute a special case for the ML method of estimation. ML produces a *consistent* and *asymptotically efficient* estimate of the parameter.

must impose restrictions on other parameters in the model. Researchers may have *a priori* reasons for choosing certain kinds of restrictions. In this case, we arbitrarily fix $\gamma_2 = \gamma_3 = 0$ for illustrative purposes, and this allows us to estimate the measured-to-unobserved regressions, given that they are constrained equal, and $\rho_{X_1 u_3}$. For ease in interpretation, we can discuss the standardized solution for this model for selected important parameters given below:

$$\hat{\beta}_1 = 0.99 \qquad\qquad \hat{\alpha}_3 = 0.66$$

$$\hat{\beta}_2 = 1.13 \qquad\qquad \hat{\rho}_{X_1 u_3} = -0.52$$

$$\hat{\alpha}_1 = 0.74 \qquad\qquad \hat{\gamma}_1 = -0.31$$

$$\hat{\alpha}_2 = 0.66$$

The estimate of $\rho_{X_1 u_3}$ does not, in fact, represent a significant path despite its size, due to the relatively large standard error in comparison to the corresponding unstandardized parameter (Z value $= -1$). However, the χ^2 for this model is 4.58 with 1 degree of freedom, denoting a relatively good fit. Note that the stabilities in this case are again close to one.

For a final model, we removed the education variable from the model — returning to the single-variable case — and assumed $\rho_{X_1 u_3} = 0$. It should be noted that we have no way in single-indicator models of attempting to estimate the possible influence of correlated measurement error. We suggest, therefore that our *best* estimate of the stability is, in fact, one. We add the restriction in our final model for social distance that $V(u_2) = V(u_3) = 0$. In effect, this assumes that the correlations among the constructs are each one. Forcing the model to lag-1 form (as in Figure 2) produces estimates of $\hat{\beta}_1 = 1$ and $\hat{\beta}_2 = 1$. The fit of this model is, of course, better than the last, with a χ^2 value of 0.59 with 2 degrees of freedom (probability level for the model $= 0.74$). Given the alternatives, our conclusion is that the best estimate is that "Latin American social distance" is perfectly stable over this five-year period.

In sum, we feel that estimates of reliabilities and stabilities in single-indicator models are difficult to interpret in view of the limited alternatives available to these models. Our *ad hoc* procedures for exploring the reasonableness of Wileys' specification are, at best, risky. The inherent lack of flexibility is the most important limitation in applying these models, and we are led to suggest that the increased flexibility in multiple indicator models makes them more useful for estimating both reliability and stability parameters.

Multivariate Panel Models with Multiple Indicators

In this section we will estimate several multivariate models for panel data in which we incorporate, as above, parameters representing the magnitude of measurement error and the stability of the variables over time. Now, however, we wish to include a variety of forms and extensions of the general model presented in Figure 4 and discussed previously. We will focus on one variable with multiple indicators (in this case, alienation) in successive specifications for the purpose of facilitating comparisons across models. The models which we present begin to specify more completely the relationships between indicators of alienation and other variables. In placing alienation in a substantive context, we wish to assume a "social structure and personality" perspective. Our interest is in the possible consequences that position in the social structure can have for the individual's psychological functioning. This is, of course, a classic sociological issue, one which is pertinent in a search for causal variables which can be added to single-variable models involving attitudes.

We have included two aspects of a person's position in the social structure—educational achievement and occupational status—as a way of placing alienation in a more completely specified, albeit rudimentary, theoretical context. Although there may be important mediating processes which more thoroughly explain how such aspects of social structure affect these variables, our main interest here is in estimating their total effects.

The correlation matrix for all observed variables that appear in our earlier analyses of single-indicator models, and all subsequent analyses, is presented in Table 2. It is apparent from a perusal of this matrix that there are consistent patterns of relatively strong negative correlations between the selected attitude variables, on the one hand, and the two measures of social position, on the other. These results are consistent with the findings of a number of other studies (Thompson and Horton, 1960; Middleton, 1963; Photiadis and Schweiker 1971; Simpson, 1970; and Anderson, 1973).

TABLE 2
Correlation Matrix for all Attitude and Status Variables Used.

	X_1	X_2	X_3	X_4	X_5	X_6	X_7	X_8	X_9	X_{10}	X_{11}	X_{12}	X_{13}
Education (1966) X_1													
SEI (1966) X_2	0.54												
Anomia (1966) X_3	−0.34	−0.25											
Powerlessness (1966) X_4	−0.41	−0.30	0.70										
Latin American social distance (1966) X_5	−0.25	−0.21	0.27	0.31									
SEI (1967) X_6	0.53	0.82	−0.26	−0.31	−0.14								
Anomia (1967) X_7	−0.36	−0.30	0.67	0.55	0.26	−0.30							
Powerlessness (1967) X_8	−0.41	−0.29	0.55	0.63	0.28	−0.33	0.66						
Latin American social distance (1967) X_9	−0.16	−0.19	0.27	0.26	0.49	−0.11	0.25	0.28					
SEI (1971) X_{10}	0.54	0.81	−0.25	−0.25	−0.21	0.78	−0.28	−0.26	−0.18				
Anomia (1971) X_{11}	−0.35	−0.29	0.53	0.50	0.27	−0.32	0.56	0.47	0.29	−0.31			
Powerlessness (1971) X_{12}	−0.37	−0.28	0.42	0.51	0.24	−0.26	0.44	0.52	0.23	−0.28	0.67		
Latin American social distance (1971) X_{13}	−0.22	−0.16	0.26	0.26	0.47	−0.14	0.25	0.27	0.41	−0.19	0.29	0.28	
Mean	10.90	37.49	21.22	14.85	1.11	36.72	13.61	14.76	0.89	37.47	14.13	14.90	0.78
S. D.	3.10	21.22	3.60	3.31	1.40	21.00	3.44	3.06	1.27	20.98	3.54	3.16	1.25

We can begin by estimating a baseline model for alienation,[9] which can be used as a starting point for comparison. This model is represented as a sub-model of Figure 4, including all paths *except* those involving Z_1, z_{11}, and e_1. Also, we assume that $p_{X_1 u_3} = \gamma_3 = 0$. The underlying model involving X_1, X_2, X_3, and their indicators is a familiar one and in various forms has been discussed elsewhere (Costner, 1969; Blalock, 1970). We need only remind the reader that it is overidentified. Each alienation construct at each point in time (X_1 = alienation (1966); X_2 = alienation (1967); X_3 = alienation (1971)) has two indicators, an anomia sub-scale (x_{A1}, x_{A2}, x_{A3}) and a powerlessness sub-scale (x_{P1}, x_{P2}, x_{P3}).

We should lay out our general strategy in estimating this and subsequent models. Of course, the first issue is one of identification. By identification we specifically mean that no two sets of distinct parameter values should be able to produce the same Σ matrix.[10] Before attempting to estimate any model, one should check for identification by ensuring analytically that a solution exists for every distinct parameter in terms of the variance-covariance elements of the population Σ matrix. We will not describe this process for every model (see Jöreskog and Sörbom, 1976a, for a discussion of identification in selected panel models). However, the specification consequences which follow from consideration of identification issues will be made explicit where necessary.[11]

In all the following models we analyze, we will incorporate the assumption that the unstandardized regressions of observed measures on constructs (the so-called "factor loadings" — see Werts, Linn, and Jöreskog, 1974, p. 273) are equal at each point in time for

[9] These models implicitly take a stand on the conceptualization of alienation that must be mentioned. There has been controversy as to the generality versus specificity of the alienation concept. Our position is that anomia and powerlessness can be interpreted as indicators of the more general and abstract construct of alienation, even though anomia and powerlessness can be distinguished as separate dimensions by some factor analytic criteria.

[10] Equivalently, in the case of *exact* multinormality of the observed variables, the model is not identified if for a given sample the same likelihood value can result from different sets of values for our parameters.

[11] We discourage using the LISREL program itself to decide issues of identification. It is true that if the program suceeds in computing standard errors of the estimates this is a good indication that the model is identified. However, this may be a costly trial-and-error procedure. Also, the program does not tell the user what the implications of different restrictions are in terms of identifying the model.

each indicator of alienation. In Figure 4 this means constraining λ_{A1} = λ_{A2} = λ_{A3} and λ_{P1} = λ_{P2} = λ_{P3}. This regression weight λ states the relationship between the unit of measurement of the observed variable and that of the construct (Werts, Linn, and Jöreskog, 1974, p. 273). In the case of the anomia measure, for instance, the equations are:

$$x_{A1} = \mu_{A1} + \lambda_{A1} X_1 + e_2$$

$$x_{A2} = \mu_{A2} + \lambda_{A2} X_2 + e_4$$

$$x_{A3} = \mu_{A3} + \lambda_{A3} X_3 + e_6$$

The λs are unstandardized regression coefficients (and when standardized they correspond to validity coefficients). The equality assumption stated above has a specific empirical interpretation: for a given alienation true score X, a unit change in alienation will produce the same amount of change in x_{A1}, x_{A2}, and x_{A3}. This amounts to specifying that each of the measures of alienation are the "same" measures across time. We include this set of restrictions for reasons of parsimony, and in order to emphasize that we feel successive applications of the same measure are tapping the same construct. These restrictions are not necessary for identification and are testable by the χ^2 test in the case of multiple indicators.

The earlier definition of reliability given by equation (1) for the single-indicator model should be modified for the more general multiple indicator case. Here we define the reliability as:

$$\alpha^2 = \frac{\lambda^2 \sigma_X^2}{\lambda^2 \sigma_X^2 + \sigma_E^2} \tag{10}$$

This definition is the same as the previous expression (where λ is implicitly assumed to be 1) in the sense that the ratio is the portion of the observed variance "explained" by the construct and it is, in fact, the square of the correlation between the observed measure and its construct. Thus, the square root of this expression is the validity (defined operationally as the correlation between an observed measure and its construct). The definition we use points out the fact that λ and σ_X^2 cannot be identified separately in the classical test theory model underlying our earlier definition for the single-indicator case. Note that, although we have restricted these loadings to be equal, the true score variances, the measurement errors — and thus the reliabilities — can vary over time.

Throughout our analyses we will fix the scale of the alienation construct by setting the variance of X_1 to one. The scale for X_2 and X_3 is then determined by setting construct loadings equal at each point in time. The variance of the endogenous constructs X_2 and X_3 may, thereby, vary in relation to the variance of X_1. The endogenous variances are, in fact, determined by the model, since

$$V(X_2) = \beta_1^2 V(X_1) + \sigma_{u_2}^2$$
$$V(X_3) = \beta_2^2 V(X_2) + \sigma_{u_3}^2$$

in the Figure 4 sub-model involving alienation measures only. Thus we should not assume these variances are known (for example, equal to 1), but rather let the model generate estimates of these variances.

To summarize, the consequences of these features of our application of the explicated *CFA* model are important in comparing multiple-indicator panel models with the single-indicator versions. The Heise model necessitates the assumption of equal reliability at three points in time, and this assumption implies that the ratio of true score to observed variance remains invariant; either due to no change in the true score variance and error variance, or to a change in both which happens not to effect the ratio (Wiley and Wiley, 1970, pp. 112–113). This rather restrictive assumption was relaxed in the Wileys' case to allow for changes in reliability, but it was necessary in their case to assume constant error variance even though the true score variance could vary. With models as in Figure 4, however, we can allow both error variance and true score variance to vary for the variables with multiple indicators; and, thus, reliability will vary as a function of changes in both. This is especially useful in estimating reliabilities of the same measure in different populations and across different models in the same population.

The proper data matrix to use as input in these analyses is the sample variance-covariance matrix *S*. It will be true that for many panel models this will be equivalent to using the correlation matrix *R* as input. In this case the model is said to be scale-free; that is, "a change in the unit of measurement in one or more of the observed variables can be appropriately absorbed by a corresponding change

in the parameters" (Werts, Linn, and Jöreskog, 1971, p. 404). The
models we estimate cannot be scale-free because of the equality
restrictions on the loadings for similar measures. This means that if
we had used the R matrix instead of the S matrix, the results of our
models would have been different in terms of fit and in terms of the
specific parameter estimates — possibly leading to quite different
interpretations.

This does not mean that we are uninterested in the standardized estimates of the parameters of our panel models. In order to
produce reliability and stability estimates we re-scale the unstandardized estimates produced by an analysis of the S matrix. The
standardized solution we report sets the construct variances at 1, so
that the regression coefficients for relations between constructs are
path coefficients. For the regressions of observed measures on constructs, we report the validities, that is, the path coefficients where
the measured variances are also set to 1. Note that this standardized
solution does not reproduce the same Σ matrix as the unstandardized version. It is scaled so as to reproduce the input correlation
matrix R with the same overall fit, but it is *not* the same standardized
solution that would have been produced from a direct analysis of the
R matrix. Our standardized solution is the accurate description of
the relationships in the model when the model is not scale-free.

The estimates for the three-wave two-indicator model for
alienation are presented in the first two columns of Table 3, under
the heading of sub-model IA. Table 3 includes estimates from a
succession of models which are all varieties of Figure 4, and the
parameters labeled in Figure 4 are listed in Table 3. Models are
numbered according to the following scheme: roman numerals are
changed due to respecification of Figure 4 by either adding or
changing a variable, and letters A and B stand for whether the
assumption is made that $p_{X_1 u_3} = \gamma_3 = 0$ or it is free in the model.

Recalling our definition of reliability, we can illustrate the
relationship between the unstandardized loadings λ and the standardized loadings λ^*. Given, for example, $\hat{\lambda}_{P2} = 2.66$, $\hat{V}(X_2) =$
0.823, and the estimated observed variance of $x_{P2} = 9.3636$, we can
calculate the reliability as follows, using equation (10):

$$\hat{\alpha}^2 = \frac{\hat{\lambda}^2 \hat{\sigma}_X^2}{\hat{\lambda}^2 \hat{\sigma}_X^2 + \hat{\sigma}_E^2} = \frac{\hat{\lambda}^2 \cdot \hat{V}(X_3)}{\hat{V}(x_{P2})}$$

$$= \frac{(2.66)^2 \cdot 0.823}{9.3636} = 0.622$$

We note that $\hat{\alpha} = \sqrt{0.622} = 0.787$, which is the reported $\hat{\lambda}_{P2}^*$, the validity coefficient.

The reported validities range from $\hat{\lambda}_{A1}^* = 0.859$ to $\hat{\lambda}_{P2}^* = 0.787$, and in general the validities for the anomia measure are slightly higher. The two stabilities estimated by this model are $\hat{\beta}_1^* = 0.897$ and $\hat{\beta}_2^* = 0.768$. These are, of course, the total estimated correlations $r_{X_1 X_2}$ and $r_{X_2 X_3}$ as well, with $r_{X_1 X_3}$ estimated as 0.689. Though these estimates are the standard we will use in comparisons with subsequent models, we should point out first the difference between the single-indicator stabilities for alienation, anomia, and powerlessness and these stabilities in the multiple-indicator case. The estimates of β_1 and β_2 are, in fact, slightly lower here — although not markedly so (see Table 1). This model produces a $\chi^2 = 184.08$ with 9 d.f., which results in a descriptive fit ratio of 20.45. According to most criteria, this is an unsatisfactory fit.

The upper diagonal of Table 4 gives the residuals for model IA($\hat{\Sigma} - S$) expressed as a signed proportion of the corresponding sample variances and covariances S. We have avoided reporting the residuals as correlations since our $\hat{\Sigma}$ matrix is attempting to reproduce the observed variances as well. Also, however, the raw residuals given by the differences between corresponding elements in $\hat{\Sigma}$ and S have little intuitive value for purposes of interpretation. Therefore, we have divided each residual by the absolute value of the corresponding element in S in order to present residuals as a proportion of input variance or covariance unexplained by the model. It should be made clear at this point that we do not advocate using the residuals as evidence for modifications in specification (see Costner and Schoenberg (1973) and Sörbom (1975) for discussions of the problems inherent in such a procedure), and we do not use the residuals for these purposes in this chapter. Residuals are presented in order to asses the *overall* magnitude of unexplained covariances and variances in the model. We should emphasize that our fitting function, Equation 8, is not aiming at the simple minimization of the $(\Sigma_{ij} - S_{ij})/|S_{ij}|$ elements, but at the minimization of F_0. Of course, the two are related, and we compare residuals to varying χ^2/d.f. ratios (where χ^2 for a given N is determined by F_0) in order to assess the level of correspondence between them, and in order to show what types of residuals accompany models whose fit we deem as unsatisfactory or satisfactory.

The residuals for model IA are often near ten percent and range up to fifteen percent of the original S covariance elements. Although these levels are not extremely high, the magnitude of these residuals do suggest that important relationships among these variables are presently left unspecified. With a large sample size such as ours we can explore some of these possibilities without inordinately capitalizing on chance.

We choose to specify "real" alternatives to this model before including "hypothetical" alternatives. Thus, we include first the causal influence of variables which we have measured and which have substantive relevance to the phenomenon of alienation before including paths involving unmeasured alternatives, $\gamma_3 \neq 0$ for example. We estimate now a model for Figure 4 in which Z_1 is educational attainment (unobserved) and z_{11} is the measured score for this variable. According to this model, the education construct is assumed to be perfectly correlated over this time period—thus, the 1967 and 1971 measures are not included in the model. In order to render the model identified, some assumptions must be made about the relationship between Z_1 and z_{11}. For this purpose we assume that the reliability of the education measure is known a $priori$, based on the Siegel and Hodge (1968) reported reliability of educational attainment of 0.9332.[12] In the present data our assumption of a perfect cross-temporal education correlation given this reliability is not inappropriate: the validity is $\sqrt{0.9332} = 0.966$, and the cross-temporal correlations between measures are $0.956, 0.915$, and 0.910; which would result in stability estimates near unity in the Heise model. In order to estimate σ_{e1} in Figure 4, we fix $V(Z_1) = 1$ and constrain λ_z so that it corresponds to a validity of 0.966 when transformed to λ_z^*. Here we do this by solving for λ in the formula:

$$\alpha = \frac{\lambda \sigma_X}{\sigma_0}$$

[12] Siegel and Hodge (1968) report a test-retest correlation of $(0.966)^2 = 0.9332$ for educational attainment based on matches from the 1960 census and the March, 1962 Current Population Survey.

derivable from equation (10), and where σ_0 is the population standard deviation of the observed measure. Since we know that for an exogenous indicator in this situation the ML-estimate for σ_0 is equal to the corresponding sample standard deviation:

$$0.966 = \hat{\lambda}(1)/3.10$$

$$\hat{\lambda} = (0.966) \cdot (3.10) = 2.99$$

In this and the following models we should note that, as usual, comparisons of absolute sizes of parameters should be between unstandardized coefficients (see Schoenberg, 1972). However, the standardized estimates are more interpretable in many situations and are the source of our validity and stability coefficients. We shall discuss them as well.

In model IIA, we assess the causal influence of education on alienation in 1967 and 1971 and thereby hope to account for a portion of the unanalyzed stability paths in model IA via indirect paths betweeen X_1 and X_2, and X_1 and X_3. The result is a corresponding drop in the stabilities of about 0.04 (see Table 3). This we assess to be important enough to justify the inclusion of education in the model—since the education effects denoted by γ_1 and γ_2 are significant in the negative direction, and education and alienation in 1966 are rather strongly correlated, $r_{x_1 z_1} = -0.46$. In other words, the model as it stands lends some support to a social structure and personality hypothesis about attitude influence, although it does not address the possibility of reciprocal influence—and there are numerous possibilities for spuriousness in γ_1 and γ_2. The descriptive fit ratio here is $200.08/12 = 16.67$, which reflects an overall improvement in fit compared to model IA.

The residuals for this model are presented in the lower diagonal of Table 4 (without parentheses). For the relationships among alienation measures, this model is no more effective than IA: some residuals are slightly lower and others are slightly higher for model IIA. Also, residuals for the relationship between education and alienation measures are, on the average, not much better. There are clearly not large differences in residuals corresponding to the change in the descriptive fit ratio. In short, we feel the fit is still, on the whole, unsatisfactory—despite the fact that certain residuals are fairly low. We should point out that both of these first two models

TABLE 3

Parameter Estimates for a Variety of Specifications of Figure 4 for the Alienation Construct, $N = 932$. [1,2]

	Sub-Model IA		Model IIA		Model IIB		Model IIIA		Model IIIB	
	U	S	U	S	U	S	U	S	U	S
λ_z			2.990[f]	0.967	2.990[f]	0.968	19.820[f]	0.934	19.82[f]	0.934
λ_{A1}	3.120[a]	0.859	3.090[a]	0.850	3.090[a]	0.849	3.110[a]	0.857	3.110[a]	0.856
λ_{P1}	2.660[b]	0.813	2.690[b]	0.822	2.690[b]	0.823	2.670[b]	0.815	2.670[b]	0.815
λ_{A2}	3.120[a]	0.824	3.090[a]	0.815	3.090[a]	0.822	3.110[a]	0.822	3.110[a]	0.830
λ_{P2}	2.660[b]	0.787	2.690[b]	0.797	2.690[b]	0.803	2.670[b]	0.789	2.670[b]	0.795
λ_{A3}	3.120[a]	0.846	3.090[a]	0.836	3.090[a]	0.836	3.110[a]	0.844	3.110[a]	0.845
λ_{P3}	2.660[b]	0.794	2.690[b]	0.803	2.690[b]	0.803	2.670[b]	0.796	2.670[b]	0.795
β_1	0.814	0.897	0.772	0.852	0.764	0.836	0.786	0.866	0.778	0.850
β_2	0.806	0.768	0.756	0.721	0.513	0.493	0.772	0.736	0.518	0.497
γ_1			-0.091	-0.100	-0.095	-0.103	-0.083	-0.091	-0.085	-0.094
γ_2			-0.093	-0.098	-0.201	-0.211	-0.080	-0.084	-0.170	-0.178
γ_3	0.000[f]	0.000	0.000[f]	0.000	0.174	0.270	0.000[f]	0.000	0.202	0.309
$\mathrm{Cov}(X_1, Z_1)$			-0.460	-0.460	-0.459	-0.459	-0.347	-0.347	-0.347	-0.347
$V(X_1)$	1.000[f]	1.000	1.000[f]	1.000	1.000[f]	1.000	1.000[f]	1.000	1.000[f]	1.000
$V(Z_1)$			1.000[f]	1.000	1.000[f]	1.000	1.000[f]	1.000	1.000[f]	1.000
σ_{u2}	0.400	0.442	0.391	0.429	0.420	0.459	0.392	0.432	0.423	0.463
σ_{u3}	0.611	0.641	0.603	0.694	0.645	0.678	0.605	0.636	0.655	0.687
σ_{e1}			0.784	0.253	0.781	0.252	7.580	0.357	7.580	0.357
σ_{e2}	1.860	0.512	1.920	0.527	1.920	0.529	1.870	0.516	1.880	0.517
σ_{e3}	1.910	0.583	1.860	0.569	1.860	0.568	1.900	0.580	1.890	0.579
σ_{e4}	1.950	0.567	1.990	0.579	1.960	0.570	1.950	0.569	1.910	0.557
σ_{e5}	1.890	0.617	1.850	0.605	1.830	0.596	1.890	0.614	1.860	0.606
σ_{e6}	1.870	0.533	1.930	0.549	1.930	0.549	1.880	0.536	1.880	0.535
σ_{e7}	1.940	0.608	1.900	0.596	1.900	0.596	1.930	0.606	1.940	0.606

$V(X_2)$	0.823	1.000	0.822	1.000	0.836	1.000	0.823	1.000	0.838	1.000
$V(X_3)$	0.908	1.000	0.904	1.000	0.904	1.000	0.907	1.000	0.908	1.000
χ^2	184.080		200.080		195.930		190.200		185.670	
d.f.	9.000		12.000		11.000		12.000		11.000	
Probability level	0.000		0.000		0.000		0.000		0.000	

f = fixed parameters
a = parameters constrained equal
b = parameters constrained equal
U = unstandardized solution
S = standardized solution

[1] All coefficients in this table exceed twice their standard error.
    Variable designations common to all models are: X_1 = Alienation (1966); X_2 = Alienation (1967); X_3 = Alienation (1971); x_{A1} = Anomia (1966); x_{A2} = Anomia (1967); x_{P1} = Powerlessness (1966); x_{A3} = Anomia (1971); x_{P3} = Powerlessness (1971).

For models IIA and IIB: Z_1 = Education (unobserved) 1966 and z_{11} = years of education in 1966 (measured).
For models IIIA and IIIB: Z_1 = SEI (unobserved) 1966 and z_{11} = SEI score in 1966.

[2] The "^" notation is not included for estimated parameters, but it is to be understood that all parameters are sample estimates.

TABLE 4

Relative Evaluation of Fit of Models IA, IIA, and IIIA to Observed Variances and Covariances (S Matrix), Residuals expressed as a Proportion of S Values

$$\hat{\Sigma}_{ij} - S_{ij}/|S_{ij}|$$

Model IA above diagonal; Model IIA below diagonal without parentheses; Model IIIA below diagonal in parentheses.

	z_{11}	x_{A1}	x_{P1}	x_{A2}	x_{P2}	x_{A3}	x_{P3}
Covariances							
z_{11}							
x_{A1}	−0.1217 (−0.1213)		−0.0051	−0.0455	0.1149	−0.0547	0.1398
x_{P1}	0.1173 (0.1291)	−0.0029 (−0.0048)		0.0786	−0.0970	−0.0704	−0.1292
x_{A2}	−0.0752 (−0.0007)	−0.0648 (−0.0494)	0.0812 (0.0794)		−0.0170	−0.0534	0.1512
x_{P2}	0.0739 (0.0026)	0.1175 (0.1156)	−0.0742 (−0.0922)	−0.0158 (−0.0167)		0.0815	−0.0659
x_{A3}	−0.0365 (−0.0021)	−0.0714 (−0.0586)	−0.0659 (−0.0699)	−0.0736 (−0.0570)	0.0827 (0.0823)		0.0053
x_{P3}	0.0416 (0.0036)	0.1453 (0.1405)	−0.1049 (−0.1246)	0.1525 (0.1521)	−0.0435 (−0.0608)	0.0033 (0.0048)	
Variances							
IA		0.0173	−0.0215	−0.0030	0.0035	−0.0155	0.0210
IIA	0.0004	0.0183	−0.0204	−0.0038	0.0043	−0.0157	0.0193
IIIA	−0.0001	0.0182	−0.0221	−0.0039	0.0046	−0.0155	0.0205

reproduce the variances in S fairly well, with approximately 2 percent the highest proportion of unexplained variance.

Model IIB adds the possibility that X_1 is correlated with the disturbance term for X_3. With multiple indicators, we can identify this path without adding further restrictions to the model. There are at least two possible interpretations of a covariance between X_1 and u_3: another exogenous variable or set of variables presently excluded from the model could covary with X_1 and have a causal effect on X_3, or X_1 could affect X_3 directly. We do not have the space to explore these alternatives here, so we will leave γ_3 specified as in Figure 4. We see that $\hat{\gamma}_3^*$ for model IIB in Table 3 denotes a significant correlation between X_1 and u_3 ($= 0.27$); and the influence on our stabilities is important — $\hat{\beta}_1$ is only reduced to 0.764 from 0.772, but $\hat{\beta}_2$ drops from 0.756 to 0.513, amounting to a -0.243 change in this stability estimate. The effect of education on alienation at time 3 appears to be larger than its effect on alienation at time 2 in this model, but there is more than one possible interpretation of this result: either the one year lag underestimates the true causal lag for this relationship or there are factors excluded from the model prior to time 1 which covary with X_1 and Z_1 and affect X_3 directly (resulting in an inflated γ_2).

The resulting stability coefficients are now 0.836 and 0.493 respectively. The question is: how do we assess the improvement in fit of this model? In this case we compare the change in χ^2 from model IIA to IIB, which *itself* is a χ^2 variable with degrees of freedom equal to the difference in degrees of freedom of the two models, and not the descriptive fit ratio across the two models. This is true in comparing all "nested" models; that is, models where no new variables are specified, and we impose or relax constraints while holding specification in the rest of the model constant. Comparing model IIB to IIA, we see that the χ^2 difference is:

$$\chi_1^2 = \chi_{12}^2 - \chi_{11}^2 = 200.08 - 195.93 = 4.05$$

meaning that the decrease in χ^2 due to respecification is significant beyond the 0.05 level ($\chi_{\text{1d.f.}, p=0.05}^2 = 3.84$), and that model IIB stands for an improvement in fit.[13]

---

[13] Of course, this significant χ^2 value is merely a re-statement of the significant Z-value for the correlation between X_1 and u_3. This is true in our analyses when nested models differ only in one parameter that is fixed to zero in the first model.

Before proceeding to our next model, we must discuss other possible specifications of model IIB. There are other kinds of correlated error between disturbance terms and exogenous variables $(p_{X_1 u_2})$ and between disturbance terms $(p_{u_2 u_3})$ which could affect stability estimates. However, $p_{X_1 u_2} \neq 0$ cannot be identified. The same possibility for indirect relationships through other variables between X_2 and X_3 would be reflected by $p_{u_2 u_3} \neq 0$, and this path can be identified. We cannot identify both $p_{u_2 u_3}$ and $p_{X_1 u_3}$ since the disturbance terms are free parameters in this model. We did estimate a variant of model IIB in which $p_{u_2 u_3}$ was not constrained to zero and $p_{X_1 u_3} = \gamma_3$ was constrained to zero. The results of this model are not reported in Table 3, but they are important to the ensuing discussion. The estimated correlation $\hat{p}_{u_2 u_3}$ is -0.193, which fails to be significant according to our criterion. Our expectation is that this "test" is not seriously affected by constraining γ_3 to zero and forcing this covariance through other paths in the model. The fit of the model reflected by the χ^2_{11df} is 195.93, exactly the same as model IIB. This reflects the fact that the construct part of the model is just-identified in both cases. Given that we can specify either $p_{X_1 u_3} \neq 0$ or $p_{u_2 u_3} \neq 0$, and it turns out in the above case that $p_{u_2 u_3} = 0$, we choose to specify subsequent models with $p_{X_1 u_3}$ unconstrained as the alternative, and we will not discuss the possibilities connoted by $p_{u_2 u_3}$ further.

Model IIIA replaces education and its measure with SEI (unobserved) and its measure in 1966. For this model Z_1 in Figure 4 is now occupational status, as measured by Duncan's SEI Index (z_{11}). Again, our specification assumes that Z_1 is stable over the five-year period in the sample. Using the Siegel and Hodge (1968) reliability for occupational reporting of 0.8726, we estimate the autocorrelations of SEI over time to be near unity and, thus, we use the specification as in Figure 4. Again, we must constrain the construct loading for z_{11}, but in this case we want to set λ_z such that $\lambda_z^* = 0.9341 = \sqrt{0.8726}$. By fixing $V(Z_1) = 1$, we calculate λ_z to be 19.82. Loadings for anomia and powerlessness are again set equal.

The model estimates the stabilities for alienation to be higher than for Model IIA, although they are very close. Our hope in specifying occupational status as Z_1 was that this variable would improve on previous estimates of stability by accounting, in part, for γ_3 in Model IIB. In fact, SEI is slightly less correlated with alienation in 1966 (-0.347 compared to -0.46 for education), and its lagged effects are also slightly smaller. However, these effects are still significant, although we do not yet know how confounded they are with the education effects. The fit for this model as evaluated by our fit ratio is $190.12/12 = 15.85$, the best overall fit to this point.

We add the specification that $\gamma_3 \neq 0$ for model IIIB, and the results reflect the changes in estimates between models IIA and IIB. Most importantly, there is a significant reduction in the estimate of the stability of alienation between 1967 and 1971 (β_2^* drops from 0.736 to 0.497). γ_3 is still significant in this model and is higher than for model IIB, reflecting the fact that *SEI* accounts for indirect effects less effectively. The χ^2 change from model IIIA to IIIB of -4.53 denotes a significant improvement in fit for a model for the relationship between occupational status and alienation.

Finally in Table 3, we should note the similarity in validity estimates across all models estimated to this point. Changes in validities are slight, amounting to ± 0.01. Model IA does as well as any in estimating these parameters. This invariance should be expected, however, since we have not changed either the measurement specification or the type of concomitant theoretical construct in the model. Estimates of these validities suggest that the reliabilities of similar measures across time may change slightly; and, of course, longer time periods could produce larger differences. Since differences in estimates of reliability for similar measures across time range up to 0.06 here, the ability to allow validity to vary is of some importance.

In Table 4 we compare the residuals for models IIA and IIIA in the lower diagonal. Proportional residuals for model IIIA are in parentheses, while entries for model IIA are not. In line with the similarity of the fit ratios for these two models, the residuals are also similar; the major difference being the residuals between z_{11} and the alienation measures at time 2 and time 3. Column one shows the superiority of model IIIA in reproducing these covariances, which may account for the slightly better fit ratio for this model.

The logical next step is to estimate a model in which the effects of both education and occupational status are included simultaneously in order to assess the confounding in previous models. The model in Figure 5 can be used for this purpose. This model allows for some instability in *SEI* (designated as S_1 through

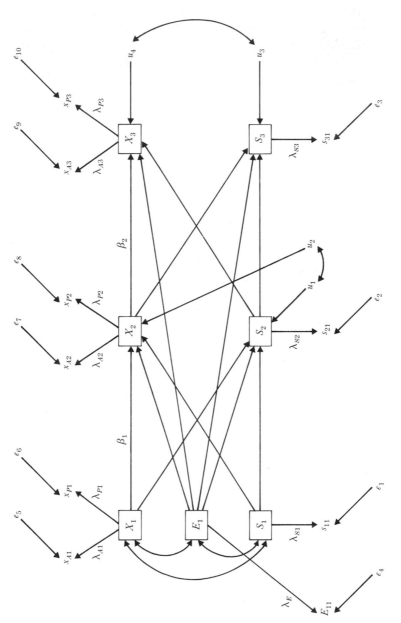

Figure 5. Explicated Causal Model for Alienation with Both Education and *SEI* Included as Separate Constructs, *SEI* at Three Time Points.

S_3 in the model). Thus, we include measures in 1966 (s_{11}), 1967 (s_{21}), and in 1971 (s_{31}). We must allow for the possibility here that education (E_1) will account for a portion of the previous stability estimates for *SEI*. This model will be useful for social researchers who might want to assume some instability in more than one variable in their panel models. Figure 5 represents just one type of cross-lagged model that can be used with panel data, and it is based on the Heise (1970) model extended to three time points.

We saw in Figure 4 that education and occupational status exhibited very similar effects on alienation. Figure 5 is mainly concerned with the size of the correlation between E and S variables, and the distribution of their individual effects. Without reporting the complete solution of this model, we do wish to summarize the estimates we derive. First, the correlation between education and occupational status is substantial, $r_{E_1 S_1} = 0.642$; and the consequences for the rest of the model are far-reaching. Lagged effects for education and *SEI* separately on alienation are all now nonsignificant, and in this sense their individual effects are similar. The estimates of β_1 and β_2 in this model are thus close to those for model IA. The model is unsatisfactory in that it does not describe parsimoniously the relationships between these variables. Evidence from this model and models II and III suggests that education and *SEI* do not affect alienation differently in this sample. Moreover, the argument could be advanced that the *SEI* and education measures are tapping the common construct of socioeconomic status, and that this construct explains the covariance between these measures.

This leads us to estimate a final set of models which are all variants of the model in Figure 6. This model argues that occupational status in 1966, s_s, and education in 1966, s_E, measure in common a construct S_1 we call socioeconomic status (*SES*). For certain substantive purposes this specification may be questionable; however, introducing *SES* as a summary concept here may, in fact, increase the interpretive value of the model since now we do not have to assume reliabilities for education and *SEI*. Also, this measurement specification is a possibility clearly suggested by previous models. The *SES* part of the model can be identified by fixing $V(S_1)$ = 1, and allowing both λ_S and λ_E to be free. Also, we need not restrict σ_{e1} and σ_{e2}.

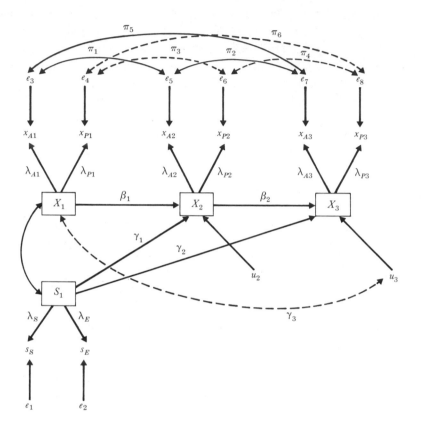

Figure 6. Final Explicated Model for the Relationship between *SES* and Alienation, with a
Two-Indicator Specification for an *SES* Construct Assumed Perfectly Stable,
1966–1971.

Panel Models with Multiple Indicators
and Correlated Error between Measures

The other major change in specification in Figure 6 concerns
the possibility of correlated measurement errors. Thus, we now wish
to relax assumption (2) for the single-indicator models. These correlated errors stand for sources of nonrandom measurement error in
the measures, such as a yeasaying or naysaying bias, "memory
effects," etc. (Costner, 1969; Alwin, 1974). The first source is a real

possibility in statements containing judgments, and the second becomes important when the time lag is not sufficient to create independence of successive measures. If this second type of problem is, in fact, the source of correlated error, we have no *a priori* reason for expecting correlated errors to be equal across successive lags in this model. Our error specification allows us to assess the influence of both sources of nonrandom error, although we do not separate the total covariance into different "methods bias" components. To represent these possibilities, we include all error correlations for similar measures across time. Thus, we are not detecting correlated errors by the more systematic stepwise procedure suggested by Sörbom (1975), which is intended to produce the best-fitting error model; rather, we impose the *a priori* restriction that correlated error should occur between the same measures only, and then we estimate the most flexible error model possible given this restriction. Changing the measurement specification with these error correlations can affect *both* validity and stability estimates and, indirectly, our estimates of other parameters.

We wish to emphasize that the correlated errors in Figure 6 can be identified without imposing any equality restrictions, which allows the differential time lag to have the effect it should. The identification issues which arise in this model are worthy of discussion since equality restrictions on correlated errors have often been assumed in identifying these errors over time, for example, $\pi_1 = \pi_2$ and $\pi_3 = \pi_4$. Also, separate parameters for π_5 and π_6 are sometimes assumed not to be identifiable in two-indicator models. First, consider a version of Figure 6 in which S_1 and its accompanying measures are excluded from the model. In making a preliminary inspection of the identifiability of the model, we introduce the possibility that a new $\lambda'_{A1} = \lambda_{A1} \cdot a$, where a is any nonzero constant not equal to one. Our definition of identification demands that no two sets of parameters can reproduce the same population variance-covariance matrix Σ. However, we *can* compensate for the change in λ_{A1} by a change in λ_{P1} equal to $1/a$, thereby reproducing the same covariance between x_{A1} and x_{P1}, and the same holds as a result of equivalent changes in λ_{Ai} at later points in time. In order to reproduce the same cross-temporal covariance for the same indicators, we must compensate in the error covariances π_i, which is possible since they are all free parameters. Finally, in order to reproduce the same Σ variances, we can compensate by the proper changes in the error variances since they are also all free. Since we can produce two sets of parameters for the model that both reproduce Σ, the model is not identified—even where we have equality restrictions for the construct loadings of the same indicators across time.

Now we can consider the consequences of adding S_1 to the model. For example, in order to leave the covariance between x_{A1} and s_S in Σ intact, and assuming for the moment that we leave the variances and covariances for constructs the same, we would have to divide λ_S by a. However, in order to avoid changing the covariance between x_{P1} and s_S we would have to *multiply* λ_S by a. Therefore, we have a contradiction, implying that we cannot obtain the same Σ with these two sets of parameters. We could, without changing λ_S, change the parameters for relationships between constructs in order to reproduce Σ, but this would change the reproduced covariances for alienation indicators. For instance, we could attempt to alleviate the above contradiction by compensating in $\mathrm{Cov}(X_1, S_1)$, but this would reproduce either the covariance between s_S and x_{A1} or s_S and x_{P1}, but not both. For example, if we have divided λ_S and λ_{P1} by a as above, then in order to reproduce $\mathrm{Cov}(s_S, x_{P1})$ we would have to multiply $\mathrm{Cov}(X_1, S_1)$ by a^2. However, this would again change the reproduced covariance between s_S and x_{A1}. Now we know that none of the parameters at the first time point can be altered. Changes in the λs at later points in time for the alienation measures result in similar contradictions in attempting to reproduce covariances with s_S. Using this approach, it seems unlikely that the same matrix could be reproduced by two different sets of parameters. A rigorous analysis of identifiability will prove this to be correct in this case. Therefore, the model becomes identifiable as we specify it due to the inclusion of the concomitant variable S_1 (of which only one indicator is necessary for identification pruposes). There àre two indirect paths that the observed cross-temporal covariances between alienation indicators can take: through the constructs, and through the error correlations. S_1 helps to determine the λs for these indicators, and we can thereby separate the indirect path through the constructs from the indirect path through the error terms—two components which are otherwise inseparable.

Our first specification of Figure 6, however, assumes there is no correlated error, as in previous models (that is, $\pi_1 = \pi_2 = \pi_3 =$

$\pi_4 = \pi_5 = \pi_6 = 0$). We include $\gamma_3 \neq 0$ because we know that it is significant in all versions of Figure 4. Results for this model are under model VA in Table 5. First we see that our validity for *SEI* in the *SES* construct is somewhat lower than what was assumed for the single-indicator construct in Figure 4. As a consequence of this S_1 specification, relationships between *SES* and alienation are affected: the correlation at time 1 is now -0.525, and the lagged effects of *SES* on alienation are also correspondingly larger than in Figure 4 versions, $\hat{\gamma}_1^* = -0.137$ and $\hat{\gamma}_2^* = -0.263$. As a result, the estimate of $p_{X_1 u_3}$ is a bit smaller, but still significant. The effect on the stabilities is also predictable.

The standardized estimates are slightly lower still, than for previous models, with $\hat{\beta}_1^* = 0.812$ and $\hat{\beta}_2^* = 0.467$. This is a reasonable model for assessing the influence of position in the social structure on a generalized attitude such as alienation, and we are beginning to produce stability estimates which are closer to expectation. We should expect, however, that for attitudes which are not object-specific there should be some stability over a five year period. The descriptive fit ratio is $200.64/16 = 12.54$, and we judge this specification to be somewhat superior to models IIB and IIIB in which education and *SEI* are considered separately. Despite the general interpretative use of this model, it is still unsatisfactory in terms of fit; and there are other specifications we must now consider. By changing the theoretical specification in various ways, we have reduced the fit ratio from 20.54 to 12.54. Considering the fact that changes at this level of specification have not been incorporated in the reliability/stability literature, this is an important improvement in fit. Of course, what we have illustrated with one concomitant variable states our point only to a degree, and other variables could by added to this model which would specify the context within which alienation changes over time more completely.

We turn finally to changes in measurement specification with model VB. In this model, π_1 through π_6 are free (as outlined above), but in all other respects the model is the same as model VA.[14] The results of this model are interesting in terms of estimating reliability and stability. First we inspect the results for π_1 through

---

[14] In Jöreskog and Sörbom (1976a) it is shown how correlated errors are specified in LISREL.

TABLE 5
Parameter Estimates for Various Specifications of Figure 6.[1,2]

	Model VA		Model VB		Model VC	
	U	S	U	S	U	S
λ_S	13.670	0.645	13.500	0.636	13.480	0.635
λ_E	2.600	0.838	2.630	0.848	2.640	0.850
λ_{A1}	3.090[a]	0.849	2.880[a]	0.792	2.860[a]	0.788
λ_{P1}	2.690[b]	0.823	2.900[b]	0.886	2.920[b]	0.889
λ_{A2}	3.090[a]	0.823	2.880[a]	0.764	2.860[a]	0.759
λ_{P2}	2.690[b]	0.803	2.900[b]	0.863	2.920[b]	0.871
λ_{A3}	3.090[a]	0.837	2.880[a]	0.780	2.860[a]	0.775
λ_{P3}	2.690[b]	0.802	2.900[b]	0.859	2.920[b]	0.866
β_1	0.742	0.812	0.648	0.711	0.651	0.712
β_2	0.486	0.467	0.359	0.346	0.383	0.370
γ_1	-0.125	-0.137	-0.170	-0.187	-0.167	-0.183
γ_2	-0.250	-0.263	-0.310	-0.327	-0.295	-0.312
γ_3	0.157	0.246	0.210	0.302	0.198	0.287
$Cov(X_1, S_1)$	-0.525	-0.525	-0.527	-0.527	-0.526	-0.526
$V(X_1)$	1.000[f]	1.000	1.000[f]	1.000	1.000[f]	1.000
$V(S_1)$	1.000[f]	1.000	1.000[f]	1.000	1.000[f]	1.000
σ_{u2}	0.415	0.454	0.516	0.566	0.520	0.569
σ_{u3}	0.638	0.671	0.695	0.733	0.689	0.727
σ_{e1}	16.220	0.765	16.370	0.771	16.390	0.772
σ_{e2}	1.690	0.546	0.164	0.529	1.630	0.526
σ_{e3}	1.920	0.528	2.220	0.611	2.240	0.616
σ_{e4}	1.860	0.569	1.520	0.464	1.500	0.458
σ_{e5}	1.950	0.569	2.220	0.645	2.240	0.651
σ_{e6}	1.830	0.597	1.550	0.505	1.500	0.491
σ_{e7}	1.920	0.548	2.190	0.626	2.220	0.633
σ_{e8}	1.910	0.597	1.640	0.512	1.600	0.501
π_1	0.000[f]	0.000	2.300	0.467	2.380	0.474
π_2	0.000[f]	0.000	1.740	0.357	1.830	0.368
π_3	0.000[f]	0.000	0.077*	0.033	0.000[f]	0.000
π_4	0.000[f]	0.000	0.202*	0.080	0.000[f]	0.000
π_5	0.000[f]	0.000	1.450	0.297	1.500	0.302
π_6	0.000[f]	0.000	-0.012*	-0.005	0.000[f]	0.000
$V(X_2)$	0.836	1.000	0.831	1.000	0.836	1.000
$V(X_3)$	0.905	1.000	0.898	1.000	0.900	1.000
χ^2	200.640		16.900		18.180	
d.f.	6.000		10.000		13.000	
Probability level	0.000		0.0767		0.1507	

f   = fixed parameters
a   = parameters constrained equal
b   = parameters constrained equal
*   = coefficients less than twice their standard error (designated nonsignificant)
U   = unstandardized solution
S   = standardized solution

[1] Variables are the same as in previous models except S_1 = socioeconomic status (1966), $s_S = SEI$ (1966), s_E = education (1966).

[2] The "^" notation is not included for estimated parameters, but it is to be understood that all parameters are sample estimates.

π_6. The correlated errors for the anomia measure are significant and surprisingly strong: $\hat{\pi}_1^* = 0.467$, $\hat{\pi}_2^* = 0.357$ and $\hat{\pi}_5^* = 0.297$. We can see that relaxing equality restrictions in this case is an important feature of the model. On the other hand, the evidence suggests that there is no correlated error for the powerlessness measure, with $\hat{\pi}_3$, $\hat{\pi}_4$, and $\hat{\pi}_6$ near zero.

The consequences for our validity estimates are as one would expect: for the first time, estimates of validity for anomia are now lower than for powerlessness. Estimates of validity for anomia drop about 0.06, while estimates for powerlessness increase about 0.06. The distortion due to assuming there is no correlated measurement error in previous models is considerable. In fact, powerlessness is the more reliable measure of alienation, and its reliability is higher when we specify correlated errors over time for the anomia measure. This specification also has important effects on the stability parameters. Note that $\hat{\beta}_1$ is affected more in this model than any estimated previously. The change in the unstandardized estimate is -0.094, resulting in a stability $\hat{\beta}_1^* = 0.711$. We now see that alienation in 1966 accounts for only about fifty percent of the variance in alienation in 1967. $\hat{\beta}_2$ is also drastically affected in this model, dropping -0.127 from 0.486 to 0.359 in the unstandardized case and resulting in a stability of just 0.346. This estimate is still significant, but rather low.

The correlated error across anomia measures also indirectly affects estimates of the substantive relationships in the model. The effects of SES on alienation are somewhat larger than in model VA. This suggests that the correlated error in the model was previously manifested as both a component of the stabilities (causing inflated estimates) and a counteractive component of indirect effects on X_2 and X_3 through S_1, causing inhibition of the S_1 effects. Also, $\hat{\gamma}_3^*$ is larger again, now an estimated correlation of 0.302. The fact that γ_3 remains significant in these models can be interpreted in at least two ways, as noted earlier.

The single most succinct reflection of the change in this model is our measure of overall fit. χ^2 is now 16.90 with 10d.f., producing a fit ratio of 1.69. For the first time we see that the probability level for the model differs from zero. This we judge to be a satisfactory model in terms of fit, except that we should re-estimate the model with $\pi_3 = \pi_4 = \pi_6 = 0$, since this is indicated in model VB. Given the number of different specification possibilities we have now considered, we can start to believe the reliability/stability estimates this model produces. Also, we have shown that changes in both theoretical and measurement specification are necessary in producing more reasonable reliability and stability estimates.

Thus we go on to specify model VC with $\pi_3 = \pi_4 = \pi_6 = 0$, producing our final model for the alienation construct. Estimates for model VC are quite similar to VB, except that here there is even more of a difference between the anomia and powerlessness validities, there is a slight increase in $\hat{\beta}_2$ and in $\hat{\pi}_1$, $\hat{\pi}_2$, and $\hat{\pi}_5$, and there are slight decreases in SES effects and $\hat{\gamma}_3$. All effects are significant in this model. The correlated errors are substantial, with $\hat{\pi}_1^* = 0.474$, $\hat{\pi}_2^* = 0.368$ and $\hat{\pi}_5^* = 0.302$. This is a potentially disturbing result for many researchers interested in panel models, but it does reflect a real possibility which one can address only with multivariate multiple indicator models. Our final estimates of the validities for anomia are below 0.8, and for powerlessness they range from 0.87 to 0.89. These validities reflect reliability estimates $\hat{\lambda}_i^{*2}$ ranging from 0.58 for anomia in 1967 to about 0.79 for powerlessness in 1966. This is a considerable range and reflects the importance of allowing both true score variance and error variance to vary in these models. Our final stability estimates are 0.712 and 0.370, and we consider these as approaching a lower limit. Owing indirectly to the effect of correlated measurement error in the model, the total correlations between alienation constructs estimated by the model are somewhat lower for model IIA: $r_{X_1 X_2} = 0.804$, $r_{X_2 X_3} = 0.689$, and $r_{X_1 X_3} = 0.684$. These are still in marked contrast with our stability estimates.

The descriptive fit ratio for this model is the best we have achieved, equal to 1.40 (with an accompanying improvement in the probability level). Residuals for model VC are compared with those for model VA in Table 6 (entries for VC are in parentheses). Differences in fit of the two models are clearly reflected by these residuals, especially for covariances among alienation indicators. Model VC is a clear improvement here and in reproducing relationships of these indicators with s_E, but it seems less effective in reproducing relationships between s_S and the alienation indicators at times 2 and 3. This is the only area in which the residuals increase across the two models, and the problem is especially noticeable in the case of the latter two anomia indicators. We see that the negative covariances between s_S and x_{A2} and s_S and x_{A3} are overestimated by the model (taking into account the sign of the residual). Despite this, the overall fit of model VC suggests that this model is adequately specified for interpretative purposes. It is true that this fit can be improved, but we do not feel that further modification will seriously affect our estimates of reliabilities and stabilities.

We began with the constraint that the loadings for the same alienation indicator over time would be assumed equal. This is an important assumption in reliability/stability models, and it merits further attention. First, we feel that this equality is implied in any model that purports to interpret a variable's stability: it is the specification of equal loadings when using the same measures over time, which means that we are expecting to measure the same construct. Strictly speaking, the concept of stability demands this specification, but we *can* test for the equality assumption by comparing χ^2 differences between a constrained "same construct" model and an unconstrained model in which loadings for the same indicators are not set equal.[15] We first tested model IA for the efficacy of this equality assumption by specifying an alternative model in which the loadings for anomia and powerlessness are both free at time 1 (with $V(X_1) = 1$), and the loadings for anomia at times 2 and 3 are set at 1 (in order to give the construct a metric),

---

[15] A word of caution is in order here: successive application of this χ^2 difference test to a series of nested models affects the validity of its probability level and forces an analysis of specification problems to become exploratory and speculative without further data.

TABLE 6

Relative Evaluation of Fit of Models VA and VC to Observed Variances and Covariances (S Matrix), Residuals Expressed as a Portion of S Values

$$\hat{\Sigma}_{ij} - S_{ij}/|S_{ij}|$$

Model VA without parentheses; Model VC in parentheses.

	s_S	s_E	x_{A1}	x_{P1}	x_{A2}	x_{P2}	x_{A3}	x_{P3}
Covariances								
s_S	−0.0001 (−0.0000)							
s_E	−0.1607 (−0.0613)	−0.1095 (−0.0450)						
x_{A1}	0.0828 (0.0197)	0.1275 (−0.0000)	−0.0032 (0.0004)					
x_{P1}	0.0072 (0.1037)	−0.0756 (−0.0001)	−0.0714 (0.0157)	0.0727 (−0.0158)				
x_{A2}	−0.0067 (−0.0622)	0.0743 (−0.0061)	0.1088 (0.0173)	−0.0821 (−0.0156)	0.0006 (0.0039)			
x_{P2}	0.0306 (0.1312)	−0.0442 (0.0361)	−0.0392 (−0.0065)	−0.0342 (−0.0938)	−0.0893 (−0.0123)	0.0635 (−0.0173)		
x_{A3}	0.0193 (−0.0273)	0.0352 (−0.0410)	0.1843 (0.1111)	−0.0752 (0.0142)	0.1320 (0.0460)	−0.0611 (0.0140)	0.0036 (0.0018)	
x_{P3}								
Variances								
VA	0.0001	−0.0000	0.0200	−0.0222	−0.0045	0.0048	−0.0168	0.0207
VC	0.0000	0.0000	−0.0188	−0.0178	0.0030	−0.0005	−0.0200	0.0227

and the loadings for powerlessness are free. The test assesses whether the *set* of loadings at times 2 and 3 differs from the *set* of loadings at time 1. The χ^2 test for improvement in fit is

$$\chi^2_{9df} - \chi^2_{7df} = 184.08 - 181.47$$

$$\chi^2_{2df} = 2.60$$

which is not significant at the 0.05 level, $p = 0.27$. Thus, the equality assumption holds for this model. We can apply the same test to model VC, since this model includes a concomitant variable, correlated error, and a construct-to-endogenous disturbance correlation not included in model IA. Here, respecification of the constrained version with the free loading version reduces the χ^2 value 5.3, which with 2d.f. just fails to be a significant difference at the 0.05 level, $p = 0.08$. Thus, the assumption of loading equality is more in question in our final model, but it is still not unreasonable. This is especially true when we consider the residuals for model VC: excluded correlations between s_S and the errors for the anomia indicators, for instance, would presently operate through paths in the model which include the construct loadings—and this could distort these estimates slightly. We conclude that the equality assumption is still tenable and that we are discussing the same construct over time in this model.

The conclusions one can infer from this model can now be summarized. First, powerlessness is a more reliable measure of alienation than anomia. Second, this anomia measure exhibits some nonrandom measurement error which is correlated over time. Third, alienation shows a moderate amount of stability over a one year period, but a considerable amount of instability over a four year period. Fourth, in terms of an analysis of trends over a five year period in this sample, higher *SES* in 1966 leads to lower levels of alienation in 1967 and 1971. Fifth, evidence indicates that either other causal variables are related to alienation in 1966 and cause alienation in 1971, or that alienation in 1966 is directly related to alienation in 1971. This second explanation is possible, for instance, if alienation in 1971 depends on original position in the alienation distribution in 1966.

SUMMARY AND CONCLUSIONS

It should be obvious at this point that specification flexibility is a mandatory requirement in the adequate estimation of reliability and stability parameters with panel data. Our presentation has emphasized that the issue of stability should be addressed within a thoroughly specified theoretical and measurement context. There is a statistical basis for this assertion in that stability coefficients are subject to bias if obtained from single-indicator single-variable models. Also, we have seen that only with multiple-indicator multivariate models can we begin to test our reliability and stability estimates.

We should point out that the stability of a variable over time should be an issue in the theory needed to explain that variable. Basically, we could speculate that stable variables should be less sensitive to situationally based influences, and unstable variables should be more sensitive to these sources of influence. This is the sense in which the stability issue is inseparable from the substantive context and, thus, the causal system within which the variable operates. We should be sensitive to the point at which estimates of stability begin to "bottom out" in the light of successive respecifications of a model, since evidence for completeness of a causal system partially depends on this lower-limit stability value.

We began with stability estimates for alienation in model IA of 0.897 and 0.768, and finally concluded with model VC that the stabilities were probably closer to 0.712 and 0.370, respectively. Obviously, there is some danger in taking a "barefaced" approach to single-indicator or single-construct models. Additionally, we can best address theoretical issues only when measurement issues are also incorporated into our models.

The superiority of multiple-indicator models is not only on methodological grounds. In fact, these models are in harmony with meta-theoretical arguments which suggest the need for multiple-indicators of all theoretical concepts. This argument is usually made in terms of the increased content validity of the unobserved construct with increasing numbers of indicators. Thus, there are convenient rationales available at both the empirical and meta-theoretical levels for choosing multiple-indicator panel models where possible.

In general, our conclusion is that there is a need to be explicit about both measurement and theoretical specification in stating relationships between variables in panel models in order to maximize the accuracy of estimation of parameters in these models. We have shown that concerns at one level of specification can affect the estimation of parameters at another. And since we believe the stability coefficient has implications for our definition and interpretation of a concept in the process of theory construction, these specification issues are important for theorists to consider as well. Where we depend on parameter estimates to make decisions with theoretical implications, adequacy at both levels of specification is necessary if our decisions are to be taken seriously.

REFERENCES

ALTHAUSER, R. B., AND HEBERLEIN, T. A.

    1970   "Validity and the Multitrait-multimethod Matrix." In E. F. Borgatta and G. W. Bohrnstedt (Eds.), *Sociological Methodology 1970.* San Francisco: Jossey-Bass, pp. 151–169.

ALWIN, D. F.

    1974   "Approaches to the Interpretation of Relationships in the Multitrait-multimethod Matrix." In H. L. Costner (Ed.), *Sociological Methodology 1973-1974.* San Francisco: Jossey-Bass, pp. 79–105.

ANDERSON, B. D.

    1973   "School Bureaucratization and Alienation from High School." *Sociology of Education* 46:315–334.

BLALOCK, H. M., JR.

    1970   "Estimating Measurement Error Using Multiple Indicators and Several Points in Time." *American Sociological Review* 35:101–111.

BOGARDUS, E. S.

    1925   "Measuring Social Distances." *Journal of Applied Sociology* 9:299–308.

BOHRNSTEDT, G. W.

    1969   "Observations on the Measurement of Change." In E. F. Borgatta (Ed.), *Sociological Methodology 1969.* San Francisco: Jossey-Bass, pp. 113–133.

BURT, R. S.

    1973   "Confirmatory Factor-Analytic Structures and the Theory Construction Process." *Sociological Methods and Research* 2:131–190.

COSTNER, H. L.
    1969 "Theory, Deduction, and Rules of Correspondence." *American Journal of Sociology* 75:245–263.

COSTNER, H. L., AND SCHOENBERG, R.
    1973 "Diagnosing Indicator Ills in Multiple Indicator Models." In A. S. Goldberger and O. D. Duncan (Eds.), *Structural Equation Models in the Social Sciences*. New York: Seminar Press, pp. 167–199.

DUNCAN, O. D.
    1969 "Some Linear Models for Two-Wave, Two-Variable Panel Analysis." *Psychological Bulletin* 72:177–182.
    1972 "Unmeasured Variables in Linear Models for Panel Analysis." In H. L. Costner (Ed.), *Sociological Methodology 1972*. San Francisco: Jossey-Bass, pp. 36–82.
    1975 "Some Linear Models for Two-Wave, Two-Variable Panel Analysis, with One-Way Causation and Measurement Error." In H. M. Blalock, Jr., A. Agankegian, F. N. Borodkin, R. Boudon, and V. Capecchi (Eds.), *Quantitative Sociology: International Perspectives on Mathematical and Statistical Modeling*. New York: Academic Press, pp. 285–306.

HANNAN, M. T., RUBINSON, R., AND WARREN, J. T.
    1974 "The Causal Approach to Measurement Error in Panel Analysis: Some Further Contingencies." In H. M. Blalock, Jr. (Ed.), *Measurement in the Social Sciences: Theories and Strategies*. Chicago: Aldine, pp. 293–323.

HAUSER, R. M., AND GOLDBERGER, A. S
    1971 "The Treatment of Unobservable Variables in Path Analysis." In H. L. Costner (Ed.), *Sociological Methodology 1971*. San Francisco: Jossey-Bass, pp. 81–117.

HEISE, D. R.
    1969 "Separating Reliability and Stability in Test-Retest Correlation." *American Sociological Review* 34:93–101.
    1970 "Causal Inference from Panel Data." In E. F. Borgatta and G. W. Bohrnstedt (Eds.), *Sociological Methodology 1970*. San Francisco: Jossey-Bass, pp. 3–27.

JÖRESKOG, K. G.
    1969 "A General Approach to Confirmatory Maximum Likelihood Factor Analysis." *Psychometrika* 34:183–202.
    1973 "A General Method for Estimating a Linear Structural Equation System." In A. S. Goldberger and O. D. Duncan (Eds.), *Structural Equation Models in the Social Sciences*. New York: Seminar Press, pp. 83–112.

1976   "Structural Equation Models in the Social Sciences: Specification, Estimation, and Testing." Department of Statistics, University of Uppsala. Invited paper for the Symposium on Applications of Statistics, Ohio, June 14–18, 1976.

JÖRESKOG, K. G., AND SÖRBOM, D.
1976a "Statistical Models and Methods for Analysis of Longitudinal Data." In D. J. Aigner and A. S. Goldberger (Eds.), *Latent Variables in Socioeconomic Models*. Amsterdam: North-Holland.

1976b "LISREL — Estimation of Linear Structural Equation Systems by Maximum Likelihood Methods." A computer program manual. Chicago: International Educational Services.

KENNY, D. A.
1973   "Cross-Lagged and Synchronous Common Factors in Panel Data." In A. S. Goldberger and O. D. Duncan (Eds.), *Structural Equation Models in the Social Sciences*. New York: Seminar Press, pp. 153–165.

LORD, F. M., AND NOVICK, M. R.
1968   *Statistical Theories of Mental Test Scores*. Reading, Mass.: Addison-Wesley.

MERTON, R. K.
1957   *Social Theory and Social Structure*. Glencoe: Free Press.

MIDDLETON, R.
1963   "Alienation, Race, and Education." *American Sociological Review*. 28:973–977.

O'MEARA, J.
1966   *Sample Design: Bench-Mark Survey*. Memoranda No. 1 to Project No. 007. Urbana, Ill.: Survey Research Laboratory, University of Illinois.

PELZ, D. C., AND ANDREWS, F. M.
1964   "Detecting Causal Priorities in Panel Data." *American Sociological Review* 29:836–848.

PHOTIADIS, J. D., AND SCHWEIKER, W. F.
1971   "Correlates of Alienation: the Marginal Businessman." *Rural Sociology* 36:20–30.

ROZELLE, R. M., AND CAMPBELL, D. T.
1969   "More Plausible Rival Hypotheses in the Cross-Lagged Panel Correlation Technique." *Psychological Bulletin* 71:74–80.

SCHOENBERG, R.
1972   "Strategies for Meaningful Comparison." In H. L. Costner (Ed.), *Sociological Methodology 1972*. San Francisco: Jossey-Bass, pp. 1–35.

SIEGEL, P. M., AND HODGE, R. W.
    1968   "A Causal Approach to the Study of Measurement Error." In
           H. M. Blalock, Jr. and A. B. Blalock (Eds.), *Methodology in Social
           Research.* New York: McGraw-Hill, pp. 21–59.

SIMPSON, M. E.
    1970   "Social Mobility, Normlessness, and Powerlessness in Two
           Cultural Contexts." *American Sociological Review* 35:1002–1013.

SNELL, P. AND MIDDLETON, R.
    1961   "Dimensions and Correlates of Religious Idiologies." *Social
           Forces* 39:285–290.

SÖRBOM, D.
    1975   "Detection of Correlated Errors in Longitudinal Data." *British
           Journal of Mathematical and Statistical Psychology* 28:138–151.

SROLE, L.
    1956   "Social Integration and Certain Corollaries: An Exploratory
           Study." *American Sociological Review* 21:709–716.

SUMMERS, G. F., HOUGH, R. L., SCOTT, J. T., AND FOLSE, C. L.
    1969   *Before Industrialization: A Rural Social System Base Study.* Bulletin
           No. 736. Urbana, Ill.: Illinois Agricultural Experiment Station,
           University of Illinois.

THOMPSON, W. E., AND HORTON, J. E.
    1960   "Political Alienation as a Force in Political Action." *Social
           Forces* 38:190–195.

WERTS, C. E., JÖRESKOG, K. G., AND LINN, R. L.
    1971   "Comment on 'the Estimation of Measurement Error in Panel
           Data'." *American Sociological Review* 36:110–113.

WERTS, C. E., LINN, R. L., AND JÖRESKOG, K. G.
    1971   "Estimating the Parameters of Path Models Involving Un-
           measured Variables." In H. M. Blalock, Jr. (Ed.), *Causal Models
           in the Social Sciences.* Chicago: Aldine, pp. 400–409.

    1974   "Quantifying Unmeasured Variables." In H. M. Blalock, Jr.
           (Ed.), *Measurement in the Social Sciences: Theories and Strategies.*
           Chicago: Aldine, pp. 270–292.

WILEY, D. E., AND WILEY, J. A.
    1970   "The Estimation of Measurement Error in Panel Data."
           American Sociological Review 35:112–117.

Received April 15, 1975.

4

ON ANALYZING THE EFFECTS OF POLICY INTERVENTIONS: BOX-JENKINS AND BOX-TIAO VS. STRUCTURAL EQUATION MODELS*

Douglas A. Hibbs, Jr.
MASSACHUSETTS INSTITUTE OF TECHNOLOGY

In recent years, interest in applying quantitative methodologies to policy-related problems has increased markedly throughout the social sciences. This chapter outlines and contrasts two approaches to estimating the effects of reforms, policy innovations, and similar discontinuous "interventions" or "treatments" on phenomena that are observed through time. The diverse range of

*I am grateful to James Bennett, Arthur Goldberger, and Peter Lemieux for comments on an earlier draft of this chapter. I retain the usual responsibilities of authorship.

137

substantive problems for which the intervention analysis techniques developed here are applicable include, for example: the impact of the introduction or repeal of capital punishment on murder rates; the effect of government incomes policies on wage and price inflation; and the contribution of women's suffrage, personal registration, residency laws, new ballot forms, and so on, to the secular decline in American electoral turnout since the 1890s.

The first scheme for intervention analysis treated in this chapter is based on the time-series models of Box, Jenkins, and Tiao (Box and Jenkins, 1970; Box and Tiao, 1965, 1975). This approach owes much to the conceptual work of D. T. Campbell (Campbell, 1963, 1969; Campbell and Stanley, 1966), which emphasizes that post-hoc time-series analysis can be viewed quasi-experimentally to evaluate the impact of interventions by government agencies and other institutional actors. Box-Tiao and Box-Jenkins models[1] represent time-series observations as the realization of a linear stochastic process of a autoregressive moving average or a mixed autoregressive moving average form. Hence, no attempt is made to model the causal structure generating the time-series data. Intervention occurrences are represented by binary variables (0, 1) or by related coding schemss (+1, −1, for example), and the effects of interventions (changes in the slope and/or level of the time-series) are assessed by estimating simple "transfer functions."

The second approach to intervention analysis considered here is the socalled structural equation method. Structural techniques were developed primarily in economics, but have subsequently gained wide acceptance in all of the social sciences. (See, for example, Blalock (Ed.), 1971; Goldberger, 1972; and Goldberger and Duncan (Eds.), 1973.) The principal difference between the structural equation approach and the Box-Tiao scheme is that the former involves specification and estimation of intervention effects in the context of a system of equations designed to represent the

---

[1] Simple versions of these models have been explicitly linked to Campbell's methodological perspective by the educational methodologists Glass, Gottman, Maguire, and Willson (Glass, 1968, 1972; Glass, Willson, and Gottman, 1972; Maguire and Glass, 1967). A number of studies by political scientists have also employed Campbell's perspective, but these analyses have relied on statistical procedures that have weak justification in the time-series context. See, for example, Caporaso and Pelowski, 1971; and Duvall and Welfling, 1973, which are conveniently collected along with related studies in Caporaso and Ross (Eds.), 1973.

causal relationships underlying the realizations of endogenous time-series. The structural approach is therefore geared to determining how and to what extent reforms or policy innovations influence endogenous phenomena as they are transmitted through a dynamic causal structure.

I discuss what appear to be lines of convergence between the two approaches in the final section.

THE BOX-TIAO (BOX-JENKINS) APPROACH

Imagine that we are dealing with a time-series of equally spaced observations on some endogenous or dependent variable Y_t, $t = 1, 2, ..., T$, and that we want to determine the impact of some exogenous treatments or policy motivated interventions. The Box-Tiao approach employs a model of the general form

$$Y_t = \sum_k \mathbf{y}_{tk} + N_t \qquad (t = 1, 2, ..., T) \qquad (1)$$

where N_t denotes stochastic noise and deterministic time trends and $\sum_k \mathbf{y}_{tk}$ represents the additional effects of the interventions over noise.

Suppose that the interventions occur, say, at the nth period and thereafter, $Y_1, ..., Y_n, ..., Y_T$. The pre-intervention Y_t series is therefore driven entirely by stochastic noise and deterministic time trends. Hence:

$$N_t = Y_t - \sum_k \mathbf{y}_{tk} \qquad (2)$$
$$= Y_t \quad \text{for } t < n$$

Since these Y_t observations are unperturbed by external intervention, they may be analyzed to determine a time-series model for the N_t component of (1).[2] This N_t model provides a stochastic benchmark against which functions for the intervention effects ($\mathbf{y}_{tk}$) can be specified and estimated. In the Box-Tiao framework the N_t process takes the form of an autoregressive, moving average, or mixed autoregressive-moving average model of order p, d, q:

---

[2] In many situations the model for N_t can be developed by analyzing all Y_t observations. This would apply, for example, in cases in which a sustained intervention is believed to produce a change in the level of the series—or in cases which a one-shot nonsustained intervention produces an effect that dies out quickly. See the discussion below.

$$\Delta^d Y_t = \theta_0 + \varphi_1 \Delta^d Y_{t-1} + \cdots + \varphi_p \Delta^d Y_{t-p} \tag{3}$$
$$- \theta_1 a_{t-1} - \cdots - \theta_q a_{t-q} + a_t$$

where $\Delta^d Y_t$ denotes the dth backward difference of Y_t, for example,

$$\Delta Y_t \equiv Y_t - Y_{t-1}$$
$$\Delta^2 Y_t \equiv \Delta Y_t - \Delta Y_{t-1}$$

and so on; θ_0 is a constant that indexes a deterministic polynomial time trend of degree d in the Y_t;[3] φ_p and θ_q are autoregressive and moving average coefficients, respectively; and a_t is a sequence of independently distributed random variables with mean zero and variance σ_a^2.

The noise or benchmark model in (3) asserts that the dth difference of the Y_t series is generated by a linear combination of autoregressive terms and moving average shocks. Hence $\Delta^d Y_t$ depends on p lagged terms $\Delta^d Y_{t-p}$ with coefficients $(\varphi_1, \ldots, \varphi_p)$ and on a moving linear sum of q random shocks a_t with coefficients $(1, -\theta_1, \ldots, -\theta_q)$. A nonzero constant term θ_0 accomodates deterministic time trends of order d in the undifferenced Y_t; for example, if $Y_t = \mu + \theta_0 t^d +$ stochastic terms, then $\Delta^d Y_t = \theta_0 +$ stochastic terms.

Introducing the lag operator L, such that $L Y_t \equiv Y_{t-1}$ and in general $L^i Y_t \equiv Y_{t-i}$, allows the noise model in (3) to be rewritten in the form that will prove to be convenient later. Rearranging terms in (3) a bit and noticing that Δ^d may now be expressed $(1 - L)^d$, we have

$$(1 - L)^d Y_t = \theta_0 + \sum_p \varphi_p L^p (1 - L)^d Y_t + a_t - \sum_q \theta_q L^q a_t \tag{4}$$

$$Y_t (1 - L)^d (1 - \varphi_1 L - \cdots - \varphi_p L^p)$$
$$= \theta_0 + (1 - \theta_1 L - \cdots - \theta_q L^d) a_t$$

$$Y_t = \frac{\theta_0 + (1 - \theta_1 L - \cdots - \theta_q L^q) a_t}{(1 - L)^d (1 - \varphi_1 L - \cdots - \varphi_p L^p)}$$

[3] Notice that this implies that $\Delta^d Y_t$ has a nonzero mean equal to $\theta_0 / 1 - \varphi_1 - \cdots - \varphi_p$.

The autoregressive-moving average ($ARMA$) model for stochastic noise, therefore, can be written as the ratio of polynomials in L. Although the representation at first appears somewhat formidable, it will be useful when developing the examples presented below.

The first task in the Box-Tiao method is to derive a model for the N_t component in (1) by fitting an appropriately specified version of (3) or (4) to the Y_t observations that are not perturbed by external interventions. As developed by Box and Jenkins (1970), this involves an iterative process of tentative model *specification*, preliminary *estimation*, a series of *diagnostic checks*, possible model respecification, and so on.

Specification

The basic noise model in (3) or (4) is fully specified by choosing the degree of differencing d, the order of the autoregressive component p, and the order of the moving average component q.

The degree of differencing d is chosen such that the differenced series is stationary and, hence, varies about a fixed mean or equilibrium level with variance independent of displacements in time and autocovariance dependent only on the magnitude of lags in time. Stationarity, therefore, means that

$$E(Y_t) = E(Y_{t-m})$$

and

$$\mathrm{Cov}(Y_t, Y_{t-k}) = \mathrm{Cov}(Y_{t-m}, Y_{t-m-k})$$

for all t, k, and m. A stationary series will exhibit an autocorrelation function (ρ_k) that dies out after moderate-to-large lag. (A "large" lag is on the order of $k = T/5$.) Figure 1 shows hypothetical examples of the autocorrelation functions of a nonstationary and a stationary time-series. Sample estimates of the lag k autocorrelations ($\hat{\rho}_k$) are given by

$$\hat{\rho}_k = \frac{\sum_{t=k}^{T} (Y_t - \bar{Y})(Y_{t-k} - \bar{Y})}{\sum_{t=1}^{T} (Y_t - \bar{Y})^2} \quad k = 1, 2, \ldots, T/5$$

1(a) Autocorrelation Function of a Stationary Time-Series.

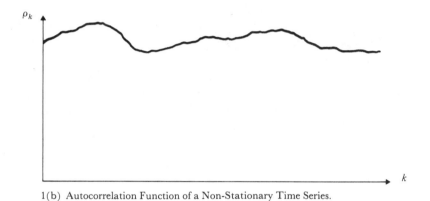

1(b) Autocorrelation Function of a Non-Stationary Time Series.

Figure 1. Hypothetical Autocorrelation Function for Non-Stationary and Stationary
           Time-Series.

and those successive differences, $\Delta^d Y_t$, $d = 1, 2, \dots$ are calculated
analogously. In practice it is rarely necessary that d exceed 2 and,
typically, $d = 1$ is sufficient to induce stationary behavior.[4]

[4] All *homogeneous* nonstationary series will exhibit stationary behavior after
suitable differencing, that is, the autocorrelations of the differences $\Delta^d Y_t$ will go to
zero as the lag k becomes large. Occasionally it may be necessary to apply a
transformation to the Y_t in order to obtain a stationary series. For example, a series
driven by an exponential function of time is *nonhomogeneous* nonstationary and,
therefore, should be logarithmically transformed prior to specification and
estimation.

Having settled upon a degree of differencing sufficient to ensure stationarity, the orders of the moving average and autoregressive components of (3) are tentatively specified by comparing the sample autocorrelation and partial autocorrelation functions of $\Delta^d Y_t$ to the theoretical functions of various autoregressive-moving average models. The theoretical behavior of autocorrelation and partial autocorrelation functions, denoted as ρ_k and φ_{kk}, respectively, are readily derived through algebraic manipulation of (3) for varying values of p and q. Such manipulations show that:

(1) Purely autoregressive processes of order $p[AR(p)]$ have autocorrelation functions that tail off (gradually approach zero) and partial autocorrelation functions that cut off (go to zero) after lag p. Hence ρ_k tails off, and $\varphi_{kk} = 0$ for $k > p$ in autoregressive models.

(2) Purely moving average processes of order $q[MA(q)]$ have autocorrelation functions that cut off after lag q and partial autocorrelation fumctions that tail off. Hence, $\rho_k = 0$ for $k > q$, and φ_{kk} tails off in moving average models.

(3) Mixed autoregressive-moving average processes of order $p, q[ARMA(p, q)]$ have autocorrelation functions that are a mixture of exponential and damped sine waves after the first $q - p$ lags, and partial autocorrelation functions that are dominated by a mixture of exponentials and damped sine waves after the first $p - q$ lags. Hence, neither ρ_k nor φ_{kk} cut off in mixed models.

Since AR, MA, and $ARMA$ time-series models are distinguishable by thcir autocorrelation and partial autocorrelation functions, sample estimates of these functions facilitate preliminary identification of p and q and permit calculation of initial guesses of the parameters φ_p and θ_q. Figure 2 and Table 1 put this into somewhat sharper focus by displaying the autocorrelation functions, partial autocorrelation functions, and related theoretical properties of some simple autoregressive moving average and mixed autoregressive-moving average models.

Estimation

The specification process outlined above leads to a tentative choice of p, d, and q, and yields preliminary guesses of the parameters φ_p and θ_q. Letting Y_t^* denote the dth difference of Y_t (that is, $Y_t^* \equiv$

$(1 - L)^d Y_t \equiv \Delta^d Y_t)$, the autoregressive moving average model can be expressed very generally

$$Y_t^* = \theta_0 + \sum_p \varphi_p Y_{t-p}^* - \sum_q \theta_q a_{t-q} + a_t \tag{5}$$

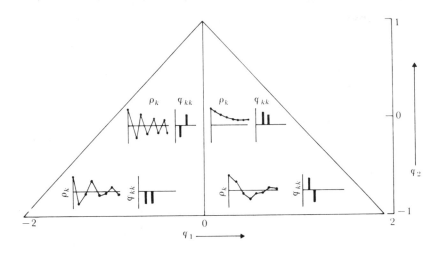

2(a) Autocorrelation and Partial Autocorrelation Functions for Various $AR(2)$ Models:

$$Y_t = q_1 Y_{t-1} + q_2 Y_{t-2} + a_t$$

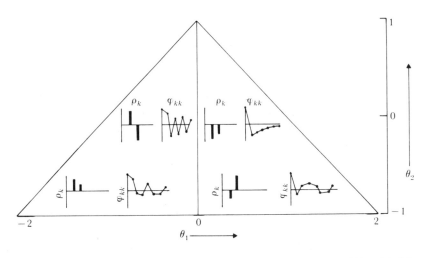

2(b) Autocorrelation and Partial Autocorrelation Functions for Various $MA(2)$ Models:

$$Y_t = a_t - \theta_1 a_{t-1} - \theta_2 a_{t-2}$$

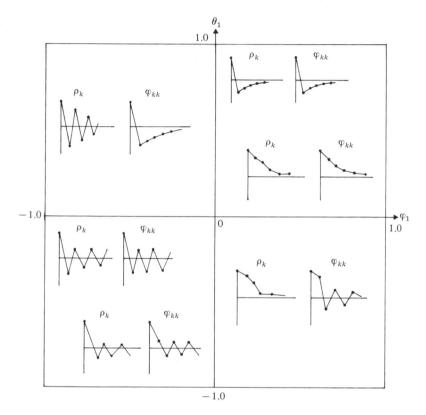

2(c) Autocorrelation and Partial Autocorrelation Functions for Various $ARMA(1, 1)$ Models:

$$Y_t = \varphi_1 Y_{t-1} + a_t - \theta_1 a_{t-1}$$

Figure 2. Typical Autocorrelation (ρ_k) and Partial Autocorrelation (φ_{kk}) Functions for Various Stationary AR, MA, and $ARMA$ Models.
(Box and Jenkins, 1970; by permission of the authors and the publisher.)

Rewriting (5) as

$$a_t = Y_t^* - \theta_0 - \sum_q \varphi_p Y_{t-p}^* + \sum_q \theta_q a_{t-q} \qquad (6)$$

yields an equation for the (independently distributed) "error" term a_t. The model is estimated by choosing (φ_p, θ_q, θ_0) in the admissible

TABLE 1

Some Properties of Simple $ARMA$ Models of Order (p, q)

Adapted from Box and Jenkins, 1970, by permission of authors and publisher.

Order	$AR(1)$	$MA(1)$
Behavior of ρ_k	$\rho_k = \varphi_1^k$	$\rho_k = 0, \quad$ for $k > 1$
Behavior of φ_{kk}	$\varphi_{kk} = 0, \quad$ for $k > 1$	tails off, dominated by damped exponential
Preliminary estimates from	$\varphi_1 = \rho_1$	$\rho_1 = -\theta_1/(1 + \theta_1^2)$
Asmissible region	$-1 < \varphi_1 < 1$	$-1 < \theta_1 < 1$

Order	$AR(2)$	$MA(2)$
Behavior of ρ_k	$\rho_k = \varphi_1 \rho_{k-1} + \varphi_2 \rho_{k-2}$ (mixture of exponentials or damped sine wave)	$\rho_k = 0, \quad$ for $k > 2$
Behavior of φ_{kk}	$\varphi_{kk} = 0, \quad$ for $k > 2$	tails off, mixture of exponentials or damped sine wave
Preliminary estimates from	$\varphi_1 = \dfrac{\rho_1(1 - \rho_2)}{1 - \rho_1^2}$ $\varphi_2 = \dfrac{\rho_2 - \rho_1^2}{1 - \rho_1^2}$	$\rho_1 = \dfrac{-\theta_1(1 - \theta_2)}{1 + \theta_1^2 + \theta_2^2}$ $\rho_2 = \dfrac{-\theta_2}{1 + \theta_1^2 + \theta_2^2}$
Admissible region	$-1 < \varphi_2 < 1; \varphi_2 + \varphi_1 < 1;$ $\varphi_2 - \varphi_1 < 1$	$-1 < \theta_2 < 1; \theta_2 + \theta_1 < 1;$ $\theta_2 - \theta_1 < 1$

Order	$ARMA(1, 1)$	
Behavior of ρ_k	$\rho_k = \varphi_1^{k-1} \rho_1, \quad$ for $k > 1$ (decays exponentially after first lag)	
Behavior of φ_{kk}	$\varphi_{11} = \rho_1$, thereafter tails off dominated by damped exponential	
Preliminary estimates from	$\rho_1 = \dfrac{(1 - \varphi_1\theta_1)(\varphi_1 - \theta_1)}{1 + \theta_1^2 - 2\varphi_1\theta_1}$	
Admissible region	$-1 < \varphi_1 < 1; -1 < \theta_1 < 1$	$\rho_2 = \rho_1\varphi_1$

parameter space[5] such that the sum of squares function

$$S(\varphi_p, \theta_q, \theta_0) = \sum_t [Y_t^* - \theta_0 - \sum_q \varphi_p Y_{t-p}^* + \sum_q \theta_p a_{t-q}]^2 \qquad (7)$$

$$= \sum_t [a_t / \varphi_p, \theta_q, \theta_0]^2$$

is minimized.

Estimates $(\hat{\varphi}_p, \hat{\theta}_q, \hat{\theta}_0)$ corresponding to a minimum of (7) are least squares estimates, and evaluating (6) at $(\hat{\varphi}_p, \hat{\theta}_q, \hat{\theta}_0)$ generates the residuals $\hat{a}_t$. (Notice that we ignore the problem of initiating the series.) In practice, the minimization of (7) may be undertaken by a number of acceptable nonlinear least-squares procedures—such as grid search, steepest descent, successive linearizations, or some combination thereof.[6] (Marquardt's (1963) compromise between the latter two methods has been popular.)

Diagnostic Checks

If the fitted model is adequate, then the calculated residuals $\hat{a}_t$ should behave as independently distributed random variates. This may be formally tested by computing the residual autocorrelations

[5] Admissibility requires that the roots of the characteristic equations

$$(1 - \varphi_1 L - \cdots - \varphi_p L^p) = 0,$$
$$(1 - \theta_1 L - \cdots - \theta_q L^q) = 0$$

(with L treated as an algebraic quantity) have roots outside the unit circle—the solutions $L_1, L_2, ..., L_p$ and $L_1, L_2, ..., L_q$ must all be greater than one in absolute value. This means that the process is stationary (if autoregressive) and invertible (if moving average) and, therefore, converges to an equilibrium level. Notice that Table 1 gives the admissible coefficient values for some simple $ARMA$ models. For further discussion see Box and Jenkins, 1970; or Nelson, 1973a.

[6] Computer programs for Box-Jenkins $ARMA$ model specification, estimation, and forecasting are described in Box and Jenkins, 1973, appendix (batch process programs are distributed by the Data and Program Library Service, Social Systems Research Institute, University of Wisconsin, Madison), Nelson, 1973a, appendix (batch proress programs available by writing to the author, Professor C. R. Nelson, Graduate School of Business, University of Chicago), TSP/DATA-TRAN manual (Cambridge Project, M.I.T., interactive computer system accessible via the ARPA national network), the TROLL Reference Manual (available from Support Staff Coordinator, NBER Computer Research Center, 575 Technology Square, Cambridge, Mass., interactive computer system accessible via the NBER's national network); and Wall, 1975 (interactive program available from the author at 575 Technology Square, Cambridge, Mass.).

$$r_k(\hat{a}) = \frac{\sum \hat{a}_t \hat{a}_{t-k}}{\sum \hat{a}_t^2}$$

and evaluating the test statistic (developed by Box and Pierce, 1970)

$$Q = (T - d) \sum_{k=1}^{K} r_k^2(\hat{a}) \qquad K \geqq 20$$

which for large K is distributed as χ^2 with $(K - p - q)$ degrees of freedom. Q serves as a general or "portmanteau" criterion of model adequacy. A large value is evidence of significant lack of fit and indicates that model respecification is necessary. Patterns in the residual autocorrelations are usually informative about the nature of the misspecification and should be analyzed along the lines proposed earlier for specification of p and q.

A well-specified *ARMA* model should, of course, also satisfy more conventional ststistical criteria of adequacy. Thus, the coefficient estimates $\hat{\varphi}_p, \hat{\theta}_q, \hat{\theta}_0$ should be significantly different from zero, and the estimated error variance $\hat{\sigma}_a^2$ should be less than that of alternative *ARMA* specifications.

Dynamic Intervention Models

The techniques outlined so far pertain to the specification, initial estimation, and diagnostic checking of the N_t component of the general Box-Tiao model in (1). As I noted earlier, the N_t process provides a stochastic benchmark against which intervention-induced changes in the slope and/or level of the endogenous Y_t series can be determined. Let us confine attention for the moment to the case of a single intervention occurring at the nth period, which is sustained thereafter. Such an intervention might be represented by the binary variable,

$$I_t = 0 \quad \text{for } t < n$$
$$= 1 \quad \text{for } t \geqq n$$

Previously, the impact of an intervention on the endogenous variable, that is, the effect of I_t on Y_t, was represented simply by y_t. A general, dynamic model for the effects of exogenous interventions is given by the linear difference equation

$$y_t = \delta_1 y_{t-1} + \dots + \delta_r y_{t-r} + \omega_0 I_{t-b} - \omega_1 I_{t-b-1} - \dots - \omega_s I_{t-b-s} \tag{8}$$

which also can be written as the ratio of two polynomials L of degree s and r, respectively:

$$y_t(1 - \delta_1 L - ... - \delta_r L^r) = (\omega_0 - \omega_1 L - ... - \omega_s L^s)I_{t-b} \quad (9)$$

$$y_t = \frac{(\omega_0 - \omega_1 L - ... - \omega_s L^s)}{(1 - \delta_1 L - ... - \delta_r L^r)} I_{t-b}$$

where: b is a delay (lag) parameter, and the system is stable.[7] Notice that when the intervention is sustained indefinitely ($I_t = 1$ for all $t \geqq n$), the effect will eventually reach the equilibrium or steady state value.[8]

$$y^* = \frac{\omega_0 - \omega_1 - \cdots \omega_p}{1 - \delta_1 - \cdots - \delta_r} \quad (10)$$

The general intervention effects model in (8) and (9) clearly admits a wide range of possibilities, however, in most empirical work, very simple versions are likely to suffice. Figure 3 shows a few examples (from Box and Tiao, 1975). Suppose that the (sustained) intervention is believed to have produced a change in the level of the endogenous series immediately following a one period delay. The appropriate function would be

$$y_t = \omega_0 I_{t-1} \quad \text{(Figure 3a)} \quad (11)$$

An intervention that generated a gradual change in the level of a series could be represented by the first-order dynamic model.

$$y_t = \delta_1 y_{t-1} + \omega_0 I_{t-1}$$

---

[7] Stability requires that the roots of the characteristic equation

$$(1 - \delta_1 L - ... - \delta_r L^r) = 0$$

(with L treated as an algebraic quantity) lie outside the unit circle, that is, the solutions $L_1, L_2, ..., L_r$ must all be greater than unity in absolute value, which implies that the system eventually converges to an equilibrium level. This exactly parallels the stationarity and invertibility conditions for the $ARMA$ model in (3) and means that the admissible regions for the parameters are the same as those given in Table 1.

[8] Since y_t is a stable or stationary process $E(y_t) = E(y_{t-1}) = \cdots = E(y_{t-r})$ equals a constant say y^*. Taking y^* as the initial conditions of (8) gives

$$y^* - \delta_1 y^* - \cdots - \delta_r y^* = \omega_0 I_{t-b} - \cdots - \omega_s I_{t-b-s}$$

Hence, if I_t is held indefinitely at the value $+1$, then

$$y^* = \frac{\omega_0 - \omega_1 - \cdots - \omega_s}{1 - \delta_1 - \cdots - \delta_r}$$

is the equilibrium value of of y_t. Structural equation modelers will recognize this as the equilibrium multiplier which is discussed in a following section.

$$y_t(1 - \delta_1 L) = \omega_0 I_{t-1} \qquad \text{(Figure 3)}$$

$$y_t = \frac{\omega_0}{1 - \delta_1 L} I_{t-1} \qquad (12)$$

$$y_t = \delta_1^t y_0 + \omega_0 \sum_{i=0}^{t-1} \delta_1^i I_{t-1-i}$$

in which the rate of adjustment to a new equilibrium depends on δ_1. A slope change intervention effect can be represented by taking δ_1 to unity, which gives

$$y_t = y_{t-1} + \omega_0 I_{t-1}$$

$$y_t(1 - L) = \omega_0 I_{t-1}$$

$$y_t = \frac{\omega_0}{1 - L} I_{t-1} \qquad (13)$$

$$y_t = y_0 + \omega_0 \sum_{i=0}^{t-1} I_{t-1-i}$$

This model never adjusts to a new equilibrium level and might be used to characterize empirical situations in which convergence is very slow and occurs far beyond the period of observation.

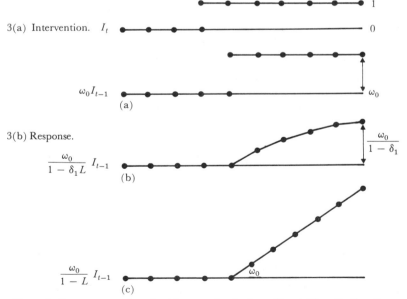

3(a) Intervention. I_t

$\omega_0 I_{t-1}$

(a)

3(b) Response.

$\dfrac{\omega_0}{1 - \delta_1 L} I_{t-1}$

(b)

$\dfrac{\omega_0}{1 - L} I_{t-1}$

(c)

Figure 3. Responses to a Sustained Intervention for Some Simple Transfer Functions.

After a theoretically plausible intervention function has been specified (in practice, several alternatives might be entertained), it should be adjoined to the noise model whose functional form has been established by the procedures outlined previously. The parameters of the complete model can then be estimated simultaneously in order to make inferences about the impact of interventions. The scheme readily accommodates multiple interventions, a wide variety of effect patterns, and seasonal or cyclical movements in a time-series. An empirical example will undoubtedly make matters clearer.

Macroeconomic Policy and Unemployment Rate in Great Britian

An illustrative example of the Box-Tiao approach to intervention analysis is provided by my own recent study of postwar macroeconomic policy in advanced industrial societies (Hibbs, 1975). One of the central propositions in this study was that macroeconomic outcomes—especially rates of unemployment—systematically covary with the political orientation of governments. In particular, it is argued that left-wing governments assign higher priority to full employment than center- and right-wing governments; and, therefore, in *net* of trends, seasonal dependencies, and stochastic fluctuation in the unemployment time-series data, we should observe downward movement in the unemployment rate during the tenure of leftist government and upward movements in the unemployment rate during periods of centrist and rightest rule. Here we focus on the analyses for Great Britian that were designed to assess the net impact of Labour versus Conservative macroeconomic policies on the unemployment rate, as well as the effect of an important change in the British unemplotment compensation law that was initiated in 1966.

Given the general intervention analysis model $Y_t = \sum_k y_{tk} + N_t$, the first step in the model building process is to develop a preliminary specification of the stochastic $ARMA$ component N_t by analyzing the sample autocorrelation functions of the endogenous unemployment variable. The sample autocorrelation function r_k for seasonally unadjusted, quarterly observations on the British unemployment rate over the 1948(1)–1972(4) period is graphed in Figure 4.[9] The sample autocorrelations decay steadily as the lag k increases,

[9]Unemployment is defined as wholly unemployed as a percentage of the civilian labor force. Since the government is always controlled by either Labour or the Conservatives, there is no "pre-intervention" time-series. Therefore, we analyze the entire unemployment series in order to develop a tentative noise model.

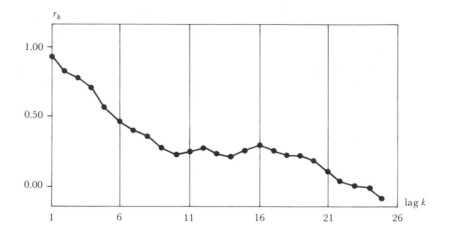

Figure 4. Sample Autocorrelation Function of British Unemployment Rate Data, 1948(1)–1972(4).

which indicates that a low order autoregressive process is compatible with the British unemployment observations (cf. Table 1 and Figure 2). Since the partial autocorrelations (which are not reported here) are insignificant for $k > 1$, we tentatively entertain a first-order autoregressive specification. Letting U_t designate the unemployment rate, we have

$$U_t = \varphi_1 U_{t-1} + e_t \qquad (14)$$

or

$$(1 - \varphi_1 L) U_t = e_t$$

Figure 5 presents the sample autocorrelations of the residuals $\hat{e}_t$, that is, the autocorrelations of the transformed $U_t - \hat{\varphi}_1 U_{t-1}$. The autocorrelations exhibit distinct peaks every 4th quarter, that is, at $k = 4, 8, 12, 16, \ldots$; which suggests a strong seasonal dependence between unemployment rates of the same quarter in different years. The seasonal dependence identified in Figure 5 shows no tendency to die out as the lag k increases and, therefore, four-quarter seasonal differencing is called for. Hence we propose the model

$$(1 - L^4) e_t = \theta_0 + a_t \qquad (15)$$

or

$$e_t = \frac{\theta_0 + a_t}{(1 - L^4)}$$

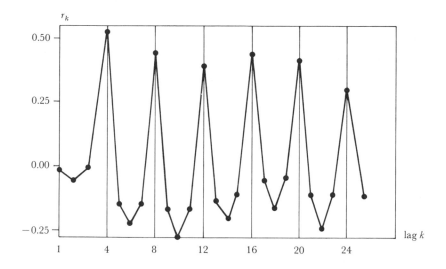

Figure 5. Sample Autocorrelation Function of the Transformed British Unemployment Rate Data $(1 - \hat{\varphi}_1 L) U_t$, 1948(1)–1972(4).

Substituting (15) into (14) yields the following expression for the stochastic noise component N_t of the general intervention analysis model:

$$(1 - \varphi_1 L) U_t = \frac{\theta_0 + a_t}{(1 - L^4)} \qquad (16)$$

or

$$U_t = \frac{\theta_0 + a_t}{(1 - L^4)(1 - \varphi_1 L)} = N_t$$

Having tentatively settled on the *ARMA* specification in (15), we now propose functions for the interventions briefly described earlier. The first intervention concerns the impact of Labour versus Conservative macroeconomic policies on the postwar British unemployment rate. In view of the fact that Socialist-Labor parties typically attach much greater importance to full employment than Center or Conservative parties, we expect the unemployment rate to be driven downward during the tenure of Labour governments and to move upward during periods of Conservative rule. These effects are likely to take the form of gradual changes in the unemployment level (cf. Figure 3b) and, therefore, can be represented by the first-order dynamic expression $\mathbf{u}_{t1} = (\omega_{01}/1 - \delta_1 L) G_{t-1}$, where G_t equals $+1$ during Labour governments and -1 during Conservative governments. The intervention term G_t is specified with a one period (quarter) delay or lag, since we assume that the macroeconomic policies of a new government are not introduced or implemented instantaneously.

An important change in the British employment compensation law, which took effect in October 1966, comprises the second intervention. Until 1966 the unemployed in Great Britian received a relatively flat rate benefit that was not tied to previous earnings. The change in the unemployment system initiated in 1966 provided for an "earnings related supplement" equal to about one third of the employed person's weekly earnings, between £9 and £30. This represented a substantial increase in benefits for most wage earning groups. As a result, unemployed workers were under less financial pressure to accept unattractive jobs and presumably spent more time searching for new employment. It is therefore widely believed that the new compensation scheme increased the duration and, hence, the rate of unemployment. (See, for example, Feldstein, 1973.) Since it is reasonable to suppose that the new compensation scheme produced a *gradual* increase in the level of unemployment, we define a new variable C_t taking a value of $+1$ in 1966 (4) and thereafter, and a value of 0 otherwise; and introduce a second intervention expression $\mathbf{u}_{t2} = (\omega_{02}/1 - \delta_2 L) C_t$.

Combining the noise function proposed in (16) and the intervention expression introduced above yields the following model for the British unemployment rate

$$U_t = \mathbf{u}_{t1} + \mathbf{u}_{t2} + N_t \tag{17}$$

$$= \frac{\omega_{01}}{1 - \delta_1 L} G_{t-1} + \frac{\omega_{02}}{1 - \delta_2 L} C_t + \frac{\theta_0 + a_t}{(1 - L^4)(1 - \varphi_1 L)}$$

where:

U_t = the percentage of the civilian labor force wholly unemployed (quarterly data)

G_t = $+1$ during Labour administrations
 -1 during Conservative administrations

C_t = $+1$ for 1966 (4) and thereafter, and 0 otherwise.

Equation (17) permits a simultaneous test of the hypotheses that (independent of trends, seasonal dependencies, and stochastic fluctuation in the data) the new unemployment compensation system and unrelated interparty differences in macroeconomic policy gradually altered the level of British unemployment.

The estimation results are reported in Table 2.[10] All coefficients (except the constant or trend term θ_0) are substantially larger than their estimated standard errors and, therefore, are significant by conventional statistical criteria. Before considering the implications of these estimates, let us first evaluate the adequacy of the fitted model. Figure 6 shows the actual and predicted levels of the unemployment time series.[11] The predicted unemployment observations track the actual data quite well, which of course is expected in view of the highly significant parameter estimates and small residual variance reported in Table 2. Diagnostic checks applied to the

TABLE 2

Estimation Results for the British Unemployment Rate Model (Equation 17)

	Parameter Estimates	Standard Errors
C_t	$\hat{\omega}_{01} = +0.511$	0.155
	$\hat{\delta}_1 = +0.407$	0.228
G_{t-1}	$\hat{\omega}_{02} = -0.094$	0.035
	$\hat{\delta}_2 = +0.692$	0.118
Trend (4 quarter)	$\hat{\theta}_0 = +0.002$	0.023
Autoregressive	$\hat{\varphi}_1 = +0.773$	0.071
Residual variance	$\hat{\sigma}_a^2 = 0.045$	$R^2 = 0.950^a$

[a]The R^2 reported here pertains to the level data rather than the four-quarter difference data. The four-quarter difference R^2 is 0.850.

[10] The model was estimated with Kent D. Wall's *ERSF* program, which provides full information maximum likelihood estimates of rational distributed lag structural form equations. Details are given in Wall, 1975.

[11] The predicted level data are obtained by summing the predicted four-quarter difference series

$$\hat{U}_t = U_0 + \Sigma_t(1 - L^4)U_t$$

The summation operator Σ is just the inverse of difference operator $(1 - L)$ in the same way that integration is the inverse of differentiation in continuous time problems.

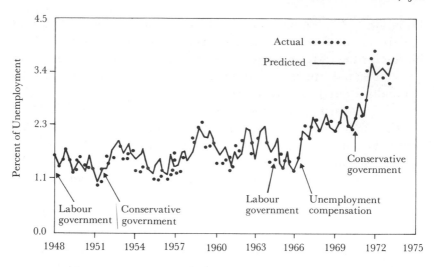

Figure 6. Actual and Predicted Values from the British Unemployment Rate Model (Equation 17).

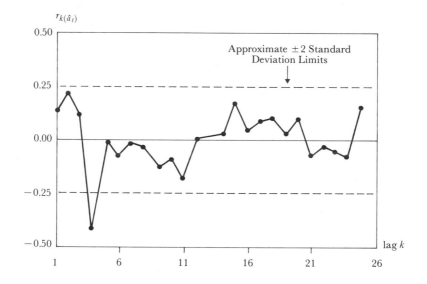

Figure 7. Residual Autocorrelations from the British Unemployment Rate Model.

residuals provide more convincing evidence of the model's adequacy. Figure 7 presents the residual autocorrelations $r_k(\hat{a}_t)$ for lags 1 through 25. The autocorrelations exhibit no systematic patterns and, except for $k = 4$, fall within the approximate ± 2 standard deviation limits.[12] The mean of the residuals is $\bar{a} = 0.0000003$ and the estimated standard error $\sigma_{\bar{a}}^2 = 0.023$. The sample evidence strongly suggests, therefore, that the a_t are independently distributed random variates with zero means.

Returning to the parameter estimates in Table 2, interest centers on the intervention coefficients $\hat{\omega}$ and $\hat{\delta}$. The coefficients associated with the unemployment compensation dummy variable $C_t(\hat{\omega}_{01}, \hat{\delta}_1)$ indicate that the additional unemployment benefits available since October 1966 produced a net increase of about 0.86 percent in the unemployment rate, that is

$$+ \frac{\hat{\omega}_{01}}{1 - \hat{\delta}} = \frac{+0.511}{1 - 0.407} = 0.86$$

Holding fixed the G_{t-1} variable and the stochastic $ARMA$ terms in the model, we see that the expression

$$U_t = (\hat{\omega}_{01}/1 - \hat{\delta}_1 L) C_t$$

implies

$$U_t = \hat{\omega}_{01} \sum_{i=0}^{\infty} \hat{\delta}_1^i \, C_{t-i} \qquad (18)$$

$$= \hat{\delta}_1^t U_0 + \hat{\omega}_{01} \sum_{i=0}^{t-1} \hat{\delta}_1^i C_{t-i}$$

Imposing the initial condition $U_0 = 0$ and applying the coefficient estimates $\hat{\omega}_{01} = 0.511, \hat{\delta}_1 = 0.407$, we obtain the dynamic response on the unemployment rate to the change in the unemployment compensation law by simulating (18) for C_t held at $+1$. The effect is graphed in Figure 8. In view of the fact that the dynamic response parameter $\hat{\delta}_1 = 0.407$, the steady state effect of 0.86 percent was almost fully realized rather quickly — after only 4 or 5 quarters.

---

[12] The lag 4 autocorrelation is, of course, significant and therefore the model might be improved by specifying $a_t = (1 - \theta_4 L^4) v_t$ where the v_t are $N(0, \sigma_v^2)$. Since the $k = 4$ autocorrelation was essentially induced by the seasonal differencing (which overcompensates for the four-quarter seasonal dependency) — and we are primarily interested in predicting the level unemployment series, modification of the model in this way is not advantageous.

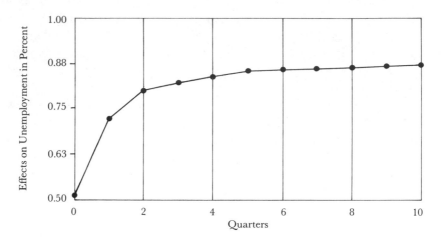

Figure 8. Simulated Net Effects of the 1966 Unemployment Compensation Law on the Unemployment Rate.

The maximum liklihood estimates of ω_{02} and δ_2 also clearly support our initial proposition concerning the impact of partisan change on the British unemployment rate. The estimates indicate that the unemployment rate is driven downward during the tenure of Labour governments and moves upward during periods of Conservative rule. The estimated steady state effects are ± 0.31 percent, that is

$$\pm \frac{\hat{\omega}_{02}}{1 - \hat{\delta}_2} = \pm \frac{0.094}{1 - 0.692} = \pm 0.31$$

which implies a difference of about 0.62 percent between the equilibrium unemployment levels associated with Labour and Conservative governments. Holding constant all other terms in the model, the expression

$$U_t = (\hat{\omega}_{02}/1 - \hat{\delta}_2 L) G_{t-1}$$

implies

$$U_t = \hat{\omega}_{02} \sum_{i=0}^{\infty} \hat{\delta}_2^i G_{t-1-i} \qquad (19)$$

$$= \hat{\delta}_2^t U_0 + \hat{\omega}_{02} \sum_{i=0}^{t-1} \hat{\delta}_2^i G_{t-1-i}$$

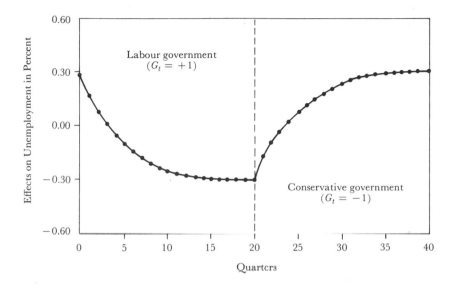

Figure 9. Simulated Net Effects of Labour and Conservative Governments on the
Unemployment Rate.

Again, imposing the arbitrary initial condition $U_0 = 0$ and applying
the coefficient estimates $\hat{\omega}_{02} = -0.094$ and $\hat{\delta}_2 = 0.692$, we obtain
the dynamic time-paths of the unemployment rate that can be
attributed to Labour and Conservative macroeconomic policies by
simulating (19) for G_t held at $+1$ and -1, respectively. Figure 9
depicts the unemployment time-paths for regimes of 20 quarters (5
years) duration. Notice that the steady state of ± 0.31 percent are
fully realized after about 16 quarters, or 4 years.

THE STRUCTURAL EQUATION APPROACH

In contrast to the Box-Tiao scheme, which employs a sophisticated noise model as the point of reference for assessing intervention effects, the structural equation approach attempts to represent explicitly the behavioral processes generating movements in
endogenous variables. Stochastic noise in structural models is
usually given little attention and is typically specified as a sequence
of additive, independently distributed random variates perturbing
each equation in the model.

Consider a model of m simultaneous equations ($m = 1 \dots M$) taking the structural form

$$p_{11}y_{1(t)} + \dots + p_{1M}y_{M(t)} + \sum_i a_{11(i)}y_{1(t-i)}$$

$$+ \dots + \sum_i a_{1M(i)}y_{M(t-i)} + b_{11}x_{1(t)}$$

$$+ \dots + b_{1K}x_{K(t)} + \sum_j c_{11(j)}x_{1(t-j)}$$

$$+ \dots + \sum_j c_{1K(j)}x_{K(t-j)} = u_{1(t)}$$

$$\vdots \tag{20}$$

$$p_{M1}y_{1(t)} + \dots + p_{MM}y_{M(t)} + \sum_i a_{M1(i)}y_{1(t-i)}$$

$$+ \dots + \sum_i a_{MM(i)}y_{M(t-i)} + b_{M1}x_{1(t)}$$

$$+ \dots + b_{MK}x_{K(t)} + \sum_j c_{M1(j)}x_{1(t-j)}$$

$$+ \dots + \sum_j c_{MK(j)}x_{K(t-j)} = u_{M(t)}$$

where: $y_{M(t)}, y_{M(t-i)}$ denote current and lagged endogenous variables, respectively; $x_{K(t)}, x_{K(t-j)}$ denote current and lagged exogenous variables, respectively; and $u_{M(t)}$ denotes stochastic disturbances. Without sacrificing the generality of subsequent analysis, it is convenient to confine lags in endogenous and exogenous variables to one period (any higher-order system of difference equations can be translated to a first-order system) and to write the model more compactly in matrix notation as

$$PY_t + AY_{t-1} + BX_t + CX_{t-1} = U_t \qquad (t = 1, 2, \dots T)$$

where: P and A are $M \times M$ coefficient matrices; B and C are $M \times K$ coefficient matrices; Y_t and Y_{t-1} are M-component column vectors of current and lagged endogenous variables, respectively; X_t and X_{t-1} are K-component column vectors of current and lagged exogenous variables, respectively; and U_t is an M-component column vector of current disturbances.

If identification conditions are satisfied (see Fisher, 1966 for an exhaustive analysis), simultaneous equation models can be estimated by a variety of consistent methods; the most common being two-stage least-squares.[13] In the special case of recursive models in which P is triangular (there are no simultaneous relationships) and the cross-equation disturbance covariance matrix is diagonal (the disturbances are uncorrelated across equations), ordinary least-squares regression yields consistent parameter estimates. Throughout the discussion in this section it is assumed that the functional form of the hypothetical structural model is well established and, hence, that model validation is not an issue.[14] Attention will be confined, therefore, to techniques for intervention effects analysis in the context of a well-defined model.

Interventions and Direct Manipulation of Exogenous Variables

Intervention analysis is least problematic when the intervention or policy change is known to have been implemented by direct manipulation of exogenous variables or policy parameters. Notable examples are policy motivated, exogenously induced changes in government spending, tax rates, and the like, which figures prominently in econometric analysis of macroeconomic policy experiments.

If the structural model consists of a relatively small number of *linear* simultaneous difference equations, the response of endogenous "target" variables to exogenous interventions can be assessed analytically by the method of multiplier analysis. (See Goldberger, 1959; and Thiel and Boot, 1962.) The first step in multiplier analysis is to derive the "reduced form" of the system by solving all

---

[13] Note, however, that the appearance of lagged endogenous variables in (20) and (21) introduces additional complications. Briefly, consistency is not ensured unless the U_t are serially uncorrelated. If this condition fails, there are essentially two options: (1) treat the Y_{t-1} as endogenous for estimation purposes (which has obvious implications for identification); or (2) combine two-stage least-squares with generalized least squares so that the transformed disturbances are properly behaved. On the latter procedure see Fair, 1970. A general review of this and related problems is provided by Fisher, 1970a.

[14] It is hardly necessary to mention that establishing the functional form of a structural model is a substantial task, particularly in areas in which theory is not well developed and the processes under investigation are behaviorally complex. A very useful review of model evaluation procedures (which is geared to econometric systems) is given by Dhrymes *et al.*, 1972.

right-hand side current endogenous variables as functions of the predetermined lagged endogenous and exogenous variables. Thus, given the estimated structural form

$$\hat{P}Y_t = -\hat{A}Y_{t-1} - \hat{B}X_t - \hat{C}X_{t-1} + \hat{U}t \qquad (22)$$

the reduced form can be secured by premultiplying by $\hat{P}^{-1}$

$$Y_t = -(\hat{P}^{-1}\hat{A})\,Y_t - (\hat{P}^{-1}\hat{B})X_t$$

$$-(\hat{P}^{-1}\hat{C})X_{t-1} + \hat{P}^{-1}\hat{U}_t \qquad (23)$$

which for convenience may be rewritten as

$$Y_t = A^*Y_{t-1} + B^*X_t + C^*X_{t-1} + V_t \qquad (24)$$

where

$$A^* = -\hat{P}^{-1}\hat{A}; \qquad B^* = -\hat{P}^{-1}\hat{B};$$
$$C^* = -\hat{P}^{-1}\hat{C}; \qquad \text{and } V_t = \hat{P}^{-1}\hat{U}_t$$

Notice that every predetermined variable appears in each reduced form equation. Hence, derivation of the reduced form of the model makes explicit what is implied by the structural form; namely, that all predetermined variables directly and/or indirectly influence all endogenous variables.[15] The effects of policy motivated interventions now can be readily assessed by analyzing the reduced form in (24). Assuming that the expectation of $U_t = V_t = 0$, the immediate effects if induced changes in exogenous variables x_{kt} on the expected values of endogenous variables y_{mt} taking account of all contemporaneous feedbacks in the system, are given by elements of B^*, the so-called *impact multiplier* matrix. The elements of B^*, therefore, estimate the instantaneous impact of a unit change in x_{kt} on the *conditional* expectation of y_{mt} with the remaining exogenous variables held constant. Thus, the impact multipliers correspond to the reduced form derivatives $\partial y_{m(t)}/\partial x_{k(t)} = b^*_{mk}$. Since the model at

[15] This of course also means that the reduced form parameters can be *consistently* estimated by regressing each endogenous variable on all predetermined variables. The trade-offs between the derived reduced form estimation procedure shown in (23) and the unrestricted least-squares method mentioned here are developed in Fisher, 1965; and Goldberger, 1964, Chapter 7, Section 9.

hand is linear, endogenous responses to multiple interventions (packages of policy changes) are determined by summing over the appropriate elements of B^*; that is, by calculating

$$\sum_k \partial y_{m(t)}/\partial x_{k(t)} = \sum_k b^*_{mk} \qquad {}^{16}$$

Typically, interest will not be confined to the immediate consequences of policy treatments or interventions but will center instead on the dynamic, long-run implications of exogenously induced change. This amounts to investigating how the time-paths of endogenous variables are affected by external manipulation of exogenous policy instruments. Lagged, cross-temporal feedbacks in the system are now of central importance.

The effects of exogenous interventions, as they are transmitted dynamically through the model, are evaluated by lagging (24) repeatedly and substituting for lagged endogenous variables. For example, lagging (24) one period gives

$$Y_{t-1} = A^* Y_{t-2} + B^* X_{t-1} + C^* X_{t-2} + V_{t-1} \qquad (25)$$

which upon substitution yields

$$Y_t = A^{*2} Y_{t-2} + B^* X_t + (C^* + A^* B^*) X_{t-1} \qquad (26)$$
$$+ A^* C^* X_{t-2} + V_t + A^* V_{t-1}$$

Applying this procedure s times, we obtain

$$Y_t = A^{*s+1} Y_{t-s-1} + B^* X_t$$

$$+ \sum_{\tau=1}^{s} A^{*\tau-1}(C^* + A^* B^*) X_{t-\tau} \qquad (27)$$

$$+ A^{*s} C^* X_{t-s-1} + \sum_{\tau=0}^{s} A^{*\tau} V_{t-\tau}$$

[16] The response to a change of any order is simply $\Delta y_{m(t)} = \sum_k b^*_{mk} \cdot \Delta x_{k(t)}$. Sociologists and political scientists will recognize that algebraic computation of the reduced form coefficients is the simultaneous equation analog of compound path analysis, which is commonly applied to static recursive models. See, for example, Stokes, 1971.

If the system is stable[17] (in which case $\lim_{s \to \infty} A^s = 0$), letting s go to infinity yields

$$Y_t = B^* X_t + \sum_{\tau=1}^{\infty} A^{*\tau-1}(C^* + A^* B^*) X_{t-\tau}$$

$$(28)$$

$$+ \sum_{\tau=0}^{\infty} A^{*\tau} V_{t-\tau}$$

which is known as the *final form* of the model.[18]

The period-by-period responses of endogenous variables to induce shifts in exogenous variables, which are known as *dynamic multipliers,* now can be obtained from (27) and (28). If the exogenous change is sustained for only one period, the effects on subsequent (expected) values of endogenous variables are given by the *delay* multiplier matrices. Hence, the estimated influence of a one-shot exogenous intervention s periods later is

---

[17] The stability assumption is identical to that of the previous section and essentially means that the system cannot grow or oscillate explosively without growth in exogenous variables and/or without impulses from the disturbances. Introductory accounts of the formal conditions for stability of simultaneous difference equations are given by Baumol, 1970; and Goldberg, 1958. Samuelson, 1947, provides an advanced treatment.

[18] The final form of the model can also be derived by applying the algebra of lag operators. Given the lag operator L, such that $L^i Y_t \equiv Y_{t-i}$, the reduced form of the system given in (24) can be expressed

$(I - A^*L)Y_t = B^* X_t + C^* X_{t-1} + V,$

$\qquad Y_t = (I - A^*L)^{-1} B^* X_t + (I - A^*L)^{-1} C^* X_{t-1}$

$\qquad\quad + (I - A^*L)^{-1} V_t$

Since $(I - A^*L)^{-1}$ is the limit of the convergent geometric series $(I + A^*L + A^{*2}L^2 + \cdots)$ we have

$\qquad Y_t = (I + A^*L + A^{*2}L^2 + \cdots)B^* X_t$

$\qquad\qquad + (I + A^*L + A^{*2}L^2 + \cdots)C^* X_{t-1}$

$\qquad\qquad + (I + A^*L + A^{*2}L^2 + \cdots)V_t$

$\qquad Y_t = B^* \sum_{\tau=0}^{\infty} A^{*\tau} X_{t-\tau} + C^* \sum_{\tau=0}^{\infty} A^{*\tau} X_{t-\tau-1}$

$\qquad\qquad + \sum_{\tau=0}^{\infty} A^{*\tau} V_{t-\tau}$

$\qquad Y_t = B^* X_t + \sum_{\tau=1}^{\infty} A^{*\tau-1}(C^* + A^* B^*) X_{t-\tau}$

$\qquad\qquad + \sum_{\tau=0}^{\infty} A^{*\tau} V_{t-\tau}$

$$A^{*\,s-1}(C^* + A^*B^*) \qquad s \geqq 1 \qquad\qquad (29)$$

The response of endogenous variables to one-shot exogenous impulses can, therefore, be tracked through time by evaluating the impact and successive delay multiplier matrices $B^*, (C^* + A^*B^*)$, $A^*(C^* + A^*B^*)$, $A^{*2}(C^* + A^*B^*)$, ..., the elements of which correspond to the reduced form derivatives $\partial y_{m(t+s)}/\partial x_{k(t)}$. Since the assumption of system stability implies that $\lim_{s\to\infty} A^s = 0$, it is clear that unsustained exogenous interventions will produce responses (displacements from equilibrium) in the Y_t that die out after sufficiently long lags.

Frequently, however, policy motivated interventions will be sustained through time. The dynamic implications of (unit) changes in exogenous variables that are continued, say, over s periods are given by the *cumulated multiplier* matrices

$$B^* + \sum_{\tau=1}^{s} A^{*\,\tau-1}(C^* + A^*B^*) \qquad\qquad (30)$$

$$= B^* + (I + A^* + A^{*2} + \cdots + A^{*\tau-1})(C^* + A^*B^*)$$

which have elements corresponding to the summed reduced form derivatives

$$\sum_{\tau=0}^{s} \partial y_{m(t+\tau)}/\partial x_{k(t)}$$

The time paths of endogenous responses to sustained exogenous interventions can therefore be determined by evaluating (30) over the index τ.

Finally, by taking $\tau \to \infty$ we obtain the *equilibrium multiplier* matrices

$$
\begin{aligned}
B^* + \sum_{\tau=1}^{s} A^{*\,\tau-1}(C^* + A^*B^*) & \\
&= B^* + (I + A^* + A^{*2} + \ldots)(C^* + A^*B^*) \\
&= B^* + (I - A^*)^{-1}(C^* + A^*B^*) \qquad (31) \\
&= (I - A^*)^{-1}[(I - A^*)B^* + C^* + A^*B^*] \\
&= (I - A^*)^{-1}[B^* - A^*B^* + C^* + A^*B^*] \\
&= (I - A^*)^{-1}(B^* + C^*)
\end{aligned}
$$

(by the convergence rule for a geometric series).

The elements of (31) give the equilibrium or steady-state responses of endogenous variables to unit changes in exogenous variables that are sustained indefinitely.

Perhaps a simple analytic example will help clarify the results of this section. Suppose that the system under investigation is adequately represented as a pair of simultaneous equations in the structural form

$$y_{1(t)} + p_{12}y_{2(t)} + a_{11}y_{1(t-1)} + b_{11}x_{1(t)} = u_{1(t)} \tag{32}$$

$$p_{21}y_{1(t)} + y_{2(t)} + a_{22}y_{2(t-1)} + b_{22}x_{2(t)} = u_{2(t)} \tag{33}$$

In order to determine the consequences of hypothetical policy manipulations of the exogenous variables x_1 and x_2 we need to derive the reduced form of the system, which is obtained by applying simple matrix operations in the manner of (23) or, alternatively, by solving algebraically the current endogenous variables as functions of the lagged endogenous and exogenous variables. Either approach yields the reduced form equations

$$y_{1(t)} = \frac{-a_{11}}{1 - p_{12}p_{21}} y_{1(t-1)} + \frac{p_{12}a_{22}}{1 - p_{12}p_{21}} y_{2(t-1)}$$

$$- \frac{b_{11}}{1 - p_{12}p_{21}} x_{1(t)} + \frac{p_{12}b_{22}}{1 - p_{12}p_{21}} x_{2(t)} \tag{34}$$

$$+ \frac{1}{1 - p_{12}p_{21}} (u_{1(t)} - p_{12}u_{2(t)})$$

$$y_{2(t)} = \frac{p_{21}a_{11}}{1 - p_{12}p_{21}} y_{1(t-1)} - \frac{a_{22}}{1 - p_{12}p_{21}} y_{2(t-1)}$$

$$+ \frac{p_{21}b_{11}}{1 - p_{12}p_{21}} x_{1(t)} - \frac{b_{22}}{1 - p_{12}p_{21}} x_{2(t)} \tag{35}$$

$$+ \frac{1}{1 - p_{12}p_{21}} (u_{2(t)} - p_{21}u_{1(t)})$$

In accordance with the earlier convention (c.f. equation 24) these equations are conveniently rewritten as

$$y_{1(t)} = a_{11}^{*}y_{1(t-1)} + a_{12}^{*}y_{2(t-1)} + b_{11}^{*}x_{1(t)} + b_{12}^{*}x_{2(t)} + v_{1(t)} \tag{36}$$

$$y_{2(t)} = a_{21}^{*}y_{1(t-1)} + a_{22}^{*}y_{2(t-1)} + b_{21}^{*}x_{1(t)} + b_{22}^{*}x_{2(t)} + v_{2(t)} \tag{37}$$

The instantaneous effects of unit changes in the exogenous x_{kt} on the conditional expectations of the endogenous y_{mt}, the impact multipliers, are given by the b^*_{mk}; which, as (34) and (35) make apparent, are nonlinear functions of the underlying structural coefficients in (32) and (33). The responses of the $y_{mt}s$ periods later to interventions (which, for simplicity, are again taken to be unit changes in the x_{kt}) that are initiated at time t and sustained only 1 period are given by the delay multipliers. For example, taking $s = 2$ and applying (29) to the model at hand yields

$$\frac{\partial y_{m(t+2)}}{\partial x_{k(t)}} = A^{*2}B^* \tag{38}$$

$$= \begin{bmatrix} a^*_{11} & a^*_{12} \\ a^*_{21} & a^*_{22} \end{bmatrix}^2 \begin{bmatrix} b^*_{11} & b^*_{12} \\ b^*_{21} & b^*_{22} \end{bmatrix}$$

$$= \begin{bmatrix} (a^{*2}_{11} + a^*_{12}a^*_{21})b^*_{11} & (a^{*2}_{11} + a^*_{12}a^*_{21})b^*_{12} \\ + (a^*_{11}a^*_{12} + a^*_{12}a^*_{22})b^*_{21} & + (a^*_{11}a^*_{12} + a^*_{12}a^*_{22})b^*_{22} \\ (a^*_{21}a^*_{11} + a^*_{22}a^*_{21})b^*_{11} & (a^*_{21}a^*_{11} + a^*_{22}a^*_{21})b^*_{12} \\ + (a^*_{21}a^*_{12} + a^{*2}_{22})b^*_{21} & + (a^*_{21}a^*_{12} + a^{*2}_{22})b^*_{22} \end{bmatrix}$$

Hence, the impact of a one-shot (or pulse) unit increment in x_{1t} on $y_{1(t+2)}$ is given by the northwest entry of the matrix, that of x_{1t} on $y_{2(t+2)}$ by the southwest entry, that of x_{2t} on $y_{1(t+2)}$ by the northeast entry, and that of x_{2t} on $y_{2(t+2)}$ by the southeast entry. Delay multipliers for longer lags (leads) and/or for more complex models will obviously require even more tedious calculations, if undertaken analytically.

The cumulative effects of interventions that are sustained over some finite period are determined by application of (30), that is, by simply summing the impact and delay multiplier matrices over the appropriate time index. The ultimate impact of induced changes in exogenous variables that are maintained indefinitely are calculated by employing the equilibrium multiplier expression in (31). To illustrate for the system of (32)–(37) we derive

$$\sum_{\tau=0}^{\infty} \frac{\partial y_{m(t+\tau)}}{\partial x_{k(t)}} = (I - A^*)^{-1} B^* \tag{39}$$

$$= \begin{bmatrix} 1 - a_{11}^* & -a_{12}^* \\ \\ -a_{21}^* & 1 - a_{22}^* \end{bmatrix}^{-1} \begin{bmatrix} b_{11}^* & b_{12}^* \\ \\ b_{21}^* & b_{22}^* \end{bmatrix}$$

$$= \frac{1}{D} \begin{bmatrix} (1 - a_{22}^*)b_{11}^* + a_{12}^* b_{21}^* & (1 - a_{22}^*)b_{12}^* + a_{12}^* b_{22}^* \\ a_{21}^* b_{11}^* + (1 - a_{11}^*)b_{21}^* & a_{21}^* b_{12}^* + (1 - a_{11}^*)b_{22}^* \end{bmatrix}$$

where: $D = (1 - a_{11}^*)(1 - a_{22}^*) - a_{21}^* a_{12}^*$. The elements of (39) give the ultimate or equilibrium responses of the y_m to unit changes in the x_k that are sustained forever.

Although the analytic approach taken thus far has considerable heuristic value, the dynamic multipliers associated with changes in exogenous variables are, in practice, usually derived numerically by computer simulation. The reason, of course, is that simulated solutions are vastly more convenient computationally, even for relatively small models.[19] Simulation-based estimates of the intervention multipliers are secured by simulating the model dynamically in order to obtain an "intervention" endogenous series and a "nonintervention" endogenous series.[20] The intervention or "policy-on" solution is designed to depict actual endogenous outcomes during the post-intervention periods. Accordingly, these outcomes, which we denote as $\hat{y}_{mt}^i$, are generated by supplying initial conditions (values) for the y_{mt} and allowing exogenous variables and parameters to take on their historical, post-intervention values. On the other hand, the nonintervention or "policy-off" solution attempts to replicate endogenous outcomes that would have occurred

---

[19] Multiplier analysis in nonlinear models (that is, models in which one or more endogenous variables appear in two or more linearly independent functional forms) requires a simulation approach, since explicit analytical solutions for the reduced form equations are difficult, if not impossible, to obtain. For further discussion see Howrey and Kelejian, 1969.

[20] Dynamic simulation simply means that actual historical values of lagged endogenous variables are used only for initial conditions; all subsequent endogenous values are generated sequentially by the model. Thus, the current period's endogenous calculations form the lagged inputs to the next period, and so on.

in the absence of exogenously induced change. These outcomes, which we denote as $\hat{y}^n_{mt}$, are obtained by imposing values on exogenous variables and/or parameters that would have prevailed without the external manipulation (that is, by subtracting the known magnitude of induced changes from the historical values).

Comparison of differences $(\hat{y}^i_{mt} - \hat{y}^n_{mt})$, $(\hat{y}^i_{mt+1} - \hat{y}^n_{mt+1})$, ..., $(\hat{y}^i_{mt+\tau} - \hat{y}^n_{mt+\tau})$ yields estimates of the endogenous responses to exogenous interventions. Simulation estimates of the intervention multipliers corresponding to a sustained exogenous variable change of, say, $\delta - (x_{kt} + \delta)$, ..., $(x_{kt+\tau} + \delta)$ — would be given the ratios $(\hat{y}^i_{mt} - \hat{y}^n_{mt})/\delta$, ..., $(\hat{y}^i_{mt+\tau} - \hat{y}^n_{mt+\tau})/\delta$. Studies of the consequences of specific policy changes (hypothetical and actual) that have been undertaken in this way include Fromm and Taubman's (1967) analysis of the effects of the U.S. excise tax cut of 1965, and Klein's (1969) similar investigation of the U.S. income tax cut of 1964, and Klein's (1968) study of the economic consequences of Vietnam peace.

It is clear that static and dynamic multipliers are the structural equation equivalents of the Box-Tiao intervention function response schemes. However, an important advantage of the structural method is that endogenous responses to exogenous interventions can be interpreted causally in the light of structural information. That is, the behavioral mechanisms underlying intervention multipliers are made apparent by inspection of the interdependent structure of the system. Naturally, such multipliers have meaning only within the framework of the model from which they are derived. If the model does not square well with reality, then the estimated multipliers cannot be informative about real-world intervention effects.

Interventions and Structural Shifts

In most empirical situations, at least outside of macroeconomics, policy interventions are not likely to consist of direct manipulation of exogenous variables or policy parameters. On the contrary, the typical intervention will involve a change in the law, government regulation, or administrative procedure, or perhaps not an intervention in the usual sense at all — but, rather, a dramatic event such as a war, strike, critical electoral outcome, important international agreement, and so on. In such situations, the manner in which an exogenous intervention or event potentially affects a particular endogenous variable or an entire system of variables is not known a priori.

If it can be assumed that the intervention does not perturb the *values* of exogenous variables, but affects only the *parameters* of the model, the problem is readily approached by structural shift estimation. Recall that the general (*m* equation) linear dynamic structural model was expressed previously as

$$PY_t + AY_{t-1} + BX_t + CX_{t-1} = U_t \qquad (40)$$

Rearranging terms and assuming that the system has been normalized (such that the coefficient of one endogenous variable in each structural equation is taken as $+1$ a priori) allows the equation of the model to be written in the scalar form of, for example, the *j*th equation:

$$y_{j(t)} = -\sum_{m \neq j} p_{jm} y_{m(t)} - \sum_{m} a_{jm} y_{m(t-1)} \qquad (41)$$
$$-\sum_{k} b_{jk} x_{k(t)} - \sum_{k} C_{jk} x_{k(t-1)} + u_{j(t)}$$

Suppose that the intervention event under investigation occurs at the *n*th period and continues thereafter. Shifts in the structural parameters associated with the intervention can be determined by defining a binary variable, say, *D*

$$D = 0 \quad \text{for } t < n$$
$$= 1 \quad \text{for } t \geq n$$

and estimating the revised, unrestricted equation(s)

$$y_{j(t)} = -\sum_{m \neq j} P_{jm} y_{m(t)} - \sum_{m \neq j} P'_{mj} [y_{m(t)} \cdot D]$$
$$-\sum_{m} a_{jm} y_{m(t-1)} - \sum_{m} a'_{jm} [y_{m(t-1)} \cdot D]$$
$$-\sum_{k} b_{jk} x_{k(t)} - \sum_{k} b'_{jk} [x_{k(t)} \cdot D]$$
$$-\sum_{k} c_{jk} x_{k(t-1)} - \sum_{k} c'_{jk} [x_{k(t-1)} \cdot D] + u^*_{j(t)}$$

Equations in the form of (42) allow detection of structural shifts or breaks induced by the exogenous intervention by permitting all parameters to have different values in the pre- and post-intervention periods.[21] Of course, any prior (theoretical) information about the location of intervention shift effects should be exploited by setting the relevant cross-product terms equal to zero. The t ratios of p'_{jm}, a'_{jm}, b'_{jk} and c'_{jk} provide direct tests of the null hypothesis that the post-intervention parameters are not significantly different from the corresponding pre-intervention parameters. The joint hypothesis that all coefficients (or some subset thereof) are common across the pre- and post-intervention observations may be evaluated by computing the F ratio(s)[22]

$$ F_{(j)} = \frac{\left[\sum_t \hat{u}_{j(t)}^2 - \sum_t \hat{u}_{j(t)}^{*2} \right] \Big/ r}{\left[\sum_t \hat{u}_{j(t)}^{*2} \right] \Big/ T - G} $$

which is (are) distributed with r, and $T - G$ degrees of freedom, where: $\sum_t \hat{u}_{j(t)}^2$ and $\sum_t \hat{u}_{j(t)}^{*2}$ are estimates of the restricted and unrestricted residual sums of squares, respectively, and are derived by applying the structural coefficient estimates to the original data,[23] r denotes the number of restrictions or constraints in (41) and $T - G$ denotes the degrees of freedon of the residual sum of squares in (42)—G being the number of parameters in that equation.

Once the magnitude of parameter shifts attributable to the exogenous intervention(s) has been determined for each equation in

---

[21] Intercept-constants are not shown explicitly in (41) or (42), but may be considered to be among the b_{jk}. Also, there are alternative ways to set up the problem, for example, one might estimate equations in the model separately for the pre- and post-intervention periods in the spirit of analysis of covariance.

[22] If the number of parameters to be estimated exceed the available post-intervention observations, the F test of Chow, 1960, should be used in place of that given above. A unifying exposition of these and related tests is given by Fisher, 1970b.

[23] Because the the residual sums of squares are necessarily calculated in this way in simultaneous equation models, t and F statistics do not have full classical justification in the sample. They might be viewed as tests of "quasi-significance." If the model under investigation consists of a single equation that can be estimated consistently by ordinary least-squares (rather than by a simultaneous equations estimator such as two-stage least squares), $\sum_t \hat{u}_{j(t)}^2$ and $\sum_t \hat{u}_{j(t)}^{*2}$ are, of course, computed directly from the residuals of the estimating equations.

the model, the methods outlined previously for calculating intervention effects can be employed. However, the structural equation approach would appear to be of little value in situations in which the external intervention not only perturbs the model's parameters but also affects the values of exogenous variables. Unless the investigator knows which exogenous variables are affected, and by how much (a case treated earlier), there is simply no way to determine the consequences of an intervention within the structural framework. This general point is illustrated by the British unemployment example presented in the previous section. In a typical neo-Keynesian structural model, employment would depend heavily on the rate of growth of current and lagged real national income; which, in turn, would hinge on changes in government spending, taxation, investment and consumption. The impact of the supplementary unemployment benefits available since 1966 could be successfully determined in this framework by defining an intervention dummy variable (denoted earlier as C_t) and estimating revised structural eqations in the form of (42), which allow direct and indirect intervention effects. However, it is unlikely that the net effects of Labour versus Conservative macroeconomic policies on the unemployment rate could be estimated by using such techniques. The principal instruments of government macroeconomic policy are public spending and taxation, which are taken as *exogenous* in structural models. Hence, unless precise information was available about the alterations in these variables due to partisan change in the system, the structural equation approach would not permit estimation of interparty effects.

LIMITATIONS AND LINES OF CONVERGENCE

Limitations

Box-Tiao or Box-Jenkins methods are essentially models for "ignorance" that are not based on theory and, in this sense, are void of explanatory power. Although these models are in many situations likely to yield good estimates of endogenous responses to external interventions, they provide no insight into the causal structure underlying the transmission of exogenous impulses through a dynamic system of interdependent social, economic, or political relationships.

Moreover, the Box-Tiao approach is potentially susceptible to errors of inference due to "omitted variables." Discontinous movements in endogenous variables that are actually responses to discontinous changes in omitted exogenous (causal) variables are easily attributed by Box-Tiao methods to external interventions that happen to covary with sudden changes in the omitted variables. However, the multiple contrast design ("multiple-group time-series design") proposed by Campbell (1963; 1966) to deal with this problem and successfully applied in the Box-Tiao framework by Glass (1968) and Glass, Willson, and Gottman (1972) is likely to be at least somewhat effective in coping with this potential source of spurious interence.[24]

Perhaps the most obvious constraint on the use of the structural approach to intervention analysis is that many areas of inquiry, especially outside of macroeconomics, are simply not sufficiently rich in theory and/or data to permit specification and estimation of adequate structural models. In such situations the causally naive Box-Tiao scheme—which merely requires time-series observations on endogenous variables, knowledge of the time-span of external interventions, and some hunches about the form of endogenous responses—would appear to have no serious rival. However, as I noted earlier, even in areas in which acceptable structural models have been developed, the empirical data cannot be informative about intervention effects unless it can be assumed that exogenous variables do not respond to external treatments (or, at least, do not respond in ways that are not fully known a priori).

Lines of Convergence

It has been noted several times that Box-Jenkins and Box-Tiao methods are essentially sophisticated noise models that make no attempt to represent the behavioral structure generating endogenous time-series. However, recent Box-Tiao papers hint at the need to elaborate the basic "noise plus intervention function" model

---

[24] A good example of this design is provided by Glass' 1968 study of the effectiveness of Governor Abraham Rubicoff's 1955 "crackdown" on speeding in reducing traffic fatalities in Connecticut. In order to ensure that the effects attributed to this intervention were genuine, Glass analyzed the fatality rates of four "control" states that did not experience a comparable alteration of law enforcement practices.

to incorporate additional exogenous variables and interdependent relationships among "output" or endogenous variables. Progress along these lines has already been made by Wall (1974) and Wall and Westcott (1974) and this work clearly points in the structural equation direction.

Conversely, the structural equation tradition has placed great emphasis on behavioral sophistication but has given much less attention to noise or disturbance processes. Error models other than first-order autoregressive schemes are rarely entertained in empirical studies; indeed, in simultaneous equation models the disturbances are nearly always assumed at the outset to be white noise. This may, in part, underlie the rather poor short-term forecasting performance of econometric models in relation to that of naive, especially Box-Jenkins, alternatives. (Cf. Cooper, 1972; Naylor et al., 1972; Nelson, 1973; Stekler, 1968).

However, structural modelers are becoming more sensitive to the need for stochastic sophistication. A number of recent state of the art papers have urged that greater attention be given to error processes (Dhrymes, et al., 1972; Klein, 1971), and work on the specification and estimation of more complex disturbance models in the structural context is beginning to appear with regularity in the technical literature. (See, for example, Chow and Fair, 1973; Fair, 1970, 1973; Hannan and Nichols, 1972; Hibbs, 1974; Sarris and Eisner, 1974; and Schmidt, 1971.) As I have tried to show in an earlier paper (Hibbs, 1974), Box-Jenkins techniques are ideally suited to the characterization of structural disturbance processes, which, after all, represent our ignorance. Finally, the traditional econometric commitment to the maintained hypothesis and strong axiomatization of models appears to be giving way to a renewed emphasis on experimentation with functional forms. These developments in the structural equation camp have much in common with the explicit empiricism of the *ARMA* approach and clearly point in the Box-Jenkins direction. Indeed, Box-Jenkins techniques applied to the final autoregressive equations of econometric models have been shown to be useful in validating the adequacy of the presumed causal structure. (See Pierce and Mason, *n.d.*, and Zellner and Palm, 1973.)

Convergence will be fully realized when structural models corrupted by *ARMA* noise are used routinely in empirical work.

REFERENCES

BAUMOL, W. J.
    1970   *Economic Dynamics.* 3rd ed. New York: Macmillan.

BLALOCK, H. M., JR.
    1971   (Ed.), *Causal Models in the Social Sciences.* Chicago: Aldine Atherton.

BOX, G. E. P., AND JENKINS, G. M.
    1970   *Time Series Analysis; Forecasting and Control.* San Francisco: Holden-Day.

BOX, G. E. P., AND PIERCE, D. A.
    1970   "Distribution of Residual Autocorrelations in Autoregressive-Integrated Moving Average Time-Series Models." *Journal of the American Statistical Association* 64.

BOX, G. E. P., AND TIAO, G. C.
    1965   "A Change in Level of a Nonstationary Time Series." *Biometrika* 52:1 and 2.
    1975   "Intervention Analysis with Applications to Economic and Environmental Problems." *Journal of the American Statistical Association* 70 (Mar.).

CAMPBELL, D. T.
    1963   "From Description to Experimentation: Interpreting Trends as Quasi-Experiments." In C. W. Harris (Ed.), *Problems in Measuring Change.* Madison, Wisc.: University of Wisconsin Press.
    1969   "Reforms as Experiments." *American Psychologist* 24 (Apr.).

CAMPBELL, D. T., AND STANLEY, J. C.
    1966   *Experimental and Quasi-Experimental Designs for Research.* Chicago: Rand McNally.

CAPORASO, J. A., AND PELOWSKI, A. L.
    1971   "Economic and Political Integration in Europe: A Time-Series Quasi-Experimental Analysis." *American Political Science Review* 65 (June).

CAPORASO, J. A., AND ROOS, L.
    1973   *Quasi-Experimental Approaches.* Evanston, Ill.: Northwestern University Press.

CHOW, G. C.
    1960   "Tests of Equality Between Subsets of Coefficients in Two Linear Regressions." *Econometrica* 28 (July).

CHOW, G. C., AND FAIR, R. C.
    1973   "Maximum Likelihood Estimation of Linear Equation Systems with Autoregressive Residuals." *Annals of Economic and Social Measurement* II (Jan.).

COOPER, R. L.

    1972   "The Predictive Performance of Quarterly Econometric Models of the United States." In B. G. Hickman (Ed.), *Econometric Models of Cyclical Behavior.* New York: National Bureau of Economic Research, Columbia University Press.

DHRYMES, P. J., AND OTHERS.

    1972   "Criteria for Evaluation of Econometric Models." *Annals of Economic and Social Measurement* 1 (July).

DUVALL, R., AND WELFLING, M.

    1973   "Determinants of Political Institutionalization in Black Africa: A Quasi-Experimental Analysis." *Comparative Political Studies* 5 (Jan.).

FAIR, R. C.

    1970   "The Estimation of Simultaneous Equation Models with Lagged Endogenous Variables and First Order Serially Correlated Errors." *Econometrica* 38 (May).

    1973   "A Comparison of Alternative Estimators of Macroeconomic Models." *International Economic Review* 14 (June).

FELDSTEIN, M.

    1973   "The Economics of the New Unemployment." *The Public Interest* 33 (Fall).

FISHER, F. M.

    1965   "Dynamic Structure and Estimation in Economy-Wide Econometric Models." In J. Duesenberry *et al.* (Eds.), *The Bookings Quarterly Econometric Model of the United States.* Chicago: Rand-McNally.

    1966   *The Identification Problem in Econometrics.* New York: McGraw-Hill.

    1970a "Simultaneous Equations Estimation: The State of the Art." *Institute for Defense Analysis, Economic Papers* (July).

    1970b "Tests of Equality Between Sets of Coefficients in Two Linear Regressions: An Expository Note." *Econometrica* 28 (Mar.).

FROMM, G., AND TAUBMAN, P.

    1967   *Policy Simulations with an Econometric Model.* Washington, D.C.: Brookings.

GLASS, G. V.

    1968   "Analysis of Data on the Connecticut Speeding Crackdown as a Time-Series Quasi-Experiment." *Law and Society* 3 (Aug.).

    1972   "Estimating the Effects of Intervention into a Nonstationary Time-Series." *American Educational Research Journal* 9.

GLASS, G. V., WILLSON, V. L., AND GOTTMAN, J. M.

1972 *Design and Analysis of Time-Series Experiments.* University of Colorado. Mimeo.

GOLDBERG, S.

1958 *Introduction to Difference Equations.* New York: John Wiley.

GOLDBERGER, A. S.

1959 *Impact Multipliers and Dynamic Properties of the Klein-Goldberger Model.* Amsterdam: North-Holland.

1964 *Econometric Theory.* New York: John Wiley.

1972 "Structural Equation Methods in the Social Sciences." *Econometrica* 40 (Nov.).

GOLDBERGER, A. S., AND DUNCAN, O. D.

1973 (Eds.), *Structural Equation Models in the Social Sciences.* New York: Seminar Press.

HANNAN, E. J., AND NICHOLS, D. F.

1972 "The Estimation of Mixed Regression, Autoregression, Moving Average, and Distributed Lag Models." *Econometrica* 40 (May).

HIBBS, D. A.

1974 "Problems of Statistical Estimation and Causal Inference in Time-Series Regression Models." In H. L. Costner (Ed.), *Sociological Methodology 1974.* San Francisco: Jossey-Bass.

1975 "Economic Interest and the Politics of Macroeconomic Policy." Cambridge, Mass.: Center for International Studies, forthcoming in *American Political Science Review,* Dec. 1977.

HOWREY, P., AND KELEJIAN, H. H.

1969 "Computer Simulation vs. Analytical Solutions." In Naylor (Ed.), *The Design of Computer Simulation Experiments.* North Carolina: Duke University Press.

KLEIN, L. R.

1968 "Economic Consequences of Vietnam Peace." *Wharton Quarterly* (Summer).

1969 "Econometric Analysis of the Tax Cut of 1964." In J. Duesenberry *et al.* (Eds.), *The Brookings Model: Some Further Results.* Chicago: Rand-McNally.

1971 "Whither Econometrics?" *Journal of the American Statistical Association* 66 (June).

MAGUIRE, T. O., AND GLASS, G. V.

1967 "A Program for the Analysis of Certain Time-Series Quasi-Experiments." *Educational and Psychological Measurement* 27 (Autumn).

MARQUARDT, D. W.

1963 "An Algorithm for Least Squares Estimation of Nonlinear Parmeters." *Journal of the Society od Industrial and Applied Methematics* 11 (June).

NAYLOR, T. H., SEAKS, T. G., AND WICHERN, D. W.

1972 "Box-Jenkins Methods: An Alternative to Econometric Models." *International Statistical Review.*

NELSON, C. R.

1973a *Applied Time-Series Analysis.* San Francisco: Holden-Day.

1973b "The Predictive Performance of the *FRB-MIT-PENN* Model of the U.S. Economy." *American Economic Review.*

PIERCE, D. A., AND MASON, J. M.

"On Estimating the Fundamental Dynamic Equations of Structural Econometric Models." Mimeo.

SAMUELSON, P. A.

1947 *Foundations of Economic Analysis.* Cambridge, Mass.: Harvard University Press.

SARRIS, A. H., AND EISNER, M.

1974 "Parameter Estimation of *ARMA* Models Using a Computationally Efficient Maximum Likelihood Technique." National Bureau of Economic Research.

SCHMIDT, P.

1971 "Estimation of a Distributed Lag Model with Second Order Autoregressive Disturbances: A Monte Carlo Experiment." *International Economic Review* 12 (Oct.).

STEKLER, H. O.

1968 "Forecasting with Econometric Models: An Evaluation." *Econometrica* 36 (July-Oct.).

STOKES, D. E.

1971 "Compound Paths in Political Analysis." In J. F. Herndon and J. L. Bernd (Eds.), *Mathematical Applications in Political Science V.* Charlottesville, Va.: University Press of Virginia.

THEIL, H., AND BOOT, J. C. G.

1963 "The Final Form of Econometric Equation Systems." *Review of the International Statistical Institute* 30, 2.

WALL, K. D.

1974 "An application of Simultaneous Estimation to the Determination of Causality Between Money and Income." Discussion Paper 8, Department of Computing and Control, Imperial College of Science and Technology, University of London (Apr.).

1975   "*FIML* Estimation of Rational Distributed Lag Structural Form Models." Working Paper No. 77. Cambridge, Mass.: National Bureau of Economic Research (Mar.).

WALL, K. D., AND WESTCOTT, J. H.
1974   "Macro-Economic Modelling for Control." Discussion Paper 7, Department of Computing and Control, Imperial College of Science and Technology, University of London (Jan.).

ZELLNER, A., AND PALM, F.
1973   "Time Series Analysis and Simultaneous Equation Models." H. G. B. Alexander Research Foundation, Graduate School of Business, University of Chicago.

Received January 21, 1975.

5

ESTIMATES FOR DIFFERENTIAL EQUATION MODELS OF SOCIAL PHENOMENA

Patrick Doreian
UNIVERSITY OF PITTSBURGH

Norman P. Hummon
UNIVERSITY OF PITTSBURGH

The attempts of sociologists to understand social phenomena are increasingly concerned with strategies for analyzing data referenced by time. These strategies vary with the nature of (available) data and with the substantive character of the phenomena.

We are grateful to Thomas J. Fararo for his helpful comments. Comments by the referees prompted us to expand on certain problems and to improve the communicative style of the chapter. Any errors contained in this chapter are our own responsibility.

Singer and Spilerman (1974, 1976) have significantly extended our knowledge of modeling social processes by time referenced Markov models that are probabilistic multistate models usually applied to panel data. The work of Box and Jenkins (1970) on time series analysis is beginning to make an impact (see Hibbs 1974 and Chapter four of this volume). Their approach is primarily concerned with models of a few stochastic variables and sophisticated time relations estimated on time series observations. Sociologists are becoming more and more knowledgeable about econometric models (such as the Klein-Goldberger model, Theil, 1971, pp. 468 ff) and their applications to multivariate deterministic systems of equations generally estimated on time series data.

The class of models discussed in this chapter represent yet another approach. We are concerned with models represented by systems of linear differential equations. These models are not new to sociology — Coleman (1968) and Land (1970) have written articles discussing their use and merits. It is our purpose to extend the range of application of these models to further discuss their theoretical properties and to firm up the principles of their empirical estimation.

In the next sections we present three applications of differential equation system models. In the final section we summarize and extend our results to a broad range of empirical situations.

A BIVARIATE HOMOGENOUS MODEL

The first empirical example we consider involves only two endogenous variables. The example and the data were first presented by Gowler (1969). For a particular manufacturing firm let X_1 denote the labor turnover rate per annum and X_2 denote overtime hours per man per annum. Suppose that the level of overtime demanded by management responds systematically to the level of labor turnover in the work force, and that the level of labor turnover also systematically responds to the level of overtime worked. We need, then, to represent these responses. In order to produce a given level of output, some level of labor input is required that—with technology unchanging—is made up of some combination of regular labor and overtime. If X_2^* is the required level of overtime at any point in time (given the size of the workforce), then management can be thought of as trying to move X_2 towards X_2^*. The mechanism of change can be represented as

$$\Delta X_2 = c_2 \, \Delta t (X_2^* - X_2) \tag{1}$$

where ΔX_2 represents the incremental change in X_2 during an increment of time Δt. The parameter c_2 indicates how sensitive the system is (for X_2) with respect to the discrepancy between X_2^* and X_2. In this simple model the level of overtime demanded, X_2^*, is a simple function of the level of labor turnover

$$X_2^* = a_{21}^* X_1 \tag{2}$$

In the same manner, the level of labor turnover can be thought to respond to overtime demands via a mechanism represented by

$$\Delta X_1 = c_1 \, \Delta t (X_1^* - X_1) \tag{3}$$

where

$$X_1^* = a_{12}^* X_2 \tag{4}$$

If equation (4) is substituted into (3), equation (2) substituted into (1), and the limits taken for each equation; then the following pair of equations result:

$$\begin{aligned} \dot{X}_1 &= a_{11}X_1 + a_{12}X_2 \\ \dot{X}_2 &= a_{21}X_1 + a_{22}X_2 \end{aligned} \tag{5}$$

where $a_{11} = -c_1$, $a_{12} = c_1 a_{12}^*$, $a_{21} = c_2 a_{21}^*$, $a_{22} = -c_2$ and $\dot{X}_i$ denotes dX_i/dt. In matrix form these equation can be written as

$$\dot{X} = AX \tag{6}$$

where

$$X' = [X_1, X_2] \qquad \text{and } A = \begin{bmatrix} a_{11} & a_{12} \\ a_{21} & a_{22} \end{bmatrix}$$

While the solution to equation (6) can be readily obtained,[1] it is not a form that directly permits estimation of the matrix A.

---

[1] The solution form is $X(t) = e^{At}X(0)$. For a readable discussion of the solution and theory of differential equations, see Platt (1971).

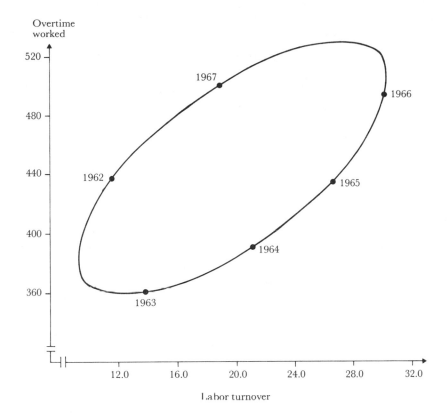

Figure 1. Phase Space: Scattergram of Overtime Against Labor Turnover.

Estimation can proceed, however, through use of the phase space, which can be visualized as the geometric representation of the relation between X_1 and X_2 viewed along the time axis. In effect time is eliminated from the relation between X_1 and X_2.

In the labor turnover example, the scattergram of X_2 plotted against X_1 yields an ellipse, as shown in Figure 1. From an inspection of the data, Gowler noted that both X_1 and X_2 behaved in a sinusoidal manner which can be represented by

$$X_1 = X_{10} + p \sin\theta \tag{7}$$

$$X_2 = X_{20} + q \sin(\theta - \varphi) \tag{8}$$

The parameters of these equations are interpreted in the following way. First, X_{10} and X_{20} are co-ordinates of the center of the ellipse; second, p and q give the amplitude of the excursions of X_1 and X_2, respectively; and third, φ represents the phase lag of X_2 with respect to X_1. The variable θ is an auxiliary variable that is a function of time.

Brée (1971) provided a procedure for obtaining a differential equation form, as in equation (6), from equations (7) and (8). We repeat his results. The auxiliary variable θ is assumed to be a simple linear function of time,

$$\theta = a_0 + a_1 t + \varepsilon \tag{9}$$

(This is, of course, an approximation, as Gowler (1969) showed θ to be a higher order polynomial function of t, but it is one that introduces only minor distortion.)

Differentiation of equations (7) and (8) with respect to time yields

$$dX_1/dt = p \cos \theta \, d\theta/dt$$
$$dX_2/dt = q \cos(\theta - \varphi) \, d\theta/dt \tag{10}$$

The rate at which θ changes with time is obtained directly from equation (9) and is

$$d\theta/dt = a_1 \tag{11}$$

It is necessary to eliminate $d\theta/dt$ from equation (10). By expanding equation (8) and substituting it into (7) it is possible to obtain

$$\cos \theta = (1/p \cot \varphi) X_1 - (1/p \operatorname{cosec} \varphi) X_2 \tag{12}$$

If equations (12) and (11) are then substituted into equations (10), the following equations result:

$$dX_1/dt = (a_1 \cot \varphi) X_1 - 1/q (a_1 p \operatorname{cosec} \varphi) X_2$$
$$dX_2/dt = 1/p (a_1 q \operatorname{cosec} \varphi) X_1 - (a_1 \cot \varphi) X_2 \tag{13}$$

Equations (13) are exactly the form of equation (6), which indicates that the general form of the differential equation can be obtained from more than one starting point. While we prefer the differential equation representation substantively, the phase space representation is useful in defining an estimation form. Expanding $\sin(\theta - \varphi)$ in equation (8) and substituting into equation (7) gives

$$
\frac{X_2 - X_{20}}{q} \tag{14}
$$

$$
= \frac{(X_1 - X_{10})}{p} \cos\varphi - \left[1 - \frac{(X_1 - X_{10})^2}{p} \right]^{1/2} \sin\varphi
$$

Now the sine and the cosine functions are linked via the identity $\sin^2\varphi + \cos^2\varphi = 1$. Use of this identity and equation (14) in a series of straightforward but tedious algebraic manipulations leads to the equation.

$$
\beta_0 + X_2^2 + \beta_1 X_1^2 + 2\beta_2 X_1 X_2 + 2\beta_3 X_1 + 2\beta_4 X_2 = 0 \tag{15}
$$

where

$$
q = p\beta_1^{1/2}
$$

$$
p = \left[\frac{\beta_4^2 - \beta_0}{\beta_1 - \beta_2^2} + X_{10}^2 \right]
$$

$$
X_{20} = (\beta_2\beta_3 - \beta_1\beta_4)/(\beta_1 - \beta_2^2) \tag{16}
$$

$$
X_{10} = (\beta_2\beta_4 - \beta_3)/(\beta_1 - \beta_2^2)
$$

$$
\cos\varphi = -\beta_2/\beta_1^{1/2}
$$

Equation (15) represents a general second order conic (Rektorys, 1969, p. 266) and, if estimates of the βs can be determined, it is possible to recover any of the parameters given in equations (7) and (8)—whence it is also possible to determine the process model parameters of equations (13).

To estimate equation (15), it is convenient to divide by β_0; making the coefficient of $X_2^2 = 1/\beta_0$, and the other coefficients β_i/β_0, and let $Z_1 = X_2^2, Z_2 = X_1^2$, etc. Then the equation becomes

$$
\sum_{i=1}^{5} \alpha_i Z_i + 1 = 0 \tag{17}
$$

a structural form representation that is linear in the parameters. To fit this model to data, we assume that the left hand side equals a disturbance term ε that is distributed $N(0, \sigma^2)$. The equation in matrix form becomes

$$Z^\alpha + i = \varepsilon \qquad (18)$$

where i is a unit vector of dimension n, the number of observations.

The maximum likelihood procedure is an attractive way to estimate α, the structural form parameters. The likelihood function is

$$L = (2\pi\sigma^2)^{-n/2} \exp[-(2\sigma^2)^{-1} \, \varepsilon'\varepsilon]$$

and the more convenient log-liklihood function is

$$L^* = n/2 \ln(2\pi\sigma^2) - (2\sigma^2)^{-1}\varepsilon'\varepsilon \qquad (19)$$

On substituting for ε,

$$L^* = n/2 \ln(2\pi\sigma^2) - (2\sigma^2)^{-1}(Z\alpha + i)'(Z\alpha + i)$$

and maximizing L^* by taking partial derivatives and setting them equal to 0 yields

$$\partial L^*/\partial\alpha = -(2\sigma^2)^{-1}(2Z'Z\alpha + 2Z'i) = 0$$

$$\partial L^*/(\partial(\sigma^2)) = n/2(\sigma^2)^{-1} + 1/2(\sigma^2)^{-2}\varepsilon'\varepsilon = 0$$

Solving for $\hat{\sigma}$ and $\hat{\sigma}^2$ yields

$$\hat{\alpha} = -(Z'Z)^{-1}Z'i$$
$$\sigma^2 = 1/n(\hat{\varepsilon}'\hat{\varepsilon}) \qquad (20)$$

where $\hat{\varepsilon}$ is computed for $\hat{\sigma}$.

Variance of the estimates can also be derived from the log-liklihood function.[2] Namely,

$$V^{-1} = -E \begin{bmatrix} \partial^2 L^*/\partial\alpha^2 \\ \partial^2 L^*/\partial(\sigma^2)\partial\alpha \end{bmatrix} \begin{bmatrix} \partial^2 L^*/\partial\alpha\,\partial(\sigma^2) \\ \partial^2 L^*/\partial(\sigma^2)^2 \end{bmatrix}$$

Taking the appropriate partial derivatives and substituting $\hat{\alpha}$ for α and $\hat{\sigma}^2$ for σ^2 yields

[2] For a complete discussion of this method see Kendall and Stuart, 1973, Chapter 18.

$$V^{-1} = 4/\hat{\sigma}^2 \begin{bmatrix} Z'Z \\ -2/\hat{\sigma}^2(Z'Z) \end{bmatrix} \begin{bmatrix} -2/\hat{\sigma}^2(Z'i) \\ n/8(\hat{\sigma}^2)^2 \end{bmatrix} \qquad (21)$$

Algebraically inverting this matrix to obtain V is too complicated for this presentation. However, V can be obtained numerically to statistically evaluate the model's parameters. Of course, this estimation procedure adds another step to the computational backtracking by which we obtain numerical estimates of the original models.[3]

When all these transformations are employed the estimated form of the differentiated model is

$$dX_1/dt = 1.0078X_1 - 0.179X_2 \qquad (22)$$

$$dX_2/dt = 12.61X_1 - 1.078X_2$$

The parameters in this equation can be straightforwardly interpreted. Gowler remarked, "As it has often been observed, the disruptive effects of high labor turnover can lead to even more labor turnover" (Gowler, 1969, p. 83). This can be taken as a description of a situation where there is a positive feedback reflected by the positive estimate of the parameter a_{11} in equation (22). By way of contrast, overtime worked is characterized by negative feedback — which is also in accord with empirical reality — as increased levels of overtime diminish the need for further overtime demands. When the two variables (one intrinsically unstable and the other intrinsically stable) are coupled together they form a system of dynamic equilibrium suggested by a phase space that is an ellipse (see Platt, 1971, p. 187). Further substantive discussion of the estimates of this model can be found in Brée (1971) and in Doreian and Hummon (1976).

A NON-HOMOGENOUS MODEL
WITHOUT EXOGENOUS INPUT

Our second empirical example concerns a model that was constructed to address the theory of formal organizational structure

---

[3] Gowler's data set formed an almost perfect ellipse and estimation produced parameters that were multiples of their standard errors.

advanced by Blau (1970). At the core of the model lies the assumption that formal organizations, and particularly bureaucracies, have structures that control the development and change of organizational components. Our first step in explicitly constructing the model is to define the variables that make up the state space of the organizational system. We are interested in the empirical realization of two pairs of variables in response to a comparison with a corresponding pair of variables in the control process. The first pair of observable variables represents the productive subsystem of an organization.[4]

1. P, the number of employees primarily performing the output tasks of the organization, for example, the production employees.

2. D, the number of divisions which functionally differentiate the work force.

The second pair of observable variables represents the administrative subsystem of the organization:

3. S, the number of supervisory employees in the organization.

4. L, the number of hierarchical levels in the organization.

For each of the observable variables, we define unobservable counterparts P^*, D^*, S^*, and L^*. These unobservable variables represent what the values of the real system variables would be if the configuration of the organization were "properly" structured. With these two types of variables a structural control process can be formulated. Let X_i be any of the four observable variables and X_i^* be its structural control counterpart. Then

$$\Delta X_i = c_i \Delta t(X_i^* - X) \tag{23}$$

where ΔX_i is the "correction" value for X_i, $c \leqq 0$ is a parameter of the process, and Δt is an increment of time.[5] The parameter c is dimensioned t^{-1} and is a measure of the sensitivity of a variable to structural control. To complete the specification of the control process, it

---

[4] It is common practice in organizational research to use the variable size ($=$ $P + S$) in an analysis of organizational structure. For reasons which will become apparent, we prefer to partition variable size into P and S.

[5] The parameter c is required to be greater than 0. If $X_i > X_i^*$, then the control process demands a decrease in X_i in the time increment Δt; and if $X_i < X_i^*$, then the control process demands an increase in X_i in Δt.

is necessary to state the relationships that determine the values of the structural control variables X_i^*. These relationships are given by

$$P^* = e_{12}D + e_{13}S + e_{14}L + f_1$$
$$D^* = e_{21}P + e_{23}S + e_{24}L + f_2$$
$$S^* = e_{31}P + e_{32}D + e_{34}L + f_3 \tag{24}$$
$$L^* = e_{41}P + e_{42}D + e_{43}S + f_4$$

These equations incorporate one of the important ideas mentioned above: that the development of organizational structure is a process where all components of an organization can influence the change of all other components.

When equations (24) are substituted into equation (23), and terms are rearranged, we have

$$\Delta P/\Delta t = -c_1 P + c_1 e_{12}D + c_1 e_{13}S + c_1 e_{14}L + c_1 f_1$$
$$\Delta D/\Delta t = c_2 e_{21}P - c_2 D + c_2 e_{23}S + c_2 e_{24}L + c_2 f_2 \tag{25}$$
$$\Delta S/\Delta t = c_3 e_{31}P + c_3 e_{32}D - c_3 S + c_3 e_{34}L + c_3 f_3$$
$$\Delta L/\Delta t = c_4 e_{41}P + c_4 e_{42}D + c_4 e_{43}S - c_4 L + c_4 f_4$$

When the limit is taken, equations (25) become a system of linear differential equations that can be expressed in matrix form. Let

$$X = \begin{bmatrix} P \\ D \\ S \\ L \end{bmatrix} \qquad A = \begin{bmatrix} -c_1 & c_1 e_{12} & c_1 e_{13} & c_1 e_{14} \\ c_2 e_{21} & -c_2 & c_2 e_{23} & c_2 e_{24} \\ c_3 e_{31} & c_3 e_{32} & -c_3 & c_3 e_{34} \\ c_4 e_{41} & c_4 e_{42} & c_4 e_{43} & -c_4 \end{bmatrix}$$

$$b = \begin{bmatrix} c_1 f_1 \\ c_2 f_2 \\ c_3 f_3 \\ c_4 f_4 \end{bmatrix}$$

Then the differential equation system can be written

$$dX/dt = \dot{X} = AX + b \qquad (26)$$

The solution of (20)[6] is

$$X = e^{At}X_0 + (e^{At} - I)A^{-1}b \qquad (27)$$

where X_0 is the vector of initial conditions. We now define $\tilde{A} = e^{At}$ and $\tilde{b} = (e^{At} - I)A^{-1}b$ for known t, and rewrite (27) as

$$X = \tilde{A}X_0 + \tilde{b} \qquad (28)$$

Equation (20) expresses the relation between the set varia-bles at time t as a linear function of the same set variables at time $t = 0$. This is our basic estimating equation. The empirical values of $\tilde{A}$ and $\tilde{b}$ can be estimated if observations are available for two points in time and the time lapse known.

To obtain estimates of A and b (the parameters of the process model) from the estimated values of $\tilde{A}$ and $\tilde{b}$ (the parameters of the solution or observation model) we must present some additional mathematics. As one might suspect, we are interested in an expres-sion for the (natural) logarithm of matrix a^A.

Under certain conditions, the following relation holds for a square matrix C: $C = V\Lambda V^{-1}$, where Λ is a diagonal matrix of eigenvalues[7] λ_i, and the corresponding columns of V are eigenvectors v_i. Furthermore, a function of a matrix can be expressed in terms of its eigenstructure: $f(C) = Vf(\Lambda)V^{-1}$.

We are interested in the log function, and this presents an additional problem because it is multiple-valued. If Z is an arbitrary complex number, $Z = a + b_i$, then

$$\ln_K Z = \sqrt{a^2 + b^2} + i(\theta + 2\pi K)$$

$$(K = 0, \pm 1, \pm 2, \pm 3, ...)$$

[6] Again, we refer the reader interested in the solution to a text on differential equations such as Platt (1971).

[7] Eigenvalues and eigenvectors are defined by the equation $(A - \lambda_i I)v_i = 0$. The condition we are assuming in this presentation is that the eigenvalues are distinct. For a more general discussion of this mathematical theory, see Singer and Spilerman (1976).

with $\theta = \tan^{-1} b/a$. We can see that even if Z is a real number (that is, $b = 0$), its natural logarithms will be complex for $K \neq 0$; namely, $Z = a + i2\pi K$.

This problem is generally resolved by taking the principle branch $K = 0$ when the eigenvalues of the matrix are distinct and real. When this is not the case, the situation becomes much more complex and is beyond the scope of this chapter.

Applying the expression for the log of the matrix $\tilde{A} = e^{At}$, and assuming the eigenvalues of $\tilde{A}$, $\tilde{\lambda}_i$, are distinct and real yields the following expression for A:

$$A = V \begin{bmatrix} & & 0 \\ & \ln(\tilde{\lambda}_i)/t & \\ 0 & & \end{bmatrix} V^{-1} \tag{29a}$$

In addition, the equation for b is

$$b = A(e^{At} - I)^{-1}\tilde{b} \tag{29b}$$

with A and b expressed as functions of $\tilde{A}$ and $\tilde{b}$. By identifying the c_i in the main diagonal of A, the sensitivity parameters are obtained; and then by dividing the rows of A and b by the corresponding c's, the e_{ij} and f_i are also obtained.

The panel study reported by Meyer (1972) on the size and structure of city, county, and state departments of finance satisfies the data requirements of two waves of data obtained with a known time interval between them. Meyer collected data from 194 finance departments in both 1966 and 1971. The variable definitions for P, D, S, and L are taken from Meyer's study, although Meyer, in accordance with general convention, employed size as a variable rather than as the size of the productive component.

In applying equation (28) to this empirical context, X is considered a vector of dependent variables whose values correspond to the observations on P, D, S, and L in 1971; and X_0 is taken as a vector of independent variables whose values correspond to the observations in 1966.

At this point another technical problem rears its head. We are interested in the values of A and b, yet must estimate $\tilde{A}$ and $\tilde{b}$. Thus, our estimation procedure must take account of the log transformation of $\tilde{A}$ to A.

Again, maximum likelihood estimation provides a reasonable estimation procedure. If a stochastic disturbance term ε is added to the right hand side of equation (28), the equation takes the form of the classical linear regression model. Furthermore, if we assume ε is distributed $N(0, \sigma^2)$ the likelihood function is exactly the same as the one used to estimate the structural form model of the labor turnover process; however, in this example the appropriate substitution is $\varepsilon = X - \tilde{A} X_0 - \tilde{b}$. In the earlier example we simply stated that the more convenient functional form for determining the maximum likelihood estimates was the log-likelihood function, L^* $= \ln L$. This transformation is possible because the estimates that maximize L^* also maximize L. If $\hat{\theta}$ is the solution to $\partial L/\partial \theta = 0$, then the solution to $\partial \ln L/\partial \theta = 0$ is also $\hat{\theta}$ because

$$\partial \ln L/\partial \theta = 1/L \cdot \partial L/\partial \theta \qquad \text{for } L > 0 \text{ [8]}$$

It should be noted that this property of maximum likelihood estimation is precisely the property we desire. Thus, maximum likelihood estimates for our observation model are also maximum likelihood estimates of the process model.

The log-likelihood function of our model is

$$\ln L = -N/2 \ln(2\pi\sigma^2) - (2\sigma^2)^{-1}\varepsilon'\varepsilon \qquad (30)$$

It can be seen that maximizing this function with respect to $\tilde{A}$ and $\tilde{b}$ is equivalent to minimizing $\varepsilon'\varepsilon$ with respect to the same parameters. But for this model, minimizing $\varepsilon'\varepsilon$ is equivalent to ordinary least squares estimation of $\tilde{A}$ and $\tilde{b}$.[9]

The actual estimates obtained by this procedure are given by Hummon and others (1975) and need not be repeated here. However, two points can be made in this context. First, examination of the eigenvalues of the estimated matrix A showed all eigenvalues to be distinct, real and negative. That the eigenvalues were real means

---

[8] It is realized that second order conditions also exist for $\hat{\theta}$ to be the maximum solution, but they will not be discussed here. See Kendall and Stuart, 1973, Chapter 18.

[9] More specifically, joint generalized least squares as discussed by Theil (1971, Chapter 7) is appropriate. There may well be other empirical problems to be considered. Organizational data tend to exhibit skewed distributions; and in the empirical example referred to, careful attention had been given to the problem of outliers.

that the principal branch solution to $\ln\tilde{A}$ is indeed appropriate. Their negative values indicate that the process is one leading to a stable equilibrium.

The second general observation concerns strategies for evaluating the differential consequences, or importance, of the endogenous variables in the system. This was done by means of examining the propagated effects of changes of any given variable. The system being studied is one that is richly interconnected, and the impact of changes needs to be examined throughout the entire system, taking into account direct and indirect effects as well as feedback loops. By examining how standardized changes in each of the variables impact upon all of the other variables in the system, the set of major mechanisms of structural change that are shown in Figure 2 were inferred. Details of this are given by Hummon and

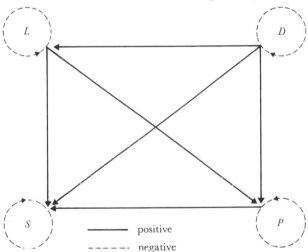

Figure 2. Major Mechanisms of Structural Change for Organizations.

others (1975) together with a discussion relating work to the propositions of Blau (1970) concerning structural change in organizations.

A NON-HOMOGENOUS MODEL WITH EXOGENOUS INPUT

Our final empirical example features a model constructed to account for the through-time variation in the public support for parliamentary parties in Great Britain, and requires genuine time series data. The exogenous variables for this particular model are made up of economic performance measures and measures of political cycles. The endogenous variables are measures of support for the Government, the Opposition, and the Liberal parties. A fuller discussion of the kinds of variables used in this area of study can be found in Goodhart and Bhanhali (1970) or Miller and Mackie (1973), and a more extended discussion of the model itself can be found in Doreian and Hummon (1976).

We assume there are two distributions and that, further, we need to link them together. Let $X^* = (X_1^*, X_2^*, X_3^*)$ be the latent underlying distribution of support for each party.[10] This distribution may or may not be reflected (or revealed) at any particular point in time. Let $X = (X_1, X_2, X_3)$ be the publicly declared support for the Government, Opposition, and Liberal parties (respectively) that can be either an electoral outcome or the result of a particular poll. There is no inherent reason for X^* to equal X, especially in the light of short run economic and political cycle arguments. At the same time, X is not likely to be markedly different from X^* — and will indeed equilibrate about X^*, which, in turn, can vary through time. Let ΔX denote the change in X in an increment of time Δt, then the basic equilibrating mechanism can be written as

$$\Delta X_i = c_i \Delta t (X_i^* - X_i), \qquad c_i \geqq 0 \qquad (31)$$

Included in the X^* distribution are both the hard core supporters and those less committed. Shifts do occur in the X distribution, but it is highly unlikely that the hard core supporters shift in their allegiance. The higher X_i gets for the government, say, or for a particular party, the less likely it is that X_i will increase. Equation (25) reflects this: if the c_i are positive, the greater the discrepancy between X_i and X_i^*, the more marked the tendency for X_i to move back to X_i^*. The higher the value of the parameter c_i, the quicker the response of the corresponding variable to a discrepancy between the two distributions. When $X_i > X_i^*$, the rate at which increases in support occur would be expected to be negative. The reverse argument occurs when the declared support for a party is

[10] The following discussion is couched in terms of a three party model as the data base to be employed subsequently does refer to Great Britian, but it does generalize readily to an n party model.

very low—and well below the underlying distribution figure. The rate at which support is lost is diminishing. At the same time, however, X^* is not fixed. Further, if the X distribution moves away from the X^* distribution and stays there, then we no longer can talk plausibly about the old X^* as the underlying distribution. X^* will have changed, and this change can be due to the operation of a slow changing variable (for example, demographic structure).

We consider now the determinants of the X^* distribution. Let Z_j denote the set of economic variables and political variables that determine government popularity. We shall assume that the level of support in the X^* distribution is, for a particular party, determined partially by the declared level for the other parties in the system and by the exogenous variables Z_j that are included in the analysis. This would lead us to specify the following equations:

$$X_1^* = a_{12}^* X_2 + a_{13} X_3 + \sum_{j=1}^{k} b_{1j}^* Z_j + b_{10}^*$$

$$X_2^* = a_{21}^* X_1 + a_{23}^* X_3 + \sum_{j=1}^{k} b_{2J} Z_j + b_{20}^* \qquad (32)$$

$$X_3^* = a_{31}^* X_1 + a_{32}^* X_2 + \sum_{j=1}^{k} b_{3j} Z_j + b_{30}^*$$

Here b_{i0}^* denotes the mean effect of omitted variables. If equations (32) are substituted into equation (31), we have, on dividing by Δt,

$$\Delta X_1/\Delta t = -c_1 X_1 + c_1 a_{12}^* X_2 + c_2 a_{13}^* X_3$$
$$+ \sum_{j=1}^{k} c_1 b_{1j} Z_j + c_1 b_{10}^*$$
$$\Delta X_2/\Delta t = c_2 a_{21}^* X_1 - c_2 X_2 + c_2 a_{23}^* X_3 \qquad (33)$$
$$+ \sum_{j=1}^{k} c_2 b_{2j}^* Z_j + c_2 b_{20}^*$$
$$\Delta X_3/\Delta t = c_3 a_{31}^* X_1 + c_3 a_{32}^* X_2 - c_3 X_3$$
$$+ \sum_{j=1}^{k} c_3 b_{3j}^* Z_j + c_3 b_{30}^*$$

Letting $\Delta t \to 0$, we obtain the differential equation system

$$\dot{X}_1 = -c_1 X_1 + a_{12} X_2 + a_{13} X_3 + \sum_{j=0}^{k} b_{1j} Z_j$$
$$\dot{X}_2 = a_{21} X_1 - c_2 X_2 + a_{23} X_3 + \sum_{j=0}^{k} b_{2j} Z_j \qquad (34)$$
$$\dot{X}_3 = a_{31} X_1 + a_{32} X_2 - c_3 X_3 + \sum_{j=0}^{k} b_{3j} Z_j$$

where

$$a_{ij} = c_i a_{ij}^*(i \neq j) \quad \text{and} \; b_{ij} = c_i b_{ij}^*$$

Also, we have defined a column of Z as a column of 1's, and incorporated the constant terms into the corresponding summations. Finally, if we write

$$Z(t) = [Z_0(t) = 1, Z_1(t), ..., Z_k(t)]'$$

and define

$$A = \begin{bmatrix} -c_1 & a_{12} & a_{13} \\ a_{21} & -c_2 & a_{23} \\ a_{31} & a_{32} & -c_3 \end{bmatrix}$$

then equation (34) can be written as

$$\dot{X}(t) = AX(t) + BZ(t) \tag{35}$$

Equation (35) is the basic state space linear differential equation representation of the model.

Again, once we have estimates of the matrices A and B we are in a position to interpret the dynamic behavior of the system. The next issue, then, is to determine how we estimate these matrices. The data are in the form of monthly observations on each of the endogenous and exogenous variables. This turns out to be precisely what control engineers refer to as "conventional sampling," if we think of the samples being drawn at regular intervals from a time function of each of the variables. In particular, we are concerned with the exogenous variables being represented as sampled input. Consider one exogenous variable, say $Z_j(t)$, as a function of time. Such a function is represented in Figure 3, where the samples are taken at equally spaced points in time, $T, 2T, 3T, \ldots$.

The dotted line represents the function being sampled, and the horizontal bars the sampled values. The sampling function, denoted here as $Z_{js}(t)$, is constant between the sampling times. More precisely, $Z_{js}(t)$ is piecewise constant with points of discontinuity at sampling times

$$Z_{js}(t) = Z_j(nT)$$

$$nT \leqq t < (n+1)T \qquad n = 0, 1, 2, \ldots \qquad 1 \leqq j \leqq k$$

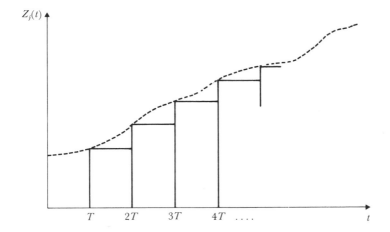

Figure 3. A Time Sampled Function.

In the model, $Z_{js}(t)$ is regarded as a sampled *input* to the system. In vector notation, let $Z_s(t)$ be the sampled inputs given by

$$Z_s(t) = Z(nT)$$

$$nT \leqq t < (n + 1)T \qquad n = 0, 1, 2, ...$$

where the subscript s denotes the sample value.

In order to obtain a tractable estimation form for the model contained in equation (35), define $t' = t - nT$. Then the model becomes

$$\dot{X}(t') = AX(t') + BZ_{s0} \tag{36}$$

where Z_s is constant (taking the value Z_{s0}) over the interval $(0, T)$ defined in terms of t', or over the interval $(nT, \overline{n + 1} \, T)$ defined in terms of t. Let $e^{-At'}$ be an integrating factor. Then

$$e^{-At'} X(t') - e^{-At'} AX(t') = e^{-At'} BZ_{s0}$$

Equivalently,

$$d/dt' [e^{-At'} X(t')] = e^{-At'} BZ_{s0}$$

Integrating yields

$$e^{At'} X(t') \Big|_0^T = \left[\int_0^T e^{-At'} dt' \right] BZ_{s0}$$

Or,

$$e^{-AT}X(T) - X(0) = A^{-1}e^{-At'}\Big|_0^T BZ_{s0}$$

or,

$$e^{-At}X(T) = X(0) - [A^{-1} - A^{-1}e^{-AT}]BZ_{s0}$$

Rearranging this equation yields

$$X(T) = e^{AT}X(0) + A^{-1}[e^{AT} - I]BZ_{s0}$$

In terms of the original time parameterization,

$$X(\overline{n+1}\,T) = e^{AT}X(nT) + A^{-1}[e^{AT} - I]BZ_s(nT) \qquad (37)$$

which is the basic estimating equation for the model given in equation (35).

If the observations are spaced regularly in time, then, without loss of generality, T can be taken to be unity. If $\Phi = e^A$ and $D = A^{-1}[e^A - I]B$, then the estimating equation can be written as

$$X(\overline{n+1}\,T) = \Phi(nT) + DZ(nT) \qquad (38)$$

and the empirical procedure would be to estimate Φ and D, then work back to estimates of A and B. Let $\hat{e}^A$ be the estimate of e^A, and $\hat{\lambda}_i$ be the eigenvalues of this estimated matrix. Then, as before, assuming the λ_i are distinct and real and taking the principle branch of the log function

$$\hat{A} = V \begin{bmatrix} & & 0 \\ & \ln(\hat{\lambda}_i) & \\ 0 & & \end{bmatrix} V^{-1} \qquad (39)$$

where V is the matrix of eigenvectors of $\hat{e}^A$. Further, if $\hat{D}$ is the matrix of estimated coefficients of D from equation (38), then the estimating equation for B is given by

$$\hat{B} = (\hat{e}^A - I)^{-1}\hat{A}\hat{B} \qquad (40)$$

Estimating equation (38) presents some of the same problems we faced in the organizational model; maximum likelihood estimates are desired because we are interested in the parameters of the process model. However, we are fitting the observation model to time series data, and that can create additional problems. Each of the individual equations in (38) is of a form having a lagged endogenous variable. This type of equation usually requires specifying a disturbance term that is auto-correlated. Thus, we require an estimation procedure that is maximum likelihood and accounts for a lagged endogenous variable and an auto-correlated disturbance term.

In order to discuss an estimation procedure in this context, we change our notation to one that is more in accord with econometric conventions. If we focus on the equation for X_1, then we can denote $y_t = X_{1t}$. Then if $W_t = [X_{2t}, X_{3t}, Z_{jt}]$, and Γ denotes the vector of the corresponding coefficients, the first equation can be written

$$y_{t+1} = \beta y_t + W_t \Gamma + \varepsilon_{t+1} \tag{41}$$

where ε_t is the disturbance term. We explore the proposed estimation procedure for an $AR(1)$ process specified by

$$\varepsilon_{t+1} = \rho \varepsilon_t + U_{t+1} \tag{42}$$

where U_t is a white noise term, and ρ is the auto-regressive parameter. Suppose now that equation (41) is lagged through one time period, multiplied by ρ and the resulting equation subtracted from equation (41). This yields

$$y_{t+1} - \rho y_t$$
$$= \beta y_t - \rho \beta y_{t-1} + W_t \Gamma - \rho W_{t-1} \Gamma + (\varepsilon_{t+1} - \rho \varepsilon_t)$$

On rearranging we have

$$y_{t+1} = (\rho + \beta) y_t + \rho \beta y_{t-1}$$
$$= (W_t - \rho W_{t-1}) \Gamma + U_{t+1} \tag{43}$$

If we define

$$y^*_{t+1} = y_{t+1} - (\rho + \beta) y_t + \rho \beta y_{t-1}$$

and

$$W^*_t = W_t - \rho W_{t-1}$$

then equation (37) can be written

$$y^*_{t+1} = W^*_t \Gamma + U_{t+1} \qquad (44)$$

If we now specify that the white noise disturbance term is distributed $N(0, \sigma^2)$, we can use the same likelihood function we have previously.

$$L^* = -n\ln(2\pi\sigma^2)/2 - (2\sigma^2)^{-1}U'U$$

where, dropping the time subscripts,

$$U'U = (y^* - W^*\Gamma)'(y^* - W^*\Gamma)$$

After simplification, the solution equations become

$$\partial U'U/\partial\rho = 0$$

$$\partial U'U/\partial\beta = 0$$

$$\partial U'U/\partial\Gamma = 0$$

and

$$\partial U'U/\partial(\sigma^2) = -n/2\sigma^2 + U'U/2\sigma^4 = 0$$

An analytic solution to the above implied equations is not readily apparent because one must solve a system of nonlinear matrix equations. However, we would again point out that finding the parameter values that maximize L^* is equivalent to finding the $\hat{\rho}$, $\hat{b}$, and $\hat{\Gamma}$ that minimize $U'U$. This is a task which can be accomplished numerically. We used a two-stage iterative procedure. First, for fixed ρ and β, compute $\Gamma = (W^{*'}W^*)^{-1}W^{*'}y^*$ and then compute $U'U$. Second, increment either ρ or β in some systematic manner and repeat the first stage.

In the empirical example reported by Doreian and Hummon (1976) the popularity model was estimated for two distinct time periods, and it turned out that for only one of the periods the value of ρ was zero. The model is estimable, however, irrespective of the value of ρ (whose absolute value has to be less than unity).

All of the estimation results, and substantive interpretation of those results, are provided in the source reference (Doreian and Hummon, 1976), and need not be repeated here. However, some of the results will be given in order to illustrate the approach and to focus on certain further potential estimation difficulties. While the time series was for the period between the late 1940s through the early 1970s, we chose to estimate the model separately in two time periods—as both the academic and journalistic writings suggested that the 1950s and the 1960s were different. The dividing point was the general election of 1959; and, in this chapter, we focus only on the second time period (where the fit was superior).

The summary measures are given in Table 1.

TABLE 1

Summary of Results for Estimation Form

Education	$U'U$	ρ	R^2
Government	833.4	−0.30	0.80
Opposition	620.0	−0.30	0.57
Liberal	293.7	−0.15	0.80

As a further check on the adequacy of the fit and the procedure, we took the final estimates of A and B (together with the data for only the first time period) and used the recursive estimating form to "simulate" the entire time series. The results of this are shown in Figure 4, together with the original time series. The fit appears to be, and is, a good one.

Estimates of the matrix A are given in Table 2. The diagonal elements of this matrix are estimates of sensitivity parameters c_i.

TABLE 2

Estimates of A

	Government (G)	Opposition (O)	Liberal (L)
$\dot{G}$	−0.57	−0.40	−0.07
$\dot{O}$	−0.32	−0.76	−0.32
$\dot{L}$	0.15	0.04	−0.42

Eigenvalues of A : −0.23, −0.95, −0.57

These indicate that the response mechanism operates most rapidly for the Opposition and least rapidly for the Liberal (third) Party. Given the form of the equation, these sensitivity parameters (without the minus sign) can be interpreted as the reciprocal of what Box and Jenkins (1970, p. 341) refer to as the time constants of such a system. They advise that when a choice is available, samples should

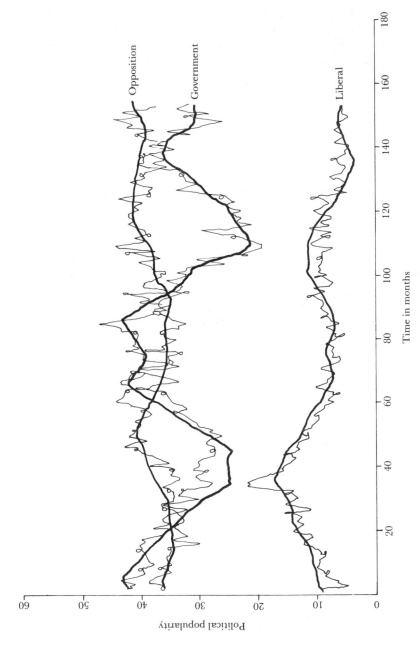

Figure 4. Empirical and Simulated Trajectories.

be taken more frequently than the values that would be anticipated for the time constants. In this case we had no choice, given the nature of the data base,[11] but we can note that the sampling would have been more frequent than the values of the time constants actually obtained.[12]

Another potential problem with this approach to estimation that could be raised is that of aliasing.[13] Strictly speaking, this applies to the situation of estimating the spectral density of a function in the frequency domain — which is not being considered in this chapter. It arises as a problem where the continuous data are periodic and are being sampled at regular intervals. If the sampling interval is, say, T, then no information can be obtained from frequencies higher than those with a period $2T$ corresponding to a frequency $w_{max} = \pi/T$. The problem is illustrated in Figure 5, which has been adopted from Himmelblau's (1970) treatment.

The two functions $f(t)$ and $g(t)$ are shown, and each is sampled with the same interval. The sampling frequency for $f(t)$ is well below w_{max}, and the form of the sampled function (shown on the right of Figure 5) approximates $f(t)$. For the function $g(t)$, however, the sampling frequency is higher than w_{max}, and the

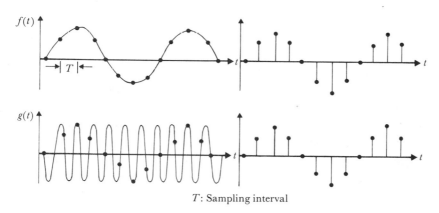

T: Sampling interval

Figure 5. An Example of Aliasing (adapted from Himmelblau).

---

[11] While data on the popularity variables were available more frequently, data on key economic indicators were published monthly.

[12] In the first time period, one sensitivity parameter was very close to -1, implying a time constant not much greater than 1.

[13] Indeed, one reviewer did raise this as a problem.

sampled function appears to be that of $f(t)$. The higher frequencies are "folded" back into lower frequencies when aliasing occurs. When the through-time variation of the endogenous variables of our example are examined, they are not periodic in the short term; and where long run periodicities can be discerned, the sampling frequency is well above that usually recommended (which is five to ten times the highest frequency of interest). In this context, aliasing is not likely to be a problem.

Once estimates of A and B have been obtained, then limited predictions for given mixes of the exogenous variables can be made by means of equation (38). This was done in generating the time series shown in Figure 4. It is also possible to engage in a kind of equilibrium analysis in order to examine the relative importance, or political salience, of various measures of economic performance with respect to political popularity. If equilibrium were assumed, that is, $\dot{X} = 0$, then

$$X_{\text{equil}} = -A^{-1}BZ_{\text{const}} \tag{45}$$

which is an equation transforming some fixed exogenous input Z_{const} into an equilibrium distribution of support X_{equil}. By taking the mean value of the exogenous variables, a base line distribution can be established against which the propagated effects of standardized changes of each exogenous variable, or any combination of standardized changes, can be compared. The five exogenous variables considered in the original analysis (Doreian and Hummon, 1976) were (i) a measure of the political cycle, (ii) the bank rate, (iii) the balance of payments, (iv) unemployment, and (v) a measure of price changes relative to wage changes. By examining the changes in government lead due to standardized changes in these exogenous variables, it was possible to infer the rank order of importance, or political salience, of these exogenous variables. These are shown in Table 3. Examination of the columns shows the similarities and differences between the two periods. This summary discussion does, however, mask the fact that during the 1960s the political salience of each of the economic indicators was higher than during the 1950s.

In this presentation, most of the detailed comparison of the empirical results has been omitted, and the interested reader is refered to the source reference. The point to be stressed is that a general dynamic model in the form of a non-homogenous linear differential equation system with exogenous input can be formulated, empirically estimated, and interpreted.

TABLE 3

Rank Order of Political Salience

Exogenous Variables	1950s	1960s
Price	2	4
Unemployment	4	2
Balance of payments	3	3
Bank rate	5	5
Political cycle	1	1

SUMMARY AND EXTENSION OF RESULTS

We have presented three examples that use differential equation system models to understand social processes. Each involved a different combination of mathematical form (homogenous, non-homogenous with exogenous input constant, and non-homogenous with exogenous time varying input—respectively) and observation form (phase space, panel series, and time series, respectively). All the models were substantively constructed and interpreted using the concept of structural control, and all the models were estimated by maximum likelihood methods. We can comment on these differences and commonalities and, thereby, extend some of our results.

First, it should be obvious that construction of a model depends on the substantive properties of the social process. Others may not find structural control an interesting or even applicable concept.

Second, the "labor turnover-phase space" model illustrates the importance of examining multiple time point data using a scatter plot. The unusual, but distinctive, patterns typical of dynamic equilibria might be missed if this is not done. Furthermore, estimation in phase space is often simpler than in the time series because non-linearities are less likely. We recognize, however, that the possibility of constructing a phase space model is small; seldom do the observations describe an ellipse, or circle, or figure eight, and so on. We turn now to the more likely cases.

In their most general solution form, the class of models we have been considering can be written

$$X(t) = e^{\int A dt}c + e^{\int A dt}\int e^{-\int A dt}BZ(t)dt \tag{46}$$

where c is the vector of initial conditions. If we now define $t_1 = t_0 + \Delta t$ and evaluate the integrals on the interval t_0 to t_1 then

$$X(t_1) = e^{A(t_1 - t_0)}c + e^{A(t_1 - t_0)}\int_{t_0}^{t_1} e^{-A\tau}BZ(\tau)d\tau \tag{47}$$

If $t_1 \to t_0$; $X(t_0) = c$, and by substitution for any $t = t_0$

$$X(t + \Delta t) = e^{A\Delta t}X(t) + e^{A\Delta t}\int_{t}^{t+\Delta t} e^{-A\tau}BZ(\tau)d\tau \tag{48}$$

Equation (48) characterizes the class of models we are interested in. Applied to panel observations, Δt describes the time between any pair of panels. If more than two panels are available; projection of interpolation to the unused panel(s) can be used to test invariant structure, or the model could be estimated on successive pairs of panels to study *changes in structure*. Applied to time series data, with observations made Δt apart, the model becomes a recursive time series model.

The three mathematical forms mentioned earlier (homogenous, non-homogenous with exogenous constant, and non-homogenous with exogenous time functions) depend on B or $Z(t)$. If B or $Z(t)$ equals zero, equation (48) becomes the homogenous model of the labor turnover example. If $Z(t)$ is a constant vector, then $B \cdot Z = b$, and the model simplifies to a form like the organizational example. The third model, with $Z(t)$ neither zero nor constant, requires either specification of the functional form of $Z(t)$ or a strategy like time sampling that was used in the government popularity example. It should be noted, however, that even if the functional form of $Z(t)$ is known, estimation may be problematic. For example, if $BZ(t) = e^{Kt}$, then we have an exponential forcing function

$$\begin{aligned} X(t + \Delta t) = {}& e^{A\Delta t}X(t) \\ & + e^{A\Delta t}(-A + K)^{-1}[e^{(-A+K)\Delta t} - I]e^{(-A+K)t} \end{aligned} \tag{49}$$

Equation (49) is linear in X, but non-linear in t, with the term $e^{(-A+K)t}$ causing the difficulty. Further, the difficulty remains if K is known. Thus, practical limits do exist for this third model.

In conclusion, we have discussed how differential equation system models can be estimated on either panel or time series data sets. We stressed the importance of maximum likelihood estimation methods and, also, indicated the condition under which the required mathematical transformations hold, for example, taking the log of a matrix. Finally, we hope we have indicated the analytic power of these models for unraveling the complexity of social processes.

REFERENCES

BLAU, P. M.

    1970   "A Formal Theory of Differentiation in Organizations." *American Sociological Review* 35:201–218.

BOX, G. E. P., AND JENKINS, G. M.

    1970   *Time Series Analysis: Forecasting and Control.* San Francisco: Holden-Day.

BREE, D. S.

    1971   "Causal Relationships with Two Variables in Dynamic Equilibrium: Labour Turnover and Overtime." *Journal of Management Studies* 8:13–25.

COLEMAN, J. S.

    1968   "The Mathematical Study of Change." In H. M. Blalock and A. B. Blalock (Eds.), *Methodology in Social Research.* New York: McGraw-Hill.

DOREIAN, P., AND HUMMON, N. P.

    1976   *Modeling Social Processes.* Amsterdam: Elsevier.

GOLDBERGER, A. S.

    1964   *Economic Theory.* New York: Wiley.

GOODHART, C. A. E., AND BHANHALI, R. J.

    1970   "Political Economy." *Political Studies* 18:43–106.

GOWLER, D.

    1969   "Determinants of the Supply of Labor to the Firm." *Journal of Management Studies* 6:73–95.

HIBBS, D.

    1974   "Problems of Statistical Estimation and Causal Inference in Time Series Regression Models," *Sociological Methodology 1974.* San Francisco: Jossey-Bass.

HIMMELBLAU, D. M.
  1970   *Process Analysis by Statistical Methods.* New York: Wiley.

HUMMON, N. P., DOREIAN, P., AND TEUTER, K.
  1975   "A Structural Control Model of Organizational Change."
         American Sociological Review 40:813–824.

KENDALL, M. G., AND STUART, A.
  1973   *The Advanced Theory of Statistics: Vol 2.* 3rd ed. London: Hafner.

LAND, K.
  1970   "Mathematical Formalization of Durkheim's Theory of Divi-
         sion of Labor." *Sociological Methodology 1970.* San Francisco:
         Jossey-Bass.

MEYER, M. W.
  1972   *Bureaucratic Structure and Authority: Coordination and Control in 254
         Government Agencies.* New York: Harper & Row.

MILLER, W. L., AND MACKIE, M.
  1973   "The Electoral Cycle and the Asymmetry of Government and
         Opposition Popularity: An Alternative Model of the Rela-
         tionship between Economic Conditions and Political Popular-
         ity." *Political Studies* 21:263–279.

PLATT, O.
  1971   *Ordinary Differential Equations.* San Francisco: Holden-Day.

REKTORYS, K.
  1969   *Survey of Applicable Mathematics.* Cambridge, Mass.: MIT Press.

SIMON, H. A.
  1957   *Models of Man.* New York: Wiley.

SINGER, B., AND SPILERMAN, S.
  1974   "Social Mobility Models for Heterogenous Populations."
         Sociological Methodology 1974. San Francisco: Jossey-Bass.

  1976   "The Representation of Social Processes by Markov Models."
         American Journal of Sociology.

THEIL, H.
  1971   *Principles of Econometrics.* New York: Wiley.

Received May 15, 1975.

﹌6﹌

ESTIMATING RATES FROM RETROSPECTIVE QUESTIONS

Aage B. Sørensen

UNIVERSITY OF WISCONSIN

INTRODUCTION

In certain areas of sociological research, variables that measure the rate at which persons carry out a certain act are of central importance. This is the case in the analysis of social and geographical mobility and in the analysis of population processes. In most areas of sociology, rate variables are less frequently used. Variables that are measures of attitudes are generally preferred to variables

I am indebted to Frank Montfort and Rachel Rosenfeld for their assistance and to James Coleman and Paul Allison for helpful suggestions and discussion. Computer facilities were provided by the Center for Demography and Ecology, University of Wisconsin-Madison under a grant from the National Institute of Child Health and Human Development.

that are direct measures of overt behavior. Still, direct measures of the rate at which a person exhibits some behavior would, in many instances, be preferable. Further, variables expressing rates are in general attractive because they are not plagued by the metric problems many attitudinal measures raise.

Rate variables are usually derived from counts of events or acts over a period of time. Such counts demand detailed over-time information—not only for observations at discrete intervals of time, as in the panel design preferred by sociologists for obtaining over-time data. Obtaining retrospective information appears, in many instances, to be the only way to obtain the needed counts. With events that are infrequent—or where the occurrence of an event is easily distorted, so that only counts over short intervals of time are possible—retrospective information on counts would however seem to be of dubious reliability.

This chapter will show that it is, nevertheless, possible to get estimates of rates from even very rudimentary over-time information that is obtained retrospectively. In fact, given certain assumptions about the process, it is possible to obtain an estimate knowing only the time interval between the last event or act before the interview and the interview itself. The paper will demonstrate this for the case where events occur according to a Poisson process, that is, for events that occur randomly in time at a constant rate or intensity. However, using retrospective information on time intervals between events to estimate rates at which events occur will, further, be shown to produce an apparent paradox. The paradox is that the "interruption" of the process that takes place when the retrospective information is gathered in an interview will affect the distribution of events. The major part of this chapter will be devoted to describing this result and its implications.

When events occur according to a Poisson process, the inverse of the mean interval of time between events will estimate the intensity of events. This provides the motivation for using reports on duration between events, rather than counts of events, to estimate rates—in particular, the censored interval from last event to the interview may be used. This is useful in situations where events are rare and retrospective information has to be relied on. However, Feller (1971) has shown that the interruption of a stochastic process (in the context of this paper, "caused" by the interview) will tend to select a long rather than a short interval among the randomly distributed intervals between events. This has important implications for how retrospective information may be used to estimate time intervals between events and the rates at which events occur.

Feller gives a general formulation of the phenomenon produced by the interruption of a stochastic process (1971, p. 326) and a specific illustration with the "waiting for the bus" paradox (1971, p. 11). A justification of the result in terms of Baysian probabilities is given by Morrison (1973), who also mentions the relevance of the phenomena to the analysis of recall data from surveys. Finally, Cox and Lewis (1966) give a treatment of the problem for renewal processes.

The main result does not seem well-known among sociologists, even though retrospective information is increasingly often being gathered—most elaborately in life-history studies, but also for events occurring between waves in a panel, and in cross-sectional surveys. This provides the motivation for restating the main result here. The results obtained in the technical literature mentioned above are, however, restricted to the long-run behavior of processes. This paper will further extend the results to the situation where the process is interrupted shortly after its start, that is, when a proportion of respondents will answer "never" to a question about when an event of a certain kind last occurred.

The main restriction of the results to be presented is the reliance on the Poisson process. It may seem too simple for most social processes. It is well-known, however, that sources of failure of this process are variations in intensity of events among persons in a sample (or heterogeneity) and time dependence in the rate (or nonstationarity). Both problems may be abetted by obtaining separate estimates for homogeneous subgroups of the sample and/or for different periods. The techniques described here should be useful for such purposes as the use of intervals between events is an efficient way of utilizing over-time information. Further, in connection with the empirical example brought in at the end of the chapter, it will be shown that a simple modification of the Poisson model will enable adequate description of an important type of nonstationarity: time dependence due to aging. Finally, as a point of departure in the absence of any a priori knowledge about a process, the Poisson process is an attractive choice because of its simplicity.

The problems discussed in this paper should be taken into account before modifications of the simple Poisson process are attempted. Otherwise, the Poisson process may be rejected in situations where its apparent failure is due to the phenomena to be described here.

THE POISSON PROCESS

If a social process can be described by a Poisson process, then events should occur randomly with a constant intensity α. This means that the probability that an event will occur is the same in any small interval of time dt and equal to αdt. In particular, this assumption implies that the occurrence of an event has no effect on the probability that another event occurs; that is, the process lacks memory.

Well-known properties of the Poisson process may be utilized to obtain estimates of α or the rate at which events occur. When counts of events are available, one may use the property that the number of events in a time period t will be Poisson distributed or—if r denotes the number of events:

$$p(r) = e^{-\alpha t}(\alpha t)^r/r! \tag{1}$$

The mean of the distribution is αt, and by knowing the number of events in a period we may use this property to estimate the intensity or rate of events α. However, when dealing with a retrospective question, one may only know the duration since the last event before the interview. It is, therefore, necessary to focus on the distribution of intervals between events, rather than events. Let X_i be the time interval from the occurrence of an event to the next event. The distribution function for this random variable is

$$P(X_i \leqq t) = 1 - e^{-\alpha t} \tag{2}$$

This is the exponential distribution, and by differentiation its density is obtained as

$$f(x) = \alpha e^{-\alpha x} \tag{3}$$

The mean of X_i or the mean duration between events will be

$$E(X_i) = \int_0^\infty \alpha x e^{-\alpha x} = \frac{1}{\alpha} \tag{4}$$

Hence, the mean duration between events is the inverse of the intensity or rate. This means that rather than counting the frequency of events in a period t, we may estimate α as the inverse of the mean duration between events.

The first part of this chapter will consider the situation where information is available not on the interval of time between events in general, but only on the interval between the last event before an interview (or other interruption) and the interview. Denote this time interval X_w. Suppose the interview takes place at time t, and the last event before the interview takes place at time $y < t$. The lack of memory of the Poisson process may seem to imply that X_w is distributed as any other interval X_i with mean α^{-1}. It will be demonstrated that this is, in fact, the case, with some modifications. But, consider now the interval from the interview until the first event after the interview. Suppose this event takes place at time $z > t$. The length of the interval from t to z will be a random variable X_v, and its distribution, because of the lack of memory of the Poisson process, will again be exponential. Hence, X_v will also have the mean α^{-1}. But, consider now the interval X_t between the events happening at y and at z. The interview presumably occurs independently of the process. Hence, X_t should also be exponentially distributed with mean α^{-1}. But $X_t = X_w + X_v$, hence we have a contradiction: if the mean of X_w and the mean of X_v both are α^{-1}, it cannot be the case that the mean of the interval X_t also is α^{-1}.

The contradiction means that something is wrong in our argument. The error is the assumption that X_t is exponentially distributed. It is not, even when all the other intervals X_i's are assumed to be identically and independently exponentially distributed. The proof of this apparent paradox by Feller shall now be presented, and subsequently the distribution of the intervals X_w and X_v will be derived.

THE WAITING TIME PARADOX

Assume that the interview takes place at time $t > 0$, where 0 is the origin of the process. Suppose the last event before the interview takes place at time y. The next event after the interview will take place at time $y + X_t$, where $X_t = X_w + X_v$, that is, the sum of the interval of y until t and the interval from interview until the first event after it, denoted X_v.

Denote further by $X_1, X_2, \ldots X_n$ the intervals from the origin to the first event, from the first event to the second, and so forth up to the nth event. The intervals are assumed mutually independent and identically distributed according to Equation (2). The sum of these intervals $X_1 + X_2 + X_3 \cdots + X_n$ will be the time at which the nth event occurred. The probability that this event takes place at time y has the sensity (cf., Feller, 1971, p. 11):

$$g_n(y) = (\alpha(\alpha y)^{n-1}/(n-1)!)e^{-\alpha y} \tag{5}$$

The density $g_n(y)$ is a gamma density. It reduces to (3) when $n = 1$, and represents the density of the distribution of a sum of exponentially distributed variables. We will need this quantity shortly.

Consider now the probability $P(X_t < x)$, where x is an arbitrary number, so that $0 < x < \infty$. It is necessary to consider two situations: the case where $x \leqq t$, and the case where $x > t$. The distinction is necessary because if $x \leqq t$, then an event must have happened in the period 0 to t; but if $x > t$, then the first event of the process may have happened after t.

If $x < t$ then the situation $X_t < x$ will happen if and only if the nth event ($n = 1, 2, \ldots \infty$) at time y *and* the interval between this event and the next is greater than $t - y$, or $t - y < X_{n+1} \leqq x$. The density of the probability of the nth event occurring at y is given by (5). The probability that $t - y < X_{n+1} \leqq x$ is given by the exponential distribution function as

$$P(t - y < X_{n+1} \leqq x) = P(X_{n+1} \leqq x) - P(X_{n+1} \leqq t - y)$$
$$= 1 - e^{-\alpha x} - 1 - e^{-\alpha(t-y)} \tag{6}$$
$$= e^{-\alpha(t-y)} - e^{-\alpha x}$$

The condition $t - y < X_{n+1} \leqq x$ implies that $t - x \leqq y \leqq t$, which then is the range of variation for y. Summing over all possible n's and y's we obtain

$$P(X_t \leqq x) = \sum_{n=1}^{\infty} \int_{t-x}^{t} g_n(y) \cdot P(t - y < X_{n+1} \leqq x)dy$$

$$= \sum_{n=1}^{\infty} \int_{t-x}^{t} \alpha \frac{(\alpha y)^{n-1}}{(n-1)!} e^{-\alpha y} [e^{-\alpha(t-y)} - e^{-\alpha x}] dy \qquad (7)$$

$$x \leqq t$$

However, the sum of $g_n(y)$ for all the values of n is

$$\sum \alpha \frac{(\alpha y)^{n-1}}{(n-1)!} e^{-\alpha y} = \alpha \cdot e^{\alpha y} \cdot e^{-\alpha y} = \alpha \qquad (8)$$

Hence,

$$P(X_t \leqq x) = \alpha \int_{t-x}^{t} [e^{-\alpha(t-y)} - e^{-\alpha x}] \qquad (9)$$

$$= 1 - e^{-\alpha x} - \alpha x e^{-\alpha x} \qquad x \leqq t$$

This is the desired distribution function for $x < t$. By differentiation we obtain its density as

$$f(x) = \alpha^2 x e^{-\alpha x} \qquad x \leqq t \qquad (10)$$

The derivation of $P(X_t < x)$ for $x > t$ follows the same line of reasoning. However, $x > t$ implies that the range of variation for y is $0 \leqq y < t$, since no event may have happened before t. If no event occurs before t we count the interval from 0 to the occurrence of the first event as the interval of interest. The probability of interest $P(X_t < x)$ is the outcome either of the nth event occurring at time y and X_{n+1} being greater than $t - y$, or of the interval until the first event being greater than t and less than x. Hence

$$P(X_t \leqq x) = \sum_{n=1}^{\infty} \int_{0}^{t} g_n(y) \cdot P(t - y < X_{n+1} \leqq x)$$

$$+ P(t < X_1 \leqq x) \qquad (11)$$

$$= 1 - e^{-\alpha t} - \alpha t e^{-\alpha x} + e^{-\alpha t} - e^{-\alpha x}$$

$$= 1 - \alpha t e^{-\alpha x} - e^{-\alpha x} \qquad x > t$$

with density

$$f(x) = \alpha(\alpha t + 1) e^{-\alpha x} \qquad x > t \qquad (12)$$

The derivation of the distribution of X_t, the interval interrupted by the interview, given here closely follows Feller's argument

(1971, p. 13). It is apparent that the distribution X_t is not exponential, although the process is assumed to be a Poisson process. In fact, the distribution of X_t is gamma with index 2 in the case where $x \leqq t$, that is, at least one event occurs before the interruption.

The break in the formula at $x = t$ is due to the influence of the origin. It reflects the occurrence of no event before t. If t is large, so that the probability of this event is negligible, then Equation (9) applies. The mean of X_t under this condition is

$$E(X_t) = \int_0^\infty x^2 \alpha^2 e^{-\alpha x} = \frac{2}{\alpha} \qquad x \leqq t \qquad (13)$$

If the interview takes place a long time after the origin of the process, the mean of X_t, the interval interrupted by the interview, has twice the expectation of the mean of all other intervals. The apparent paradox, mentioned above, then is formally solved: the distribution of X_t is not exponential. Intuitively, the reason for the phenomenon is that the interruption at t is more likely to select longer intervals between the event than short.

The interview presumably takes place independently of the process. For reasons of symmetry, one should expect that, on the average, this will cut the interval in half. Hence,

$$E(X_w)_{t \to \infty} = E(X_v) = 1/\alpha \qquad (14)$$

The length of the interval from the last event before the interruption to the interruption and the length of the interval from the interruption to the first event after the interruption both have expectation α^{-1}, as isolated consideration of the Poisson process dictates. The expectation of the two intervals sums up to the expectation of the total length of the interval interrupted, as is appropriate.

In our example, this means that we may use the mean reported time since last event as an estimate of the intensity of events. It also follows that the expected time between events interrupted by the interview will be twice the expectation of the intervals between other events. These results, however, only apply for t far removed from the origin. If t is close to the origin of the process, then modifications are necessary, for Equation (9) will not always apply. To obtain the exact result, we need to obtain expectations of X_w and X_v without the assumption that t is far removed from the origin.

For X_v an argument identical to the one used for the derivation of X_t can be used to derive its distribution function. X_v is the interval from t to the first event after t. The probability $P(X_v \leqq x)$ will occur either (1) if the nth event before t happens at time y and the length of the interval from the $n + 1$st event X_{n+1} is greater than $t - y$ and smaller than $t - y + x$, or (2) if the first event happens after t and the interval from the origin to this event X_1 is greater than t and less than $t + x$. Hence,

$$P(X_v \leqq x) = P(t < X_1 \leqq t + x)$$

$$+ \sum_{n=1}^{\infty} \int_0^t g_n(y) \cdot P(t - y < X_{n+1} \leqq t + x - y) dy$$

$$= e^{-\alpha t} - e^{-\alpha(t+x)} + \alpha \int_0^t [e^{-\alpha(t-y)} - e^{-\alpha(t+x-y)}] dy \tag{15}$$

$$= e^{-\alpha t} - e^{-\alpha(t+x)} + 1 - e^{-\alpha t} - e^{-\alpha x} + e^{-\alpha(x+t)}$$

$$= 1 - e^{-\alpha x}$$

The interval X_v is exponentially distributed and will have mean α^{-1} regardless of when the interruption takes place. The distribution of X_w—the interval between the interruption and the last event before the interruption—is, however, not independent of when the interruption takes place. If no event occurs before t, then $X_w = t$.

The mean of X_w may be derived in several ways. One way is to derive the mean of X_t over all ranges of x, that is, for x greater and smaller than t. This gives, using Equation (10) and (12),

$$E(X_t) = \int_0^{\infty} \alpha^2 x^2 e^{-\alpha x} dx + \int_t^{\infty} \alpha(\alpha t + 1) e^{-\alpha x} dx$$

$$= (2/\alpha)[1 - e^{-\alpha t}(1 + \alpha t + (1/2)\alpha^2 t^2)] + e^{-\alpha t}(1 + \alpha t)(t + 1/\alpha)$$

$$= 2/\alpha - e^{-\alpha t}/\alpha e \tag{16}$$

Since we know that $E(X_v)$ is $1/\alpha$ always, it follows that

$$E(X_w) = E(X_t) - E(X_v)$$

$$= 2/\alpha - e^{-\alpha t}/\alpha - 1/\alpha \tag{17}$$

$$= (1 - e^{-\alpha t})/\alpha$$

This is finally the quantity desired — the expectation of the interval from the last event before the interruption until the interruption. It will be seen that $E(X_w)$ approaches α^{-1} asymptotically as $t \to \infty$, in accordance with our previous results. However, for t close to zero, the observed mean of X_w will underestimate the inverse of the intensity.

Equation (17) shows that it is indeed possible to estimate the intensity of events from a retrospective question concerning the occurrence of the last event, even when the process is recently started — and some may answer "never." The appropriate strategy for estimating α will be to compute the mean interval since the last event from the time of the interview and use this quantity to estimate α^{-1}, if it can be assumed that the probability of no event is negligible. If the probability of no event is not negligible — then equation (17) applies. A simple solution is obtained if everyone in the sample has been exposed to the process for the same amount of time. Note that $(1 - e^{-\alpha t})$ is the proportion with at least one event since the origin of the process. Denote the proportion with no event P_0. Then α may be estimated as

$$\alpha = \frac{1 - P_0}{w_t} \tag{18}$$

where w_t is the observed mean of X_w.

The effect of an interruption of a stochastic process on the intervals between events can be generalized to any stationary process. The general expression for the expectation of the interval being interrupted is (see Morrison, 1973; and Cox and Lewis, 1966)

$$E(X_t) = E(X_i) + \frac{V(X_i)}{E(X_i)} \tag{19}$$

where $V(X_i)$ is the variance of the distribution. It is easily seen that our result is a special case of Equation (19), since the variance of an exponentially distributed variable is α^{-2}. However, Equation (19) only holds for interruptions far removed from the origin, so that the probability of no event before the interruption is negligible.

EXTENSION TO SEVERAL INTERVALS
BEFORE INTERRUPTION

In the example considered, we have so far only dealt with

observations on one interval. However, it might be desirable to obtain information on other intervals as well. If heterogeneity of the process is a problem, then it may be desirable to estimate the intensity of events for each individual separately. Assuming no time dependence, a mean duration between events should then be obtained for each person. This quantity could then be used as the dependent variable in a causal analysis of the sources of heterogeneity. Suppose, therefore, that the intervals between events are recorded for respondents over a certain period t. The problem is whether the waiting time paradox just described has any implication for how we can treat these variables.

Denote again the interval between the events $X_1, X_2, \ldots X_t$, where X_t is the length of the interval following the last event before the interview. It was demonstrated above that if the process is Poisson with parameter α, X_t will have a mean of $2/\alpha$. The interruption will tend to select the longer of the randomly distributed intervals. But if this is so; then, with a small number of observed intervals, the remaining intervals will tend to be shorter.[1] Hence, the quantity

$$\frac{X_1 + X_2 \ldots X_w}{n} \tag{20}$$

where n is the number of intervals, will underestimate α^{-1}, if n is small. The solution is to double X_w to obtain an estimate of X_t and use this quantity in the computation of the mean. It is apparent that it is no solution to exclude the interrupted interval. Then the bias will be even more serious.

When dealing with several intervals, the choice of origin becomes important. If the origin corresponds to the occurrence of an event, then no special problem occurs. But, if the origin is chosen arbitrarily, as it will be if we ask for a report in a given period (say, six months), then the origin will "interrupt" an interval just as the interview does. Hence, the same consideration applies to X_1—the interval from the arbitrary origin to the first event. To avoid underestimating α^{-1} also, this interval must then be doubled. In the examples to be presented below, no such origin problem occurs.

These considerations apply when the number of events sampled per person is small. When the number of events is large, no

---

[1] I am indebted to James S. Coleman (personal communication) for this observation.

bias will occur if the process is stationary (cf., Cox and Lewis, 1966). But, in social science applications, the number of events may often be small.

It sometimes happens, and the empirical illustration given below is an example, that it is desired that any X_i, regardless of its occurrence, will be an estimator of α^{-1}. It is then necessary to adjust the X_i's preceding the interruption to account for the tendency of the interruption to select large intervals. A simple argument will provide the needed adjustment.

The expected number of events in period 0 to t, where 0 is assumed to coincide with the occurrence of an event, is αt. Each event is then preceded by an interval with mean value w_y. Denote w_t the expected value of X_w. The following identity holds:

$$w_t + \alpha t \cdot w_y = t \tag{21}$$

Rearranging gives

$$\frac{1}{\alpha} = \frac{w_y \cdot t}{t - w_t} \tag{22}$$

Hence, by multiplying the observed noninterrupted intervals with $t/(t - w_t)$, we obtain that each X_i has the same expectation. It is obvious that as t goes to infinity the adjustment goes to 1. Hence, it is only needed when a small number of events is sampled.

AN EMPIRICAL APPLICATION

In life-history data, series of events are of major interest and often the analysis of such series is the rationale for collecting such data. A situation where the result arrived at above is relevant occurred in the analysis of life-histories of a national sample of 30–39 year-old men. These data contain information on all jobs held by the respondents from their entry into the labor force until the time of their interview. The durations of these jobs are known, but for jobs held at the time of the interview the actual duration is, of course, not known. The average number of jobs held by a respondent is five, hence we are dealing with a situation where relatively few events are available for analysis.[2] The results of this paper should be highly relevant, if job durations were exponentially distributed.

[2]No person had only one job in the period of observation; hence, the probability of no event before t in Equation (17) is assumed to be zero.

It is apparent that job durations are not exponentially distributed. They are quite strongly dependent on age, and the process clearly is not stationary. A possible solution to this problem is to assume durations exponentially distributed, not in real time but in a transformed time scale; that is, in operational time (Sørensen, 1975a). A candidate for the redefinition of time is

$$v(t) = \frac{1}{\gamma} (1 - e^{-\gamma t}) \tag{23}$$

where t is a person's age, $v(t)$ is his age in the new time scale, and γ is a constant that measures the rate of decline in the likelihood of job shift. In $v(t)$ durations are measured as $X_i = v_2(t) - v_1(t)$, where $v_2(t)$ and $v_1(t)$ are departure and arrival times for a job. The rate of job shifts in $v(t)$, α^*, is then measured by $E(\hat{X}_i)^{-1}$.

In order to establish that the durations of jobs indeed are independent of age in $v(t)$, it is necessary that $\hat{X}_i$ has expectation $1/\alpha^*$ regardless of when it occurs; hence, it is necessary to use the adjustment procedure described above to eliminate the effect of the interruption of the process on the distribution of the durations of jobs preceding the job held at interview. This process starts with an event — the shift into the labor force — so there is no need to adjust for an arbitrary origin.

The model (23) can be tested in several ways, and it can be shown that the model does describe the observed nonstationarity in the process (Sørensen, 1975a). The best fitting estimate of γ is 0.007. Using this value, $\hat{X}_i$'s were computed for all jobs held by all respondents in the sample. Table 2 gives the means of $\hat{X}_u$, the interrupted duration, and $\hat{X}_i$, the durations preceding the job held at interview before and after adjustment.

TABLE 1

Interrupted and Noninterrupted Job Durations
in Time Scale $v(t)$ Before and After Adjustment

Mean of noninterrupted durations before adjustment	0.817
Mean of noninterrupted durations after adjustment	0.992
Mean of interrupted durations	1.025

The adjustment indeed brings the means of the noninterrupted durations close to the mean of $\hat{X}_w$ that should be a consistent estimator of $1/\alpha^*$ (provided there is no effect of the origin).

In Table 3 the mean duration of all jobs by age leaving the job is presented to demonstrate that the redefinition of time and the adjustment does make the mean $\hat{X}_i$'s estimators of $1/\alpha^*$ that are constant in time. It is apparent that there is no systematic variation in the mean $\hat{X}_i$ with age.

TABLE 2

Mean Duration of All Jobs in Time Scale $v(t)$ by Age

Age	Mean Duration in $v(t)$	N
18	1.07	165
20	1.00	220
22	0.98	229
24	0.97	250
26	1.02	268
28	1.03	245
30	0.90	293
32	1.00	212
34	0.93	162
36	0.90	132
38	1.02	108

It should be noted that the transformation of time (23) can be derived as the transformation of time that will make $y(t)$ in the process

$$dy(t)/dt = a + by(t) \tag{24}$$

change at a constant rate. The solution to (24) is

$$y(t) = a(e^{bt} - 1)/b + e^{bt}y(0) \tag{25}$$

Substituting $v(t)$ in (25) and rearranging gives (see Sørensen, 1975b for further details)

$$y(v) = y(0) + v(t)(a - by(0) \tag{26}$$

Equation (26) shows that $y(v)$ will increase linearly in $v(t)$. If change in y is brought about by an act—as, for example, increases in occupational status that are brought about by job shifts—the act should be time independent in $v(t)$. If $y(t)$, alternatively, is a continuous variable approximation to a count, Equation (24) is a deterministic formulation of a contagious Poisson process, and the transformation (23) should remove the time dependency of such a process. The contagious Poisson (Coleman, 1964) is a promising model for social influence processes. Hence, the time transformation (23) should enable the investigator to use the results of this paper, derived from the simple Poisson process, also on a wide variety of time dependent phenomena.

CONCLUSION

The waiting time paradox and the effect of an interruption in a stochastic process on the distribution of time intervals preceding the interruption have obvious practical implications for the analysis of retrospective reports on intervals between events. Retrospective data will obviously always have an interruption at the time of interview; and we have shown that if this truncated interval is eliminated, biased estimates of the preceding interval will result. Also, the result that knowledge of the length of the time period from last event before interview until interview can be used to estimate the intensity of events, and it has obvious practical utility.

REFERENCES

COLEMAN, J. S.
    1964   *Introduction to Mathematical Sociology.* New York: Free Press.
COX, D. R., AND LEWIS, P. H.
    1966   *The Statistical Analysis of Series of Events.* London: Meuthen.
FELLER, W.
    1971   *An Introduction to Probability Theory and Its Applications.* Vol. 2. New York: Wiley.
MORRISON, D. G.
    1973   "Some Results for Waiting Times with an Application to Survey Data." *The American Statistician* 27:226–227.
SØRENSEN, A. B.
    1975a   "The Organization of Activities in Time." Center for Demography and Ecology Working Paper 72–1. Madison: University of Wisconsin.
    1975b   "The Structure of Intragenerational Mobility." *American Sociological Review* 40:456:471.

Received May 22, 1975.

7

NETWORK TIME SERIES
FROM ARCHIVAL RECORDS*

Ronald S. Burt

UNIVERSITY OF CALIFORNIA, BERKELEY

Nan Lin

STATE UNIVERSITY OF NEW YORK, ALBANY

INTRODUCTION

Social scientists have demonstrated that sociometric methodologies can provide significant and meaningful insights into the

*This chapter is a by-product of research supported by a grant from the
National Science Foundation (SOC73–05504 A02) and a fellowship from the
National Institute of Mental Health (3–5690–43–3453). Participants in the Corporate Actor Project at the National Opinion Research Center were helpful in
pointing out confusing aspects of an early draft of the chapter, portions of which
were presented in the network analysis session of the 1975 annual meetings of the
American Sociological Association.

224

structure of relations within large systems of actors (for example, see Bott, 1957; Coleman et al., 1966; Mitchell, 1969; Crane, 1972; Barton et al., 1973; Boissevain and Mitchell, 1973; Laumann, 1973; Kadushin, 1974; Laumann and Pappi, 1976). Such demonstrations are likely to wax with recent developments in the conceptualization of systems of actors qua social topologies; namely, as systems of positions or statuses jointly occupied by structurally equivalent actors, since these new developments enable traditional sociometric methodologies to be brought to bear more directly on theories of the etiology and consequences of social structure.[1]

Accumulated accomplishments and conceptual developments notwithstanding, theories concerning the historical etiology of topologies of statuses in large systems of actors are difficult to assess if research is limited to the use of existing sociometric methodologies. First, the cost involved in collecting first-hand sociometric data can become prohibitive quickly as the number of actors to be included in the system increases. Most studies are concerned with less than one hundred actors and few approach one thousand. Yet a social system of one thousand actors is quite small when one thinks in terms of communities, regions, states, or nations. Second, actors that are unobservable to the researcher cannot be specified in the traditional sociometric analysis. Examples of such actors are persons who cannot be reached for interviewing, and unorganized collective groups or corporate bodies with several representatives. Third, sociometric data collected through either personal interviews or informants are reactive to the interests of the respondents. To what extent is a sociometric citation motivated by social or political interests of a respondent? Fourth, and finally, sociometric data are usually temporally confined to the time of the interview. Retrospective sociometric data would be expected to lose its reliability quickly as an investigator goes back in time, and panel studies of actors are inadequate due to the propensity for actors to die, refuse to continue, or otherwise become unobservable to the researcher over long periods of time.

[1] Given a hypothesized topology of statuses for a system of actors and observed sociometric choices (or other relational measures) among actors in the system, White et al (1976) provide a conceptualization within which each actor is mapped into a particular status, and Burt (1976b, 1976d) provides a conceptualization within which each actor exists—to varying extents—within each of the hypothesized statuses.

This chapter outlines a perspective on network analysis which avoids the above four problems. The perspective uses the content analysis of archival records to describe the relations between actors in terms of their joint involvement in events of consequence for actors in the social system.

CONCEPTUALIZING NETWORKS OF RELATIONS REFLECTED IN A CONTENT ANALYSIS

Let N equal the number of actor categories to be considered. Actor category i constitutes a category in the content analysis. It can be either an individual actor or a set of actors that are to be treated as identical within the content analysis, (for example, actors fulfilling identical roles within the social system, structurally equivalent actors in the social system). The purpose of the content analysis of archival records is to assign empirical meaning to elements in an (N, N) matrix where: diagonal elements reflect the attention given to actors in individual categories, and off-diagonal elements reflect the attention given simultaneously to actors in different categories.

The archives of a society are usually recorded within distinct (but not necessarily equal) intervals of time. For example, a daily newspaper is produced at the rate of one per day, textbooks are adopted by educational systems for the interval of one academic year, court records are gathered together by years, minutes of executive meetings are recorded within fiscal years, non-fictional accounts have specific copyright and distribution dates. Refer to the archival records produced within a single interval of time as a "document."

A document within archival records can be divided into K "sections" that are easily distinguishable portions of the entire document. The relative importance of each section within a single document can be measured as the proportion of the total document which is devoted to each section. The metric in terms of which proportions will be measured is dependent on the type of archival records being analyzed. For example, consider the situation where a document is an issue of a newspaper and a section is an article within the newspaper. The proportion of the total newspaper that is devoted to a particular article can be measured as the ratio of column inches in the article over the total number of column inches in the newspaper. Another example is the situation where a document is a volume of court records for a year and a section is a single case tried during the year. The proportion of the total document which is devoted to a particular case can be measured as the ratio of time spent by the court on the specific case over the total amount of time in thich the court was in session.

The network of relations among the N actor categories can be studied in terms of the occurence of actors in individual categories and the joint occurrence of actors in different categories within the sections of a document. The occurrences of actors in sections can then be weighted according to the proportion of the total document which is given to the sections. The more often that actors in a category are involved in the events discussed by particular archives, then the more often the actors should appear in the sections of the documents in the archives. Similarly, the more often that actors in pairs of categories have transactions with one another in regard to the events discussed by particular archives, then the more often the actors should appear together in the sections of the documents in the archival records.

Networks of Symmetric Relations

Given N as the number of categories of actors being considered, let K equal the number of sections in a document, and p^k be the proportion P of a document which is devoted to the kth section:

$$p^k = \frac{\text{Units of measurement in section } k}{\sum\limits_{j=1}^{K} \text{Units of measurement in section } j} \tag{1}$$

Let M_{nn}^k be an (N, N) binary matrix associated with section k, where elements of the matrix indicate the actor categories mentioned M in section k:

$$m_{ij}^k = 1 \text{ if actors in categories } i \text{ and } j \text{ are}$$
$$\text{mentioned in section } k \text{ as either initiating}$$
$$\text{or being affected by action} \tag{2}$$

$$= 0 \text{ otherwise}$$

Then a network of symmetric relations among the N actor categories being considered can be represented in an (N, N) matrix given as

$$Z_{nn} = \sum_{k=1}^{K} p^k M_{nn}^k \tag{3}$$

so that $\{z_{ii}\}$ is the sum of weighted occurrences of actors in category i in the document, and $\{z_{ij}\}$ is the sum of weighted joint occurrences of actors in categories i and j in the document.

As an example application, Burt (1975, 1976a) treated the front page of an issue of The New York Times as a document, and separate articles were treated as sections of the document. The proportion of a document devoted to a single section was quantified in terms of column inches so that equation (1) was given as

$$p^k = \frac{\text{Column inches in article } k}{\sum\limits_{j=1}^{K} \text{Column inches in article } j}$$

If one or more actors from the ith category of actors were mentioned as initiators or objects of action in either the largest headline associated with the kth article or the first paragraph of the kth article, then $\{m_{ii}^k\}$ was set equal to "1," otherwise the element was equal to zero. Similarly, if one or more actors from both categories i and j were mentioned as initiators or objects of action in either the largest headline or the first paragraph of the kth article, then $\{m_{ii}^k\}$ and $\{m_{ji}^k\}$ were set equal to "1," otherwise the elements were equal to zero.

Consider two general categories of actors—person actors versus corporate actors—and a three article front page of The New York Times in which the first article discusses both person actors and corporate actors and covers twenty-five percent of the front page, the second article discusses only person actors and covers twenty-five percent of the front page, and the third article discusses only corporate actors and covers fifty percent of the front page. Z_{nn} for the example front page is the sum of three products:

$$Z_{nn} = \begin{array}{cc} \text{Person} & \text{Corporate} \end{array} \\ Z_{nn} = \begin{bmatrix} 50\% & 25\% \\ 25\% & 75\% \end{bmatrix}$$

$$= 0.25 \begin{bmatrix} 1 & 1 \\ 1 & 1 \end{bmatrix} + 0.25 \begin{bmatrix} 1 & 0 \\ 0 & 0 \end{bmatrix} + 0.50 \begin{bmatrix} 0 & 0 \\ 0 & 1 \end{bmatrix}$$

The off-diagonal elements of Z_{nn} equal the percentage of the front page of an issue of The New York Times that discusses pairs of categories of actors, and the diagonal elements equal the percentage of the front page which discusses each category of actors.

Networks of Asymmetric Relations

Let P_{kk} be a (K, K) diagonal matrix defined in terms of the proportions P given in equation (1) where

$$\{p_{kk}\} = p^k \tag{4}$$

Let M_{nk} be an (N, K) binary matrix indicating the actor categories Mentioned in each section of the document, given in terms of equation (2) as

$$\{m_{ik}\} = \{m_{ii}^k\} \tag{5}$$

Finally, let A_{nk} be an (N, K) binary matrix indicating the actor categories discussed in each section of the document as Active rather than passive participants in events and given as

$$\{a_{ik}\} = 1 \text{ if actor(s) in category } i \text{ are mentioned}$$
$$\text{in section } k \text{ as initiating action} \tag{6}$$
$$= 0 \text{ otherwise}$$

Then a network of asymmetrical relations between pairs of categories of actors can be represented in an (N, N) matrix given as

$$Z_{nn} = M_{nk} P_{kk} A'_{nk} \tag{7}$$

so that diagonal elements of Z_{nn} equal the sum of weighted occurrences of actors in each category where they initiated action themselves:

$$\{z_{ii}\} = \sum_{k=1}^{K} m_{ik} p_{kk} a_{ik}$$

and off-diagonal elements z_{ij} equal the sum of weighted joint occurrences of actors in categories i and j where actors in category j initiated action involving the actors in category i:

$$\{z_{ij}\} = \sum_{k=1}^{K} m_{ik} p_{kk} a_{jk}$$

Equation (7) is a general specification of the network of relations among the N categories of actors being considered. It subsumes the specification in (3). Z_{nn} in equation (7) will be identical to Z_{nn} in equation (3) when $M_{nk} = A_{nk}$. In other words, the asymmetric network reduces to a symmetric network when actors in categories i and j always initiate action involving one another whenever they are mentioned together in a section of the document.

Consider the example given for $Z_{nn}^{(3)}$, the estimated Z_{nn} in equation (3) for The New York Times content analysis. Let the matrices M_{nk} and A_{nk} be equivalent, that is, $\{m_{ik}\} = \{a_{ik}\}$. Then Z_{nn} and $Z_{nn}^{(3)}$ are also equivalent;

$$Z_{nn} = \begin{bmatrix} 1 & 1 & 0 \\ 1 & 0 & 1 \end{bmatrix} \begin{bmatrix} 0.25 & 0.00 & 0.00 \\ 0.00 & 0.25 & 0.00 \\ 0.00 & 0.00 & 0.50 \end{bmatrix} \begin{bmatrix} 1 & 1 \\ 1 & 0 \\ 0 & 1 \end{bmatrix}$$

$$= \begin{bmatrix} 50\% & 25\% \\ 25\% & 75\% \end{bmatrix} = Z_{nn}^{(3)}$$

Imagine, however, that in the first article persons were discussed as the objects of action, and only corporate actors were discussed as initiating action so that

$$A_{nk} = \begin{bmatrix} 0 & 1 & 0 \\ 1 & 0 & 1 \end{bmatrix}$$

and Z_{nn} now becomes asymmetric;

$$Z_{nn} = \begin{bmatrix} 1 & 1 & 0 \\ 1 & 0 & 1 \end{bmatrix} \begin{bmatrix} 0.25 & 0.00 & 0.00 \\ 0.00 & 0.25 & 0.00 \\ 0.00 & 0.00 & 0.50 \end{bmatrix} \begin{bmatrix} 0 & 1 \\ 1 & 0 \end{bmatrix}$$

$$= \begin{bmatrix} 25\% & 25\% \\ 0\% & 75\% \end{bmatrix} \neq Z_{nn}^{(3)}$$

The diagonal elements of Z_{nn} equal the percentage of the front page of an issue of The New York Times, which discusses categories of actors in relation to events that they initiate. The off-diagonal elements $\{z_{ij}\}$ equals the percentage of the front page that discusses actors in categories i and j together, where actors in category j initiate action.

In both equation (3) and equation (7), attention is focused on relations between pairs of categories of actors. Subsequent analysis of the overall network of relations will consider pairs of categories in terms of the other N-2 categories, however, the occurence of triads or higher order interactions among categories of actors within sections are ignored. Separate Z matrices could be generated to analyze higher order interactions by only specifying a "1" in M_{nn}^{k} if a specific higher order interaction occurs in the content.

THE ANALYSIS OF THE NETWORK TIME SERIES

The previous section specifies the network of relations among N actor categories corresponding to a single document within archival records. Since the time frame of individual documents is known, the multiple Z_{nn} corresponding to multiple documents observed during a given time interval can be aggregated to estimate the overall Z_{nn} matrix for the time interval. Imagine that T matrices of the form Z_{nn} have been estimated from a content analysis of documents observed in T different time intervals. There will be time series on three types of variables available from equation (7) from which to make inferences about historical change in the structure of relations among actors in the N categories.

1. Time series on the prominence of actors in category i; $\hat{z}_{ii}^{t}$ = a diagonal element from $\hat{Z}_{nn}$ as easimated for time interval T,

2. Time series on the association between actor categories i and j; $\hat{z}_{ij}^{t}$ and $\hat{z}_{ji}^{t}$ = off-diagonal elements from $\hat{Z}_{nn}$ as estimated for time interval T, and

3. Time series on the tendency for the overall structure of associations among pairs of actor categories to approach some hypothetical structure; ℓ_{a}^{t} = the Euclidean distance between the structure of associations observed during time interval T and some hypothesized structure of associations A:

$$\ell_{a}^{t} = \sqrt{\left[\sum_{i=1}^{N} \sum_{j=1}^{N} (w_{ij})(\hat{z}_{ij}^{t} - z_{ij}^{a})^2 \right]} \qquad (8)$$

where $\hat{z}_{ij}^t$ is the estimated value of $\{z_{ij}\}$ during the tth time interval in the time series, z_{ij}^a is the hypothesized value of $\{z_{ij}\}$, and w_{ij} is a weight for the element $\{z_{ij}\}$ under some hypothesis (for example, by forcing all w_{ii} to equal zero, l_{at} would ignore all diagonal elements in Z_{nn}). Equation (8) can be used to assess the similarity over time of the structure of relations among the N actor categories to some hypothesized structure. For example, by setting all w_{ii} equal to zero, all w_{ij} equal to one for $i \neq j$, and all z_{ij}^a equal to zero; the time series l_a will measure the degree to which there is no interaction between the n actor categories over time. When l_a^t is small, then the $\hat{Z}_{nn}$ observed in time interval t is similar to Z_{nn}^a, that there is little interaction among the N actor categories. When l_a^t is high, then the $\hat{Z}_{nn}$ observed in time interval i is dissimilar to Z_{nn}^a, that is, there are extensive interaction among the actor categories. Alternative hypothesized network structures can be located in the network time series by clustering the observed networks to see if particular types of structures reoccur frequently at separate points in time (for example, see Burt, 1975, pp. 286–293, 1976a, Chapter six). Given the three types of time series, analysis can follow usual methods (for example, Anderson, 1971).

ASSESSING AND IMPROVING THE ADEQUACY OF INFERENCE FROM THE ANALYSIS OF THE NETWORK TIME SERIES

A major methodological problem in utilizing equation (7) to assess theories of structural change is the usually low level of adequacy of content analysis data as a basis for statistical inference. Of the three types of time series available to bring to bear on theories of structural change, since equation (8) is stated in terms of the $\{z_{ii}\}$ and $\{z_{ij}\}$, the adequacy of the time series will be a function of the adequacy of the elements of Z_{nn}.

Sampling Variability of the Elements of Z_{nn}

An overall Z_{nn} matrix can be estimated for a given time interval as the arithmetic mean of multiple Z_{nn} corresponding to multiple documents within the time interval. Let z be an element of the overall Z_{nn} matrix given as

$$z = \{\hat{z}_{ij}\} = \sum_{d=1}^{D} \{\hat{z}_{ij}^d\}/D$$

where D equals the number of documents to be content analyzed to estimate an overall Z_{nn} matrix for a time interval, and $\{\hat{z}_{ij}^d\}$ is the estimated value of $\{z_{ij}\}$ in equation (7), computed from the content analysis of the dth document. $A (1 - \alpha)$ confidence interval around an estimated z will be given as

$$CI_{(1-\alpha)} = z + (s/\sqrt{D})|t_{d-1}|_{(1-\alpha/2)} \qquad (9)$$

where $|t_{d-1}|_{(1-\alpha/2)}$ is the value of the t distribution for a (two-tailed) probability level of $(1 - \alpha/2)$, with D minus one degree of freedom, and s is the standard deviation of the D values of $\{z_{ij}^d\}$ that are combined to estimate z. The width of $CI_{(1-\alpha)}$ for a given value of alpha will decrease (that is, estimation of z will become more efficient) as N decreases and/or D increases.

In approaching an analysis of network time series, an individual will usually have in mind alternative typologies of actor categories and will want to content analyze a minimum number of documents within each time interval while maintaining reasonably efficient estimation of z. Given some test time interval, the sampling variability in z can be assessed by comparing equation (9) for alternative values of N and/or D within multiple samples of documents. Since D will usually be small, the jacknife estimation procedure for multiple samples can be used to advantage here. Instead of comparing values of equation (9) in multiple samples of size D of documents within the same time interval, the significance of the difference between z and ζ can be tested. The z is an element of Z_{nn} based on the sample of D documents for each time interval. ζ is the same element of Z_{nn} when estimated from all of the $K = D$ multiplied by the number of different samples of size D taken within the test time interval. Since ζ will be based on more documents than will z, if z is significantly different from ζ, then we know that D documents are not sufficient to estimate Z_{nn} for a time interval at a given number of actor categories. The use of the jacknife estimation, rather than the direct assessment of variability by comparing alternative confidence intervals, capitalizes on the availability of multiple samples in order to estimate an overall value of z, and CI, (see Mosteller and Tukey, 1968:128–160).

Recalling the example content analysis introduced above, two issues of the New York Times were selected per year using a constrained random sampling procedure from 1877 to 1972.[2] The front page of each issue was content analyzed as described for the

example associated with equation (3). Four different levels of aggregation of actors into actor categories were considered; $N = 2, 4,$
11 and 25.[3] Two different time intervals were considered in order to
assess the number of documents required to estimate an overall Z_{nn}
for a time interval; four-year intervals and one-year intervals. Z_{nn} for
the one-year intervals was the arithmetic mean of the two Z_{nn}
computed from equation (3). Z_{nn} for the four-year intervals was
then the arithmetic mean of eight matrices computed from equation
(3) — two matrices for each of four years. Three test time intervals
were selected over the time period studied — one at the beginning of
the time series (1877–1880), one in the middle time series
(1925–1928), and one at the end of the time series (1968–1972). For
each of these test time intervals, sixteen additional issues of The New
York Times were randomly selected to be content analyzed. K for a
four-year interval then equalled twenty-four, (eight issues from the
constrained random sample and sixteen issues from two random
samples of size eight). The four-year interval value of ζ was then
computed for twenty-four values of $\{\hat{z}_{ij}^d\}$:

$$\zeta = \sum_{d=1}^{24} \{\hat{z}_{ij}^d\}/24 \tag{10}$$

and z was computed for a four-year interval as the average of the
eight values of $\{\hat{z}_{ij}^d\}$ from the constrained random sample. The
ninety-five percent confidence interval around ζ, $CI_{0.95}$, was computed as given in equation (9) for D equal to twenty-four, and s
replaced by the jacknife estimate of the standard deviation σ given
as

$$\sigma = \sum_{k=1}^{K} (s_k/K) \tag{11}$$

[2] Given the small number of issues of The New York Times being used, issues
were randomly selected to be content analyzed under two constraints in order to
maximize the representativeness of the eight selected issues for the four years in a
four-year interval: 1) for each year an issue was selected shortly after the first of
April and shortly after the first of October, and 2) the entire set of issues from 1877
to 1972 were randomly assigned to days of the week (Monday through Friday)
following the first of April and October so that there would not be large percentages
of issues selected from particular days of the week. The sampling procedure is
explained in detail in Burt (1976a, Appendix B).

[3] The content and rationale for these alternative typologies of actor categories are given in Burt (1975, Appendix A, 1976a, Appendix A).

where s_k is a value in the sampling distribution of sigma based on the available estimates $\{\hat{z}_{ij}^d\}$:

$$s_k = (K)s_{all} - (K - 1)s_{(all\text{-}issue\ k)}$$

where s_{all} is the estimated sigma based on all twenty-four issues in the four year interval (s_{all} is the usual estimate of the standard deviation), and $s_{(all\text{-}issue\ k)}$ is the estimated sigma based on all twenty-four issues excluding the kth issue.

Table 1 presents the frequency with which the estimated

TABLE 1

Frequency of Inadequate Four-Year Estimates of the Elements of Z_{nn} at Different Levels of Actor Aggregation.*

	Four-year intervals		
Levels of aggregation	1877–1880	1925–1928	1968–1972
Two categories of actors	0 (0%)	0 (0%)	0 (0%)
Four categories of actors	0 (0%)	0 (0%)	0 (0%)
Interactions among four categories of actors	0 (0%)	1 (17%)	0 (0%)
Eleven categories of actors	0 (0%)	0 (0%)	0 (0%)
Twenty-five categories of actors	1 (4%)	2 (8%)	2 (8%)

*Entries in cells are the number of estimates which fall outside of a 95% confidence interval around the overall mean ζ (percentage of possible estimates which could have been inadequate is given in parenthesis).

TABLE 2

Frequency of Inadequate One-Year Estimates of the Elements of Z_{nn} at Different Levels of Actor Aggregation.*

	One-year intervals		
Levels of aggregation	1878	1926	1970
Two categories of actors	0 (0%)	0 (0%)	0 (0%)
Four categories of actors	0 (0%)	0 (0%)	0 (0%)
Interactions among four categories of actors	0 (0%)	0 (0%)	0 (0%)
Eleven categories of actors	2 (18%)	1 (9%)	2 (18%)
Twenty-five categories of actors	4 (16%)	2 (8%)	2 (8%)

*Entries in cells are the number of estimates which fall outside of a 95% confidence interval around the overall mean ζ (percentage of possible estimates which could have been inadequate is given in parenthesis).

elements of Z_{nn} for four-year intervals were significantly different from ζ. As an indication of the stability of the four-year eatimates of z, the confidence intervals around ζ ranged from zero to ± 10, with a mean confidence interval of ± 3.2 percent. Table 1 demonstrates that the estimation of z were adequate (that is, within a ninety-five percent confidence interval around ζ) when two categories of actors were distinguished in the content analysis, as well as when four or eleven categories were distinguished (the one $z - \zeta$ that was significant was one percentage point outside the confidence interval around ζ). When twenty-five categories of actors were distinguished, however, five of the possible seventy-five z were outside a ninety-five percent confidence interval.

Table 2 presents the frequency with which the estimated elements of Z_{nn} for one-year intervals were significantly different from ζ. Values of ζ were computed from equation (10) for one year intervals for the year within each of the test time intervals that had the most issues sampled from it (for 1878, $K = 11$; for 1926 and 1970, $K = 10$). As would be expected, the sampling variability of the annual estimates of elements of Z_{nn} is higher than the four-year interval estimates that were based on four times as many documents (confidence intervals for annual estimates ranged from zero to ± 18 percent with a mean of ± 5.2 percent). What is striking about the results in Table 2 is that even though annual estimates of the elements in Z_{nn} are only based on two issues of The New York Times, the estimates are adequate when there are two or four categories of actors distinguished by the content analysis coding. Five of the possible thirty-three estimates were inadequate when eleven categories were distinguished, and eight of the possible seventy-five estimates were inadequate when twenty-five categories of actors were distinguished. When eleven or twenty-five categories of actors were distinguished, therefore, annual estimates had to be combined into four-year intervals or more in order to provide adequate point estimates of the elements of Z_{nn}.

Reliability of the Elements of Z_{nn}

A perennial problem in content analysis is the reliability of the assignment of content to categories in a coding scheme. If the purpose of the content analysis of documents is to generate network time series for specific actors over time, then each of the N actor categories contains known actor(s). Each actor category is identifiable in terms of a set of alternative symbols. For example, the government actor "United States" can be referenced with several alternative empirical symbols: "U.S.," "United States," "America," et cetera. The coding process in this situation can most reliably be approached through computer coding of documents that code the presence of an actor whenever one records one or more of the symbols referring to an actor in a discussion (see, for example, Stone et al., 1966; Holsti, 1968, pp. 663–673). It is likely, however, that the specification of exhaustive sets of alternative symbols referencing those actors to be assigned to particular actor categories is inadequate. Actor categories often will be defined in terms of an abstract set of characteristics, which can then be applied to a wide range of empirical symbols describing actors in documents. Examples are actors engaging in similar role behavior or general classes of actors in the social system. In this situation, actors are assigned to actor categories assording to the number of characteristics which they share with a specified ideal type that defines each actor category. Willey (1926, Chapter two) remains a succinct discussion of guidelines for constructing a general set of categories for content analyzing varied documents.

In regard to network time series from archival records, reliability entails different problems to defining actor categories under these two approaches. For networks among actor categories, where each category is composed of known actors; the content analysis will be as reliable as the list of alternative symbols used to reference actors in each category is exhaustive. For the more abstract procedure, where actor categories are defined in terms of characteristics of ideal type actors; the reliability of the content analysis of documents will increase as 1) the aggregation of actors into polythetic actor categories increases (see, for example, Janis, Fadner and Janowitz, 1943), and 2) the characteristics of ideal type actors defining each actor category are increasingly stated as a series of binary (yes-no) decisions on whether or not a particular actor shares the given characteristic with the ideal type, (see, for example, Stempel, 1955; Schultz, 1958).[4]

---

[4] As pointed out by Markoff et al. (1974, pp. 35–38), additional problems stem from the necessary treatment of humans as consistent measuring instruments

TABLE 3

Mean Inter-Coder Reliability Coefficients for Elements of Z_{nn}
at DIfferent Levels of Actor Aggregation.*

| | Mean inter-coder reliability | |
| | Four-year intervals $n = 11\dagger$ | One-year intervals $n = 28\dagger$ |
Levels of aggregation		
Two categories of actors	0.93	0.79
Interaction between two categories of actors	0.90	0.75
Four categories of actors	0.67	0.49
Interactions among four categories of actors	0.46	0.43
Eleven categories of actors	0.56	0.43
Interactions among eleven categories of actors	0.34	0.31
Twenty-five categories of actors	0.50	0.44
Interactions among twenty-five categories of actors	0.28	0.25

*Correlations presented are the average correlations between the estimates of Z_{nn} computed from equation (3) based on the two coders content analyzing the same documents, for e; (for example, for the two category typology, the inter-coder reliabilities for annual estimates of z_{11} and z_{22} where 0.765 and 0.817, respectively, so that the mean reliability given above is 0.79 = (0.765 + 0.817)/2.

$\dagger n$ equals the number of estimates of the elements of Z_{nn} for four- and one-year time intervals that were correlated between the two coders.

Table 3 presents average inter-coder reliability coefficients for the elements of Z_{nn} at the four levels of aggregation of actors into categories for the example New York Times network time series. Since they are solely a function of the coding instructions used for the example New York Times data, the generalizability of the reliabilities in Table 3 to other applications of equation (7) is limited. What Table 3 does illustrate, however, is that the reliabilities decline as the number of actor categories distinguished in the

over the time spent content analyzing. This problem is particularly dangerous in the content analysis of archival records to generate network time series since coding at the beginning of the time series can change over the course of time spent coding and confound trends observed in the analysis. In order to avoid this problem in The New York Times content analysis, four-year intervals were randomly arranged in terms of their order of coding, thereby randomizing the effects of informal changes in coding on the trends later assessed.

coding increases. As N increases, off-diagonal elements of Z_{nn} (the $\{\hat{z}_{ij}\}$) decline in reliability more rapidly than do the diagonal elements (the $\{\hat{z}_{ii}\}$).

Given less than desirable reliability coefficients for one or more elements of Z_{nn} over time, the adequacy of inferences from the network time series can be improved in two ways. The first, and most obvious, method is to improve the reliability of the coding used to generate the network estimates following the guidelines given above. Given existing network time series, another method of dealing with the problem is to improve the estimation of the elements of Z_{nn} over time by specifying the elements over time as unobserved variables in structural equation models.

Structural Equation Models Specifying Elements of Z_{nn} over Time

When network time series generated from equation (7) have high sampling variability and/or low reliability, it is to be expected that an individual will make inferences from an analysis with extreme caution. When reliability and/or sampling variability is marginally adequate and two or more indicators of Z_{nn} over time are available, however, then structural equation models can be used to increase the confidence with which an individual can make inferences from time series analysis. The use of structural equation models to improve confidence in the estimation of elements of Z_{nn} over time involves a single characteristic of factor analysis. The estimation of any one parameter in a factor analysis is affected, to some extent, by every indicator variable specified in the factor analytic model. The estimation of Z_{nn} as a composite of its multiple indicator Z_{nn}'s can be improved by weighting the indicator Z_{nn}'s according to their covariances with a priori known concomitants of the elements of Z_{nn}.[5]

Let z^* be an element of Z_{nn}^* to be estimated from multiple indicators; $Z_{nn}^1, Z_{nn}^2, ..., Z_{nn}^q$. The multiple indicators of Z_{nn}^* can be computed from the content analyses of alternative coders, content analysis conducted using alternative coding schemes, content analyses based on alternative documents, et cetera. The estimated element z^* for a time interval will be a weighted composite of the Q indicators for the time interval

[5] This deliberate use of structural criteria in the construction of multiple indicator unobserved variables is an effort to improve the construct validity of the network time series. The strategy is discussed in detail in Burt (1976c).

$$z^* = \sum_{q=1}^{Q} w_q(z^q) \tag{12}$$

If the indicators are to be weighted equally, as in the previous discussion, then $w_1 = w_2 = \cdots = w_q = 1/Q$. Alternatively, if z^* is specified as an unobservable variable in a structural equation model containing known concomitants of z^*, as $(m - 1)$ unobserved variables with their $(y - Q)$ indicator variables, then allowing one indicator and one unobserved variable to represent "time" (cf., Lawley and Maxwell, 1971, pp. 108–109, on factor scores given correlated factors):

$$W_{ym} = (S_{yy})^{-1} \Delta_{ym} \Phi_{mm} \tag{13}$$

given

$$S_{yy} \simeq \Sigma = \Delta_{ym} (\Phi_{mm}) \Delta'_{ym} + \Theta^2_{yy} \tag{14}$$

$$= \Delta_{ym} (B^{-1}_{mm} \Psi^2_{mm} B^{-1}_{mm}) \Delta'_{ym} + \Theta^2_{yy} \tag{15}$$

where y and m, respectively, are the total number of indicators and unobserved variables in the structural equation model, S_{yy} is the observed variance-covariance matrix among the y indicators, Φ_{mm} is the variance-covariance matrix among the m unobserved variables, Δ_{ym} is the matrix of factor loadings linking the m unobserved variables with the y indicator variables, Θ^2_{yy} is a diagonal matrix of residual variances in the y indicators, $-B_{mm}$ is an $(m$ by $m)$ asymmetric matrix of path coefficients among the m unobserved variables, and Ψ^2_{mm} is the variance-covariance matrix of exogenous influences on the m unobserved variables. Equation (14) is the basic factor analytic model. Equation (15) expresses the variances and covariances among the m unobserved variables in terms of path corfficients. Assuming a population multivariate normal distribution of values of the indicator variables, maximum likelihood estimates of unknown parameters in equation (15) will minimize the chi-square approximation (see, for example, Jöreskog, 1973, p. 90):

$$\chi^2_0 = [N - 1][\ln|\Sigma| + \text{tr}(\Sigma^{-1}S) - \ln|S| - y]$$

which is distributed with degrees of freedom equal to the number of over-identifying restrictions in the structural equation model under the null hypothesis H_0 that the model is correct.[6]

The columns in W_{ym} in equation (13) are vectors of path coefficients leading from the y indicators to each unobserved variable in the structural equation model. The column corresponding to z^* will provide the weights in (12). When estimated within a structural equation model, z^* will be a function of not only its own indicators, but will be partially determined by indicators of other unobserved variables as well. The indicators of z^* that will be most heavily weighted in the estimation of values of z^* will be those indicators that covary the most with other indicators of z^* and, also, have the highest covariances with the specified concimitants of z^* as an unobserved variable in the structural equation model. As the covariances among the indicators of z^* decrease because of low reliability and/or high sampling variability, the weights of the indicators of z^* will be increasingly determined by the covariances of the indicators with the specified concomitants of z^* in the structural equation model.

Figure 1 presents three structural equation models, each specifying a type of unobserved concomitants of z^* in order to increase the confidence in the estimation of z^*. The symbols in the path diagrams correspond to the parameter matrices in equation (15). Figure 1A specifies simultaneous measures of other elements of Z_{nn}^* as unobserved variables to be estimated with z^*. The indicators of z^* are weighted according to their covariances with indicators of other elements of Z_{nn}^*, when their reliability is low or when they have high sampling variability. Figure 1B specifies confounding influences on the estimated attention given to actor categories. It is hypothesized that the attention given to specific types of actors will vary depending on the economic and/or political conditions in the social system. When they have low reliability or high sampling variability, indicators of z^* in Figure 1B are weighted according to

---

[6] Jöreskog and van Thillo (1972) provide a computer routine, LISREL, that numerically computes maximum liklehood estimates of unknown parameters in (15). The assumption of multivariate normality will never hold in models specifying time as an unobserved variable since time has a rectangular distribution. The estimates in the forthcoming model are not maximum likelihood, although χ_0^2 is minimized. The chi-square approximation in this situation is reduced to a qualitative indicator.

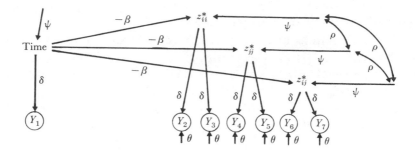

(a) Simultaneous Estimates of Other Elements in Z_{nn}.

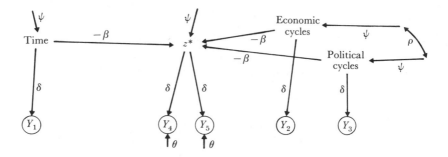

(b) Confounding Influences on Estimates of an Element in Z_{nn}

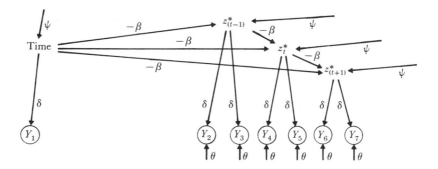

(c) Autocorrelation in Estimates of an Element in Z_{nn}

Figure 1. Improving the Estimation of Network Time Series via Structural Equation Models
$(\rho_{ij} = \psi_{ij}/\psi_i\psi_j)$. (Observed variables are circled.)

their covariances with exogenous confounding influences. Figure 1C specifies prior and subsequent estimations of $z*$ as concomitants of the value of $z*$ estimated for the tth time interval. When the indicators of $z*$ in Figure 1C have low reliability and/or high sampling variability, they are weighted according to their covariances with prior and subsequent measures of $z*$.

As a numerical illustration, Figure 2 presents a structural equation model that specifies diagonal elements of Z_{nn} as unobserved variables; attention to the actor categories of government agencies, business corporations, and political parties in The New York Times network time series (z_{ii} computed from equation 3). Figure 2 utilizes the first and second types of concomitants of $z*$ given in Figure 1; simultaneous measures of multiple elements of Z_{nn}^* are specified as unobserved variables and indicators of confounding influences on the attention to actor categories are specified in the model (EC, PCA, PCB).[7] The coefficients in Figure 2 have been estimated from the correlations and standard deviations in Table 4. Since only trends were to be corrected by the model in Figure 2, and in order to insure unique estimates of unstandardized

[7] As indication of economic fluctuations in the United States could have confounded the estimation of the elements of Znn, EC is the annual average short-term loan (90-day) interest rate on the New York market. The political fluctuations in the national social structure are hypothesized to be periodic within the four-year interval from one presidential election to the next. In order to control for spurious attention given to the actor categories due to elections, the total sample of ninety-six annual Z_{nn} matrices was divided into four subsamples corresponding to the year of the national election and each of the three years following a national election. For each of these four subsamples, means were computed of the diagonal elements of Z_{nn} using the four actor category topology: persons, aggregates of persons, corporate actors, and agents. These yearly means were then subtracted from the overall mean of attention given to each category of actors. Two separate profiles of deviations of yearly means from overall means were observed among the four categories: 1) a profile of attention given to persons and aggregates of persons which was high just after an election year and decreased over the next three years (the vector of mean yearly deviations was 2.7, 1.2, -1.5, and -2.4 percentage points), and 2) a profile of attention given to corporate actors and agents which was low just after an election, but was high during the year before an election (the vector of mean yearly deviations was -2.4, 0.1, 2.7, and -0.7 percentage points), (see Burt, 1976a, Figure C.1). These three confounding influences on the observed network time series are referenced in the text as EC—economic cycles, PCA—political cycle A (attention to persons), and PCB—political cycle B (attention to corporate actors and agents).

TABLE 4

Correlations and Standard Deviations for Indicators in Figure 2.*

	Y_1	Y_2	Y_3	Y_4	Y_5	Y_6	Y_7	Y_8	Y_9	Y_{10}	Standard Deviations	Means
Y_1	1.00										27.8	1924.5
Y_2	−0.02	1.00									1.8	3.8
Y_3	0.00	0.02	1.00								2.1	2.4
Y_4	0.00	0.09	−0.58	1.00							1.8	2.3
Y_5	0.64	−0.14	0.00	0.09	1.00						18.3	64.1
Y_6	0.67	−0.10	0.00	0.05	0.87†	1.00					18.6	64.9
Y_7	−0.29	−0.06	−0.11	0.09	−0.24	−0.30	1.00				8.3	13.9
Y_8	−0.28	0.10	−0.13	0.17	−0.25	−0.29	0.62†	1.00			8.1	14.0
Y_9	−0.42	−0.02	−0.11	0.04	−0.36	−0.34	0.09	0.09	1.00		11.8	14.5
Y_{10}	−0.40	−0.02	−0.10	0.03	−0.31	−0.32	0.08	0.08	0.52†	1.00	12.3	14.8

*Variable definitions: Y_1 — time in years; Y_2 — economic cycle as represented in short-term loan interest rates for year on New York Stock Exchange, Series X305 in Statistical History of the United States from Colonial Times to the Present, Horizon Press; Y_3 — political cycle A from footnote three; Y_4 — political cycle B from footnote three; Y_5 and Y_6 — estimated attention to government agencies and agents by coder A and B; Y_7 and Y_8 — estimated attention to business corporations and agents by coder A and B; Y_9 and Y_{10} — estimated attention to political parties and agents by coder A and B.

†These three reliabilities are computed from the twenty-eight annual estimates computed by the two coders. Other correlations are based on ninety-six observations.

$$\Delta'_{ym} =$$

	Y_1	Y_2	Y_3	Y_4	Y_5	Y_6	Y_7	Y_8	Y_9	Y_{10}
	1.00*	0.00*	0.00*	0.00*	0.00*	0.00*	0.00*	0.00*	0.00*	*0.00
	0.00*	1.00*	0.00*	0.00*	0.00*	0.00*	0.00*	0.00*	0.00*	*0.00
	0.00*	0.00*	1.00*	1.00*	0.00*	0.00*	0.00*	0.00*	0.00*	*0.00
	0.00*	0.00*	0.00*	0.00*	0.00*	0.00*	0.00*	0.00*	0.00*	*0.00
	0.00*	0.00*	0.00*	0.00	0.91	0.95	0.78	0.80	0.73	0.71
	0.00*	0.00*	0.00	0.00	0.00*	0.00*	0.00*	0.00*	0.00*	*0.00

$$(0.00^* \quad 0.0^* \quad 0.00^* \quad 0.00^* \quad 7.19 \quad 6.03 \quad 5.33 \quad 4.76 \quad 7.89 \quad 8.79) = \text{diagonal of } \Theta_{yy}$$

$$-B_{mm} =$$

1.00*	0.00*	0.00*	0.00*	0.00*	0.00*	*0.00
0.00*	1.00*	0.00*	0.00*	0.00*	1.00*	*0.00
0.00*	0.00*	1.00*	0.00*	1.00*	0.00*	*0.00
0.00*	0.00*	0.00*	1.00*	0.00*	0.00*	*0.00
0.47	-1.26	0.66	1.28	1.00*	0.00*	*0.00
-0.11	0.10	-0.33	0.55	0.00*	1.00*	*0.00
-0.25	-0.21	-0.99	-0.33	0.00*	0.00*	*1.00

$$\Psi^2_{mm} =$$

770.06	0.00*	0.00*	0.00*	0.00*	0.00*	*0.00	Time
0.00*	3.24	0.08	0.29	0.00*	0.00*	*0.00	EC
0.00*	0.08	4.41	-2.19	0.00*	0.00*	*0.00	PCA
0.00*	0.29	-2.19	3.24	0.00*	0.00*	*0.00	PCB
0.00*	0.00*	0.00*	0.00*	165.12	-18.89	-20.63	Government agencies
0.00*	0.00*	0.00*	0.00*	-18.89	56.25	-7.08	Business corporations
0.00*	0.00*	0.00*	0.00*	-20.63	-7.08	94.87	Political parties

* Marks parameters restricted during estimation process to values presented.

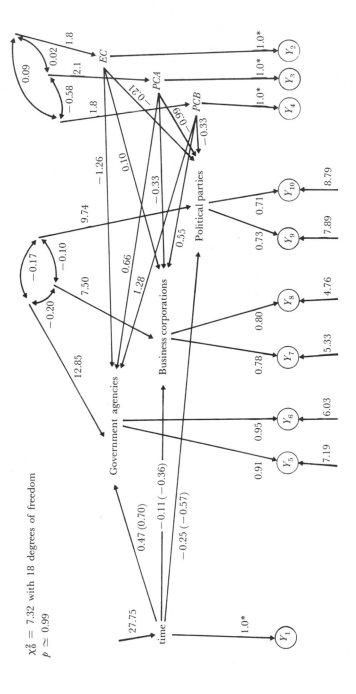

Figure 2. Structural Equation Model of Change in the Attention to the Actor Categories of Government Agencies, Business Corporations, and Political Parties (Estimates in parentheses are standardized).

parameters involving the content analysis unobserved variables, the variances of the unobserved variables are forced to equal the arithmetic averages of their indicators' variances (for example, the variance in attention to government agencies is given as : [334.9 + 346.0]/2 = 340.4).[8] The parameter matrices for equation (15) are presented with the structural equation model.

Path coefficients leading to z^* from the variable "time" express the change in z^* that occurs per year over the 1877 to 1972 time series. The attention given to government agencies has been increased in the Times at a rate of 0.47 percent per year. In contrast, the attention given to business corporations and political parties has been decreasing at an average rate of -0.11 percent and -0.25 percent per year, respectively. The chi-square approximation indicates the probable adequacy of the specified model. The chi-square approximation can be used to assess the significance of the trends of change in the three z^* in the usual manner of re-estimating parameters with a trend coefficient forced to equal zero; and, under the null hypothesis, that the trend actually is zero, the difference between the chi-square approximations for the two models will be distributed itself as a chi-square approximation with one degree of freedom (see, for example, Werts et al., 1973).

ASSUMPTIONS MADE BY THE MODEL AND CONSEQUENCES OF THEIR VIOLATION

The model specified in equation (7) depends on two major assumptions in order to realize its potential over traditional sociometric techniques.

---

[8] Necessary and sufficient restrictions for computing unique estimates of unknown parameters in structural equation models containing intercorrelated, unstandardized unobserved variables are not easily specified for the general case. However, if the variances of unobserved variables are fixed (for example, 1.0 or some unstandardized constant) and the restrictions are distributed properly in the matrix of factor loadings, then unique parameter estimates should result (see Jöreskog's 1969 discussion of restricted factor analysis, pp. 185–186, and Howe's specification of sufficient restrictions for insuring unique parameter estimates). If unstandardized, weighted estimates of the variances of the z^* are desired, then sufficient restrictions must be placed on the coefficients among the unobserved variables in order to insure unique parameter estimates. Methods of assessing the sufficiency of proposed restrictions are discussed by Wiley (1973).

Structural Equivalence of Actors
within Content Analysis Categories

The model in equation (7) assumes that the network of relations among individual actors in a system can be represented as a social topology in which those actors falling into the categories specified for the content analysis are structurally equivalent within categories over time. This assumption says that the set of actors within an actor category have similar relations with all actors relevant to the content analysis. It says, further, that when relations change over time, actors within an actor category will experience the same types of change in relations with other actors relevant to the content analysis. Knowledge of the relations involving any one actor within a set can by used to deduce the relations involving the other actors in the set—at least, those relations involving other actors relevant to the content analysis.[9]

When this first assumption is violated, actors have been combined into a single category when, in fact, they constitute multiple categories. The subsequent estimates of $\{z_{ij}\}$ will be aggregates of distinct types of relations between actors instead of being estimates of a single type of relation. The estimates of $\{z_{ij}\}$ will still reflect the relations between actors in actor categories i and j. However, that relation will be one that does not actually exist among the actors in the social system being considered. When the assumption of structural equivalence within content analysis categories is violated, therefore, the erroneously aggregated actor category(s) should be disaggregated until they are composed solely of actors who are at least equivalent under a weak criterion.[10]

---

[9] Detailed discussion of empirical conditions under which actors are to be considered structurally equivalent is given in terms of a continuum of equivalence in Burt (1976a, 1976d) and in terms of discrete values of equivalence in Breiger et al. (1975) and White et al. (1976).

[10] For example, at an early stage in the analysis of The New York Times network time series, it was hypothesized that one of the actor categories should be the set of corporate actors that make a profit by insuring political rights for their investors. Three subsets within this category termed "political corporate actors" were labor unions, political parties, and trade associations. When the data were gathered, however, these three subsets of actors had different trends of change in attention over time. The category of labor unions received increasing attention. Political parties received decreasing attention. Trade associations received a continuously low amount of attention. These differential rates of change in attention

Reliable Recording of Participation of Actors
Relevant to the Content Analysis

The model in equation (7) assumes that the content analyzed archival records left as a description over time of the joint involvement of actors in events accurately describe the relations between the sets of actors relevant to the content analysis — even if they do not accurately describe the relations between all individual actors in the social system.

There are two violations of assumption two that are likely to occur in the application of equation (7). First, bias in estimating the magnitudes of the off-diagonal elements of Z_{nn} can be manipulated by judiciously selecting the size of sections. By increasing the material to be content analyzed within a section, the observed number of interactions between actors will increase since more actors can be mentioned in a single section (c.f., Osgood's 1959 discussion of contingency analysis of the co-occurrence of content characteristics, and Geller et al., 1942, analysis of the increase in extent of coded bias as a function of increasing the size of a section). For example, the off-diagonals in the example New York Times data would have been increased by content analyzing the entire contents of articles instead of first paragraphs. The $\{\hat{z}_{ij}\}$ would have been decreased by only content analyzing the first sentence of articles. This potential bias in $\{\hat{z}_{ij}\}$ as a measure of the interaction between actors categories i and j emphasizes the point that Z_{nn} only estimates relative levels of association between categories of actors — it provides no information on specific transactions between actors in the two categories. Given an estimate of $\{z_{ij}\}$, one only has an idea of the relative tendency for actors in the ith and jth categories to be observed together. There is no information on why they are together. Due to the potentially arbitrary absolute values of $\{\hat{z}_{ij}\}$, it is useful to supplement analyses based on percentage values of $\{\hat{z}_{ij}\}$ computed from equation (7) with analyses based on deviation values of $\{\hat{z}_{ij}\}$ from mean levels of association among the N actor categories; that is,

were similarly reflected in the associations involving the three subsets of actors. The general category of political corporate actors was, therefore, discarded as a violation of assumption one, and the three subsets of actors were specified as separate actor categories.

$$\{\hat{z}_{ij}\} = (\hat{z}_{ij} - \mathbf{z})$$

where

$$\mathbf{z} = \sum_i^N \sum_j^N (\hat{z}_{ij})/(N-1)N \qquad \text{for } i \neq j \,[11]$$

A second likely source of bias in the estimation of Z_{nn} stems from the judicious selection of available information by the editors of archival records in accordance with their interests (see review by Danzer, 1975). Consider Figure 4. In the ideal research situation, $\hat{Z}_{nn}$ from equation (7) would perfectly mirror the actual network of relations among actors in the social system. Figure 4 hypothesizes two filters which can interfere with the ability of $\hat{Z}_{nn}$ to accurately reflect the network of relations among actors: 1) the error introduced during the coding of the content of documents, and 2) the selective perception of the editors of documents. The previous discussion has dealt with the problems of sampling variability, reliability, and bias in the elements of $\hat{Z}_{nn}$. Various procedures have been suggested to improve the similarity between $\hat{Z}_{nn}$ and Z_{nn}^*, where Z_{nn}^* is the "true" network of relations among the actor categories as they are discussed in the documents. Even if $\hat{Z}_{nn} = Z_{nn}^*$ however, there still exist the interests of editors as a filter between Z_{nn}^* and the actual network of relations among actors in the social system.

With few exceptions, archival records are produced within a social system for consumption by an intended audience. Persons in the intended audience have interests in events, which thay satisfy by consuming the documents in archival records, (see Stephenson, 1967, for an elaboration of this point in his play theory of mass communication, and Lin, 1973, pp. 44–86, 182–191, for general review discussion). The editors of archival records retain their posi-

---

[11] For example, in the content analysis of The New York Times, reporting practices changed over time with change in the availability of alternative sources of information to citizens. At the beginning of the time series, articles describing situations in which events occured; all attending and participating actors were mentioned. At the end of the time series, articles focused on actors involved in a specific event or issue. The raw percentage estimates of the off-diagonals of Z_{nn} were, therefore, biased downward over time—fewer actors had the opportunity to be mentioned together in later articles than they did in early articles. Consequently, deviation levels of interaction were analyzed, as opposed to raw percentage levels of interaction, (see Burt, 1975, pp. 283–287, 300–304, 1976b, Appendix A).

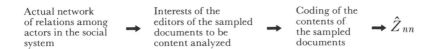

Figure 3. Filters between the Actual Network of Relations among Actors in a Social System and the Network Estimated via Equation (7).

tions as long as they can guide the content of the archival records such that it meets the interests of the intended audience of those records. The interests of editors of documents sampled to be content analyzed for equation (7) are, therefore, a function of editorial perception of the interests of the intended audience of those documents.

The second assumption of equation (7) demands that documents have been sampled for analysis whose intended audience and editors are interested in maximizing the similarity of the content in the documents and the ongoing events in the social system. The diagonal elements of $\hat{Z}_{nn}$ in equation (3) express the degree to which actors are discussed in the archival records describing the social system. The diagonal elements of $\hat{Z}_{nn}$ in equation (7) express the degree to which actors initiate action within the social system described by the archival records. It is assumed that a low $\{\hat{z}_{ii}\}$ does not mean that the editors of the coded documents are ignoring actors in the ith actor category because they do not think that their audience is interested in actors within actor category i. Failure to meet this assumption invalidates time series generated from equation (7) as a means of studying actors in category i.

Two alternative approaches can be used to guard against assumption two being violated. First, and most obvious, multiple types of archival records can be content analyzed and compared in terms of the inferences they generate. This approach depends on truly different types of records being content analyzed. Merely content analyzing multiple records can only insure lower sampling variability in the estimates of Z_{nn}. Second, exogenous determinants of differences in editorial policy can be specified as confounding influences on the observation of elements of Z_{nn} in a structural equation model (for example, economic and political cycles in Figure 1B). Controlling for variation associated with these known disturbances, inferences can be made with more confidence from the corrected time series.

REFERENCES

ANDERSON, T. W.
  1971   *The Statistical Analysis of Time Series.* New York: Wiley.
BARTON, A. H., DENITCH, B., AND KADUSHIN, C.
  1973   *Opinion-Making Elites in Yugoslavia.* New York: Praeger.
BOISSEVAIN, J., AND MITCHELL, J. C.
  1973   *Network Analysis Studies in Human Interaction.* Paris: Mouton.
BOTT, E.
  1957   *Family and Social Networks.* New York: Free Press.
BREIGER, R. L., BOORMAN, S. A., AND ARABIE, .
  1975   "An Algorithm for Clustering Relational Data with Applica-
          tions to Social Network Analysis and Comparison with Mul-
          tidimensional Scaling." *Journal of Mathematical Psychology*
          12:328–383.
BURT, R. S.
  1975   "Corporate Society: A Time Series Analysis of Network
          Structure." *Social Science Research* 4:271–328.
  1976a   *Corporate Society: A Time Series Analysis of Network Structure.*
          NORC Report, University of Chicago.
  1976b   "Positions in Networks." *Social Forces* 55: in press.
  1976c   "Interpretational Confounding of Unobserved Variables in
          Structural Equation Models." *Sociological Methods and Research*
          5: in press.
  1976d   "Positions in Multiple Network Systems: A Structural Con-
          ceptualization of Role-Set, Role Distance and Status." Paper
          presented at the annual meetings of the American Sociological
          Association.
COLEMAN, J. S., KATZ, E., AND MENZEL, H.
  1966   *Medical Innovation: A Diffusion Study.* Indianapolis, Ind.:
          Bobbs-Merrill.
CRANE, D.
  1972   *Invisible Colleges.* Chicago: University of Chicago Press.
DANZER, M. H.
  1942   "Validating Conflict Data." *American Sociological Review*
          40:570–584.
GELLER, A., KAPLAN, D., AND LASWELL, H. D.
  1942   "An Experimental Comparison of Four Ways of Coding Edi-
          torial Content." *Journalism Quarterly* 19:362–370.
HOLSTI, O. R.
  1968   "Content Analysis." In G. Linzey and E. Aronson (Eds.), *The
          Handbook of Social Psychology.* Reading, Mass.: Addison-Wesley.

JANIS, I. L., FADNER, R. H., AND JANOWITZ, M.
1943 "The Reliability of a Content Analysis Technique." *Public Opinion Quarterly* 7:293–296.

JÖRESKOG, K. G.
1969 "A General Approach to Confirmatory Maximum Likelihood Factor Analysis." *Psychometrika* 34:183–202.
1973 "A General Method for Estimating a Linear Structural Equation System." In A. S. Goldberger and O. D. Duncan (Eds.), *Structural Equation Models in the Social Sciences.* New York: Seminar Press.

JÖRESKOG, K. G., AND VAN THILLO, M.
1972 "LISREL, a General Computer Program for Estimating a Linear Structural Equation System Involving Multiple Indicators of Unmeasured Variables." Research Bulletin RB-72-56. Princeton: Educational Testing Service.

KADUSHIN, C.
1974 *The American Intellectual Elite.* Boston: Little, Brown.

LAUMANN, E. O.
1973 *Bonds of Pluralism.* New York: Wiley-Interscience.

LAUMANN, E. O., AND PAPPI, F. U.
1976 *Networks of Collective Action: A Perspective on Community Influence Systems.* New York: Academic Press.

LAWLEY, D. N., AND MAXWELL, A. E.
1971 *Factor Analysis as a Statistical Method.* New York: Elsevier.

LIN, N.
1973 *The Study of Human Communication.* Indianapolis, Ind.: Bobbs-Merrill.

MARKOFF, J., SHAPIRO, G., AND WEITMAN, S. R.
1974 "Toward the Integration of Content Analysis and General Methodology." In D. R. Heise (Ed.), *Sociological Methodology 1975.* San Francisco: Jossey-Bass.

MITCHELL, J. C.
1969 *Social Networks in Urban Situations.* Manchester University Press.

MOSTELLER, F., AND TUKEY, J. W.
1968 "Data Analysis, Including Statistics." In G. Linzey and E. Aronson (Eds.), *The Handbook of Social Psychology.* Reading, Mass.: Addison-Wesley.

OSGOOD, C. E.
1959 "The Representational Model and Relevant Research Methods." In I. de S. Pool (Ed.), *Trends in Content Analysis.* Urbana: University of Illinois Press.

SCHUTZ, W. C.
   1958   "On Categorizing Qualitative Data in Content Analysis."
            Public Opinion Quarterly 22:503–515.
STEMPEL, G. H.
   1955   "Increasing Reliability in Content Analysis." *Journalism Quarterly* 32:449–455.
STEPHANSON, W.
   1967   *The Play Theory of Mass Communication.* Chicago: University of
            Chicago Press.
STONE, P. J., DUNPHY, D. C., SMITH, M. S., AND OGILVIE, D. M.
   1966   *The General Inquirer: A Computer Approach to Content Analysis in the
            Behavioral Sciences.* Cambridge, Mass.: MIT Press.
WERTS, C. E., JORESKOG, K. G., AND LINN, R. L.
   1973   "Identification and Estimation in Path Analysis with Unmeasured Variables." *American Journal of Sociology* 78:1469–1484.
WHITE, H. C., BOORMAN, S. A., AND BREIGER, R. L.
   1976   "Social Structure from Multiple Networks: I. Blockmodels of
            Roles and Positions." *American Journal of Sociology* 81:730–780.
WILEY, D. E.
   1973   "The Identification Problem for Structural Equation Models
            with Unmeasured Variables." In A. S. Goldberger and O. D.
            Duncan (Eds.), *Structural Equation Models in the Social Sciences.*
            New York: Seminar Press.
WILLEY, M. M.
   1929   *The Country Newspaper.* Chapel Hill: University of North Carolina Press.

Received July 30, 1975.

8

AN EXAMINATION OF CONCOR
AND RELATED METHODS
FOR BLOCKING
SOCIOMETRIC DATA

Joseph E. Schwartz

HARVARD UNIVERSITY

Social scientists are interested in the patterns or structures of interactions within and between different types of individuals (or groups or organizations). In analyzing data, one often seeks to determine which types of individuals exist and then to examine their interaction. A large literature has evolved on the subject of cluster-

I am indebted to Professor Paul Holland for innumerable valuable comments and suggestions about how to refine the ideas in this chapter. The chapter has also benefited from discussions with Professor Ronald Breiger and also Professor Harrison White and Professor Fredrick Mosteller. The work for this chapter was partially funded by a grant from the National Science Foundation (GS-2689) to Harrison White.

ing algorithms[1] that attempt to do this. By aggregating individuals with similar data (attribute or relational), clusters are formed which hopefully represent meaningful types in the real world.

One recent clustering algorithm is iterative intercolumnar correlations—CONCOR.[2] This algorithm is not difficult to operationalize, but the mathematical foundation underlying its operation is not well understood. In an effort to understand this foundation, the related but simpler problem of iterative intercolumnar covariations[3] has been studied and found to be related to a special case of principal components analysis. This analysis has been extended to examine the mathematical foundations of CONCOR.

THE ALGORITHMS

The algorithms are very simplistic in concept. Begin with an $m \times n$ matrix A in which each column is a vector of data. It is the set of these column vectors that one is seeking to partition into clusters. For the CONCOR algorithm, calculate the $n \times n$ symmetric correlation matrix R where the i, j entry r_{ij} is the Pearson product-moment correlation coefficient of the ith and jth columns of A. Treat the columns of R as vectors, and compute a new $n \times n$ correlation matrix (of the correlation matrix), called $R^{[1]}$, for the first iteration of the original correlation matrix. Continue to iterate this process to obtain $R^{[2]}, R^{[3]}, R^{[4]}, \ldots$ where $R^{[j+1]}$ is the $n \times n$ correlation matrix of $R^{[j]}$. The result is that $R^{[j]}$ converges very quickly towards a limit that is, in all practical cases, a matrix of plus and minus ones.

For the iterated covariations algorithm, compute covariations instead of correlations. C will be the original covariation ma-

---

[1] See Cormack (1971) for a summary of the existing literature. Bailey (1975) also reviews a large share of the literature.

[2] This algorithm seems to have been independently discovered by several researchers. It was apparently first published by McQuitty and Clark (1968). Unaware of their work, Breiger and I discovered it, and some applications appear in papers by Breiger et al. (1975) and White et al. (1976a). Its use to date has been justified solely by the empirical results it yields.

[3] I adopt the term "covariation" as it is used by Blalock (1972, p. 572). It is the numerator of the formula for the more common covariance. Thus, the covariation and covariance matrices differ only by a multiplicative constant. This distinction is of no relevance to this chapter beyond the fact that the equations are slightly simpler if we ignore the constant.

trix of A. The first iteration $C^{[1]}$ will be the covariation matrix of C, and $C^{[j+1]}$ will be the covariation matrix of $C^{[j]}$. It will be shown that, by controlling for a scalar constant, the iterated covariation matrices also converge.

The purpose of this chapter is to examine the mathematics of why these algorithms always converge, to describe some characteristics of the results, and to ask if these results might reasonably be expected to lead to insights about the real structure underlying the data.

APPLICATIONS TO RELATIONAL DATA

Breiger and White (Breiger, 1976; Breiger et al., 1975; White et al., 1976a) have found the results of CONCOR very useful in the analysis of various types of sociometric data in the context of structural equivalence and blockmodels. CONCOR has been used to simultaneously treat, for a single population, several data-matrices of different types of relationships. As described in Breiger et al. (1975, p. 336), this can be done by vertically stacking the data-matrices in a single, very long, two-dimensional array and computing the original correlation or covariation matrix from this. It is noted in their paper that routines could be employed for weighting the different matrices before they are stacked. The column means of each data-matrix are not subtracted out before stacking and calculating a covariation or correlation matrix. Conceptually, such an operation may be ambiguous because data about several different types of relations—one of their examples includes "liking," "helping." and "antagonism"—must be added together to compute the column means of stacked matrices. However, if the column means were subtracted out of each individual data-matrix, then the column means of the stacked matrices would equal zero, the covariation matrix of the stacked matrices would equal the sum of the covariation matrices of the individual data-matrices, and computations would be easier for large datasets and/or small computers.

As will be described later, Breiger and White use CONCOR to obtain a partition of the column vectors within each cluster to obtain further subdivisions. In applying this form of heirarchical clustering, Breiger et al. (1975, pp. 343, 352) repeatedly return to the original stacked data. However, the submatrix of R, the original correlation matrix, given by r_{ij} such that i and j are in the same cluster, could be employed with the same results.

Finally, when applying CONCOR or any other method of analysis to sociomatrices in which the rows and columns represent the same population, one should carefully consider how to treat reflexive ties, that is, the diagonal of the data matrix. The possibility of obtaining data for these cells is usually limited when collecting sociometric data. In many cases the diagonal cells are assigned an arbitrary value. Any value chosen for this assignment will have a predictable, substantive effect on the interpretation of the partition resulting from the application of CONCOR. While in some cases this might be desirable, a case can usually be made for assigning the column mean to the diagonal. The result is that the (i, i) entry and (j, j) entry of the data matrix cannot contribute, either positively or negatively, to the original correlation (r_{ij}) or covariation (c_{ij}) for each i and j. This same effect can be achieved by assigning zeros to the diagonal of the data matrix after the column means have been subtracted out or by eliminating the (i, i), (i, j), (j, i), and (j, j) entries of the data matrix from the calculation of c_{ij} and r_{ij}.

MATHEMATICAL FOUNDATIONS
OF ITERATIVE COVARIATIONS

This and other sections of this chapter will use the following notational conventions in matrix formulations. The superscript "t" denotes the transpose of the preceding matrix or vector. Superscripts in brackets refer to steps in the iterative process. All other superscripts denote ordinary exponents. Finally, the word "limit" always implies "as j approaches infinity." The covariation and correlation matrices on the first iteration can by represented as follows:

$$Q^{[1]} = RMR$$

$$R^{[1]} = D^{[1]}Q^{[1]}D^{[1]} = D^{[1]}RMRD^{[1]}$$

where:

R = the original $n \times n$ correlation matrix

$R^{[1]}$ = the first iteration of R

$Q^{[1]}$ = the covariation matrix of R

$D^{[1]}$ = the diagonal matrix (the off-diagonal entries
equal zero) whose entries equal the
reciprocal square roots of the diagonal $Q^{[1]}$

$M = I - (1/n)ee^t$

I = the $n \times n$ identity matrix

$\mathbf{e}$ = the $n \times 1$ column vector of ones

The operation of iterating correlations is a complex one of repeatedly subtracting out column means and then normalizing, while iterating covariations only involves repeatedly subtracting out means. Before proceeding to discuss iterating covariations it will be helpful to examine a still simpler process that does not even involve subtracting out means.

For some types of data, it may make sense not to subtract the means from the column vectors or to normalize the column to unit length. Instead of computing either a covariation or a correlation matrix, one might simply multiply the data matrix A by its transpose. For example, consider a binary individual-by-corporation matrix A in which a_{ij} equals one if individual i is on the board of directors of corporation j, and a_{ij} equals zero otherwise. Then the matrix $B = A^tA$ will be a corporation-by-corporation interlocking directorship matrix in which b_{ij} equals the number of individuals who are members of the board of directors of both corporation i and j.[4] What would be the result of iterating the process of multiplying the matrix B by its transpose on the left?

Any matrix[5] that is the product of a matrix (of real numbers) and its transpose is symmetric and has all non-negative eigenvalues (that is, is positive semi-definite). Any symmetric matrix of real numbers has real eigenvalues, and the eigenvectors corresponding to different eigenvalues are orthogonal to each other. Thus, any symmetric matrix P can be expressed as the product VKV^t, where K is the diagonal matrix of eigenvalues ordered from largest to smallest. and the columns of V are unit-length eigenvectors of P corresponding to the eigenvalues in K. ($VV^t = V^tV = I$ because the columns of

[4] This point is discussed in Breiger (1974).
[5] Many of the following points are well known general theorems whose proofs can be found in any standard text on matrix algebra.

V are orthogonal and have unit length.) For any *P*, *K* is unique and *V* is unique up to the selection of column vectors corresponding to two or more equal eigenvalues in *K*. (The specific choice in the rare event of multiplicity of eigenvalues has no effect on the following discussion as long as an orthogonal basis is chosen for the subspace spanned by the set of vectors **x** satisfying the equation $P\mathbf{x} = k_{ii}\mathbf{x}$ where k_{ii} is the eigenvalue with multiplicity. (The equality $P = VKV^t$ is true even if we modify *K* by removing rows and columns with a zero on the diagonal and delete the corresponding columns of *V*. (Herstein, 1964, Chapter six, Section ten).

Since $B = A^tA$, there exist *K* and *V* (with the properties discussed above) such that $B = VKV^t$. It will be useful in the following discussion if we write *K* as *kL*, where *k* is the largest eigenvalue (the first diagonal entry of *K*; k_{11}), and *L* is the diagonal matrix of eigenvalues *K* divided by *k*. At the first iteration of *B*, it is observed that B^t equals *B* because of symmetry, and so

$$B^{[1]} = B^tB = BB = kVLV^tkVLV^t = k^2VLILV^t = k^2VL^2V^t$$

Similarly,

$$B^{[2]} = B^{[1]^2} = k^2VL^2V^tk^2VL^2V^{\ t} = k^4VL^4V^t$$

and

$$B^{[j]} = B^{[j-1]^2} = k^{(2^j)}VL^{(2^j)}V^t$$

Ignoring the scalar multiple (a power of *k*), the successive iterations are converging. This is seen by examining the elements of $L^{(2^j)}$ which equal the corresponding elements of *L* raised to the 2^j power because *L* is a diagonal matrix. Because all the eigenvalues are positive and we divided by the largest to arrive at *L*, all elements of *L* are between 0 and 1. For any *x* between 0 and 1, the limit of $x^{(2^j)}$ is one for *x* equal to one, and zero for *x* greater than or equal to zero and less than one.

THEOREM 1. *Let m be the multiplicity of the largest eigenvalue k of B. The limit of $k^{(-2^j)}B^{[j]}$ converges to a matrix of rank m, where B, V, and L are defined as above.*

Proof.:

$$\text{Limit } k^{(-2^j)}B^{[j]} = \text{Limit } VL^{(2^j)}V^t$$

$$= \text{Limit} \sum_{i=1}^{n} \mathbf{V}L_{ii}^{(2^j)}(\mathbf{v}_i)^t$$

where $\mathbf{v}_i$ is the ith column vector of $\mathbf{V}$,

$$= \sum_{i=1}^{n} (\text{Limit } L_{ii}^{(2^j)}) \, \mathbf{v}_i(\mathbf{v}_i)^t$$

$$= \sum_{i=1}^{m} \mathbf{v}_i(\mathbf{v}_i)^t$$

because the first m elements of Limit $L_{ii}^{(2^j)}$ equal 1, while all others equal 0.

In the normal situation in which there is a single largest eigenvalue (no multiplicity of k), it should be clear from Theorem 1 that, controlling for the scalar k, the process of iterating the "matrix multiplied by its transpose" operation converges to a matrix of rank one, $\mathbf{v}_1(\mathbf{v}_1)^t$. This iterative process reduces to zero the effect of any eigenvectors associated with lesser eigenvalues of B. Thus, most of the information contained in B is lost, while no new information is gained. However, the eigenvectors of B are analogous to the principal components of a covariance matrix and might be used in a similar fashion in an attempt to gain further understanding of the original data.

For iterated covariations and CONCOR, I will be discussing how each iterative process converges towards a matrix of small rank, almost always rank one. For example, in the above discussion about iterating B, the limit of $L_{ii}^{(2^j)}$ converges to zero for all L_{ii} less than one, so that the $B^{[j]}$ converges toward a matrix of rank m. However, in fact, $L_{ii}^{(2^j)}$ never equals zero (unless L_{ii} equals zero) for any finite j, and so the rank of $B^{[j]}$ always equals the rank of B. (The rank of a matrix equals the number of non-zero eigenvalues.) While the primary concern is that these iterations converge very quickly towards their limit, it should be recognized that one is dealing with limits, and that each successive iteration of CONCOR (iterated covariations) and the $B^{[j]}$ discussed above must produce a matrix whose rank equals the rank of the previous iteration. The proof of this statement for CONCOR and iterated covariations is presented in Appendix 1.

Suppose that one suspects that an analysis of the covariation or covariance matrix might prove fruitful. In other words, one thinks that the means of the column vectors in the original data should be controlled. This is accomplished by subtracting the vector mean from each vector so that each resulting column vector has a mean of zero. When this matrix is multiplied on the left by its transpose, we obtain the covariation matrix C of the data. When the original data are based on an interval scale, the covariation matrix has its usual statistical interpretation. For binary data, frequently used in sociometry, the covariation matrix has a direct set-theoretic or graph-theoretic interpretation.[6] Consider, again, the binary individual-by-corporation directorship matrix A, discussed in the previous section. Examining the covariation formula we see that

$$c_{jk} = \sum_{i=1}^{m} a_{ij}a_{ik} - \left(\frac{1}{m}\right)\left(\sum_{i=1}^{m} a_{ij}\right)\left(\sum_{i=1}^{m} a_{ik}\right)$$

where A is an $m \times n$ matrix,

c_{jk} = observed number of intersections

— expected number of intersections

In our hypothetical example, c_{jk} would be the difference between the number of directors the boards of the jth and kth corporation had in common and the product of the number of individuals on the board of j and the probability of an individual's being on the board of k. Similarly, the covariance obtained by dividing c_{jk} by m simply converts the difference between observed and expected *frequencies* to *proportions*.

We now examine what happens when we iterate C, computing covariation matrices of covariation matrices. Earlier it was shown that the covariation matrix of an $n \times n$ symmetric matrix, in this case C, can be expressed as $C^{[1]} = CMC$, where M again equals $I - (1/n)\mathbf{ee}^{t}$. Continuing the iterations:

$$C^{[2]} = C^{[1]}MC^{[1]} = CMCMCMC \quad \text{by substitution}$$

$$= CMCMMCMC \quad \text{since } M = MM$$

---

[6] This was pointed out by Breiger.

$$= (CM)^2(MC)^2 = (MC)^{t^2}(MC)^2$$

and, in general,

$$C^{[j+1]} = C^{[j]}MC^{[j]} = (C^{[j]}M)(MC^{[j]})$$
$$= (CM)^{(2^j)}(MC)^{(2^j)} = (MC)^{t^{(2^j)}}(MC)^{(2^j)}$$

Do the iterated covariations converge in a straightforward manner as in Theorem 1? Not quite! Examining the eigenvector decomposition of successive iterations will show that both the eigenvectors and the eigenvalues change at each iteration, although the eigenvectors do converge. This convergence can be explained by focusing on the matrix MC.

> THEOREM 2. *Let M and C be defined as above. The following statements hold for MC. First, if the rank of C is r, then the rank of MC is either r or r — 1. Second, the eigenvalues of MC are all real and non-negative. And third, MC equals SKT^t, where K is the diagonal matrix of non-zero eigenvalues of MC, the columns of S are the unit-length eigenvectors of MC with non-zero eigenvalues, and T equals CSK^{-1} where K^{-1} is the diagonal matrix containing the reciprocals of the eigenvalues. The rows of T^t are the left eigenvectors of MC with non-zero eigenvalues.*

Proof. The first statement follows directly from the observation that the rank of M is $n - 1$ and the following fact: If the ranks of two $n \times n$ matrices are p and q, respectively, then the rank of their product is less than or equal to the minimum of p and q and greater than or equal to $p + q - n$. (Herstein, 1964, pp. 142, 222). Thus the rank of MC is between $\min(r, n - 1)$ and $r - 1$. Since $\min(r, n - 1)$ must be less than or equal to r, the rank of MC must be either r or $r - 1$.

The proof of the second statement of the theorem uses the following: Given two square matrices A and B, the eigenvalues of AB equal the eigenvalues of BA. (Nomizu, 1966, p. 187). Thus the eigenvalues of $MMC(=MC)$ equal the eigenvalues of MCM. Now, from prior discussion, we can write

$$C = VKV^t$$

and so

$$MCM = MVKV^tM = (MVK^{0.5})(K^{0.5}V^tM)$$

where each entry in $K^{0.5}$ equals the square root of the corresponding entry in K. Since both $K^{0.5}$ and M are symmetric, MCM is the product of a matrix and its transpose, and MCM has real non-negative eigenvalues that, in turn, are the eigenvalues of MC.

In order to prove the more complicated third part of the theorem, we begin by showing that the right eigenvectors with non-zero eigenvalues of MC equal the eigenvectors of MCM. Let s be a right eigenvector of MC, with k its eigenvalue. Then ks equals MCs. Multiplying both sides by M yields

$$kM\mathbf{s} = MMC\mathbf{s} = MC\mathbf{s} = k\mathbf{s}.$$

Thus, for k not equal to zero, Ms equals s and, therefore,

$$MCM\mathbf{s} = MC(M\mathbf{s}) = MC\mathbf{s} = k\mathbf{s}$$

showing s to be an eigenvector of MCM, as well.

We can write $MCM = SKS^t$, where K and S are defined as above. Since the eigenvectors of MCM contained in S are orthogonal (because MCM is symmetric) and are normalized to unit length, S^tS will be the identity matrix of the same shape as K, and

$$MCS = MCMS = SKS^tS = SK$$

Since the theorem defines T equal to CSK^{-1}, it may be observed that

$$T^tMC = K^{-1}S^tCMC = K^{-1}KS^tC = KK^{-1}S^tC = KT^t$$

and, therefore, that the rows of T^t are indeed left eigenvectors of MC. By multiplying both sides of $T = CSK^{-1}$ by M on the left, it may be seen that

$$MT = MCSK^{-1} = SKK^{-1} = S$$

and, thus, for non-zero eigenvalues, the right eigenvectors of MC equal the transposes of the left eigenvectors after their means are subtracted out.

To prove that SKT^t equals MC it is sufficient to prove that $SKT^t\mathbf{x}$ equals $MC\mathbf{x}$ and that $\mathbf{x}^tSKT^t$ equals $\mathbf{x}^tMC$ for all $\mathbf{x}$. To prove that $SKT^t\mathbf{x} = MC\mathbf{x}$ for all $\mathbf{x}$, it is sufficient to prove that this holds for a set of vectors which span the vector space of all $\mathbf{x}$. The columns of S *and* all right eigenvectors of MC with zero eigenvalues form one such set. We observe that

$$SKT^t(S) = SKT^tMS = SKS^tS = SK = MCS$$

and, thus, for each column of S, $SKT^t\mathbf{s}_i$ equals $MC\mathbf{s}_i$. Next, let $\mathbf{x}$ be any right eigenvector of MC with a zero eigenvalue ($MC\mathbf{x} = \mathbf{0}$), then we see that

$$SKT^t\mathbf{x} = ST^tMC\mathbf{x} = ST^t(MC\mathbf{x}) = ST^t(\mathbf{0}) = MC\mathbf{x}$$

Similarly, the columns of T and all left eigenvectors (transposed) of MC with zero eigenvalues span the space of all $\mathbf{x}$. Proceeding as above, we see that

$$T^tSKT^t = S^tMSKT^t = S^tSKT^t = KT^t = T^tMC$$

and if $\mathbf{x}^t$ is a left eigenvector with a zero eigenvalue, then

$$\mathbf{x}^tSKT^t = \mathbf{x}^tMCST^t = (\mathbf{0})^tST^t = \mathbf{0}^t = \mathbf{x}^tMC$$

This concludes the proof of Theorem 2.

Before proceeding further, it is useful to note that

$$T^tS = S^tMS = S^tS = I$$

From this equation we derive

$$(MC)^2 = (SKT^t)^2 = SKT^tSKT^t = SK^2T^t$$

and, by induction,

$$(MC)^{j+1} = (MC)^jMC = SK^jT^tSKT^t = SK^{j+1}T^t$$

We are now in a position to explain algebraically iterated covariations. Again defining L as $(1/k)K$ (where k is the largest eigenvalue in K), and examining the earlier expression for iterated covariations, we observe

$$C^{[j+1]} = (MC)^{t(2^j)}(MC)^{(2^j)}$$

$$= (kSLT^t)^{t(2^j)}(kSLT^t)^{(2^j)}$$

$$= (kTLS^t)^{(2^j)}(kSLT^t)^{(2^j)}$$

$$= (k^{(2^j)}TL^{(2^j)}S^t)(k^{(2^j)}SL^{(2^j)}T^t)$$

$$= k^{(2^{j+1})}TL^{(2^j)}S^tSL^{(2^j)}T^t$$

$$= k^{(2^{j+1})}TL^{(2^{j+1})}T^t$$

Similarly,

$$C^{[j]} = k^{(2^j)} TL^{(2^j)} T^t$$

and, therefore,

$$\text{Limit } k^{(-2^j)} C^{[j]} = \text{Limit } TL^{(2^j)} T^t$$

$$= \text{Limit } \sum_{i=1}^{n} L_{ii}^{(2^j)} \mathbf{t}_i (\mathbf{t}_i)^t$$

$$= \sum_{i=1}^{n} (\text{Limit } L_{ii}^{(2^j)}) \mathbf{t}_i (\mathbf{t}_i)^t$$

$$= \sum_{i=1}^{m} \mathbf{t}_i (\mathbf{t}_i)^t$$

where m is the multiplicity of the largest eigenvalue, since the limits of the $L_{ii}^{(2^j)}$ are equal to either 1 or 0.

We have to now prove:

THEOREM 3. *The process of iterated covariations converges (controlling for the scalar value k) to a matrix of rank m which depends on the eigenvector(s) of MC associated with the largest eigenvalue, where m is the multiplicity of this eigenvalue, k.*

In the normal situation in which there is no multiplicity of the largest eigenvalue, the process converges to a matrix of rank one, $\mathbf{t}_1 (\mathbf{t}_1)^t$. All eigenvalues (of MC) less than k are quickly dominated by k in successive iterations and become numerically insignificant. Table 1 shows the minimum values of j for which various L_{ii} when raised to the 2^j power will be less than 0.0000001 (10^{-7}).

TABLE 1

Minimum Value of j Such That $L_{ii}^{(2^j)}$ Is Less Than 10^{-7}

L_{ii}	0.50	0.60	0.70	0.75	0.80	0.90	0.95	0.98	0.99	0.999
j	6	6	7	7	8	9	10	11	12	15

DISCUSSION

Is there any justification for advocating the iteration of covariation matrices as a method for analysis of data? The answer seems to be "no," for two basic reasons. First, it has been shown that the result of the iterative process can be deduced directly from the left eigenvectors and eigenvalues of MC without actually computing any iterations at all. Secondly, the iterative process will identify only the left eigenvector(s) associated with the largest eigenvalue, ignoring any information possibly contained in other eigenvectors.

While for the above two reasons I reject iterated covariations as an analytical method, it is reasonable to ask if T, the matrix of left eigenvectors, does not, after all, have some practical value. Recalling that S equals T with its column means subtracted out, we can answer this question by considering S and the column means of T separately. It was shown in the proof of Theorem 2 that S is also the matrix of eigenvectors of MCM. In fact, MCM is the covariation matrix of the original data matrix A with its row means subtracted out, that is, AM. Therefore, S is simply the matrix of principal components for AM, and we have arrived (needless to say, by a circuitous route) at a special case of principal components analysis. In the next section it will become clear why I do not see any real significance in the column means of T; however, they are necessary if one wants to use the first left eigenvector of T in the same way as White and Breiger apply the CONCOR algorithm.

At this point I would like to discuss briefly why this special application of principal components may be appropriate for the analysis of sociometric data. Consider a sociomatrix of relational data in which each entry represents the presence, absence, or extent of a particular relationship between the individuals (groups, organizations, etc.) associated with the row and column of that entry. This bears some similarity to a two-way analysis of variance without replication in which the levels of both independent variables are individuals and the dependent variable is the relationship. Subtracting out the row and column means of the sociomatrix controls for the overall level of the relationship experienced by each person, what remains is the interaction effect of pairs of individuals on the relationship.[7] I would suggest that this statistical concept of interaction, when applied to relational data in this manner, is related to the substantive concept of interactions among individuals, which is the focus of research on social networks. The principal components

---

[7] This modified data matrix could be considered the residuals from the additive model.

computed from *MCM* are for this matrix of interactions. The resulting components constitute a set of orthogonal axes in which the pattern and structure of interactions may be examined and clusters of individuals sought. Unlike an ordinary principal components analysis, there will be no "common factor" because the row and column means are subtracted from the data, and each principal component will be bi-polar because its mean is zero.

Before proceeding further, it should be noted that this special case of principal components analysis would probably not be appropriate for most types of data matrices. For example, in a typical person-by-variable data matrix, the entries in different columns are data for different variables, and it would, therefore, not make sense to subtract out (or even compute) row means.

AN APPLICATION
OF PRINCIPAL COMPONENTS ANALYSIS
TO SOCIOMETRIC DATA[8]

White et al. (1976a) and Breiger et al. (1975) present an analysis of sociometric data obtained as part of the study of a Western Electric plant (Roethlisberger and Dickson, 1939). For a detailed description of the data see Homans (1950) or any of the above references. For our purposes it is sufficient to know that data were collected for 14 men (known as the Bank Wiring Group) on five types of relationships: "likes," "is antagonistic towards," "helps," "plays games with," and "argues with over opening the windows." Due to lack of space, the data are not presented in their original form. They do, however, appear in their permuted form in Table 3. We now turn to the analysis.

The first step is to compute the covariation matrix from the data. If this were an original analysis, I would subtract the row means and compute a covariation matrix for each sociomatrix, excluding the diagonal from both sets of calculations. I would then sum the individual covariation matrices to arrive at the total covariation matrix *MCM*. (This is the same matrix that would be

---

[8] Factor analysis has been used in the past to study correlation matrices computed from sociometric data (MacRae, 1960). I am unaware of previous applications of the particular form of principal components analysis discussed in this chapter.

obtained by stacking the standardized data matrices and then computing the covariations.) However, since one of the purposes of this exercise is to compare the results of this principal components analysis with the results of CONCOR presented by White and Breiger, I have treated the data exactly as they did. The matrices were stacked without being individually standardized, and zeros were placed on the diagonal. The covariation matrix was computed from this stacked matrix after the row means had been subtracted.

The first three eigenvectors were computed from this covariation matrix and appear in Table 2. The code names (W1, W2, etc.) for the men are those used by Homans and in the more recent articles. Since the goal of the analysis is to find patterns in the data, the next step is to permute the rows and columns of the data to conform to the rank ordering of the loadings on the first eigenvector. These permuted data are presented in Table 3. Now, depending on

TABLE 2

Results of Four Methods Applied to Bank Wiring Group

	Eigenvectors of MCM			First left eigenvector of MC[a]	Result of CONCOR	Result of modified CONCOR
	Vector 1	Vector 2	Vector 3			
W1	−0.321	0.113	0.213	−0.300	−1	−0.530
W2	−0.261	−0.399	0.061	−0.240	−1	−0.357
W3	−0.359	0.242	0.455	−0.338	−1	−0.642
S1	−0.207	0.382	−0.414	−0.186	−1	−0.185
W4	−0.257	0.324	−0.356	−0.236	−1	−0.296
W5	−0.071	−0.553	−0.086	−0.050	−1	−0.029
W6	0.276	−0.044	−0.474	0.297	1	0.534
S2	0.000	−0.038	0.017	0.021	1	0.004
W7	0.342	0.214	0.406	0.363	1	0.759
W8	0.362	0.141	−0.026	0.383	1	0.828
W9	0.403	0.081	0.211	0.424	1	1.000
S4	0.278	−0.077	−0.054	0.299	1	0.494
I1	−0.142	−0.027	0.027	−0.121	−1	−0.105
I3	−0.042	−0.360	0.020	−0.021	−1	−0.001
Eigenvalues	0.521	0.285	0.143	0.521		
% of total variance explained	0.303	0.166	0.083	0.303		

[a]This would be the result from iterating covariations and differs from column 1 by a constant, 0.021.

one's substantive and methodological interests, one might search for meaningful partitions of the data by eyeballing the rearranged data matrix (not a bad method), or by partitioning the data according to the sign of the column vector loadings in the first eigenvector. However, there is something arbitrary about imposing a boundary between the column vectors with negative and positive loadings on the first eigenvector. This can be seen by noting in Table 3 and the

TABLE 3

Five Sociomatrices for Bank Wiring Group Permuted
to Conform with Ordering on First Principal Component

Liking

```
W3   – 1 – 1 1 1 – – – – – – – –
W1   1 – – 1 1 – – – – – – – – –
W2   – – – – – – – – – – – – – –
W4   1 1 – – 1 – – – – – – – – –
S1   1 1 – 1 – – – – – – – 1 – –
I1   1 – – – – – – – – – – – – –
W5   – – – – – – – – – – – – – –
I3   – – – – – – – – – – – – – –
S2   – – – – – – – – – – – – – –
W6   – – – – – – – – – – – – – –
S4   – – – – – – – – – – – 1 1
W7   – – – – 1 – – – – – – – 1 1
W8   – – – – – – – – – 1 1 – 1
W9   – – – – – – – – – 1 1 1 –
```

Windows

```
W3   – – – – – – – – – – – – – –
W1   – – – – – – – – – – – – – –
W2   – – – – – – – – – – – – – –
W4   – – – – – – 1 – – 1 – 1 – 1
S1   – – – – – – 1 – – 1 1 – 1 1
I1   – – – – – – – – – – – – – –
W5   – – – 1 1 – – – – 1 – – – –
I3   – – – – – – – – – – – – – –
S2   – – – – – – – – – – – – – –
W6   – – – 1 1 – 1 – – – 1 1 1 1
S4   – – – – 1 – – – – 1 – 1 1 –
W7   – – – 1 – – – – – 1 1 – 1 1
W8   – – – – 1 – – – – 1 1 1 – 1
W9   – – – 1 1 – – – – 1 – 1 1 –
```

Antagonism

```
W3   – – – – – – – – – – – – – –
W1   – – – – – – – – – – – – – –
W2   – – – – – 1 – – – – – 1 1 1
W4   – – – – – – 1 – – – – – – –
S1   – – – – – – 1 – – – – – – –
I1   – – 1 – – – – 1 – – – – – –
W5   – – – 1 1 – – 1 1 1 – 1 1 1
I3   – – – – – 1 1 – – 1 1 1 1 1
S2   – – – – – – 1 – – – – – – –
W6   – – – – – – 1 1 – – – 1 – –
S4   – – – – – – – 1 – – – – – –
W7   – – 1 – – – 1 1 – 1 – 1 – – –
W8   – – 1 – – – 1 1 – – – – – –
W9   – – 1 – – – 1 1 – – – – – –
```

Games

```
W3   – 1 1 1 1 1 1 – – – – – – –
W1   1 – 1 1 1 1 1 – – – – – – –
W2   1 1 – 1 1 1 – – – – – – – –
W4   1 1 1 – 1 1 1 – – – – – – –
S1   1 1 1 1 – – 1 – – – – – – –
I1   1 1 1 1 – – – – – – – – – –
W5   1 1 – 1 1 – – – – – – 1 – –
I3   – – – – – – – – – – – – – –
S2   – – – – – – – – – – – – – –
W6   – – – – – – – – – – 1 1 1
S4   – – – – – – – – – – 1 1 1
W7   – – – – – – 1 – – 1 1 – 1 1
W8   – – – – – – – – 1 1 1 – 1
W9   – – – – – – – – 1 1 1 1 –
```

Helping

```
W3   - - 1 - - - - - - - - - - -
W1   1 - - - 1 - - - - - - - - 1
W2   1 - - 1 1 - - - - - - - - -
W4   1 1 - - - - - - - 1 - - - -
S1   - - - - - - - - - - - 1 - -
I1   - - - - - - - - - - - - - -
W5   1 - - - - - - - - - - - - -
I3   - - - - - - - - - - - - - -
S2   - - - - - - - - - 1 - - - -
W6   1 - - - - - - - - - 1 1 1
S4   - - - 1 - - - - - - - - 1 -
W7   - - - - - - - - - - 1 - - -
W8   - - - - - - - - - 1 - 1 - 1
W9   - - - - - - - - - - 1 - - -
```

first column of Table 2 that W5, I3, and S2 are more similar to each other than to the other sets of men. It is only in the application of this arbitrary criterion that the left eigenvectors of *MC* (the first one appears in Table 2, column 4) could yield slightly different results. As will be seen in the next section, this is analogous to how Breiger and White use the results of CONCOR. They would then adopt a hierarchical clustering approach by repeating the analysis within each of the two clusters. One could also attempt to partition the data by clustering the column vectors that have "similar" loadings on the first eigenvector. With this approach, the number of clusters and the definition of "similar" are determined ad hoc from data.

Note that for all of the above approaches the permuted data are already in the right order, and the researcher must simply locate the "cluster boundaries." Alternatively, one could try any of the above methods on other eigenvectors with large eigenvalues. Finally, one could adopt a multidimensional-"factor analytic" approach that simultaneously considers the first several eigenvalues and associated eigenvectors. This might include searching for an orthogonal or oblique rotation of the principal components, which would indicate distinct clusters.

The computation of principal components is only the beginning of an analysis. Its value can only be judged by its effectiveness as a tool to help the researcher observe and study the patterns and structures of social interactions present in the data. Observe that the linear ordering of the men produced by the first principal component is strictly consistent with the two-block model obtained by White et al. (1976a) and Breiger et al. (1975) from the application of CONCOR. Since the data are fairly straightforward and there is a detailed discussion of the substantive interpretation of this and more refined blockings in both these articles, I will not present one here. However, I would like to stress one major distinction between the preceding principal components analysis and CONCOR. Whereas CONCOR produces a rigid assignment of each individual to one of two clusters or blocks, principal components analysis is more flexible; two clusters may emerge, but there are other possibilities as well. For example, the fifth column of Table 2 shows that CONCOR has assigned W5 and I3 to one block and S2 to the other.[9] However, the data for these men and their projections onto the first principal component indicate that they are more similar to each other than to the other nodes in their respective blocks and should, perhaps, be grouped together to form a third block. While they do not form a "clique" of their own (in the sense of being positively related to one another), they are structurally equivalent because of the similarity of their relationships to each other and to the two primary cliques. These results obtained by principal components analysis are similar to those obtained by Homans; he identified the two cliques and concluded that W5, I3, and S2 were not members of either.

ITERATED CORRELATIONS – CONCOR

In an earlier section of this chapter, the mathematical properties of iterated covariations were completely explained. I will extend some of the earlier results in an investigation of CONCOR. But first I begin with a theorem that provides some insight into the occurence of only plus and minus ones as CONCOR converges.

THEOREM 4. *Any correlation matrix R of rank one contains only ones and minus ones and, under a suitable premutation imposed on both the rows and columns, can be blocked into a bipartition producing four submatrices exhibiting the following form:*

[9] When CONCOR is applied as a hierarchical clustering algorithm on subsets of the original data, the problem of rigidity becomes more serious. This is due to the fact that once two nodes, such as W5 and S2, have been assigned to different blocks, they can never be reunited in a more refined blockmodel (with three or more blocks), despite their similarities.

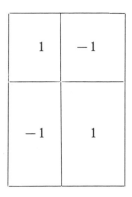

Proof. Since R is symmetric, positive semi-definite, and of rank one, it can be expressed as the product of a single eigenvector $\mathbf{w}$ (corresponding to the only non-zero eigenvalue) and its transpose: $\mathbf{w}(\mathbf{w})^t$. This means that $r_{ij} = w_i w_j$ for all i and j. From the fact that the diagonal elements of R equal one, it follows that $r_{ii} = 1 = w_i w_i = w_i^2$. Therefore, w_i must equal 1 or -1. If one permutes the n entries in $\mathbf{w}$ so that all $(h) - 1$s precede the $(n - h) + 1$s, and then compute the $r_{ij} = w_i w_j$, r_{ij} will equal one if neither i nor j is greater than h (upper left $h \times h$ block), or if both i and j are greater than (lower left $h - h \times n - h$ block), and r_{ij} will equal minus one elsewhere (that is, lower left and upper right blocks).

Theorem 4 suggests that the convergence of CONCOR to plus and minus ones is a consequence of the algorithm converging to a rank one matrix. Like iterated covariations, the eigenvalues and eigenvectors of successive iterations of correlation matrices $R^{[1]}$, $R^{[2]}$, $R^{[3]}$, ... change as they progress towards convergence. However, the process is even more complicated, since at each iteration, in addition to subtracting out the column means, the covariation matrix $Q^{[j]}$ is normalized by the $D^{[j]}$ which depends on the diagonal of $Q^{[j]}$.

To review the process, begin with the original correlation matrix R of the data. Then,

$$Q^{[1]} = RMR$$

$$R^{[1]} = D^{[1]}Q^{[1]}D^{[1]} = D^{[1]}RMRD^{[1]}$$

$$Q^{[2]} = R^{[1]}MR^{[1]} = D^{[1]}RMRD^{[1]}MD^{[1]}RMRD^{[1]}$$

$$R^{[2]} = D^{[2]}Q^{[2]}D^{[2]}$$

Similarly,

$$Q^{[j]} = R^{[j-1]} M R^{[j-1]}$$

and

$$R^{[j]} = D^{[j]} Q^{[j]} D^{[j]}$$

where M is the matrix which subtracts out column means, and $D^{[j]}$ is the diagonal matrix whose entries are the reciprocals of the square roots of the diagonal entries of $Q^{[j]}$.

In examining iterated covariations, a certain consistency was observed accross the iterations $C^{[1]}$, $C^{[2]}$, $C^{[3]}$: each was the product of a "power of MC" and its transpose. Since all powers of a matrix have the same eigenvectors, and their eigenvalues vary in a known manner, it was possible to determine the limit of the iterations. Unfortunately, no such consistency exists in the iterated correlations. At each iteration a new $D^{[j]}$ is added to the expression.

However, there is a modified version of CONCOR using an alternative method of iterating that produces the same sign pattern as the original CONCOR algorithm, but provides, as well, some additional information which is masked by the original version. Suppose, as before, that we start with the original correlation matrix R and compute its covariation matrix $Q^{[1]}$. Now, instead of computing $R^{[1]}(=D^{[1]} Q^{[1]} D^{[1]})$, create a matrix $H^{[1]} = D^{[1]} Q^{[1]}$. Each column of this new matrix $H^{[1]}$ (which is asymmetric) differs from the corresponding column of $R^{[1]}$ by a multiplicative constant. Since this is the only difference between $H^{[1]}$ and $R^{[1]}$, $R^{[2]}$ must be the correlation matrix of both. However, the covariation matrix of $H^{[1]}$ is not $Q^{[2]}$, the covariation matrix of $R^{[1]}$. The covariation matrix of $H^{[1]}$ will be designated $P^{[2]}$, which has a corresponding diagonal matrix $F^{[2]}$ by which it can be pre- and post-multiplied to obtain $R^{[2]}$. Note that $P^{[1]}$ equals $Q^{[1]}$, and $F^{[1]}$ equals $D^{[1]}$. Repeat the calculations. Instead of computing $R^{[2]}$, we compute $H^{[2]} = F^{[2]} P^{[2]}$, and again these two matrices, $R^{[2]}$ and $H^{[2]}$ are related in that they have the identical correlation matrix $R^{[3]}$. The modified version of CONCOR consists of iterating:

$$P^{[j]} = H^{[j-1]\,t} M H^{[j-1]} = P^{[j-1]} F^{[j-1]} M F^{[j-1]} P^{[j-1]}$$

where $F^{[j]}$ equals the reciprocal square roots of the diagonal of $P^{[j]}$, and $H^{[j]} = F^{[j]} P^{[j]}$. This method must parallel CONCOR because

$$R^{[j]} = H^{[j]} F^{[j]} = F^{[j]} P^{[j]} F^{[j]}$$

In particular, the limit of $R^{[j]}$ must equal the limit of $F^{[j]}P^{[j]}F^{[j]}$.[10]
Now let us examine the $P^{[j]}$.

First we note that $P^{[j]}$ is a covariation matrix and, therefore, has an eigenvector decomposition $P^{[j]} = V^{[j]}K^{[j]}V^{[j]^t}$. By thinking about the $P^{[j]}$ as linear transformations of a vector space into itself, we can observe a pattern in the successive iterations. The nullspace (or kernel) of $P^{[j]}$ is that subspace (of the n-dimensional vector space of $n \times 1$ column vectors) of vectors $\mathbf{v}$ satisfying the condition $P^{[j]}\mathbf{v} = 0$. This is simply the subspace spanned by the eigenvectors with a zero eigenvalue. The other subspace of interest is the quotient space of the n-dimensional vector space by the nullspace and is equivalent to the subspace spanned by the eigenvectors with non-zero eigenvalues (hereafter to be called "non-zero eigenvectors"). By examining the above equation for $P^{[j]}$, it is apparent that the nullspace of $P^{[j]}$ must contain the nullspace of $P^{[j-1]}$. This is because if $\mathbf{v}$ is in the nullspace of $P^{[j-1]}$, then $P^{[j-1]}\mathbf{v} = 0$ and

$$P^{[j]}\mathbf{v} = P^{[j-1]}F^{[j-1]}MF^{[j-1]}P^{[j-1]}\mathbf{v}$$

$$= P^{[j-1]}F^{[j-1]}MF^{[j-1]}0 = 0$$

Therefore, $\mathbf{v}$ is in the nullspace of $P^{[j]}$. Generalizing, the nullspace of $P^{[j]}$ is contained in the nullspace of $P^{[i]}$ for all i greater than or equal to j. The opposite argument can be made for the above-defined quotient spaces. If $\mathbf{v}$ is in the subspace spanned by the non-zero eigenvectors of $P^{[j]}$, then $\mathbf{v}$ is in the subspace spanned by the non-zero eigenvectors of $P^{[i]}$, for all i less than or equal to j. Ideally, we would like to know (without iterating) what linear combination(s) of the non-zero eigenvectors of $P^{[1]}$ equal the non-zero eigenvector(s) of the limit of $P^{[j]}$.

Assume now that the $P^{[j]}$ do converge (controlling for a scalar constant) towards a rank one matrix. Then, as in Theorem 4, the limit of $P^{[j]}$ equals $\mathbf{w}(\mathbf{w})^t$, where $\mathbf{w}$ is the single suitably normalized non-zero eigenvector. Then the diagonal entries of the limit

---

[10] There is one type of situation in which the latter limit is undefined. This is when one or more diagonal elements of the limit of $P^{[j]}$ equal zero, in which case the corresponding element of the limit of $F^{[j]}$ is undefined. (The limit of $R^{[j]}$ may still exist, and this discrepancy could be resolved by agreeing to set the corresponding elements of $F^{[j]}$ equal to 1.) However, this event (limit $P_{ii}^{[j]} = 0$) for some i, is unlikely ever to occur in real data unless one of the original data vectors has zero variance.

of $P_{ii}^{[j]}$ equal w_i^2, and the corresponding entries in the limit of $F^{[j]}$ must equal the reciprocal square root of w_i^2, that is, the reciprocal of the absolute value of w_i. Then (Limit $F^{[j]}$)w equals a vector of ones and minus ones (call it **x**) where $x_i = (w_i/|w_i|) = \pm 1$. The fact that the limit of $H^{[j]}$ equals $\mathbf{x}(\mathbf{w})^t$, and the limit of $R^{[j]} = \mathbf{x}(\mathbf{x})^t$, is related to Theorem 4 and shows that the results of the original CONCOR are simply the signs of the non-zero eigenvector **w** of the limit of $P^{[j]}$. To show that there is no inconsistency in treating **w** as the only eigenvector of successive iterations, we compute a new P from the limit of $H^{[j]}$ which yields

$$(\text{Limit } H^{[j]^t}) M (\text{Limit } H^{[j]}) = \mathbf{w}((\mathbf{x})^t M \mathbf{x}) \mathbf{w}^t$$

$$= \mathbf{w}((\mathbf{x})^t M \mathbf{x}) \mathbf{w}^t$$

$$= \mathbf{w} \left(\sum_{i=1}^{n} x_i(x_i - \bar{x}) \right) \mathbf{w}^t$$

$$= n(1 - \bar{x}^2) \mathbf{w}(\mathbf{w})^t$$

which is a scalar multiple of $\mathbf{w}(\mathbf{w})^t$, the original limit of $P^{[j]}$ ($\bar{x}$ is the mean of **x**). Finally, it might be worth noting that it can be shown that each of the $F^{[j]}$ resulting from this algorithm is the product of all the $D^{[i]}$ (for i less than or equal to j) that would be obtained by the original CONCOR that computed $R^{[j]}$ at each step. Therefore, the limit of $F^{[j]}$ equals the limit of $\prod_{i=1}^{j} D^{[1]}$, showing that the individual $D^{[j]}$ must converge to the product of a scalar (the same $n (1 - \bar{x}^2)$) and the identity matrix, and $\prod D^{[i]}$ must converge to a diagonal matrix whose entries are the reciprocal absolute value of the corresponding entries of **w**. (As before, these limits are only strictly defined if the scalar constant is controlled.)

No known equation predicts what linear combination of the non-zero eigenvectors of $P^{[1]}$ equals the non-zero eigenvector **w** of the limit of $P^{[j]}$, nor is there a mathematical proof of the empirical fact that CONCOR converges. Letting $V^{*[1]}$ be the $n \times r$ matrix whose columns are the r non-zero eigenvectors of $P^{[1]}$ normalized to unit length; and, normalizing **w** to unit length, we want to find the $r \times 1$ column vector **u** where $\mathbf{w} = V^{*[1]} \mathbf{u}$ or, alternatively, $\mathbf{u} = V^{*[1]^t} \mathbf{w}$. This **u** contains the set of weights for computing **w** from the eigenvectors in $V^{*[1]}$ and has the property that the sum of its squared elements must equal one. Empirically, the following results seem to be true, assuming that the eigenvectors in $V^{*[1]}$ are ordered with those on the left having the largest associated eigenvalues. First, the weight or loading of the first eigenvector u_1 is very large — usually greater than 0.95 — implying that the dominant eigenvector of $P^{[1]}$ has by far the largest effect on **w**. Second, in over 90 percent of a sample of over 200 random matrices, ranging in size from 5×5 to 10×10, the sign pattern of **w** exactly equalled the sign pattern of the first eigenvector in $V^{*[1]}$. For those situations in which discrepancies occurred, the elements (w_i and $v_{i1}^{*[1]}$) that were discrepant were both close to zero.

Thus it is seen that the result of CONCOR, **w**, can be reasonably approximated by the first principal component of $P^{[1]}$ (the covariation matrix of the original correlation matrix R). This matrix $P^{[1]}$ may also be thought of as the first iteration of iterated covariations if the original data have been normalized. The first principal component of $P^{[1]}$ is even more strongly related to the outcome of iterated covariations on R than to the result of the modified CONCOR algorithm. This helps to explain the empirically observed similarity between the outcomes of CONCOR and iterated covariations when applied to a correlation matrix. As can be seen from columns 4 and 6 of Table 2, the similarity can be very marked even when iterated covariations are applied to a covariation matrix.

Based on this and other evidence, it seems clear that the modified CONCOR algorithm produces something like a first principal component of *MRM*. The ways in which it differs from the principal component are not understood, except that, like the outcome of iterated covariations, the mean of **w** is not constrained to be zero. In analyses of social network data not reported here, I could find no substantive significance in the small difference between the first principal component of *MRM* and the output of the modified CONCOR algorithm. The two methods repeatedly produced almost identical linear orderings of individuals. Therefore, it is unclear why someone, given the choice, would choose to use a version of CONCOR, whose mathematical properties are still only partially understood — rather than principal components analysis, which is well understood and produces more information (*all* principal components).

Nevertheless, for those who would still choose CONCOR, I would strongly urge the use of the modified version, which produces the vector **w** which locates each individual along a single axis. The original CONCOR indicates only whether an individual is located to the left or right of zero along this axis. This is a rather arbitrary criterion which may obscure the similarities among individuals located near zero. This is demonstrated by the scores of W5, I3, and S2 in columns 5 and 6 of Table 2.

SUMMARY

The CONCOR algorithm has been introduced into the literature at least twice: by McQuitty and Clark (1968) and Breiger et al. (1975). White and Breiger have used CONCOR empirically to search for structural equivalence and blockmodels in various types of sociometric data. In order to investigate the mathematical foundations of this algorithm, the related but simpler problem of iterating covariations was examined. It was found that the limit of this process is directly interpretable in terms of the original data with row and column means subtracted out (that is, the matrix of interactions, or residuals from the additive model). Iterating covariations proved to be merely an inefficient method for computing a first principal component of this matrix.

Since the related CONCOR algorithm had been useful in the search for blockmodels, it stood to reason that this special case of principal components analysis might also prove useful. A methodological explanation was offered for why this should be true, and an application of this type of principal components analysis was presented. It was observed that the social structure of the Bank Wiring Group was reflected in the individual loadings on the first principal component. This result was compared to those obtained from both the original and a modified version of CONCOR.

It seems reasonable to conclude, from mathematical and empirical examination, that CONCOR produces results similar to a first principal component. There does not appear to be any compelling reason to apply CONCOR, since it is obscure and produces less information than principal components analysis. CONCOR has proven useful in the development of blockmodel analysis and in the study of concrete populations. The criticisms I have raised have pointed the way toward a more useful, efficient, and mathematically interpretable procedure for blockmodel analysis.

APPENDIX 1: PROOF THAT ITERATED
COVARIATION AND CONCOR
ONLY CONVERGE IN THE LIMIT

THEOREM 5. *Each successive iteration of iterated covariations or* CONCOR *has the same rank as the first.*

Proof. First we prove the theorem for iterated covariations, where $C^{[j]}$ equals the jth iteration of the original covariation matrix C. Since the product of a matrix and its transpose has the same rank as the matrix itself, and $C^{[1]} = (MC)^t(MC)$, the rank of $C^{[1]}$ equals the rank of MC. Because $C^{[j+1]} = (MC)^{(2^j)t}(MC)^{(2^j)}$, the rank of $C^{[j+1]}$ equals the rank of $(MC)^{(2^j)}$. The rank of a matrix equals the number of its non-zero eigenvalues, including any multiplicities which may occur. The eigenvalues of a matrix raised to a power equal the eigenvalues (of the original matrix) raised to the same power. Therefore, the eigenvalues of $(MC)^{(2^j)}$ equal the eigenvalues of MC raised to the 2^j power. Since a number raised to the 2^j power can only equal zero if the original number equals zero, MC and $(MC)^{(2^j)}$ have the same number of non-zero eigenvalues for any j and, therefore, have the same rank. Thus, $C^{[j+1]}$ and $C^{[1]}$ have the same rank.

To prove the theorem for CONCOR is more difficult and will be done by induction. Start with the obvious observation that the rank of $R^{[1]}$ equals the rank of $R^{[1]}$. It must now be shown that if the rank of $R^{[j]}$ equals the rank of $R^{[1]}$, than the rank of $R^{[j+1]}$ equals the rank of $R^{[1]}$.

$$R^{[j]} = D^{[j]}Q^{[j]}D^{[j]} = D^{[j]}R^{[j-1]}MR^{[j-1]}D^{[j]}$$

(by definition)

$$= (D^{[j]}R^{[j-1]}M)(MR^{[j-1]}D^{[j]})$$

(since $M = MM$)

$$= (MR^{[j-1]}D^{[j]})^t(MR^{[j-1]}D^{[j]})$$

(since M, $R^{[j-1]}$, and $D^{[j]}$ are symmetric).

Since the product of a matrix and its transpose has the same rank as the matrix itself, the rank of $R^{[j]}$ equals the rank of $MR^{[j-1]}D^{[j]}$, which must, therefore, equal the rank of $R^{[1]}$. By the same logic, it is seen that the rank of $R^{[j+1]}$ equals the rank of $MR^{[j]}D$. Applying the first part of the proof of Theorem 2, the rank of $MR^{[j]}D^{[j+1]}$ equals the rank of $MR^{[j]}$ because $D^{[j+1]}$ is non-singular (of rank n). Using the second part of the proof of Theorem 2, the eigenvalues—and, therefore, the rank—of $MR^{[j]}$ (which equals $MMR^{[j]}$) are equal to the eigenvalues of $MR^{[j]}M$. By substitution,

$$MR^{[j]}M = M(D^{[j]}R^{[j-1]}MR^{[j-1]}D^{[j]})M$$
$$= (MD^{[j]}R^{[j-1]}M)(MR^{[j-1]}D^{[j]}M)$$
$$= (MR^{[j-1]}D^{[j]}M)^t(MR^{[j-1]}D^{[j]}M)$$

Since $MR^{[j]}M$ is the product of a matrix and its transpose, the rank of $MR^{[j]}M$ equals the rank of $MR^{[j-1]}D^{[j]}M$. Applying the second part of the proof of Theorem 2 again, the eigenvalues and rank of $MR^{[j-1]}D^{[j]}$ equal the eigenvalues of $MR^{[j-1]}D^{[j]}M$. From the above statements, it follows that the rank of $R^{[j+1]}$ equals the rank of $MR^{[j-1]}D^{[j]}M$ equals the rank of $MR^{[j-1]}D^{[j]}$ equals the rank of $R^{[j]}$, which, by assumption, equals the rank of $R^{[1]}$. This concludes the proof.

APPENDIX 2: ELEMENTARY EXAMPLES
OF DATA MATRICES FOR WHICH CONCOR
DOES NOT CONVERGE TO A RANK ONE MATRIX

If we consider correlations from a geometric perspective, it is not difficult to understand some conditions under which the original version of CONCOR does not converge to a rank one matrix of plus and minus ones. Geometrically, the correlation coefficient between two vectors is the cosine of the angle they form. With this in mind, we examine two elementary examples of sociomatrices which converge to a matrix of rank two. These are presented in Figure 1. In example A each of the offff-diagonal correlations of the CONCOR result is -0.5; therefore, the angle between each pair of vectors is $120°$. When this is diagrammed with vectors of equal length, the result is an equilateral triangle. The CONCOR result reflects the fact that there is no two-cluster solution for three points in an equilateral triangle. The data in sociomatrix B form an isosceles triangle. The result of CONCOR indicate that the first and third

	Sociomatrix			CONCOR Result		
	0	1	0	1.0	−0.5	−0.5
A	0	0	1	−0.5	1.0	−0.5
	1	0	0	−0.5	−0.5	1.0
	1	0	0	1.0	0.0	−1.0
B	1	1	1	0.0	1.0	0.0
	0	0	1	−1.0	0.0	1.0

Diagram

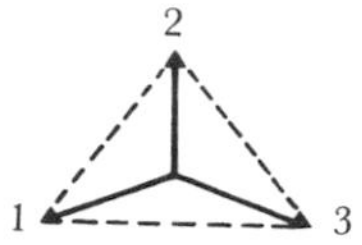

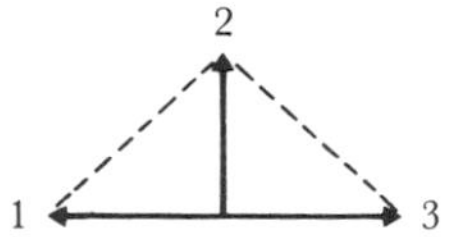

Figure 1.

points should be put in separate clusters, but there is no basis for assigning the second point to either cluster.

I have examined many other examples for which CONCOR converges to a matrix of rank greater than one. When viewed geometrically, every known example corresponds to a geometric figure displayed some form of symmetry. Thus, if the points are all equidistant—or form a square, cube, or other regular figure—then CONCOR will not produce the usual two-cluster result. However, there are figures which display some symmetry but still converge to a rank one matrix. The probability of obtaining data which do not converge to a rank one matrix is actually very, very small.

REFERENCES

BAILEY, K. D.

1975 "Cluster Analysis." In D. Heise (Ed.), *Sociological Methodology 1975.* San Francisco: Jossey-Bass.

BLALOCK, H. M., JR.

1972 *Social Statistics.* New York: McGraw-Hill.

BREIGER, R. L.

1974 "The Duality of Persons and Groups." *Social Forces* 53:181–190.

1976 "Career Attributes and Network Structure: A Blockmodel Study of a Biomedical Research Specialty." *American Sociological Review* 41:117–135.

BREIGER, R. L., BOORMAN, S. A., AND ARABIE, P.

1975 "An Algorithm for Clustering Relational Data with Applications to Social Network Analysis and Comparison with Multidimensional Scaling." *Journal of Mathematical Psychology* 12 (Aug.):328–383.

CLARK, J. A., AND MC QUITTY, L. L.

1970   "Some Problems and Elaborations of Iterative, Intercolumnar Correlational Analysis." *Educational and Psychological Measurement* 30:773–784.

CORMACK, R. M.

1971   "A Review of Classification." *Journal of the Royal Statistical Society* 134 (Series A):321–368.

HERSTEIN, I. N.

1964   *Topics in Algebra.* New York: Blaisdell.

HOMANS, G. C.

1950   *The Human Group.* New York: Harcourt Brace Jovanovich.

HOPE, K.

1969   "The Complete Analysis of a Data Matrix." *British Journal of Psychiatry* 115:1069–1079.

1970   "The Complete Analysis of a Data Matrix: Application and Interpretation." *British Journal of Psychiatry* 116:657–666.

LORRAIN, F. P., AND WHITE, H. C.

1971   "Structural Equivalence of Individuals in Social Networks." *The Journal of Mathematical Sociology* 1:49–80.

MAC RAE, D.

1960   "Direct Factor Analysis of Sociometric Data." *Sociometry* 23:360–371.

MC QUITTY, L. L.

1968   "Multiple Clusters Types and Dimensions from Interactive Intercolumnar Correlation Analysis." *Multivariate Behavioral Research* 3:465–477.

MC QUITTY, L. L., AND CLARK, J. A.

1968   "Clusters from Iterative, Intercolumnar Correlational Analysis." *Educational and Psychological Measurement* 28:211–238.

NOMIZU, K.

1966   *Fundamentals of Linear Algebra.* New York: McGraw-Hill.

ROETHLISBERGER, F. J., AND DICKSON, W. J.

1939   *Management and the Worker.* Cambridge: Harvard University Press.

WHITE, H. C., BOORMAN, S. A., AND BREIGER, R. L.

1976a "Social Structure from Multiple Networks: I. Blockmodels of Roles and Positions." *American Journal of Sociology* 81:730–780.

WHITE, H. C., AND BOORMAN, S. A.

1976b "Social Structure from Multiple Networks: Role Interlock." *American Journal of Sociology,* in press.

Received December 4, 1974.

9

STATISTICAL INFERENCE
AND STATISTICAL POWER
IN APPLICATIONS OF THE
GENERAL LINEAR MODEL

William T. Bielby

UNIVERSITY OF WISCONSIN-MADISON

James R. Kluegel

UNIVERSITY OF CALIFORNIA-RIVERSIDE

During the preparation of this paper the authors were supported by the National Institute of General Medical Sciences Training Program in Methodology and Statistics Grant 5-T01-GM01526-08. The research reported here was supported in part by funds granted to the Institute for Research on Poverty at the University of Wisconsin-Madison by the Office of Economic Opportunity pursuant to the Economic Opportunity Act of 1964. The opinions expressed are those of the authors.

INTRODUCTION

Our purpose in this chapter is to provide for a more informed use of statistical inference in tests of hypotheses in survey applications of the general linear model (*GLM*). This model, like any model, is comprised of a set of assumptions that permit the derivation of certain general principles. The assumptions of the *GLM* are of particular utility to the survey researcher in that they permit one to draw inferences about the structure of relationships among variables to larger populations on the basis of sample survey data. In this chapter we suggest that when conducting multiple statistical tests of hypotheses within the *GLM* framework, our results will be more meaningful if we know the overall probability of rejecting a false null hypothesis and the probability of finding statistically significant results when substantively meaningful effects exist.

By following the current practice for doing multiple tests for hypotheses on parameters of linear models, researchers are inadequately controlling the probability of rejecting a true null hypothesis—the probability of making a Type I error. Inference considerations in situations where multiple tests of hypotheses are conducted are qualitatively different from procedures described for single hypothesis testing in most texts. Procedures currently employed yield Type I error rates that can be considerably lower than the true probability of rejecting a true null hypothesis when a number of hypotheses are tested. Scientific norms of parsimony that dictate researchers be conservative in their claims of the empirical effects of social variables are clearly violated as social researchers systematically underestimate the likelihood that Type I errors are occurring in their analyses. Drawing on a considerable body of literature on simultaneous inference in the *GLM,* we argue that analysts of survey data must reconceptualize their approach to statistical inference. We discuss several techniques for treating the simultaneous inference problem in the *GLM,* and present, with examples, procedures for applying these techniques to survey data.

In current research practice little concern has been expressed for the power of *GLM* statistical tests. Analysts of large sample survey data often dismiss power considerations with the assertion that their tests have "more than enough power"—even trivial effects yield statistically significant results (Blau and Duncan, 1967, pp. 17–18).

We present examples below to demonstrate that for many *GLM* hypotheses, whether or not the tests are characterized by "more than enough power," can be quite problematic. Indeed, most researchers are confronted with a situation where they must take as given two important determinants of the power of statistical tests, sample size, and the configuration of independent variables.[1] Thus, we argue that it is imperative that the analyst compute the magnitudes of the effects that are likely to be detectable in a given set of data. As we shall demonstrate below, the power of *GLM* tests can be routinely calculated.

The importance of the consideration of issues in simultaneous statistical inference and power for the informed use of statistical tests of hypotheses requires that the survey researcher be aware of major issues and procedures pertaining to these two areas. In this chapter, we provide a critical examination of issues and procedures in simultaneous statistical inference and statistical power as they apply to the research. We begin our exegesis with a brief review of assumptions of the *GLM* and common hypothesis tests in survey research applications. Drawing on the body of literature on simultaneous inference in the *GLM,* we argue that analysts of survey data must reconceptualize their approach to statistical inference. We discuss several techniques for treating the simultaneous inference problem in the *GLM,* and present, with examples, procedures for applying these techniques to survey data. Following the treatment of simultaneous inference, we examine factors that influence the ability to detect substantively meaningful effects — statistical power. A procedure for estimating the power of statistical tests is discussed, and illustrative examples of the influence of various factors on statistical power are presented. We conclude with some suggestions for improving the use of statistical inference in making meaningful decisions about the merits of the hypotheses being tested.

---

[1] The choice of sample size in a survey design is always subject to cost constraints, and it is simply impossible to take into consideration the impact of sample size on all hypotheses that will be subsequently tested on the data. With multivariate sampling, it is impossible to fix *a priori* the variation in each independent variable and the covariation among the independent variables. Thus, even those analysts fortunate enough to be involved in survey design have only limited control over the power of their subsequent tests.

THE GENERAL LINEAR MODEL: ASSUMPTIONS AND COMMON HYPOTHESIS TESTS

GLM Assumptions

We shall concern ourselves with tests of hypotheses about the parameters of the *GLM,* the classical model stated in matrix terms as follows:

$$\underset{(N \times 1)}{\mathbf{y}} = \underset{(N \times K)}{\mathbf{X}} \underset{(K \times 1)}{\beta} + \underset{(N \times 1)}{\varepsilon} \tag{1}$$

$$E(\varepsilon) = \mathbf{0} \tag{2}$$

$$E(\varepsilon\varepsilon') = \sigma^2 \mathbf{I} \tag{3}$$

$$\varepsilon \sim N(\mathbf{0}, \sigma^2 \mathbf{I}) \tag{4}$$

$\mathbf{X}$ is fixed (nonstochastic) and of full column rank.[2]   (5)

While the theory of statistical inference for the *GLM* was originally developed for the above model, assumption (5), fixed $\mathbf{X}$, is clearly untenable in the application of the model to survey data. It requires that the sampling design include *a priori* stratification on all independent variables, that is, *a priori* specification of cell sizes for each combination of the levels of the independent variables. A modification of the above model allows for the typical survey design of multivariate sampling from the joint distribution of $\mathbf{y}$ and $\mathbf{X}$. We replace (2) through (5) above with the following assumptions:

$$E(\varepsilon|\mathbf{X}) = \mathbf{0} \tag{2a}$$

$$E(\varepsilon\varepsilon'|\mathbf{X}) = \sigma^2 \mathbf{I} \tag{3a}$$

$$\varepsilon|X \sim N(\mathbf{0}, \sigma^2 \mathbf{I}) \tag{4a}$$

Thus it is required that the classical assumption holds *conditionally* on $\mathbf{X}$. The disturbance must be mean independent of the independent variables[3] and be conditionally, independently normally distribut-

---

[2] In models in which an intercept is specified, the first column of $\mathbf{X}$ is a vector of ones, $(1\ 1\ ...\ 1)'$; and the first element of the β vectors is the intercept parameter. All models considered in this paper will have intercepts specified. Thus $K - 1$ rather than K is the number of independent variables.

[3] This requirement is stronger than that of uncorrelatedness of ε and $\mathbf{X}$; it is a weaker assumption than statistical independence of ε and $\mathbf{X}$.

ed with zero mean and constant variance. While this more appropriate conditional *GLM* presents no differences in the treatment of Type I error, it does complicate the treatment of power. While our results with respect to Type I error hold unconditionally, the procedures for power calculations presented in this paper give results *conditional* upon the values of **X** realized in a particular sample (Graybill, 1961, pp. 204–205; Sampson, 1974). The conditional power calculations presented herein must be considered upper bounds upon the unconditional power of the tests.[4]

Hypothesis Testing in Survey Applications of the *GLM*

In Table 1 we present an outline of the types of *GLM* hypotheses commonly tested in survey applications and the statistical tests applied to those hypotheses. In (1) we have the test of an individual coefficient, β_i. The *t*-test is just $b_i - \beta_i^*$ divided by the standard error of b_i, the usual *t*-ratio computed in regression programs. The one degree of freedom *F*-test is merely the square of the *t*-test.

Hypothesis (2) is the test that a subset of J coefficients are jointly equal to a set of J specified values. When $\boldsymbol{\beta}_{(2)}^*$ is specified to be a vector of zeros and $J = K - 1$, it is the common "overall" *F*-test of no regression. When $J < K - 1$, and $\boldsymbol{\beta}_{(2)}^*$ is a vector of zeros, it is the "increment to R_2" *F*-test for a subset of variables.

Hypotheses (1) and (2) comprise the majority of hypotheses tested in survey applications of the *GLM*. Although seldom conducted in non-experimental applications of the *GLM*, a researcher may want to test whether linear combinations of the coefficients are equal to some specified zero or nonzero values. Paralleling hypoth-

---

[4]The null distribution of *GLM* test statistics do not depend upon the configuration of the **X** matrix, and, consequently, the conditional and unconditional Type I error rates are equivalent. The non-null distributions of the *GLM* test statistics do depend upon the **X** matrix configuration (see the expression for the noncentrality parameters presented below). By ignoring sampling variability in the **X** matrix, a source of variability in the non-null distribution of the test statistics is being ignored. Consequently, the unconditional probability of Type II error is underestimated. Unfortunately, the unconditional non-null test statistic distribution theory is quite complex, and incorporating it into our presentation would take us out of the context of the classical general linear model.

TABLE 1

General Linear Hypothesis Statistical Tests

Null hypothesis	Test

(1) Individual coefficient ($J = 1$):

$H_0: \beta_i = \beta_i^*$:

$1\,df$ F-test or t-test: $t =$

$$(b_i - \beta_i^*)/s^2\,((\mathbf{X'X})^{-1})^{1/2}$$

(2) Set of J coefficients:

$H_0: \boldsymbol{\beta}_{(2)} = \boldsymbol{\beta}_{(2)}^*$

where

$\boldsymbol{\beta}' = (\boldsymbol{\beta}_{(1)}'\ \boldsymbol{\beta}_{(2)}')$

$J\,df$ F-test on increment to R^2

(3) Linear combination of coefficients ($J = 1$):

$H_0: \mathbf{a}'\boldsymbol{\beta} = \mathbf{a}'\boldsymbol{\beta}^*$.

$1\,df$ F-test or t-test: $t =$

$$\left[\frac{(\mathbf{a'b} - \mathbf{a'}\boldsymbol{\beta}^*)'(\mathbf{a'}(\mathbf{X'X})^{-1}\mathbf{a})^{-1}(\mathbf{a'b} - \mathbf{a'}\boldsymbol{\beta}^*)}{s^2} \right]^{1/2}$$

(4) Set of J independent linear combinations of coefficients:

$H_0: \underset{(J \times K)(K \times 1)}{\mathbf{A} \quad \boldsymbol{\beta}} = \mathbf{A}\boldsymbol{\beta}^*$

$J\,df$ F-test: $u =$

$$\frac{(\mathbf{Ab} - \mathbf{A}\boldsymbol{\beta}^*)'(\mathbf{A}(\mathbf{X'X})^{-1}\mathbf{A}')^{-1}(\mathbf{Ab} - \mathbf{A}\boldsymbol{\beta})/J}{s^2}$$

The test statistic for each of the above F-tests can be written as

$$u = \frac{(R^2 - R_{H_0}^2)/J}{(1 - R^2)/(N - K)}$$

where R^2 is a proportion of variance explained by the full, unrestricted model, and $R_{H_0}^2$ is the proportion of variance explained when the model is constrained by the null hypothesis. The statistic u is distributed $F_{J, N-K}$ under the null hypothesis.

eses (1) and (2), one can test a single linear combination with a t-test[5] or one degree of freedom F-test, or jointly test J linearity independent linear combinations of coefficients. Indeed, hypotheses (1) and (2) are special cases of (3).

Finally, each of the F-tests for the hypotheses can be considered "increment to R^2" tests with J numerator and $N - K$ denominator degrees of freedom as given in the equation for the u statistic found in Table 1.

SIMULTANEOUS STATISTICAL INFERENCE

In most applications of the *GLM* in survey research, more than one of a single type of the above delineated hypotheses is tested or more than one type of hypothesis is tested. Frequently, some set of interaction effects are tested jointly, and main effects are tested individually. When the effects of a categorical and one or more continuous independent variables are analyzed, often a joint test of the effects of the set of dummy variables representing the categorical variable and one or more individual tests of the coefficients for the continuous variables are performed. In applications of the *GLM* that involve a single equation, the performance of multiple t-tests on individual slope coefficients is a universal practice. Finally, it is becoming standard practice to do multiple tests on all possible slope coefficients in simple recursive structural equation models.

We have briefly noted above the researcher who performs such multiple hypotheses tests is in a qualitatively different inference situation—that of simultaneous statistical inference—than the researcher who performs only a single hypothesis test. In this section we shall consider both how the single and multiple hypotheses cases differ from the standpoint of inference and techniques of statistical inference that are appropriate to the to the multiple hypotheses test situation. First we shall examine these two issues in general, and then we shall consider them as they apply to the standard tests conducted within survey research applications of the *GLM*.

General Issues in Simultaneous Statistical Inference

An understanding of the basic difference between the single hypothesis and multiple hypotheses cases can best be achieved by

---

[5] The matrix expression for the t-test of hypothesis (3) is merely $\mathbf{a'b} - \mathbf{a'\beta^*}$ divided by the standard error of the linear combination $\mathbf{a'b}$, where the standard error in $s(\mathbf{a'(X'X)^{-1}a})^{1/2}$.

first recalling the definition of Type I error in statistical inference. Type I error is the error of falsely rejecting a true null hypothesis. For the researcher who performs only a single null hypothesis test, this definition presents no problem. The probability that he will falsely reject this single null hypothesis is the probability of Type I error in this case. The researcher can straightforwardly proceed by following the suggested standard procedure of specifying a level $1 - \alpha$ of protection against a Type I error, and then proceed to perform his statistical test accordingly. Now consider what happens if this same researcher sometime in his life performs additional tests of null hypotheses according to the suggested standard procedure. That is, he specifies a level $1 - \alpha$ of desired protection against a Type I error and conducts each of his statistical tests at this level.

If we reflect now on the definition of Type I error, we realize that for this researcher the actual level of protection against making a Type I error in the multiple null hypotheses case is less than $1 - \alpha$. Thus, this researcher is overestimating the protection he has against falsely rejecting a true null hypothesis. The problem with employing the conventional procedure for making tests of multiple null hypotheses arises because the probability of making a Type I error in this case is the probability of falsely rejecting any one of the individual null hypotheses—which equals the probability of making a Type I error for the first null hypothesis, *or* for the second null hypothesis, *or* for the nth null hypothesis, *or* for any combination of the n hypotheses. Except in the case of total dependency among the null hypotheses tested, this probability is greater than the α level under which each of the null hypotheses were tested.

Essentially, the solution to this problem is provided by the researcher's decision concerning which null hypotheses will be grouped together for the purpose of considering Type I error—generally referred to as the specification of the unit of error rate. Given this decision, the researcher can proceed to do each of the tests of individual null hypotheses in such a fashion that the desired level of protection against making a Type I error for the group of null hypotheses has been provided.

Two extreme groupings of null hypotheses can be identified. First, one could consider as a group all the null hypotheses tests that a researcher or a group of researchers will do in his or their lifetime. By grouping in this manner the researcher would be provided with protection at a specified level against ever falsely rejecting a true null hypothesis. Second, one could consider each individual null hypothesis test as a group for inference purposes. This grouping is generally called a per-comparison unit of error rate and effectively removes one from the simultaneous inference situation. The first extreme grouping essentially has been rejected in discussions of appropriate units of error rate for research, and a general agreement exists that the upper bound for grouping purposes is provided by the group of null hypotheses tested by one researcher in one study. However, there exists no consensus on what is the most appropriate unit of error rate below this upper bound (Ryan, 1959, 1962; Wilson, 1962; Miller, 1966).

The problem addressed by simultaneous statistical inference techniques is that of how to perform tests of individual hypotheses such that one has protection at a specified level against making a Type I error for a group of hypotheses. Numerous techniques of simultaneous statistical inference have been designed to address this problem (Miller, 1966; Kirk, 1968), many of which have been developed for specific types of tests within the *GLM* framework.[6] However, two techniques, the Bonferroni and Scheffé, are quite general.

The Bonferroni technique is based on the Bonferroni inequality, which states that

$$\alpha_G \leqq \sum_{i=1}^{N} \alpha_{S_i};\qquad(6)$$

where α_G equals the significance level for a group of null hypotheses, α_{S_i} equals the significance level for each individual null hypothesis in the group, and N equals the total number of null hypotheses in the group. The Bonferroni technique can be applied to virtually all situations of multiple hypotheses tests where one has prior knowledge of how many tests are to be conducted.

The Scheffé method, in the *GLM* framework, provides a means of controlling error rate for tests of all possible linear combinations of the least squares estimates of the slope coefficients. The

---

[6] Miller (1966) provides an exhaustive treatment of the statistical bases and applications of the many techniques of simultaneous statistical inference. A less exhaustive and more applications-oriented review is provided by Kirk (1968).

Scheffé technique is based on the common assumptions (distributional and otherwise) of the *GLM*. Its generality is due to the fact that it allows the researcher to perform an infinite number of tests of linear combinations of β coefficients while protecting against a specified value of Type I error for the group.

Simultaneous Statistical Inference in *GLM* Applications in Survey Research

The first question that must be addressed is, "Does one need to be concerned with issues of simultaneous inference?" The implicit answer given to this question in survey research applications of the *GLM* to date has been, "no." Virtually all analyses of survey data conducted within the *GLM* framework have implicitly employed a per-comparison error rate. In general, analyses of multiple null hypotheses based on survey data have been performed in the following manner: A value of Type I error is specified and this value is used in tests of each individual null hypothesis. No consideration is given to error rate for any group of hypotheses.

There are compelling reasons for believing that this implicit answer is insufficient. The first reason is that the implicit answer is usually based on a lack of knowledge of the issues in simultaneous inference. Basic textbook treatments of statistical inference, from which most social researchers' knowledge of this subject is obtained, generally ignore simultaneous statistical inference. Consequently, many social researchers are unaware, or vaguely aware, that a problem may exist in doing multiple tests of null hypotheses.

Beyond this lack of knowledge there are important substantive reasons for considering simultaneous inference. Perhaps the most important of these is the fact that social researchers do not limit their conern to the determination of whether or not a single variable has a statistically significant direct effect on a given dependent variable, but extend their interest to the determination of whether or not a set of independent variables affects a given dependent variable. Such analyses are frequently done in the context of a causal model of a process that determines variation in a dependent variable. This is particularly the case in analyses done within the recursive structural equation framework. Here the researcher frequently begins with a specified causal ordering among a set of variables and a set of null hypotheses about the relationships among this set of variables. It can be argued that since the researcher is interested in finding the correct model of a process in a population, the set of multiple null hypotheses used to find this model should be tested simultaneously. That is, the researcher should provide protection against a specified level α_G of finding an incorrect model of a process; since falsely rejecting any of the multiple null hypotheses is, in effect, finding an incorrect model of the process.

Another reason for being concerned with units of error rate other than the per-comparison unit is the scientific dictum of conservatism and parsimony. It is generally thought that the acceptance of a false null hypothesis is more desirable scientifically than the rejection of a true null hypothesis. Such a principle, it is proposed, keeps the scientific literature from becoming unduly confused by false research findings and keeps scientific theories from becoming overly complex. Since the employment of a unit for error rate other than the per-comparison unit makes it more difficult to capitalize on chance in conducting tests of multiple null hypotheses, the scientific dictums of conservatism and parsimony argue for the use of simultaneous inference techniques.

A final reason is specific to the practice of "data snooping," or "data dredging." Both terms are used in reference to the practice of doing some previously unspecified number of tests within a body of data in an attempt to discover relationships among the set of variables analyzed. Such a practice is undertaken either because the researcher has no prior hypotheses about the relationships among a set of variables or wishes to supplement an analysis of prior hypotheses. In this situation it is argued that since one approaches an analysis with an unspecified number of null hypotheses to be tested—the number tested could be one, several, or all possible tests—the scientifically honest procedure is to use a simultaneous inference technique that provides protection against a level of Type I error for all possible tests.

Given that one has concluded that it is desirable to employ simultaneous statistical inference techniques, the next question that must be addressed is "What unit of error rate should be employed?" The most straightforward answer that can be given to this question is simply that there are no hard and fast rules. The unit of error rate used is dependent upon the researcher's judgement of what unit best suits the research proposes. We can make suggestions, however, about what seems to be appropriate units for certain applications of the common hypotheses tests delineated in Table 1. We will consider three such applications: (1) the prediction situation, (2) the use of "theory trimming" in simple recursive structural equation models, and (3) the use of various hypothesis tests in *post hoc* analyses of linear models.

Consider first the situation in which the researcher is simply interested in determining which variables among a set of independent variables have significant, direct effects on a dependent variable. The intent here is usually that of discovering what variables are important determinants of variation in some dependent variable. The usual procedure in this case is the performance of an individual test of the hypothesis that β_i equals zero for each independent variable. We suggest that all of the individual hypothesis tests of the β's be grouped together for purposes of considering error rate. Such a grouping seems appropriate since the focus of this type of research is on the correct prediction of values of a given dependent variable. By grouping in this fashion, the researcher is protected at the level $1 - \alpha_G$ against making Type I error in predicting values of a given dependent variable.

Secondly, consider the "theory trimming" strategy (Heise, 1969) often employed in the analysis of simple recursive structural equation models. A common procedure in social research is the specification of a recursive causal ordering among a set of variables and the employment of multiple t-tests of individual β coefficients (or their standardized counterparts) to determine which effects among those possible in a recursive causal ordering are significant.[7] The intent here is usually that of determining the most plausible

---

[7] The case of "theory trimming" described here is qualitatively different from the situation of testing an *a priori* hypothesized model. A model of procedures has been proposed for testing the fit for an *a priori* model where certain structural coefficients are hypothesized to be equal to zero (Land, 1973; McPherson and Huang, 1974; Specht, 1975). McPherson and Huang (1974) present an equation-by-equation scheme for testing the fit of an hypothesized recursive structural equation model that explicitly incorporates simultaneous inference considerations. If a single test of the global fit of an hypothesized model is performed, then one is effectively removed from the simultaneous inference case. If a comparison of the fit of several models id performed (cf. Specht, 1975), or if an attempt is made to diagnose what specific structural parameters are responsible for the failure of an hypothesized model to hold, then considerations raised in our discussion of simultaneous inference issues again becomes relevant.

model of some process in a population. We propose that all of the null hypotheses tested in the "theory trimming" process be considered as a group for error rate purposes. Because, in this case, the researcher is interested in finding the correct model of a process in a population, grouping in this fashion is appropriate. Since falsely rejecting any one of the null hypotheses about the individual β coefficients means that thr researcher has found an incorrect model of the process, protecton should be provided against falsely rejecting any one of the null hypotheses. By treating all of the null hypotheses as a unit for purposes of considering Type I error the researcher does so at the level $1 - \alpha_G$.

Finally, consider the use of the common hypotheses tests in the *post hoc* case. Frequently, the results of one's analysis do not conform to the original expectations. The attainment of unexpected results may at least partially be attributed to initial assumptions not holding. For example, one may have assumed that the relationships among a set of variables are linear and additive when, in fact, they are nonlinear or not additive. Many of these assumptions are testable with the data at hand and in such a situation the researcher may wish to perform a number of hypothesis tests to determine if the unexpected results are attributable to the failure of meeting one's assumptions.

Additionally, the results of one's analysis may suggest further tests that may be interesting to the researcher, or the researcher may simply wish to snoop around in the data in the hope of discovering an interesting result. In all these *post hoc* analyses, the researcher is "data dredging." For the reasons of scientific honesty elaborated above, we suggest that the researcher employ as the unit of error rate all possible tests of the β coefficients and employ the Scheffé technique.

After one has determined the unit of error rate to be employed, a simultaneous inference technique must then be chosen. The Bonferroni and Scheffé techniques can both be applied to all of the common hypotheses tests performed on slope coefficients listed in Table 1.[8] The two techniques do differ, however, in the advan-

[8] There are, of course, other techniques that are applicable to the common hypotheses tests on slope coefficients. For example, Williams (1972) discusses the application of Tukey's technique for making pairwise multiple comparisons of means within the regression framework. We restrict our attention to the Bonferroni and Scheffé techniques because of their generality and ease of application.

tages each presents in specific situations. Two criteria are of importance in weighing the relative advantages of each technique: (1) the ability the techniques present to detect specific alternative hypotheses (that is, statistical power), and (2) their applicability to *a priori* versus *post hoc* statistical tests. We shall first consider the mechanics of applying each technique and then weigh their relative advantages in terms of these two ctiteria.

The Bonferroni Technique

To provide protection at level $1 - \alpha_G$ for a group of null hypotheses via the Bonferroni technique, one first determines the total number of individual null hypotheses to be tested, m. Then one divides α_G by m and tests each individual null hypothesis with a significance level equal to α_G/m. For example, if one wishes to test whether a subset of coefficients are jointly equal to zero and to test whether four additional coefficients are individually equal to zero, with a group probability error rate of 0.05 one would simply conduct the tests corresponding to hypotheses (1) and (2) in Table 1, each with α_{S_j} equal to 0.01.

The Scheffé Technique

The Scheffé technique is applied to the various F-tests specified in Table 1. It requires that one first perform a test of the joint null hypothesis that all of the coefficients from which subsequent tests of the nature of those in Table 1 will be conducted, with $1 - \alpha_G$ equal to the desired level of protection against a Type I error. If this test is nonsignificant, then one stops here and performs no further tests—since tests of any linear combination of these β coefficients (this includes as well hypotheses (1) and (2) in Table 1) will prove nonsignificant. If, on the other hand, one can reject this joint null hypothesis, then one carries out any and all of the tests in Table 1 by using as the critical value of the test statistic for all individual null hypotheses tests the quantity

$$JF^{\alpha_G}{}_{(J,N-K)}$$

where J equals the degrees of freedom from the joint null hypothesis test that all coefficients equal zero. For example, if the researcher wishes to conduct individual tests of three different linear combinations of four β coefficients (tests of the form of hypothesis (3) in

Table 1), one would use the specified test in Table 1 with the critical value of the test statistic equal to

$$4F^{\alpha G}_{(4, N-K)}$$

Bonferroni and Scheffé Procedures: Some Comparisons

Note first that the Bonferroni and Scheffé procedures are conservative. In general, the actual value of the group error rate will be less than that desired. Hence, one will have greater protection against a Type I error than initially specified. The Bonferroni procedure, as we had mentioned, is based on the Bonferroni inequality and the fact that it produces only approximations to the actual group error rate that can be readily seen. The Scheffé technique provides an exact value of the group error rate for all possible linear combinations. However, it is only a finite subset of these linear combinations that is ever tested, and consequently it, like the Bonferroni technique, is conservative.

The fact that the Scheffé procedure provides an error rate for all possible linear combinations while the Bonferroni procedure is based on a finite number of tests provides some insight into the ability of each to allow the rejection of individual null hypotheses. Intuitively, it appears that the Scheffé technique will be less powerful than the Bonferroni technique because the former is based on an infinite number of tests while the latter is not. In fact, the Scheffé technique will always be less powerful for the rejection of individual null hypotheses when m, the actual number of tests made, is less than or equal to J, the degree of freedom for the numerator of the F statistic. On the other hand, when m is considerably bigger than J, the inexactitude of the Bonferroni procedure is such that the Scheffé procedure provides greater power for the rejection of individual null hypotheses (Miller, 1966, pp. 62–63; Dunn, 1959). Rather than rely on the somewhat sparse literature comparing the power of simultaneous inference techniques, the researcher can apply both the Bonferroni and Scheffé techniques (or others) and use the one that provides greatest power. Doing so is fully permissible in the *a priori* case since the choice of technique is independent of the data collected.

The Scheffé procedure presents an advantage over the Bonferroni technique in *post hoc* tests. For reasons of scientific honesty elaborated earlier, the Scheffé technique is more suitable for searching one's data in an attempt to discover the nature of the relationships among a set of variables.

We turn now to an examination of issues concerning the power of statistical tests of *GLM* hypotheses. Before doing so, an important implication of the conservative nature of the Bonferroni and Scheffé procedures for the estimation of the power of *GLM* hypothesis tests must be noted. As we shall discuss below, the smaller the α level for a hypothesis test, the less power of that test (holding other factors constant). As a consequence, the ease of applicability of the two procedures is purchased at the cost of an overestimate of the power of a test (where the degree of overestimate depends on the size of the discrepency between the conservative α and the true α). This fact, together with the conditional nature of the power calculations noted above, makes it imperative that we stress that the power calculations to be presented below should be taken as absolute minimum Type II error rates.[9]

POWER

Once appropriate statistical tests and the Type I error rate have been selected; to calculate power, the probability of rejecting a false null hypothesis for any test, we must determine the probability that the test statistic for the hypothesis exceeds the critical value when a given alternative hypothesis is true. The *GLM* test statistic u is distributed as a noncentral F when an alternative hypothesis is true, with J and $N - K$ degrees of freedom and noncentrality parameter δ^2. The distribution has the property that the probability of the statistic u exceeding a given critical value (and consequently power) increases monotonically with δ^2. The noncentrality parameter is a function of (among other things) the degree to which the

---

[9] Other factors (such as departures from random sampling and measurement error) affect both Type I and Type II error rates. Again, we have slighted important issues in order to remain within the context of the classical general linear model as it is most often applied in research by sociologists. Our point is not primarily that approximate error rate calculations are better than none. A more fundamental point is that the *conceptualization* of the appropriate unit of error rate and of meaningful effects to be detected will enhance our understanding of what our statistical analyses of survey data can and cannot tell us.

null hypothesis is false. For the most general *GLM* test, the test of a set of J linear combinations of coefficients is

$$H_0: \mathbf{A\beta} = \mathbf{A\beta^*} \quad \text{and,} \tag{7}$$

the noncentrality parameter, δ^2 is

$$\delta^2 = \frac{(\mathbf{A\beta} - \mathbf{A\beta^*})'(\mathbf{A(X'X)^{-1}A'})^{-1}(\mathbf{A\beta} - \mathbf{A\beta^*})}{\sigma^2_{y \cdot x}} \tag{8}$$

Figure 1 presents a plot of power as a function of δ^2 for various combinations of Type I error rates and numerator degrees of freedom, and arbitrarily large denominator degrees of freedom.[10] It

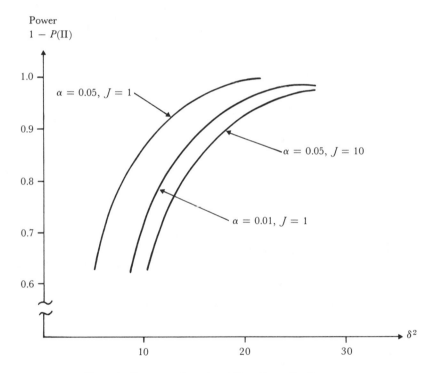

Figure 1. Power as a Function of Non-Centrality Parameter.

[10] Power tables approach an asymtope at about $N - K = 100$ denominator degrees of freedom. Since we are concerned with survey samples with generally many more than 100 observations, our calculations are based on tabled power for "infinite" denominator degrees of freedom.

can be seen that for a given α and δ^2, power decreases with numerator degrees of freedom J, and that for given J, power is monotonically related to the probability of a Type I error. All three of these relationships are important when we consider the implications of simultaneous inference for power.

In Table 2 we present alternative expressions for the noncentrality parameters for the test of an individual coefficient and the joint test of J ($J \leq K - 1$) coefficients. The noncentrality parameters are presented as functions of the original GLM parameters and standardized parameters.[11] Looking first at the test of the kth individual coefficient, we see immediately that δ^2 (and therefore power) increases with the degree β_k departs from its hypothesized value β_k^*. Noting that $\mathbf{x}' \mathbf{M}^* \mathbf{x}$ is just the sum of squared residuals for the regression of the kth independent variable on the remaining $K - 2$ independent variables, we conclude also that power increases with the orthogonality of the kth independent variable to the others. We see this again in the $(1 - R^2_{x_k \cdot X^*})$ term in the standardized expression, and note also that, of course, power increases with sample size. From the standardized expression we also see that power increases with the proportion of variance explained (that is, as $\sigma^2_{y \cdot x}/\sigma^2_y$ decreases). None of these results should be surprising. The ability to reject a false null hypothesis increases with the degree to which it is false, the degree to which the effect being tested is nonredundant with the effects of other parameters, the amount of data available, and the overall power of the linear model.

The δ^2 parameters for the joint test of $J(J \leq K - 1)$ coefficients can be interpreted as a multivariate extension of the single coefficient case. Both $\mathbf{X}_2' \mathbf{M}_1 \mathbf{X}_2$ and $\mathbf{R}_{22.1}$ are measures of the degree to which the covariation among the J variables with coefficients being tested is orthogonal to the covariation among the remaining $K - J - 1$ independent variables, and $\boldsymbol{\beta}_2 - \boldsymbol{\beta}_2^*$ is the vector discrepancy between the true values of the J coefficients and

[11] It must be assumed here that the hypotheses being tested are with respect to the *unstandardized* parameters and that the standardized parameters are merely an arbitrary rescaling of their unstandardized counterparts. The GLM distribution theory does not apply to the direct estimation of standardized parameters. The distributions of the standardized estimates and test statistics can become quite complex. The application of such distributions to direct statistical inference with respect to standardized parameters is virtually nonexistent in the social survey literature.

TABLE 2

Noncentrality

	Understandardized	Standardized

(1) The test of an individual coefficient:

$$H_0: \beta_k = \beta_k^*$$

Understandardized:
$$\delta^2 = \frac{(\beta_k - \beta_k^*)^2 \mathbf{x}_k' \mathbf{M}^* \mathbf{x}_k}{\sigma_{y.X}^2}$$

Standardized:
$$\delta^2 = \frac{n(\bar\beta_k - \bar\beta_k^*)^2(1 - R^2_{x_k \cdot X^*})}{\sigma_{y.X}^2/\sigma_y^2}$$

(2) The joint test on the last J coefficients:

$$H_0: \boldsymbol{\beta}_{(2)} = \boldsymbol{\beta}_{(2)}^*$$

Understandardized:
$$\delta^2 = \frac{(\boldsymbol{\beta}_{(2)} - \boldsymbol{\beta}_{(2)}^*)'\,\mathbf{X}_2'\mathbf{M}_1\mathbf{X}_2(\boldsymbol{\beta}_{(2)} - \boldsymbol{\beta}_{(2)}^*)}{\sigma_{y.X}^2}$$

Standardized:
$$\delta^2 = \frac{n(\bar{\boldsymbol{\beta}}_{(2)} - \bar{\boldsymbol{\beta}}_{(2)}^*)'\, R_{22.1}\, (\bar{\boldsymbol{\beta}}_{(2)} - \bar{\boldsymbol{\beta}}_{(2)}^*)}{\sigma_{y.X}^2/\sigma_y^2}$$

Notation and Definitions:

1. $\boldsymbol{\beta}$ is the $K - 1$ element vector of standardized coefficients, $\bar\beta_k = (s_x/s_y)\beta_k$ for $k = 2, ..., K$.

2. The vector $\mathbf{x}_k$ is the kth column of $\mathbf{X}$. The matrix $\mathbf{X}^*$ is the $N \times (K - 1)$ data matrix $\mathbf{X}$ with kth column omitted.

3. The coefficient vector $\boldsymbol{\beta}'$ may be partitioned as $(\boldsymbol{\beta}'_{(1)}\, \boldsymbol{\beta}'_{(2)})$, where $\boldsymbol{\beta}_{(2)}$ is the vector of the last J coefficients. The matrix $\mathbf{X}$ is similarly partitioned by columns as $(\mathbf{X}_1 \mathbf{X}_2)$.

4. $\mathbf{M}^*$ is the idempotent matrix $(\mathbf{I} - \mathbf{X}^*(\mathbf{X}^{*\prime}\mathbf{X}^*)^{-1}\mathbf{X}^{*\prime})$. $\mathbf{M}_1$ is the idempotent matrix $(\mathbf{I} - \mathbf{X}_1(\mathbf{X}_1'\mathbf{X}_1)^{-1}\mathbf{X}_1')$. For the properties of such idempotent matrices see Theil (1971: 113–114).

5. $R^2_{x_k \cdot X^*}$ is the squared multiple correlation coefficient of $\mathbf{x}_k$ on $\mathbf{X}^*$. $\mathbf{R}_{22.1}$ is the matrix of partial correlations among the J variables in $\dot{\mathbf{X}}_2$ with the variables in $\mathbf{X}_1$ partialled out. The diagonal elements of this matrix are proportions of variance in the J variables orthogonal to the $K - J - 1$ variables in $\mathbf{X}_1$.

their hypothesized values. Indeed, for all *GLM* tests we can conceptualize the noncentrality parameter as a scaler measure of the degree to which the null hypothesis is false, weighted by the amount of independent information available.

Given a substantively meaningful alternative hypothesis one would wish to be able to detect (the configuration of independent variables in the model and the completeness of the model as measured by the proportion of variance explained), it is a trivial matter to program a computer to compute δ^2 as expressed in equation (8) for any general linear hypothesis and any specified alternative. Thus, given δ^2 and n, one has enough information to determine the power of the test from Pearson and Hartley charts (Scheffé, 1959: 438–445; Kirk, 1968: 520–547). We now present examples of calculations of power as functions of n and the degree to which the null hypothesis is false.

DETERMINING THE POWER OF GLM TESTS:
SOME EXAMPLES

Is it indeed the case that survey researchers are typically confronted with testing situations where they have "too much" power, that is, is it usually true that trivial departures form the null hypothesis result in statistically significant tests? It is impossible to answer this question with any accuracy without doing power calculations. Our calculations presented below show that having too much power is by no means generally the case. Furthermore, we argue that if a researcher is to report the results of statistical tests, it is always imperative that the magnitude of the effects, trivial or nontrivial, that are likely to be detected also be presented.

Consider the following linear model:

$$y_i = \beta_1 + \beta_2 X_{i2} + \beta_3 X_{i3} + \beta_4 X_{i4} + \beta_5 X_{i5} + \beta_6 X_{i6} + \varepsilon_i \qquad (9)$$

where:

$$y = \text{Income}$$
$$X_2 = \text{Education}$$
$$X_3 = \text{Occupation}$$
$$X_4 = \text{Parental income}$$
$$X_5 = \text{Father's occupation}$$
$$X_6 = \text{Father's income}$$

When models of the socioeconomic achievement process such as equation (9) are estimated, the researcher is usually interested in hypotheses about all five coefficients (excluding the intercept), β_2, ..., β_6. To maintain an overall protection of $1 - \alpha_g = 0.95$ against Type I error, we can conduct simple t-tests on the five coefficients at the 0.01 level (Bonferroni), or compare the usual 1 degree of freedom F-tests (the square of the t-test) to the $5F_{N-K}^{0.05}$ critical value (Scheffé).

Let us consider the power of the test of the education coefficient, H_0: $\beta_2 = 0$ when the true net return to a year of education is \$150, H_0: $\beta_2 = 150$. Given this null hypothesis and a meaningful alternative hypothesis, how large a sample size is required to have a reasonable likelihood of detecting an education effect of \$150 a year in samples drawn from the United States labor force? We know from the expression for the noncentrality parameter in Table 2 that the power of the test also depends on the variation in and covariation among the independent variables and the proportion of variation explained in the model. Assuming that the five social variables explain about fifteen percent of the income variation in the United States labor force, and using published correlations and variances of the five variables from a sample of Wisconsin high school graduates (Sewell and Hauser, 1972), we can calculate the noncentrality parameter as a function of sample size. From Pearson-Hartley charts we can then plot power as a function of sample size.[12]

In Figure 2 we present the plot of power as a function of sample size for a Type I error rate of 0.05 for: (1) the Bonferroni test, (2) the Scheffé projection, and (3) a simple t-test not controlling for overall Type I error (the noncentrality parameter is identical for all three tests). We see, as noted above, that the Bonferroni test is slightly more powerful than the Scheffé projection, and that compared to the simple t-test one must pay a price in terms of power in order to control for overall error rate. Thus, if one is going to test the net education effect with a Bonferroni test, a sample size of at least 2200 observations is required to achieve a power of 0.90.

---

[12] An intermediate step is required to use these charts. They are presented in terms of a parameter Φ, where $\Phi = \sqrt{\delta^2/(J + 1)}$ and J is the numerator degrees of freedom of the test. For Scheffé projections, J is the numerator degrees of freedom from the preliminary joint test.

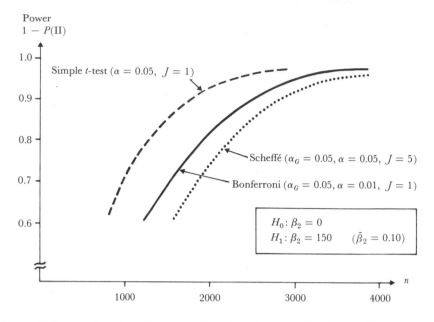

Figure 2. Income Equation—Power as a Function of sample Size for the Test on an Individual Coefficient.

Does the above result imply that for national samples of more than 10,000 observations, tests on coefficients of the income determination model will have "more than enough power"? This is only true for the specific null and alternative hypotheses specified above. Consider a different hypothesis on the same education coefficient. Suppose that from a census of the population we know that the net effect of a year of education in 1960 was $150. In 1975 we are to collect a sample in order to detect changes in β_2 through β_5, and we want to be able to detect a change in β_2 of $30 a year in either direction. In this case, we are testing a nonzero null hypothesis H_0: $\beta_2 = \beta_2^* = 150$, against a nondirectional alternative: H_1: $|\beta_2 - \beta_2^*| = 30$. Using the same information as in the previous example, we have determined power as a function of sample size for this test and present the plot in Figure 3. In order to detect a change of $30 a year with a Bonferroni test with a power of 0.90, a sample of about 60,000 observations would be required.[13]

[13] Note also that our value for β_2 in 1960 was assumed to be based on a census and, therefore, not subject to sampling variability. If this were not the case, the power curves would be still lower.

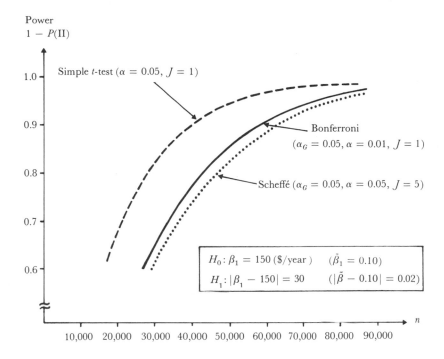

Figure 3. Income Equation—Power as a Function of Sample Size for the Test of an Individual Coefficient.

The power of *joint* tests on coefficients is generally greater for a given sample size. Figure 4 and 5 present the power of joint tests on β_2, β_3, and β_4 (where we have assumed that no hypotheses concerning β_5 and β_6 are to be treated). Figure 4 presents the power of the test of the joint null hypothesis that β_2, β_3, amd β_4 are all zero versus the alternative that they each have standardized effects of 0.10. Figure 5 presents the power to detect a joint standardized change of 0.02 in each coefficient. Once again, the sample size needed to detect the joint change with a power of 0.90 is relatively large, nearly 9,000 for $\alpha = 0.01$.

We conclude from the above examples that it is by no means guaranteed that tests based on large sample surveys have "more than enough" power. While it is true that as our theories become more powerful and our models become more precise representatives of empirical processes, the increase in the proportion of variance we can explain will unilaterally increase the power of our statistical

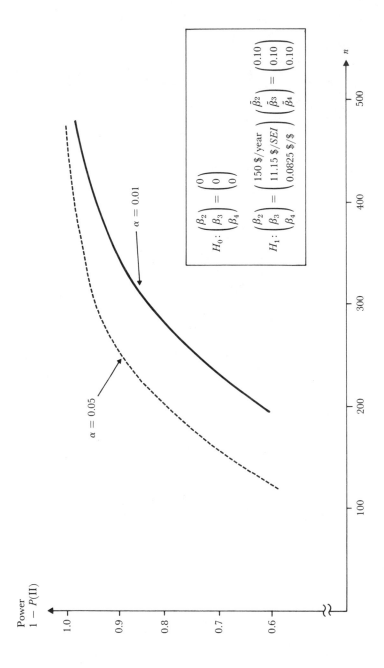

Figure 4. Income Equation—Power as a Function of Sample Size for a Joint F-test on Three Coefficients.

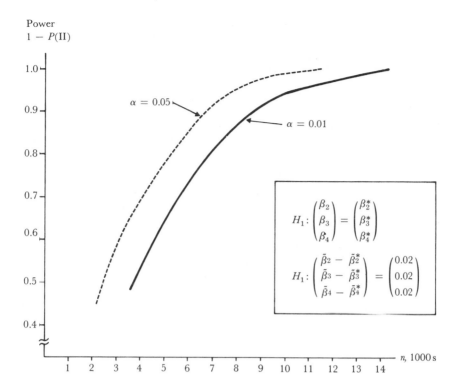

Figure 5. Income Equation — Power as a Function of Sample Size for a Joint F-test on Three Coefficients.

tests, we will also become interested in detecting increasingly smaller effects. Indeed, in situations where we are interested in detecting change through replications of surveys, it is likely that we will wish to detect relatively small effects with little or no increase in the proportion of variance explained in the replication.

Analysts of survey data are most often confronted with a situation where the data have already been collected. Sample size and the configuration of independent variables are given, and the researcher wishes to test hypotheses of the parameters of a model on the given data set. In such a situation, the relevant power calculation is power as a function of the degree to which the null hypothesis is false. From equation (8) and Table 2 we see that the only additional information needed to compute δ^2 is a value for $\sigma^2_{y \cdot x}$ or $\sigma^2_{y \cdot x}/\sigma^2_y$. Should the researcher find that one or more tests are not

powerful enough to detect substantively meaningful effects, two
actions are possible. The researcher can increase α_G, lowering the
protection against making a Type I error. If this is unacceptable, the
researcher must simply conclude that the data are inadequate for
testing those particular hypotheses.

In Figure 6 we present power as a function of the degree to
which the null hypothesis is false for our example of the Bonferroni
test of the education coefficient in the income model. For fixed
sample sizes from 250 to 10,000 observations, the power of the test of
the hypothesis $H_0: \beta_2 = \beta_2^*$ is presented as a function of the absolute
magnitude of the standardized measure of the degree to which the
null hypothesis is false, $|\tilde{\beta}_2 - \tilde{\beta}_2^*|$. With a sample size of 250, we see
that the standardized effect would need to be as large as 0.30 to be
detected with any regularity (power of 0.90), while for a sample of
10,000 observations, an effect as small as 0.07 can be detected with

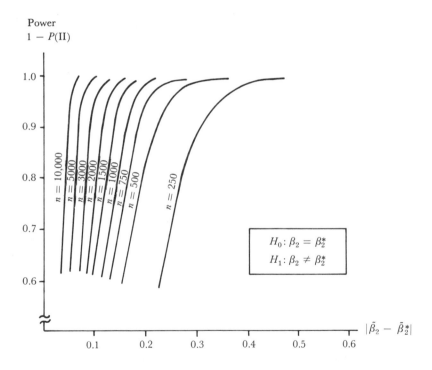

Figure 6. Income Equation—Power of the Bonferroni Test on an Individual Coefficient as a
Function of Standardized Effect to be Detected. $\alpha_G = 0.05$, $\alpha = 0.01$.

near certainty. To detect an effect of 0.15, a researcher with a sample of 250 observations would have to conclude that the data are inadequate, while a researcher with a sample of 10,000 would be in danger of finding "trivial" effects statistically significant and would perhaps decide to increase protection against Type I error substantially.

A single short FORTRAN computer program based on equation (8) has allowed us to compute all of the power calculations presented in this section. The logistics of these calculations are simple[14] and could be routinely incorporated into regression or *GLM* computer packages. If for no other reason than to force invertigators to decide what effects in the population they would find substantively important, power considerations should be incorporated into our *GLM* hypothesis testing procedures. It is our hope that by incorporating power and simultaneous inference considerations into our hypothesis testing procedures we can narrow the gap between "statistical significance" and "substantive significance."

CONCLUSION

Classical hypothesis testing as presented in most texts is a two-step procedure. One chooses a level of Type I error α and compares the test statistic to a critical value based on that α. After reviewing the neglected issues of simultaneous inference and power, we find classical hypothesis testing inadequate for the purposes of social research. The intelligent use of statistical inference demands control over the overall level of Type I error and knowledge of the magnitude of effects one is likely to detect. Our examination of specific techniques for dealing with the power and simultaneous inference problems have led us to conclude that these techniques can be routinely incorporated into our procedures for the statistical analysis of survey data. Therefore, we suggest the following procedures precede the testing of *GLM* hypothesis:

[14] While the calculations are simple, the intermediate step of calculating the Φ parameter and finding power in the Pearson-Hartley charts can be annoying. It would be much more convenient if charts were available for power as a function of δ^2 directly (as in Figure 1) for a number of α levels and numerator degrees of freedom. The Pearson-Hartley charts are further limited in that they have been tabulated only for $\alpha = 0.01, 0.05$, and 0.10.

1. Specify the hypotheses to be tested in terms of the parameters of the linear model.

2. Choose an acceptable Type I error rate α_G for the group of hypotheses.

3. Select the appropriate test statistics, Bonferroni or Scheffé, which provide protection against Type I error at the $1 - \alpha_G$ level.

4. Compute the noncentrality parameter δ^2 and power of the tests as a function of the magnitude of the effects to be detected.

The above steps will provide information such that meaningful decisions can be made about the hypotheses being tested. This information may be used in survey design for the rational choice of sample size or for assessing the adequacy of available data for hypothesis testing.

In recent years the use of statistical inference as a criteria in scientific decision-making has been the subject of increasing criticism (Morrison and Henkel, 1970). Part of this criticism has been directed at the failure of standard procedures of statistical inference to provide the kind of information required for meaningful scientific decision-making. In spite of this criticism, standard procedures of statistical inference continue to be employed. The continued use of the standard procedures can, at least in part, be attributed to the lack of a viable alternative when survey samples are analyzed. The use of our alternative precedure in our estimation can contribute to a more informed use of statistical inference in scientific decision-making. It does so by requiring that the researcher give more attention to the goals of his research in the use of statistical inference as a scientific decision-making aid. The procedure we suggest requires that the researcher consider the purpose of the research in the selection of a meaningful unit of error rate. It also requires that the researcher give attention to the size of effect believed to be substantively significant in judging the adequacy of a given sample for decision-making purposes.

REFERENCES

BLAU, P. M., AND DUNCAN, O. D.
   1967   *The American Occupational Structure.* New York: Wiley.

DUNN, O. J.
  1959   "Confidence Intervals for Means of Dependent, Normally Distributed Variables," *Journal of the American Statistical Association* 54:613–621.

GRAYBILL, F. A.
  1961   *An Introduction to Linear Statistical Models.* New York: McGraw-Hill.

HEISE, D. R.
  1969   "Problems in Path Analysis and Causal Inference." In E. F. Borgatta (Ed.), *Sociological Methodology 1969.* SanFrancisco: Jossey-Bass.

KIRK, R. E.
  1968   *Experimental Design Procedures for the Behavioral Sciences.* Monterey, Cal.: Brooks/Cole.

LAND, K. C.
  1973   "Identification, Parameter Estimation, and Hypothesis Testing in Recursive Sociological Models." In A. S. Goldberger and O. D. Duncan (Eds.), *Structural Equation Models in the Social Sciences.* New York: Seminar Press.

MC PHERSON, J. M., AND HUANG, C. J.
  1974   "Hypothesis Testing in Path Models." *Social Science Research* 3:127–139.

MILLER, R. C., JR.
  1966   *Simultaneous Statistical Inference.* New York: McGraw-Hill.

MORRISON, D. E., AND HENKEL, R. E.
  1970   *The Significance Test Controversy.* Chicago: Aldine.

RYAN, T. A.
  1959   "Multiple Comparisons in Psychological Research." *Psychological Bulletin* 56:26–47.
  1962   "The Experiment as the Unit for Computing Rates of Error." *Psychological Bulletin* 59:301–305.

SAMPSON, A. R.
  1974   "A Tale of Two Regressions." *Journal of the American Statistical Association* 60:682–689.

SCHEFFÉ, H.
  1959   *The Analysis of Variance.* New York: Wiley.

SEWELL, W. H., AND HAUSER, R. M.
  1972   "Causes and Consequences of Higher Education: Models of the Status Attainment Process." *American Journal of Agricultural Economics* 54:851–861.

SPECHT, D. A.

    1975   "On the Evaluation of Causal Models." *Social Science Research* 4:113–133.

THEIL, H.

    1971   *Principles of Econometrics.* New York: Wiley.

WILLIAMS, J. D.

    1972   "Multiple Comparisons in a Regression Approach." *Psychological Reports* 30:639–647.

WILSON, W.

    1962   "A Note on the Inconsistency Inherent in the Necessity to Perform Multiple Comparisons." *Psychological Bulletin* 59:296–300.

Received April 22, 1975.

NAME INDEX

A

AGANKEGIAN. A., 134
AIGNER, D. J., 135
ALFORD, R., 29, 31, 33–35, 38, 40, 42–44, 46
ALLISON, PAUL, 209
ALTHAUSER, R. B., 89, 133
ALWIN, D. F., 84, 89, 122, 133
AMENIYA, T., 65, 80
ANDERSON, A. R., 2–3, 20, 28, 46
ANDERSON. B. D., 105, 133
ANDERSON. T. W., 232, 252
ANDREWS, F. M., 54, 83, 86, 135
ARABIE, P., 281
ARONSON, E., 252–253
ATKINS, J., 51
ATTEWELL, P., 9, 46
AUSTIN, J. L., 1, 46

B

BAILEY, K. D., 256, 281
BALDAMUS, W., 46
BALESTRA, P., 58, 80
BARTON, A. H., 225, 252
BAUMOL, W. J., 164, 175
BENNET, J., 137

BERGUNDER, A. F., 51
BERND, J. L., 178
DERSHADY, H., 47
BHANHALI, R. J., 194, 207
BIELBY, W. T., 283
BLALOCK, A., 81, 136, 207
BLALOCK, H. M., JR., 53–55, 81, 85, 89, 91, 107, 133–134, 136, 138, 175, 207, 256, 281
BLAU, P. M., 188, 193, 207, 284, 310
BOGARDUS, E. S., 100, 133
BOHRNSTEDT, G. W., 81–82, 84–86, 133–134
BOISSEVAIN, J., 225, 252
BOORMAN, S. A., 252, 254, 281–282
BOOT, J. C. G., 161, 178
BORGATTA, E. F., 81–82, 133–134, 311
BORODKIN, F. N., 134
BOTT, E., 225, 252
BOUDON, R., 54, 81, 134
BOX, G. E. P., 137–139, 141, 145–149, 151, 159, 169, 172–175, 178, 181, 201, 207
BREE, D. S., 184, 187, 207
BREIGER, R. L., 248, 252, 254–257, 259, 262, 267–269, 271–272, 278, 281–282

313

BURLING, R., 6, 13, 47
BURT, R. S., 93, 133, 224–225, 228, 232, 234, 239, 243, 248, 250, 252

C

CAMPBELL, D. T., 54, 81, 86, 135, 138, 173, 175
CAPECCHI, V., 134
CAPORASO, J. A., 138, 175
CARTER, L. F., 54, 81
CHOMSKY, N., 1, 14–15, 47
CHOW, G. C., 174–175
CICOUREL, A. V., 10–11, 15, 47
CITIZENS BOARD OF INQUIRY, 47
CLARK, J. A., 256, 278, 282
COHEN, R., 49, 51
COLEMAN, J. S., 55–56, 60, 81, 181, 207, 209, 219, 223, 225, 252
COOPER, R. L., 174, 176
CORMACK, R. M., 256, 282
COSTNER, H. L., 81, 85, 89, 91, 107, 111, 122, 133–135, 177
COX, D. R., 211, 218, 220, 223
CRANE, D., 225, 252

D

DANZER, M. H., 250, 252
DE S. POOL, I., 253
DENTICH, B., 252
DHRYMES, P. J., 161, 174, 176
DICKSON, W. J., 268, 282
DOREIAN, P., 180, 187, 194, 200, 204, 207–208
DOUGLAS, J., 47, 50
DREITZEL, H., 47
DUESENBERRY, J., 176–177
DUNCAN, O. D., 54–55, 57, 81–82, 85–86, 92, 100, 118, 134, 138, 177, 253–254, 284, 310, 311
DUNN, O. J., 297, 311
DUNPHY, D. C., 254
DUVALL, R., 138, 176

E

EISNER, M., 174, 178

F

FADNER, R. H., 237, 253
FAIR, R. C., 161, 174–176
FARARO, T. J., 180

FELDSTEIN, M., 154, 176
FELLER, W., 210–211, 213–215, 223
FENTON, J., 4–5, 13, 21, 51
FISHER, F. M., 161–162, 171, 176
FOLSE, C. L., 136
FRAKE, C. O., 4, 47
FREIDRICHS, R., 2, 24, 47
FREIDSON, E., 47
FROMM, G., 169, 176

G

GARFINKEL, H., 10–11, 47–48
GEERTZ, C., 2, 27–28, 48
GELLER, A., 249, 252
GLADWIN, T., 48
GLASS, G. V., 138, 173, 176–177
GOLDBERG, S., 164, 177
GOLDBERGER, A. S., 52, 61, 64 68, 81–82, 85, 134–135, 137–138, 161–162, 177, 181, 207, 253–254, 311
GOODENOUGH, W. H., 4, 6–9, 11, 48
GOODHART, C. A. E., 194, 207
GOSLIN, D., 46
GOTTMAN, J. M., 138, 173, 177
GOWLER, D., 181, 183–184, 187, 207
GRAYBILL, F. A., 287, 311

H

HAMPSHIRE, S., 1, 48
HANNAN, E. J., 174, 177
HANNAN, M. T., 52, 54, 57, 63, 65, 70, 81, 83, 86, 92, 134
HANSON, N. R., 23, 48
HARRIS, C. W., 175
HARTLEY, 302–303, 309
HARVEY, O. J., 47
HAUSER, R. M., 85, 134, 303, 311
HEBERLEIN, T. A., 89, 133
HEISE, D. R., 55, 58, 82, 84–88, 90–93, 100–102, 109, 112, 121, 134, 253, 281, 294, 311
HENDERSON, C. R., 81–82
HENKEL, R. E., 310–311
HENRY, N., 52
HERNDON, J. F., 178
HERSTEIN, I. N., 260, 263, 282
HIBBS, D. A., JR., 137, 151, 174, 177, 181, 207
HICKMAN, B. G., 176

HIMMELBLAU, D. M., 203, 208
HODGE, R. W., 112, 118, 136
HOLLAND, P., 255
HOLSTI, O. R., 237, 252
HOLZNER, B., 21, 48
HOMANS, G. C., 268, 269, 272, 282
HOPE, K., 282
HORTON, J. E., 105, 136
HOUGH, R. L., 136
HOWREY, P., 168, 177
HUANG, C. J., 294, 311
HUMMON, N. P., 180, 187, 192–194, 200,
    204, 207–208
HURD, M. D., 54, 69, 82
HUSSAIN, A., 58, 83
HYMES, D. H., 6, 48

I

IMERSHEIN, A. W., 1–2, 9, 28–29, 31, 33,
    35, 39, 42, 44, 48–50

J

JANIS, I. L., 237, 253
JANOWITZ, M., 237, 253
JENKINS, G. M., 137–139, 141, 145–147,
    172–175, 178, 181, 201
JOHNSTON, J., 66, 82
JÖRESKOG, K. G., 85–88, 92–93, 95,
    97–98, 107–108, 110, 125,
    134–136,   240–241,   247,
    253–254

K

KADUSHIN, G., 225, 252–253
KAPLAN, D., 252
KATZ, E., 252
KAY, P., 49

KEESING, R. M., 7–9, 11, 15, 20, 49
KELEJIAN, H. H., 168, 177
KENDALL, M. G., 186, 192, 208
KENNY, D. A., 57, 82, 86, 135
KIRK, R. E., 291, 302, 311
KLEIN, L. R., 169, 174, 177, 181
KLUEGEL, J. R., 283
KNUTH, D. E., 82
KUH, E., 58, 82
KUHN, T. S., 2–4, 21–30, 34, 37, 41, 49

L

LAKATOS, I., 2, 23, 49
LAND, K. C., 181, 208, 294, 311
LASWELL, H. D., 252
LAUMANN, E. O., 225, 253
LAWLEY, D. N., 240, 253
LAZARSFELD, P. F., 54–55, 82
LEMIEUX, P., 137
LEVI-STRAUSS, C., 4, 49
LEWIS, P. H., 211, 218, 220, 223
LIN, N., 224, 250, 253
LINDZEY, G., 252, 253
LINN, R. L., 85, 88, 107–108, 110, 136,
    254
LORD, F. M., 88, 135
LORRAIN, F. P., 282
LOUNSBURY, F. G., 4, 49
LYMAN, S., 35, 51

M

MCHUGH, P., 10–11, 35, 50
MACKIE, M., 194, 208
MCKINNEY, J. C., 48
MCPHERSON, J. M., 294, 311
MCQUITTY, L. L., 256, 278, 282
MACRAE, D., 268, 282
MADDALA, G. S., 58, 64, 66, 82
MAGUIRE, T. O., 138, 177
MALINVAUD, E., 66, 72, 82
MARKOFF, J., 237, 253
MARQUARDT, D. W., 147, 178
MASON, J. M., 174, 178
MASTERMAN, M., 23–24, 49
MAXWELL, A. E., 240, 253
MAYRL, W. W., 10, 50
MENZEL, H., 252
MERTON, R. K., 135
MEYER, M. W., 191, 208
MIDDLETON, R., 100, 105, 135–136
MILLER, R. C., JR., 291, 297, 311
MILLER, W. L., 194, 208
MITCHELL, J. C., 225, 252–253
MONTFORT, F., 209
MOORE, O. K., 2–3, 20, 28, 46
MORRISON, D. E., 310–311
MORRISON, D. G., 211, 218, 223
MOSTELLER, F., 233, 253, 255

MUSGRAVE, A., 2, 49
MUTHÉN, B., 84

N

NAROLL, R., 49, 51
NAYLOR, T. H., 174, 178
NELSON, B., 3, 50
NELSON, C. R., 147, 174, 178
NELSON, F., 83
NERLOVE, M., 58, 63, 65–67, 71, 80, 82
NICHOLS, D. F., 174, 177
NOMIZU, K., 263, 282
NOVICK, M. R., 88, 135
NUCHRING, E., 2, 50

O

OGLIVE, D. M., 254
O'MEARA, J., 99, 135
OSGOOD, C. E., 249, 253

P

PALM, F., 174, 179
PAPPI, F. U., 225, 253
PARSONS, T., 2, 45
PASANELLA, A. K., 82
PEARSON, 302–303, 309
PELOWSKI, A. L., 138, 175
PELZ, D. C., 54, 83, 85, 135
PHOTIADIS, J. D., 105, 135
PIERCE, D. A., 148, 174–175, 178
PLATT, O., 182, 187, 190, 208
POLANYI, M., 27–28, 50
PSATHAS, G., 5, 50

R

RETORYS, K., 185, 208
RITZER, G., 2, 50
ROETHLISBERGER, F. J., 268, 282
ROOS, L., 138,175
ROSE, S. M., 51
ROSENFELD, R., 209
ROZELLE, R. M., 86, 135
RUBINSON, R., 57, 81, 86, 134
RYAN, T. A., 291, 311
RYLE, G., 1, 50

S

SACKS, H., 10, 20, 48, 50
SAMPSON, A. R., 287, 311
SAMUELSON, P. A., 161, 178

SAPIR, E., 4, 50
SARRIS, A. H., 174, 178
SHEFFÉ, H., 291–292, 295–298, 302, 303–304, 310–311
SCHMIDT, P., 174, 178
SCHNEIDER, D. M., 6
SCHOENBERG, R., 89, 111, 113, 134–135
SCHUTZ, W. C., 234, 254
SCHWARTZ, J. E., 255
SCHWEIKER, W. F., 105, 135
SCOTT, J. T., 136
SCOTT, M., 35, 51
SEAKS, T. G., 178
SEARLE, S. R., 63, 83
SEWELL, W. H., 303, 311
SHANIN, T., 46, 51
SHAPIRO, G., 253
SIEGAL, P. M., 112, 118, 136
SIMMEL, G., 2–3, 28, 51
SIMON, H. A., 208
SIMONS, R. L., 2, 49
SIMPSON, M. E., 105, 136
SINGER, B., 181, 190, 208
SMITH, M. S., 254
SNELL, P., 100, 136
SÖRBOM, D., 86–87, 92, 107, 111, 123, 125, 135–136
SØRENSEN, A., 52, 209, 221–223
SPECHT, D. A., 294, 312
SPILERMAN, S., 181, 190, 208
SROLE, L., 100, 136
STANLEY, J. C., 138, 175
STANLEY, J. S., 54, 81
STANLEY, M., 50
STEKLER, H. O., 174, 178
STEMPEL, G. H., 237, 254
STEPHANSON, W., 250, 254
STOKES, D. E., 163, 178
STONE, P. J., 237, 254
STUART, A., 186, 192, 208
STURTEVANT, W. C., 4–5, 48, 51
SUMMERS, G. F., 84, 99–100, 136
SUPPE, F., 49

T

TAUBMAN, P., 169, 176
TEUTER, K., 208
THEIL, H., 57, 83, 161, 178, 181, 192, 208, 312
THOMPSON, W. E., 105, 136

TIAO, G. C., 137–139, 141, 148–149, 151, 159, 169, 172–173, 175

TIRYAKIAN, E., 48

TUKEY, J. W., 233, 253, 295

TYLER, S. A., 47, 49, 51

V

VAN THILLO, M., 240, 253

W

WALL, K. D., 155, 174, 178–179

WALLACE, A. F. C., 6, 51

WALLACE, T. D., 58, 83

WARREN, J. T., 57, 81, 86, 134

WARREN, R. L., 2, 29, 32–33, 43–44, 51

WARTOFSKY, M. W., 46

WEBER, M., 20

WEITMAN, S. R., 253

WELFLING, M., 138, 176

WELLS, C. S., 54, 81

WERNER, O., 4–5, 13–17, 20–21, 51

WERTS, C. E., 85, 88, 107–108, 110, 136, 247, 254

WESTCOTT, J. H., 174, 179

WHEATON, B., 84

WHITE, H. C., 225, 248, 254–257, 267–269, 271–272, 278, 282

WICHERN, D. W., 178

WILEY, D. E., 247, 254

WILEY, J. A., 83, 85–86, 88, 90, 93, 100–102, 104, 109, 136

WILEY, T. D., 83, 85–86, 88, 90, 93, 100–102, 104, 109, 136, 247, 254

WILLEY, M. M., 237, 254

WILLIAMS, J. D., 295, 312

WILLSON, V. L., 138, 1 3, 177

WILSON, W., 291, 312

WITTGENSTEIN, L., 1, 3, 17–18, 25, 51

Y

YOUNG, A. A., 52, 63, 65, 70, 81, 83

Z

ZELLNER, A., 174, 179

SUBJECT INDEX

A

Aggregation, 57
Archival records, 224, 226–227, 231, 237–238, 249, 251
Autocorrelations, 53–54, 58–59, 78, 80, 141–145, 147–148, 151–153, 156–157, 199
Autoregressive moving average process, 138, 141, 143–144, 146, 148, 151, 153
Autoregressive processes, 143, 147, 174

B

Baysian analysis, 211
Blockmodels, 255, 257, 272, 278
Bonferroni technique, 291, 295, 298, 303–304, 310

C

Causal lag, 57
Causality, 53–55, 57, 85, 138–139, 172
Change, 182

Chi square, 94, 98–99, 103–104, 108, 111, 117, 119, 128–129, 131, 148, 240–241, 247
CONCOR, 255–259, 267–269, 271–272, 274, 276–281
Content analysis, 226, 232–234, 236–239, 247–249, 251
Correlated error, 122
Cross-lag correlations, 54, 56, 59
Cumulated multiplier matrices, 165
Cycles, 151–152

D

Delay multiplier, 164–165, 167
Difference equations, 160–161
Differential equations, 55–56
Differential equation models, 180–181, 190, 195–196, 205, 207
Disturbance correlation, 131
Documents, 41
Dummy variables, 64–65, 70, 73, 138, 148, 157, 170, 172, 289

Dynamic multipliers, 164, 168–169
Dynamics, 55–56, 79

E

Efficiency, 57–59, 62–63, 65–70, 73, 75, 79–80, 92, 98
Elicited action, 13, 17, 19
Entailment, 7–8
Equilibrium, 141, 149–150, 157, 166, 168, 187
Equilibrium multipliers, 167
Equilibrium multiplier matrices, 165
Estimation, 53, 61, 63–69, 71, 76, 78–80, 85–86, 91–92, 94, 98–99, 103, 133, 138, 141, 143, 145–148, 155, 161, 171, 173–174, 181, 185, 187, 190–191, 196, 198, 200–201, 203, 220, 222, 245, 247, 249–250
Ethnomethodologists, 1–3, 9–10, 35, 46
Ethnoscience, 3–5, 11–12, 15–16, 28, 32
Exemplars, 24–31, 38–39, 41–42, 44

F

Factor analysis, 92, 239–240, 271
Feedback, 53, 58
Forecasting, 147
Full information methods, 68

G

Generalized linear model (GLM), 283–288, 291–292, 298–300, 302, 309
Generalized least squares (GLS), 63–80, 161
Grammer, 8

H

Hierarchy, 4
Historical research, 33, 36, 43

I

Identification, 55, 85, 91–92, 94–95, 98, 103, 107, 118, 123–124, 143, 161
Impact multipliers, 162, 167

Instruments, 53–54, 56, 67–68, 70, 78, 80
Interaction, 71, 77–78
Intervention multipliers, 168
Interventions, 137–139, 148–151, 153–154, 157, 161–163, 165, 167, 169, 171–173
Interviews, 210, 213, 215, 221, 223

J

Jacknife estimation, 233–234

L

Lagged variables, 54, 56, 58, 62
Lags, 140–142, 149, 154, 160, 163–167, 199
Life-history data, 220
LISREL, 98, 103, 107, 125, 241
Longitudinal data, 64, 99
Loops, 53

M

Markov models, 181
Maximum likelihood estimation, 56, 65, 67, 98, 155, 158, 186, 192, 198–199, 205, 207, 240–241
Monte Carlo simulation, 53, 69
Moving average processes, 143, 147
Multiple indicators, 122, 132

N

Networks, 226–227, 229–233, 236–238, 242–243, 248, 250–251
Nonlinear models, 168
Nonstationarity, 57, 211, 221

O

Ordinary least squares (OLS), 56, 58, 62–80, 98, 161, 171

P

Panel data, 79, 85–87, 91–92, 122, 133, 205–207, 210
Panels, 52–57, 61, 69
Paradigms, 4–5, 12–19, 21–31, 33–35, 37–45
Path analysis, 57, 90
Phase space, 183–184, 187
Poisson process, 210–213, 216, 223

Pooled data, 53, 57–59, 64, 69, 71–72, 74, 79–80
Principal components analysis, 268, 272, 277

R

Rates, 209–211, 213, 221–222
Recursive models, 163
Reduced form, 161–163, 165–166
Reliability, 85–88, 90, 92–93, 100–102, 104–105, 108–110, 112, 118–119, 121, 125, 127–129, 132, 210, 236–239, 241, 243, 249–250

S

Sampling function, 196, 204
Sampling variability, 232–233, 239, 241, 243, 250–251
Simulation, 168–169, 201
Sixteen-fold table, 54
Sociometric data, 225, 247, 255, 257–258, 267–268, 278
Specification, 85–87, 91–93, 103, 117, 121–124, 128, 131–133, 138, 141, 143, 147–148, 173–174
Stability, 85–86, 88–89, 91–93, 100–105, 110–113, 117–119, 121–124, 127–129, 131–133, 149, 164–165
Statics, 55
Stationary processes, 218, 220

Stationarity, 141–143, 147, 149
Statistical power, 283, 285, 287, 296, 298–300, 302, 304–308
Structural equation models, 55, 138–139, 159–160, 166, 169, 173–174, 239–244, 247, 251, 289, 294
Structural shifts, 169–171
Survey research, 283–285, 287, 292, 302

T

Taxonomies, 4, 12–15, 17, 28, 32
Time series data, 55, 58, 61, 66, 69, 79–80, 138–139, 151, 155, 173, 181, 194, 196, 199, 205–207, 224, 231–233, 236–238, 242–243
Transfer functions, 138, 150
Two-stage least squares, 161, 171
Type I error, 284, 290–300, 303, 308–310
Type II error, 287, 298

U

Unobservable variables, 55, 60, 85, 87, 92–93, 96, 188, 240–241, 243, 247

V

Validity, 108, 110–113, 119, 123 125, 127, 132